ALONG HEROIC LINES

ALONG HEROIC LINES

CHRISTOPHER RICKS

OXFORD
UNIVERSITY PRESS

OXFORD
UNIVERSITY PRESS

Great Clarendon Street, Oxford, OX2 6DP,
United Kingdom

Oxford University Press is a department of the University of Oxford.
It furthers the University's objective of excellence in research, scholarship,
and education by publishing worldwide. Oxford is a registered trade mark of
Oxford University Press in the UK and in certain other countries

First Edition published in 2021

Impression: 2

Published in the United States of America by Oxford University Press
198 Madison Avenue, New York, NY 10016, United States of America

British Library Cataloguing in Publication Data
Data available

Library of Congress Control Number: 2020946423

ISBN 978–0–19–289465–6

Printed and bound by
CPI Group (UK) Ltd, Croydon, CR0 4YY

Contents

Prefatory Note

Along Heroic Lines is concerned with the heroic, with the English heroic line (Samuel Johnson's long-standing term for what in education is now called the iambic pentameter), and with the interactions of prose and poetry. The essays engage with these related matters, but any claim to coherence has to be a mild one, something of a disclaimer. 'Some versions of the heroic' might have done it, were it not that William Empson gave the world a work of genius in *Some Versions of Pastoral* (1935).

When tracing 'the ideal line of study', we should (Matthew Arnold suggested) 'fix a certain series of works to serve as what the French, taking an expression from the builder's business, call *points de repère*—points which stand as so many natural centres, and by returning to which we can always find our way again'.[1] To a series of works may be added a series of writers, of periods, and of literary kinds or medium, all encouraging a return to such centres as the heroic, the heroic line, and the engagements of poetry and prose.

Thomas Carlyle's lectures *On Heroes, Hero-Worship, and the Heroic in History* (delivered 1840, published 1841) stand as one of these points. The reduction of his title to *On Heroes and Hero-Worship* is unfortunate as narrowing the triangular to the binary, as making Hero-Worship even more important than it (unfortunately) already was in Carlyle, and as slighting the Heroic in History—including the imaginative slights perpetrated by the mock-heroic or by scepticism as to the heroic. One's moral bearings may even be obliged to call upon Hilaire Belloc. *A Moral Alphabet* (1899) succeeds octosyllabic quatrains with a heroic couplet, Aesop's summary injustice.

---

1. 'Johnson's Lives' (1878); included in *Selected Criticism of Matthew Arnold,* ed. Christopher Ricks (New York, 1972).

B stands for Bear.

When Bears are seen
   Approaching in the distance,
Make up your mind at once between
   Retreat and Armed Resistance.

A Gentleman remained to fight—
   With what result for him?
The Bear, with ill-concealed delight,
   Devoured him, Limb by Limb.

Another Person turned and ran;
   He ran extremely hard:
The Bear was faster than the Man,
   And beat him by a yard.

MORAL
Decisive action in the hour of need
Denotes the Hero, but does not succeed.

George Orwell began his 'Reflections on Gandhi' in 1949 with a characteristic combination of trenchancy and caveat. 'Saints should always be judged guilty until they are proved innocent, but the tests that have to be applied to them are not, of course, the same in all cases.' The clincher is *of course*. And of course what Orwell says about saints goes for heroes too. He emphasized that Gandhi's 'natural physical courage was quite outstanding'. This conviction of Orwell's was braced against a pair of further convictions: 'No doubt alcohol, tobacco and so forth are things that a saint must avoid, but sainthood is also a thing that human beings must avoid.'[2] Saints and heroes have long been brought forward, often by themselves, as the two finalist contenders. Heroes, heroism, the heroic (leave alone heroics), are all contentious.

'The Anagram' is included, I admit, because there is something about the word 'Proceedings'—*Proceedings of the British Academy*—that does rather discourage people from proceeding. And an anagram is a way with words that both prose and poetry enjoy transacting, with my opening instance being not from the poetry of Byron but from his prose. The free-standing anagram is neither poetry nor prose, being

---

2. *In Front of Your Nose* [vol. iv of *The Collected Essays, Journalism and Letters of George Orwell*], ed. Sonia Orwell and Ian Angus (Harmondsworth, 1968), 463–4, 467.

between two worlds, like an inscription. Such inscribing can honour a heroic figure (*Charles Stuart, cals true hearts*) or a heroine, 'the name of such an honour to human nature as Miss Nightingale' (*Flit on, cheering angel*). Or the heroic may give way to the far-from-heroic covert: *Tony Blair, MP: I'm Tory Plan B.* The anagram can even incarnate the tension between the saint and the hero, the sacred and the secular, between George Herbert contemplating the Virgin Mary, and Charles Tomlinson contemplating John Constable.

I

The Best Words in the
Best Order

From the inaugural lecture as Professor of Poetry at the University of Oxford,
November 2004

Gratitude is among those human accomplishments that literature
lives to realize. Art enjoys the power not only to voice gratitude
but to prompt it, even to restore us to a state in which *grateful* might
come again to mean at once *feeling gratitude* and *feeling pleasure*—as
though it once was, and ought always to be, impossible to be granted
something gratifying and not be grateful for it.

Even the fallen natural world may be alive to this paradisal possibility. A hope, at least, is to be scented. There are wafted

> *Sabean* Odours from the spicie shoare
> Of *Arabie* the blest,

whereupon

> many a League
> Cheard with the grateful smell old Ocean smiles.

> (*Paradise Lost*, iv. 161–5)

With how fine an air 'the grateful smell' turns to and into 'smiles'. We
should be grateful to Milton, and so we are. Meanwhile Satan, the
great ingrate, in this his unsmiling passage into the Garden of Eden,
seeks to darken any such passage as this of Milton.

Gratitude, not an easy thing. Fortunately, there is the gratitude felt
by all of us to—and for—the enduring poets whom the Professorship
of Poetry at Oxford exists to honour. Gratitude, moreover, as a high
calling of literary studies in particular, with *in*gratitude as then the low

answer. Not one of us is professionally immune, since what should be a triumph of literary criticism—that it exists in the same medium as its art, as, say, music criticism does not—is by the same token its special peril of professionalized triumphalism. 'The deep | Moans round with many voices': *my* moan, or (uglily) what I'd like to know, is why, since Tennyson and I work in the same medium—language, in a word— why it's always *me* giving a talk about *him* and never him giving a talk about me.

A century ago this professorship was held by one who is, in my eyes, the greatest of those who—while not themselves being poets—have ministered here to the art: A. C. Bradley, who graced the chair from 1901 to 1906. His inaugural lecture was devoted to 'Poetry for Poetry's Sake' (probably—since he was never owlish—with some memory of the countering quip about Art: *What is art, that it should have a sake?*), and he began with these words:

One who, after twenty years, is restored to the University where he was taught and first tried to teach, and who has received at the hands of his Alma Mater an honour of which he never dreamed, is tempted to speak both of himself and of her. But I remember that you have come to listen to my thoughts about a great subject, and not to my feelings about myself · · · [1]

A great subject, poetry: but as against what, exactly? There is no Oxford Professor of Prose. Not only is there no Proser Laureate (as against, over the years, many a Poetaster Laureate), there is no prose counterpart to the word 'poet', or to 'poem'. T. S. Eliot in 1921 wrote that 'we cannot speak conveniently in English, as we can in French, of "Proses" in the plural',[2] but even more tellingly we cannot speak conveniently of a prose in the singular either. Eliot pressed on ('if we admit the long poem, we surely ought to admit the short "prose"'), but, as so often, *surely* and those quotation-marks are allowed to plead but on the understanding that they concede defeat.

Samuel Johnson: 'To circumscribe poetry by a definition will only shew the narrowness of the definer.'[3] Here in Oxford the widest of predecessors, Matthew Arnold, narrowed his mind no doubt in one disrespect: 'Poetry, no doubt, is more excellent in itself than prose. In poetry man finds the highest and most beautiful expression of that

1. *Oxford Lectures on Poetry* (London, 1909), 3.
2. 'Prose and Verse', in *The Chapbook*, No. 22 (April 1921), 5–6.
3. 'The Life of Pope', in *The Lives of the Most Eminent English Poets*, ed. Roger Lonsdale (Oxford, 2006), iv. 80.

which is in him.'⁴ But such an announcement, in claiming too much for poetry, and in issuing the claim *tout court*, sets poetry up precariously. All who love music or painting may bridle or bristle at this, and must wish to hear *something* from Arnold as to why there is no conceivable competition for the accolade. The superiority of poetry to prose is asserted and reasserted by Arnold but never has to be made good since it is taken to be self-evident:

Poetry is simply the most delightful and perfect form of utterance that human words can reach. Its rhythm and measure, elevated to a regularity, certainty, and force very different from that of the rhythm and measure which can pervade prose, are a part of its perfection.⁵

'Poetry is simply ⋯'⁶: this has its work cut out, or rather cuts out the need for any work. That the rhythm and measure of poetry (or rather, the rhythms and measures of poetry) may be 'very different' from those of prose (prose itself being no one thing): this may be conceded without accepting that the differences constitute 'simply' a superiority in poetry. T. S. Eliot knew otherwise. For a start: 'poetry has as much to learn from prose as from other poetry; and I think that an interaction between prose and verse, like the interaction between language and language, is a condition of vitality in literature.'⁷ To esteem poetry should entail respecting its sibling, prose.

Not so for Coleridge, who is keen to get the better of any opponent:

A poem is that species of composition, which is opposed to works of science, by proposing for its *immediate* object pleasure, not truth; and from all other species (having *this* object in common with it) it is discriminated by proposing to itself such delight from the *whole*, as is compatible with a distinct gratification from each component *part*.⁸

But where is the making good, or even any attempt at making good, of this last assertion? How much of an artistic achievement could (say) a novel be, that did *not* propose 'to itself such delight from the *whole*, as is compatible with a distinct gratification from each component *part*'?

4. 'Johnson's Lives', in *Selected Criticism of Matthew Arnold*, 358; 'man' as mankind, but quietly enlisting the word's masculine persuasive force.
5. 'The French Play in London' (1879), ibid. 159.
6. Ellipses that are raised ⋯ indicate an omission editorially introduced in these essays. Ellipses printed in the ordinary way are from the immediate source. (The practice is that established in *The Poems of T. S. Eliot*, ed. Christopher Ricks and Jim McCue (London, 2015).)
7. *The Use of Poetry and the Use of Criticism* (London, 1933), 152.
8. *Biographia Literaria*, ed. James Engell and W. Jackson Bate (Princeton, 1983), ii. 13.

Why does this responsibility, this imaginative feat, characterize poetry, as against 'all other species' of composition? Because Coleridge will have it so. Poetry is from all other species discriminated by . . . He is not exercising discrimination, he is practising *discrimination*. Lacking respect for prose, he is a prosist.

I wish our clever young poets would remember my homely definitions of prose and poetry; that is, prose equals words in their best order; poetry equals the best words in the best order. The definition of good prose is—Proper words in their proper places;—of good Verse—the properest words in their proper places.[9]

Not altogether proper, this. Wordsworth, for whom even the familiar sibling figure-of-speech constituted an insufficient acknowledgement of the affiliation of poetry and prose, wisely differed as to whether any homely-definitional differentiation would hold:

We are fond of tracing the resemblance between Poetry and Painting, and, accordingly, we call them Sisters: but where shall we find bonds of connection sufficiently strict to typify the affinity betwixt metrical and prose composition? They both speak by and to the same organs; the bodies in which both of them are clothed may be said to be of the same substance, their affections are kindred and almost identical, not necessarily differing even in degree; Poetry sheds no tears 'such as Angels weep,' but natural and human tears, she can boast of no celestial Ichor that distinguishes her vital juices from those of prose; the same human blood circulates through the veins of both.[10]

'Thrice he assayd, and thrice in spite of scorn, | Tears such as Angels weep, burst forth · · ·' (*Paradise Lost*, i. 619–20). 'Som natural tears they drop'd, but wip'd them soon' (xii. 645). Justice, for the fallen angel even, as well as for fallen mankind. Justice to prose, then.

Great prose may constitute an elaborated cry for justice, or—in the unavoided absence of justice—for revenge, a kind of wild justice that is not without its heroism.

SALERIO   Why I am sure if he forfaite, thou wilt not take his flesh, what's that good for?
SHYLOCK   To baite fish withal, if it will feede nothing else, it will feede my revenge; he hath disgrac'd me, and hindred me halfe a million, laught at my losses, mockt at my gaines,

9. Coleridge, *Table Talk*, ed. Carl Woodring (Princeton, 1990), i. 90, 25–26 August 1827.
10. Preface to *Lyrical Ballads* (1800), in *The Prose Works of William Wordsworth*, ed. W. J. B. Owen and Jane Worthington Smyser (Oxford, 1974), i. 134.

scorned my Nation, thwarted my bargaines, cooled my friends, heated mine enemie, and what's his reason? I am a *Jewe*: Hath not a *Jew* eyes? hath not a *Jew* hands, organs, dementions, sences, affections, passions, fed with the same foode, hurt with the same weapons, subject to the same diseases, healed by the same meanes, warmed and cooled by the same Winter and Sommer as a Christian is: if you pricke us, doe we not bleede? if you tickle us, doe we not laugh? if you poison us doe we not die? and if you wrong us shall we not revenge? if we are like you in the rest, we will resemble you in that. If a *Jew* wrong a *Christian*, what is his humility, revenge. If a *Christian* wrong a *Jew*, what should his sufferance be by Christian example, why revenge? The villanie you teach me I will execute, and it shall goe hard but I will better the instruction. (*Merchant*, III. i)

Great prose may mount a rebuke to the human propensity to elude responsibility.

EDMUND   This is the excellent foppery of the world, that when we are sicke in fortune, often the surfets of our own behaviour, we make guilty of our disasters, the Sun, the Moone, and Starres, as if we were villaines on necessitie, Fooles by heavenly compulsion, Knaves, Thieves, and Treachers by Sphericall predominance, Drunkards, Lyars, and Adulterers by an inforc'd obedience of Planatary influence; and all that we are evill in, by a divine thrusting on. An admirable evasion of Whore-master-man, to lay his Goatish disposition on the charge of a Starre: My father compounded with my mother under the Dragons taile, and my Nativity was under *Ursa Major*, so that it followes, I am rough and Lecherous. Fut, I should have bin that I am, had the maidenlest Starre in the Firmament twinkled on my bastardizing. (*Lear*, I. ii)

I cannot see—more, I cannot imagine—any respect in which Shakespeare's ways with words in prose are any less supreme than in verse or poetry. The same is true of Hamlet's words, Hamlet whose heroic courage before the lethal duel could not be better, either in itself or in Shakespeare's realization of it—in prose. Nothing could be less *prosy* or *prosaic* (the epithets that a partiality for poetry is happy to visit upon prose).

HORATIO   You will lose this wager, my Lord.

HAMLET   I doe not thinke so, since he went into France, I have
          beene in continuall practice; I shall winne at the oddes.
          But thou would'st not thinke how ill all's heere about my
          heart: but it is no matter.

HORATIO   Nay, good my Lord.

HAMLET   It is but foolery; but it is such a kinde of gain-giving as
          would perhaps trouble a woman.

HORATIO   If your minde dislike any thing, obey it. I will forestall
          their repaire hither, and say you are not fit.

HAMLET   Not a whit, we defie Augury; there's a speciall Providence
          in the fall of a sparrow. If it be now, 'tis not to come: if it
          bee not to come, it will bee now; if it be not now; yet it
          will come; the readiness is all. Since no man of aught he
          leaves knows, what is't to leave betimes? Let be. (V. ii)[11]

Any presupposition that thinks less well of such realization for being
prose, not poetry, is thoughtless. Shakespeare is either the greatest
prose-writer in our literature or one of the greatest, and he is neither
working in an inferior medium, nor saddled with an inferior system of
punctuation, nor denied the very various powers that rhythm can
command.

Let me turn to another predecessor, from the great line of poet-
critics. Yet it may be that it is the poet-critics who are most tempted
to misvalue prose as against poetry, especially if they themselves wrote
their prose more to gain a living than that they might have life and that
they might have it more abundantly.[12]

Robert Graves on 'Prose and Poetry': 'Prose is the art of manifest
statement.' It depends what prose. The King James Bible? Traherne,
Johnson, Jane Austen, Ruskin, Dickens, Henry James, I. Compton-
Burnett, Beckett? True, the claim that prose is the art of manifest statement can, in a way, manifestly be shown to be true, or be made to be

---

11. Four pages in a book of mine, *The Force of Poetry* (Oxford, 1984), are devoted to the
    greatness of the prose of this scene and to the heroism of Hamlet (pp. 61–5). The
    present text of the plays draws upon both Folio and Quartos. The prose performs in
    a dramatic work: 'the best example for a sentence with a particular meaning is a
    quotation from a play' because 'the contexts of a sentence are best portrayed in a play',
    Wittgenstein, *Last Writings on the Philosophy of Psychology* (Oxford, 1982), i. 6; from Eric
    Griffiths, 'Lines and Grooves: Shakespeare to Tennyson', in *Tennyson Among the Poets*,
    ed. Robert Douglas-Fairhurst and Seamus Perry (Oxford, 2009), 155.
12. On the poet-critic in relation to the novelist as critic, see p. 135 below.

true. All you have to do is limit your chosen prose to prose of which it is true. But.

> Prose is the art of manifest statement: the periods and diction may vary with the emotional mood, but the latent meanings of the words that compose it are largely disregarded. In poetry a supplementary statement is framed by a precise marshalling of these latent meanings; yet the reader would not be aware of more than the manifest statement were it not for the heightened sensibility induced in him by the rhythmic intoxications of verse.[13]

Largely disregarded, even as (in Graves's way), genuine thought is being very largely disregarded. Can rhythmic *intoxications* really be trusted to minister to heightened sensibility? But then again if people are told, by a true poet (for all his being a fickle authority), that when they read prose they ought not to be bothered with rhythm, sadly they may be happy to go along with unawareness. But their reading, their sense of the many forms that due attention may rewardingly take, will be a thin thing. 'One doesn't "listen" when reading standard prose.' Yet Graves, secure in the confidence (justified, which cannot but complicate things) that his own prose isn't mediocre as would be *standard prose*, does count on his readers coming to count and listen to the beats at least:

> One doesn't 'listen' when reading standard prose; it is only in poetry that one looks out for metre and rhythmic variations on it. The writers of *vers libre* rely on their printers to call your attention to what is called 'cadence' or 'rhythmic relation' (not easy to follow) which might have escaped you if printed as prose; *this* sentence, you'll find, has its thumb to its nose.[14]

By the thumbing of my nose, something wicked that way goes. The campaign to elect Robert Graves to the Professorship of Poetry had been enlivened by the slogan 'We Dig Graves'. Dig him, I did, and do, but not when he came, not to praise prose as well as poetry on occasion, but to bury prose. The campaign to elect Roy Fuller was supported by a life-line from Tennyson: 'More Life, and Fuller, that I want'.

Even W. H. Auden, of this Professorship, though he did not bite his thumb at prose, did not always give it the time of day. The introduction to *The Poet's Tongue* (1935) that he wrote with John Garrett begins:

> Of the many definitions of poetry, the simplest is still the best: 'memorable speech.' That is to say, it must move our emotions, or excite our intellect, for only that which is moving or exciting is memorable ··· [15]

13. 'Observations on Poetry (1922–1925)', in *The Common Asphodel* (London, 1949), 3.
14. Ibid. 8.   15. Auden, *Prose: 1926–1938*, ed. Edward Mendelson (London, 1996), 105.

But where does this leave all such literature as is prose? Auden casually calls prose 'all those uses of words that are not poetry'. Everything that Auden said here about poetry (including that 'The test of a poet is the frequency and diversity of the occasions on which we remember his poetry'[16]—or hers) does strike me as true, but true solely because true of all literature (and of all art?) and not as genuinely characterizing, leave alone defining, poetry. Not, that is, as differentiating poetry from other things—prose, for one, 'all those uses of words that are not poetry'.

When one poet-critic thumbs his nose at another, this may because the thumber is nailing the thumbee as soft on prose. I'd have thought that A. E. Housman was quite sufficiently lauding poetry when he said that 'it may differ from prose only in its metrical form, and be superior to prose only in the superior comeliness of that form itself, and the superior terseness which usually goes along with it'.[17] (What I tell you three times is true: *superior*...) And comeliness? Come now. This would have to depend on whether comeliness itself could always be becoming. Housman persevered in this conviction that somehow all literature would be poetry if it could, but he did along the way lapse into an admission that was to earn him the fury of Ezra Pound. Housman:

> When I examine my mind and try to discern clearly in the matter, I cannot satisfy myself that there are any such things as poetical ideas. No truth, it seems to me, is too precious, no observation too profound, and no sentiment too exalted to be expressed in prose. The utmost that I could admit is that some ideas do, while others do not, lend themselves kindly to poetical expression; and that these receive from poetry an enhancement which glorifies and almost transfigures them···[18]

Uncharacteristically slippery of Housman, this, for he was not one to permit to others such rhetorical evasions as 'almost transfigures'. (Almost? Try, instead, thinking out—with precision—the ways in which *transfigures* both is and is not the right word.) But anyway Pound could hardly believe his ears, and was delightedly released to express his contempt of Housman for too much respecting prose. Pound:

> 'No truth', says Housman, 'too precious, observation too profound, sentiment too exalted to be expressed in prose'.

---

16. Auden, *Prose: 1926–1938*, 106.
17. 'The Name and Nature of Poetry' (1933), in *Collected Poems and Selected Prose*, ed. Christopher Ricks (Harmondsworth, 1988), 351.
18. Ibid. 364.

I am unqualified to speak of exalted sentiment, but I should say no idea worth carrying in the mind from one year's end to another, and no story really good enough to make me at least want to tell it, but chafes at the flatness of prose, but suffers from inadequate statement, but leaves me feeling it is but half said, or said in abstraction, defined in terms so elastic that any god's ape can stretch its definition to meet his own squalor or to fit his imbecility, until it be conjoined with music, or at least given rhythmic definition even though one do not arrive at defining its total articulation.[19]

Pound was too often keen to execute summary justice. 'I begin with poetry because it is the most concentrated form of verbal expression.'[20] (As for prose: 'One reads prose for the subject matter.'[21]) Yet nothing could be more concentrated than the verbal expression that is a proverb, and to resort then to saying that proverbs are a form of poetry would be to win at all costs, including the cost of bogus argument and of annulling any such differentiation. If whenever prose is characterized by concentration (or by any other of the things that are falsely held to characterize poetry, such as suggestiveness, rhythm, metaphor, or reaching the parts that other literary kinds fail to reach) we simply co-opt the word *poetic* or *poetry*, we evacuate the argument. Any such victory is emptily rhetorical, circularly sawing the air.

Among Auden's opinions was that 'The difference between verse and prose is self-evident, but it is a sheer waste of time to look for a definition of the difference between poetry and prose'.[22] I need to spend a moment saying where, for me, the matter stands. In 1928, T. S. Eliot remarked, 'Verse, whatever else it may or may not be, is itself a system of *punctuation*; the usual marks of punctuation themselves are differently employed.'[23] This insight into verse might be adopted and adapted within a consideration of poetry. If we set aside metre, the remaining poetry/prose distinction is that in prose the lines run the full breadth of the page. In prose, the line-endings are without significance, and may be the creation not of the composer but of the compositor; in poetry, the line-endings are significant, and they effect their significance—not necessarily of rhythm, and whether of force or of nuance—by using their

19. 'Mr Housman at Little Bethel' (1934), in *The Literary Essays of Ezra Pound* (London, 1954), 70–1.
20. *ABC of Reading* (New Haven, CT, 1934), 36.   21. Ibid. 61.
22. 'Writing', in *The Dyer's Hand* (London, 1963), 23.
23. *Times Literary Supplement*, 27 September 1928. In 1921, 'The distinction between "verse" and "prose" is clear; the distinction between "poetry" and "prose" is very obscure'. 'Prose and Verse: The Definition', in *The Chapbook*, No. 22 (April 1921), 4.

ensuing space, by using a pause which is not necessarily a pause of punctuation or timing and so may be only equivocally a pause at all.

Lines of prose have a way of ending with what could be thought
of, computer-wise, as a soft return. Learning to read may do well to
begin with nursery rhymes, where the line-units are characteristically
sense-units.

> Jack and Jill
> Went up the hill
> To fetch a pail of water

When, as children, we moved on then to prose, it meant having to
learn to disattend to line-endings; we managed it, and have by now
forgotten what a feat it was, this training in disattending.

Such a working distinction works most of the time, and in poetry it
can work wonders. The art of Milton is repeatedly and diversely an art
of realizing what it is to play the line-unit against the sense-unit;
Donald Davie wrote with exquisite precision about such flickers of
hesitation in *Paradise Lost*.[24] There is no exact equivalent in prose
(prose has its own effects unachievable *except* by soft return) to the
taunting comedy that John Berryman mounts by beginning the fourth
of his Dream Songs with a suggestive line of poetry that both is and is
not a unit of sense—and of the senses: 'Filling her compact & delicious
body'.

Pull yourself together, man. The appeal to your goatish disposition is
a temptation you'd better resist, a beckoning that will turn at once, as
you round the corner of the line, into a reckoning, a slap on the wrist:

> Filling her compact & delicious body
> with chicken páprika, she glanced at me
> twice.
> Fainting with interest, I hungered back
> and only the fact of her husband & four other people
> kept me from springing on her

But any such distinction works only most of the time. For there
exists, on occasion, the hard return within prose (and only the usual
weasel would try to evade this), the hard return that is, for instance,
paragraphing, or the one that is the inscription. It would evacuate the
argument, along the old lines, to claim that an inscription is poetry, not
prose, and yet the inscription stands in need of hard returns. Don't

---

24. 'Syntax and Music in "Paradise Lost"' (1960), in *Older Masters* (Manchester, 1992).

even think, as they threaten in the USA, of displaying an inscription
that would segregate the word UNITED within this:

THIS STONE WAS LAID
BY
THE PRESIDENT OF THE
UNITED
STATES OF AMERICA

Or, within the United Kingdom, of sectioning MOTHER:

THIS STONE WAS LAID
BY
QUEEN ELIZABETH THE QUEEN
MOTHER

But back to the larger differentiation of poetry from prose, especially as to preferential treatment or favoured-nation status.

Writing on 'The French Play in London', Matthew Arnold went so
far as unmisgivingly to disparage even Shakespeare's prose at the very
moment of consolidating the immitigable hierarchy. 'The freshness and
power of Molière are best felt when he uses prose · · · How entirely the
contrary is the case with Shakespeare; how undoubtedly is it his verse
which shows his power most!'[25] Clinched with exclamatory power!
Undoubtedly: Arnold has closed his mind and stopped his ear.

It is to a rhetorical question—'Which of us doubts · · ·?'—that he will
have recourse when, praising Shakespeare, he heightens the rhetoric as to
poetry versus prose. But the case is not only that of poetry versus prose, it
is that of England versus France. France (Arnold acknowledged) had
boasted in the person of Sainte-Beuve one critic who had his priorities
right. 'LIMITS OF PROSE': this was Arnold's heading, in his Notebooks,
for an excerpt from Sainte-Beuve on Chateaubriand, an assertion that
moves on to accord to poetry the higher flights and the higher status:

En prose, il n'y a rien au delà [Arnold: *such things as Chateaubriand's best*]. Après
de tel coups de talent, il n'y a plus que le vers qui puisse s'élever encore plus
haut avec son aile.[26]

LIMITS OF PROSE: and these needed to be understood not as limits
only, but as severe limitations. Yet some of the French, Arnold reports,

25. *Selected Criticism of Matthew Arnold*, 163.
26. *The Note-Books of Matthew Arnold*, ed. H. F. Lowry, Karl Young, and Waldo Hilary
    Dunn (London, 1952), 474.

are questioning a superiority that should not be in question; that of five lines of poetry from *Henry V*, for instance.

Which of us doubts that imaginative production, uttering itself in such a form as this, is altogether another and a higher thing from imaginative production uttering itself in any of the forms of prose? And if we find a nation—

—the French nation, *cela va sans dire*—

And if find a nation doubting whether there is any great difference between imaginative and eloquent production in verse and imaginative and eloquent production in prose, and inclined to call all imaginative producers by the common name of poets, then we may be sure of one thing: namely, that this nation has never yet succeeded in finding the highest and most adequate form for poetry. Because, if it had, it could never have doubted of the essential superiority of this form to all prose forms of utterance.[27]

'It could never have doubted'; 'no doubt'; 'undoubtedly': no stops are left unpulled. 'Which of us doubts · · ·?' Well, I, for one. Shakespeare's greatest prose is, for me, in no way lesser than his greatest poetry although it works its deep effects upon us differently, with other cadences and rhythms, voicing and interaction.

Or there is the supreme prose of Samuel Beckett. The opening of *Ill Seen Ill Said*, translated from the French by the author, envisages the very heights and depths:

From where she lies she sees Venus rise. On. From where she lies when the skies are clear she sees Venus rise followed by the sun. Then she rails at the source of all life. On. At evening when the skies are clear she savours its star's revenge. At the other window. Rigid upright on her old chair she watches for the radiant one. Her old deal spindlebacked kitchen chair. It emerges from out the last rays and sinking ever brighter is engulfed in its turn. On. She sits on erect and rigid in the deepening gloom. Such helplessness to move she cannot help. Heading on foot for a particular point often she freezes on the way. Unable till long after to move on not knowing whither or for what purpose. Down on her knees especially she finds it hard not to remain so forever. Hand resting on hand on some convenient support. Such as the foot of her bed. And on them her head. There then she sits as though turned to stone face to the night. Save for the white of her hair and faintly bluish white of face and hands all is black. For an eye having no need of light to see. All this in the present as had she the misfortune to be still of this world.

The French as published after several revisions is this: 'Garder la pose est plus fort qu'elle'. Successive drafts in English: 'She knows well this

27. *Selected Criticism of Matthew Arnold*, 159.

loss of power to move'; 'This loss of power to move she is powerless to prevent'. Final rendering in English: 'Such helplessness to move she cannot help'.[28] The thought and the feeling have reached their heroic line.[29] A loving exasperation finds itself tinged with a tender rebuke to any such loving exasperation, tender because it understands the cross-currents of feeling, the all-too-natural refusal to admit to oneself that a loved one simply *cannot*.

'From the French': Arnold thought that what came from the French was misguidance. Tennyson, looking across the English Channel, likewise feared trouble from the French, though he had in his sights not culture-wars but wars:

> Ready, be ready! they mean no good:
> Ready, be ready! the times are wild!
> Bearded monkeys of lust and blood
> Coming to violate woman and child!   (*Rifle-Clubs!!!*)[30]

A mere two years later, the Crimean War brought home that *nous avons changé tout cela* (Molière's impostor-doctor, on the relative positions of the heart and the liver, including the lily-liver), and the new cry from Tennyson had become this:

> Frenchman, a hand in thine!
> Our flags have waved together!
> Let us drink to the health of thine and mine
> At the battle of Alma River.[31]

Arnold, for his part, would have welcomed the flag waved by Paul Valéry, the flaunting of poetry, the flouting of prose. Yet, for T. S. Eliot, this is the very point at which to part company with Valéry. 'There is, however, one direction in which Valéry's theory and practice take him, which seems to me not without its dangers.' *Not without its dangers*, to put it mildly; Eliot does so, but steelily withal.

---

28. *Ill Seen Ill Said* (1982), 7. *Mal Vu Mal Dit* (1981), 7. *Mal Vu Mal Dit / Ill Seen Ill Said*, ed. Charles Krance (New York, 1996), 2–3, 43–4, 167–8.

29. See p. 314 for the opening and closing of Beckett's *Ceiling* as constituting a heroic couplet:

> On coming to the first sight is of white.
> Endless ending breath. Dread darling sight.

30. The original version (1852) of *Riflemen Form!*, in *The Poems of Tennyson*, ed. Christopher Ricks, 2nd edn (London, 1987), iii. 601.

31. Ibid. 627.

This direction is indicated, is even imposed, by the sharp distinction which he draws between poetry and prose. He supports this division by a very neat and persuasive analogy, *viz.*:

Poetry : Prose :: Dancing: Walking (or Running).

Prose, Valéry maintains, is *instrumental*: its purpose is to convey a meaning, to impart information, to convince of a truth, to direct action; once its message has been apprehended, we dismiss the means by which it has been communicated. So with walking or running: our purpose is to get to a destination. The only value of our movement has been to achieve some end that we have set ourselves. But the purpose of the dance is the dance itself. Similarly with poetry: the poem is for its own sake—we enjoy a poem as we enjoy dancing· · ·[32]

Eliot finds the analogy persuasive, or rather, momentarily persuasive; he offers what he amiably dubs a 'quibble' when it comes to dancing as never purposive ('the purpose of a war dance, I believe, is to rouse the dormant pugnacity of the dancers'), and then he moves with entire courtesy not just to a caveat but to a repudiation:

I think that much poetry will be found to have the instrumental value that Valéry reserves to prose, and that much prose gives us the kind of delight that Valéry holds to be solely within the province of poetry. And if it is maintained that prose which gives that kind of delight *is* poetry, then I can only say that the distinction between poetry and prose has been completely obliterated, for it would seem that prose can be read as poetry, or poetry as prose, according to the whim of the reader.

To turn to a successor to Valéry, Yves Bonnefoy, is to engage with another creative and critical mind of the utmost scruple and pertinacity, intent on the word *mind* itself and on how variously Shakespeare's use of the word may need to be rendered in French. I am indebted to Anthony Rudolf, himself one of M. Bonnefoy's translators, for many generosities, among them his drawing my attention to Bonnefoy's deep and wide book, *Shakespeare and the French Poet*.[33] Let me commend and recommend it, even while dissenting from it at the place where, by now, I shall be expected to dissent.

'Translating into Verse or Prose': Bonnefoy is enduringly persuasive in his central contention. 'There is a certain inevitability about translating into verse what was written in verse.'[34] But then it would follow that what was written by Shakespeare as prose should be translated

32. Introduction to Paul Valéry, *The Art of Poetry* (New York, 1958), pp. xv–xvi.
33. Edited by John Naughton (Chicago, 2004).
34. Ibid. 243. Translated by Anthony Rudolf.

into prose; fine, of course, and Bonnefoy does not dissent from this, though he does not bring himself to speak of it. For translating prose into prose might turn out to be more easily done than said. Bonnefoy can't quite bring himself to say it, since prose is to him a lesser being. True, he quotes superlatively from Shakespeare's superlative prose (Falstaff, most notably), but then there looms an unacknowledged difficulty. For Bonnefoy is one of those who believe that it is poetry alone that is superlatively good; prose is only comparatively good:

If poetry exists, it is because poets have wanted the sonorous dimensions of words to be heard, to be an active element in the elaboration of form, so that meaning alone no longer determines the phrase · · ·

But poets are not the only writers who value the sonorous dimensions of words or who aspire to larger utterance than meaning alone. 'So that meaning alone no longer determines the phrase': whereas in prose...? Bonnefoy is explicit as to poetry's being verse and prosody (which precludes the evasive move that others make, which is to lavish the word *poetic* upon such prose as passes their muster). Bonnefoy, with characteristic honesty, worries at his decision to translate—against his own principles—*Venus and Adonis* into prose. But there it is. 'Too much of the richness of this poem can survive in translation only on the level of prose.' (Going down: Lower Level: Prose, Instrumentalities, Limitations.) 'Let us say I resigned myself to prose.'

To attend—in translation or out of it—only to concepts would indeed be to fall short, but would it be exactly what Bonnefoy calls it? 'By definition this would merely be prose.' But great prose, that of Proust, say, is not a mereness. 'There may be a level of self-awareness where prose is a worthwhile instrument of expression.' Even the concession has rather a grudging air. A level of self-awareness: then from *a* to *the*. 'This is the level on which intelligence labours without any feeling for transcendence · · · seeking to know human reality only insofar as it remains an object, reducible to entirely natural laws · · ·'.[35]

Bonnefoy expresses his disappointment at the translation of Shakespeare's verse into prose; understood, but his position at once involves him in deprecating not just prose translations (of any uninspired kind) but prose in itself. His position, we are unsettlingly assured, 'in no way implies that all prose translation should be proscribed, for

---

35. Bonnefoy, *Shakespeare and the French Poet*, 232–5, 249–55.

there is still a case where, provided it is aware of its limits, the non-poetic approach to a poet can contribute to the truth'. *Thanks, I suppose*, as the urchin in Beckett says to the grown-up who hands him his marble. And what of the occasions when a great writer chooses to work not in poetry but in what is finding itself called the *non-poetic*. Prose is reduced to a non. Yet on this same page Bonnefoy repeatedly adduces Hamlet, Hamlet whose self-awareness before the duel is voiced unforgettably in prose.

'And as for feelings, which poetry lays bare as no other words can···': this very paragraph of Bonnefoy invokes again the Prince of Denmark, without confronting the critical incompatibility of a disapprobation for prose with the highest approbation for a play that again and again realizes its deepest apprehensions in the form and moving of prose, not poetry.

What a piece of worke is a man! how Noble in Reason! How infinite in faculty? in forme and moving how expresse and admirable? in Action, how like an Angel? in apprehension, how like a God? the beauty of the world, the Parragon of Animals; and yet to me, what is this Quintessence of Dust? Man delights not me; no, nor Woman neither; though by your smiling you seeme to say so. (II. ii)

And what a work of art is the prose that says so. Itself noble in reason, infinite in faculty, in form and moving how express and admirable, in action and in apprehension a beauty and a quintessence and a delight: all this, despite the inferiority of prose?

On 13 September 2019, the *Times Literary Supplement* published a 'lunchtime talk' given by Eliot in 1954, on poetry and drama.[36] Still central for him, after all his years, was the question *Why in verse?* But his answer is one that can be credited only if we avert our minds from the greatness that prose can command. Can and does command, and this within the great prose of Shakespeare himself. And of Johnson, Dickens, Henry James, Beckett...

Why in verse?

Because, I think, there is always a point beyond which words fail, without the help of verse rhythm to intensify the emotion. There are things which can be expressed in verse and not in prose, simply because the rhythm, the sound of the words, is essential for the full meaning. The words in that order have an

---

36. From the Hayward Bequest, and now in *The Complete Prose of T. S. Eliot*, vol. 8, ed. Jewel Spears Brooker and Ronald Schuchard (Baltimore, 2019).

enhanced value. You have only to try to make a prose paraphrase of any great lines of verse, to see that this is true; you have only to put some great scene of Shakespeare's into prose, to see that there is a <u>dramatic</u> loss—something that has evaporated from the emotions of the characters.

Simply because?

Eliot, when young, had been crisp and impartial on 'The Value of Verse and Prose':

I take it for granted that prose is allowed to be, potentially or actually, as important a medium as verse, and that it may cost quite as much pains to write. Also that any enjoyment that can be communicated by verse may be communicated by prose, with the exception of the pleasure of metrical form. And there is an equivalent pleasure in the movement of the finest prose, which is peculiar to prose and cannot be compensated by verse · · · the writing of prose can be an art as the writing of verse can be an art · · · prose, not being cut off by the barrier of verse which must at the same time be affirmed and diminished, can transmute life in its own way by raising it to the condition of 'play,' precisely because it is not verse.[37]

Yet by 1954: ' · · · simply because the rhythm, the sound of the words, is essential for the full meaning. The words in that order have an enhanced value.'[38] But such is the case with any imaginative meeting of *how* with *what*, of manner with matter, of style with substance, of medium with message, of form with content. Why is such a claim, a claim that is indeed happily true of great poetry—why is this *not* true of great prose? Why does 'the help' have to be '*verse* rhythm'? Great writing of any kind whatsoever lives likewise in such convictions. And though it is of course the case that 'You have only to try to make a prose paraphrase of any great lines of verse, to see that this is true', it is no less true that you have only to try to make a paraphrase of *any* great passage of writing, &c. &c. Try making a paraphrase of Shylock's 'Hath not a *Jew* eyes?', or of Hamlet's 'But thou would'st not thinke how ill all's heere about my heart: but it is no matter'. Eliot's way of setting up the disquisition—'you have only to put some great scene of Shakespeare's into prose'—is framed to ignore the great scenes of Shakespeare that *are* in prose, and to deny that any great scene could

37. 'Prose and Verse', in *The Chapbook*, No. 22 (April 1921), 5–6.
38. 'Prose equals words in their best order; poetry equals the best words in the best order' (Coleridge; p. 4 above). 'I am content to leave my theorizing about poetry at this point. The sad ghost of Coleridge beckons to me from the shadows' (the closing words of *The Use of Poetry and the Use of Criticism*).

ever be in prose already. Yet in 1921, in a page on 'One Kind of "Poetic" Prose', Eliot had deprecated a famous passage from Sir Thomas Browne (on 'these dead bones') in these terms: 'Even if it be "poetry," it is not great poetry like such sepulchral things as the Grave Digger Scene in *Hamlet* (which is prose, besides) · · ·'[39]

Alas poore *Yorick*, I knew him *Horatio*, a fellow of infinite Jest; of most excellent fancy, he hath borne me on his backe a thousand times: And how abhorred my Imagination is, my gorge rises at it. Heere hung those lips, that I have kist I know not how oft. Where be your Jibes now? Your Gambals? Your Songs? Your flashes of Merriment that were wont to set the Table on a Rore? No one now to mock your own Jeering? Quite chop-falne? Now get you to my Ladies Chamber, and tell her, let her paint an inch thicke, to this favour she must come. Make her laugh at that: prythee *Horatio* tell me one thing · · · (V. i)

'Alas poore *Yorick*.' Alas, poor critics, set to persuade themselves, in some trade-union demarcation-dispute, that such writing—being prose, not poetry—has of course had to do without 'the rhythm, the sound of the words', has had to sacrifice any possibility that 'the words in that order' might have 'an enhanced value'.

'In poetry, form is not a framework but an instrument of research' (Bonnefoy). True, if true, here only? No, true no less of all those times when prose is great writing no less than is poetry.

Yet exquisitely true, it must further be said, of the poet Yves Bonnefoy, for and to whom the deepest response is gratitude.

[*Further gratitude was and is owed to those whose voices were heard in the concluding part of the lecture in 2004: Yves Bonnefoy, for supplying a recording of Ronsard's* 'Quand vous serez bien vieille · · ·' *and of his own translation into French of Yeats's Ronsardian poem* 'When you are old and grey and full of sleep'; *Jean-Philippe Puymartin, for his recording of two poems by Baudelaire; and David Ferry, for his translations of them*: The Blind People *and* The Abyss.]

39. 'Prose and Verse', in *The Chapbook*, No. 22 (April 1921), 7.

2

The Anagram

' I was well enough treated at Cambridge, but glad to leave it, it made me "*lemancholy*" for many reasons.'[1] Byron, to Hobhouse, 2 November 1811. *Lemancholy*: melancholy because of something's having gone askew, thanks to a lover, a leman. The disorder is real but it does manage to arrive at a new order. The anagrammatic shuffling is characteristically Byronic in its combination of discomposure and composure, a state of mind intimate with a state of body, love-sick.

The terms of the British Academy's Shakespeare Lecture ask for some Shakespearean subject, philosophical, historical, or philological. One focus for a loving study of words might legitimately be a device of which the legitimacy is often impugned: the anagram.

The anagram, which may be seen and not heard, may be seen as a historical phenomenon, as a religious intimation, and as a literary and linguistic resource. Shakespeare's sonnets are one place to look for and at anagram. This, not in the interests of showing that A. N. Other wrote the sonnets or that they are coded, but because the anagram— with which the minor poets of the late sixteenth century and the seventeenth century were fascinated (and of which Donne, Jonson, and Herbert signally availed themselves)—may be understood as one form that metaphor may take, in its bringing together (as does rhyme) likeness and unlikeness revelatorily.

My hope is, first, to make good a claim on behalf of anagrams as capable of being a true assistance to art, this claim then asking that I proffer something of an anthology; second, to recollect that the particular period is the heyday of the anagram, especially in its religious

1. *Byron's Letters and Journals*, ed. Leslie A. Marchand, ii (London, 1973), 124.

intimations; and third, to illustrate from Shakespeare's sonnets the secular felicities to which the anagrammatic may variously give rise.[2] Sonnet 14 writes of reading, and it sets something before our eyes.

> But from thine eies my knowledge I deriue,
> And constant stars in them I read such art
> As truth and beautie shal together thriue

It is not only 'from thine eies' that knowledge is derived, but from mine eyes too, since it is they that do the reading—and that read the word 'art' as derivable from the word 'stars'.

Of commentators on the sonnets, it is Helen Vendler who has been quick-eyed when it comes to anagrammatic filaments, and in *The Art of Shakespeare's Sonnets* (1997) she adduces in Sonnet 14 'the graphic overlaps among *stars, astrology, constant*, and *art*'. Since vowels and consonants are manifestly both visual and audible, there will always be an overlap of the two (phonemic or phonetic, and graphic, in Vendler's terms). I should want only to point out that the overlapping can be seen to crystallize in *stars / art*, and that this enjoys the manifest guidance of 'my knowledge I deriue' and of 'I read'. Colin Burrow, in his edition of the sonnets, remarks that 'Vendler's is a fine study of the poems' aural magic';[3] true, but given that it is Vendler's emphasis on the graphic, not on the phonetic, that most distinguishes her commentary, it comes happily to mind, within a lecture today, that my voice cannot make clear the difference between 'aural' and 'oral', the eared and the mouthed, though the eye is in no doubt as to which word is proffered.

No one knows how trustworthy the text of the 1609 Quarto of the sonnets is, but 1609 remains all that we have, and for this first instance of mine there is no need to appeal even to old spelling. Yet the word 'read' does distinguish the art of the page from that of the stage. The positioning of the anagrammatic turn, there at the line-ending with 'art', bears out the aptness of William Drummond of Hawthornden, in his 'Character of a perfect *Anagram*':

---

2. I wrote briefly on anagrams in Shakespeare's sonnets and elsewhere, in *The Balcony* (Sydney, March 1965). Helen Vendler, in *The Art of Shakespeare's Sonnets* (Cambridge, MA, 1997), says of the line in Sonnet 87, 'In sleepe a King, but waking no such matter': 'the rhyme internally present in *a king* and *waking* (the only internal words in the poem ending in -*ing*) is therefore necessarily foregrounded, rendering the pun noticeable—though it does not seem, for all its flagrantness, ever to have been noticed.' The present writer noted it in the past, back in 1965.
3. *The Oxford Shakespeare: Complete Sonnets and Poems* (2002), 108.

An Anagram, which turneth in an Hemistich or half Verse, is most pleasant. However it be, in an Epigram or Sonnet it fitly cometh in mostly in the Conclusion, but so that it appeareth not indented in, but of it self naturally.[4]

In the Conclusion, the anagram can the more saliently take to itself the effect of a rhyme, a clinch. People often speak as though there were something inherently trivializing about the anagram, as against the rhyme. This, as though there were sound effects and then those other things, unsound effects. Anagrams, it must be granted, may be trivial, flippant, or empty, but then so may be rhymes, or apt alliteration's artful aid. That 'room' rhymes with 'doom' is in itself no more arbitrary than that 'room' anagrammatizes into, or may form a palindrome with, 'moor', or that 'doom' may form a palindrome with 'mood'. An anagram is no more and no less arbitrary than a rhyme. Anyway artists are arbiters, with a gift for convincing us that their acts of arbitration amount to more than the capricious or whimsical. An anagram is a coincidence, true—but you should hear the voice of the bard, and take what you have gathered from coincidence.

The anagram has been in a few respects the beneficiary of the crossword puzzle (with its incitements to be alert to what can alter), but it has mostly been the victim of pressure from the crossword puzzle and its entertainment value, pressure to disrespect the anagram, to take it to be no more than the occasion for an ephemeral puzzlement, an item with which to kill time.

For there is a prejudice against anagrams, including the *parti pris* of many poets who use them. (Not that it is unusual for poets to practise what they inveigh against; Pope deplores amphibologies, and Samuel Johnson puns.) Practice is here at odds with asseveration in three poets, in three distant ages born.

First, Ben Jonson, of whom Drummond reported that 'he scorned Anagrams & had ever in his mouth *turpe est, difficiles amara Nugas.* | *et stultus labor est ineptiarum'.*[5] But in *Hymenaei* (1606), Jonson put the following lines in another's mouth:

4. *Works* (Edinburgh, 1711), 230–1.
5. Martial 2.86.9–10, in *Ben Jonson*, ed. C. H. Herford and Percy Simpson, i (Oxford, 1925), 144. In *An Execration upon Vulcan*, Jonson mentions 'those hard trifles Anagrams'. He refers to anagrams in *A Pleasant Comedy* (II. viii), *Epicoene* (III. iii), and *The New Inne* (I. vi).

> And see, where I VNO, whose great name
> Is V NIO, in the *anagram*,
> Displayes her glistering state, and chaire,
> As she enlightned all the *ayre!*[6]

The masque, aware that it is for the stage, not the page, spells out 'in the *anagram*', while urging 'see' and while displaying the word 'Displayes'. Again, this poet who scorned anagrams avails himself of an intricate one, scarcely available to the ear (one would have thought), in *The Speeches at Prince Henry's Barriers* (1610):

> Now when the Iland hath regain'd her fame
> Intire, and perfect, in the ancient name,
> And that a *monarch* æquall good and great,
> Wise, temperate, iust, and stout, *claimes A RTHURS seat.*

In the Conclusion, he who 'claimes Arthurs seat' is Charles James Stuart, James I; the anagram is from Camden, 1605, and it recurs in Jonson's *For the Honour of Wales* (1618), where it is seconded by '*Charles Stuart, cals true hearts*'.[7] Jonson may scorn anagrams, but it is not scorn that he is using them to pour here.

The second such poet is A. E. Housman, who poured scorn on wit in poetry whenever it depended, in Dr Johnson's words, upon the 'discovery of occult resemblances in things apparently unlike': 'Such discoveries are no more poetical than anagrams; such pleasure as they give is purely intellectual and is intellectually frivolous.'[8] True, there is a frivolous Housman poem that speaks in mock-anguish of the finite intellect, and yet how inspired it was of Housman to ensure that a poem on 'The Amphisbæna' should include a palindrome:

> The question which bereaves of bliss
> My finite intellect is this:
> Who, who, oh, who will make it clear
> Which is the front and which the rear?

'Oh who' doesn't know whether it is coming or going. But there are occasions when the anagrammatic turn is anything but frivolous. Take the opening of *A Shropshire Lad* XLI, a great evocation of the enduring wishfulness that is the pathetic fallacy, nature in sorrowing sympathy with me:

---

6. *Ben Jonson*, vii (1941), 217.   7. *Ben Jonson*, vii. 323, 509.
8. *The Name and Nature of Poetry* (Cambridge, 1933), 13.

THE ANAGRAM 23

> In my own shire, if I was sad,
> Homely comforters I had:
> The earth, because my heart was sore,
> Sorrowed for the son she bore;

The earth is no more and no less than his heart, reconfigured and seen under a different aspect; and his heart's being 'sore' (there at the line-ending, 'in the Conclusion') then finds itself dilated, and doubly so: first, into the immediate expansion of 'sore' into 'Sorrowed', at the head of the line, and then into the expansion in the Conclusion of successive lines, 'sore' into 'son she bore'. Both 'Sorrowed' and 'son she bore' put before us, in order, s o r e. Heartfelt, the dilation, and creating, in its different way, something of the effect that Keats achieved in those lines of his that speak of 'mysteries | That made my heart too small to hold its blood'.[9]

The third such poet is T. S. Eliot, who, constraining his admiration for Marvell's *The Definition of Love*, declared: 'compared to the twistings of the brain of Donne, this is mere parroting of anagrams'.[10] Yet Eliot is the poet who opens the landscape that is *Rannoch, by Glencoe* with a patient succinctness that profits from something ana-grammatic. Not the 'parroting of anagrams', but the crow, and the company it keeps.

> Here the crow starves, here the patient stag
> Breeds for the rifle. Between the soft moor
> And the soft sky, scarcely room
> To leap or soar.

'Scarcely room': no more than there is room for a main verb in the second sentence. Room only for a word to re-arrange itself, in the moment when 'moor' ('in the Conclusion', to value Drummond yet again) turns to occupy the space of 'room', the perfectly fitting and patient anagram, or re-tracing of the steps, as a type of rhyme.[11] One way to appreciate Eliot's calm leap here is to recall the wrong softness, the lack of tautness, in the lines of Swinburne that went to the making of Eliot's moment, Swinburne's 'Prelude' to *Songs before Sunrise*, from stanza 9:

---

9. *The Fall of Hyperion*, i. 253–4.
10. *The Varieties of Metaphysical Poetry*, ed. Ronald Schuchard (London, 1993), 135 (the Clark Lectures, 1926).
11. Here I draw upon my book *T. S. Eliot and Prejudice* (London, 1988), 214.

> Ah, see, between soft earth and sky,
> What only good things here are ours!

Then again Eliot would not have promptly admitted an accusation—along Housman's lines—of being intellectually frivolous, since Eliot delighted in making art out of what others deemed intellectual and frivolous. For this or such was Eliot's way. As in *The Love Song of J. Alfred Prufrock*:

> No! I am not Prince Hamlet, nor was meant to be;
> Am an attendant lord, one that will do
> To swell a progress, start a scene or two,
> Advise the prince; no doubt, an easy tool,
> Deferential, glad to be of use,
> Politic, cautious, and meticulous;
> Full of high sentence, but a bit obtuse;

Everyone can sense that this invokes Polonius. Not everyone consciously notices, although many may unconsciously register, that the line 'Politic, cautious, and meticulous' is one that can swell a progress as it moves from its opening *Pol* to its Conclusion *us*, via—in sequence—o n i. Polonius lurks behind the arras of the line.[12] In the vicinity of the arras, the meticulous became the metrical in this same year in which Eliot published *Prufrock and Other Observations* (1917), when he wrote: 'We may therefore formulate as follows: the ghost of some simple metre should lurk behind the arras in even the "freest" verse; to advance menacingly as we doze, and withdraw as we rouse.'[13] In due course metre was to be transformed again, this time into motto, when the arras shook in the duly undulating line of *East Coker* (1940): 'And to shake the tattered arras woven with a silent motto'.

I

The anagram has lived as a literary and linguistic device through the ages.[14] Within Romantic poetry, for instance, it is one of Byron's

12. *The Poems of T. S. Eliot*, ed. Christopher Ricks and Jim McCue (London, 2015), i. 396; augmenting *Times Literary Supplement*, 14 March 1997.
13. 'Reflections on "Vers Libre"' (1917); *To Criticize the Critic* (1965), 187.
14. The 1911 *Encyclopaedia Britannica* article on anagrams is enduringly informative.

resources.[15] The Queen had wanted to keep to herself handsome young Don Juan (who is disguised as a woman and ensconced in the harem); now the eunuch Baba is being quizzed by her about his dereliction of duty:

> But there seemed something that he wished to hide,
>   Which hesitation more betrayed than masqued;—
> He scratched his ear, the infallible resource
> To which embarrassed people have recourse.
>
> *(Don Juan*, Canto VI, 100)

Resource / recourse: this is itself both a resource and a recourse, an anagram as well as a rhyme (in the Conclusion not only of the lines but of the stanza). There is something that the lines wish both to hide and to betray (but then 'masqued' is exactly right for this duplicity). 'Resource' pulls itself together, albeit differently, as 'recourse'. Baba is recourseful and resourceful. As is Byron. Just how much, may be appreciated if one contrasts his art with a pious anagram that mentions a resource instead of realizing one:

> When *I cry that I sin* is transposed, it is clear
> My resource *Christianity* soon will appear.

Byron likes to throw in an allusion and then guide it with something of an anagrammatic turn. As when a wife is eager to berate her husband. Of husbands:

> And even the wisest, do the best they can,
>   Have moments, hours, and days, so unprepared,
> That you might 'brain them with their lady's fan;'
>   And sometimes ladies hit exceeding hard,
> And fans turn into falchions in fair hands,
> And why and wherefore no one understands.
>
> *(Don Juan*, Canto I, 21)

The allusion is to Hotspur's contempt for 'a shallow cowardly Hinde': 'By this hand, if I were now by this Rascall, I could braine him with his Ladies Fan' (*1 Henry IV*, II. iii). Such was Byron's inspiration for the lines, but what then inspires them is his extravagantly witty play with the little letters. A fan can be expanded into a flutter or a flirt of feeling, so Byron expands the words, with a flick and a shake, into 'falchions'

---

15. For Byron and anagrams, see the essay in my book *Allusion to the Poets* (Oxford, 2002), on which I draw here.

(swords): *fans* / *falchions*; and then manages to trump even this hand with the expansion into two words, again preserving the sequence of the letters: *'fair hands'*.

> And fans turn into falchions in fair hands

—*turn into*, yes, you can say that again, and Byron does, twice. Or rather, he does better than say, he sets it flutteringly before our eyes. 'And why and wherefore no one understands'? But the *how* at any rate we can understand.

Byron is a master of indelicacy, Keats of delicacies. These, sometimes anagrammatic:

> for, every minute's space,
> The streams with changèd music interlace:
> Sometimes like delicatest lattices,   (*Endymion*, ii. 612–14)

A space of time ('every minute's space') remains at once clear and mysterious, and so is the interlacing by which 'lace' is woven into both of the words 'delicatest lattices', and this again in the Conclusion of the lines. Keats creates both a 'changèd music' for the ear and fluid streams for the eye.[16]

Again, Victorian poetry delights no less, albeit differently, in what the anagram may effect. George Meredith enforced a thoroughgoing finality for the closing lines of the closing sonnet (L) of *Modern Love*:

> In tragic hints here see what evermore
> Moves dark as yonder midnight ocean's force,
> Thundering like ramping hosts of warrior horse,
> To throw that faint thin line upon the shore!

This Conclusion may speak of hints and of that faint thin line but there is a force here that goes beyond hints and beyond anything faint and thin. Two pairs of rhymes, prised open (*evermore* / *shore* enfolding *force* / *horse*), are compounded not only by the obdurate assonance of all four conclusive lines (*more* / *force* / *horse* / *shore*) but by the final anagram, the plural *horse*, wave upon wave of them in regiment, pounding the *shore*. Ben Jonson: 'And see'; Meredith: 'here see', with the alerting of the eye to the page, 'see' being at one with the homophone 'sea' that is the groundswell of 'yonder midnight ocean's force'.

---

16. In *Musicks Empire*, Marvell, extraordinarily, brings music into apposition with the least fluid of the visual arts: 'Then Musick, the Mosaique of the Air'.

Against the tragic force of such a Victorian anagram might be set the comic darkness of the singularly different nineteenth-century poet, Emily Dickinson. A poem of hers opens:

> The Mushroom is the Elf of Plants—
> At Evening, it is not
> At Morning, in a Truffled Hut
> It stop opon a Spot
>
> As if it tarried always
> And yet it's whole Career
> Is shorter than a Snake's Delay—
> And fleeter than a Tare—

Why did she not parallel 'it is not' with the due syntax 'It stops'? *It stop?* Answer to this riddling: because of the sudden surprise, like that of the mushroom's dawning, that moves from 'stop' to 'Spot'—and this via the Dickinson spelling of 'upon' as 'opon'.[17] The closing word of the line, of the stanza, 'Spot', has no stop after it (the syntax continuing into the next stanza with 'As if'), so that the absence of punctuation is evenly at odds with the anagrammatic deftness. Meanwhile, 'Elf' has perhaps found itself in reverse, in reserve, within 'Truffled', and in the second stanza 'tarried' is to find itself both 'shorter' and 'fleeter' in the form of a 'tare'. Yet once more, both the turn upon *stop / Spot* and that upon *tarried / Tare* are precipitated in the Conclusion.

'It stop opon a Spot': the relation there of the graphic to the phonetic, at once congruent and discrepant, may be apprehended if we think of the sound effect of the sequence, at once alike and unlike, in Beatrix Potter's *The Tale of Peter Rabbit*: 'Mr McGregor came up with a sieve, which he intended to pop upon the top of Peter; but Peter wriggled out just in time, leaving his jacket behind him.'

Within twentieth-century poetry the anagram unobtrusively flourished. I think, first, of Charles Tomlinson and *A Meditation on John Constable*:

> If delight
> Describes, which wrings from the brush
> The errors of a mind, so tempered,
> It can forgo all pathos; for what he saw

17. Five manuscripts have the opening quatrain with no variants of wording, all with the spelling 'opon' (the usual spelling by Dickinson; see R. W. Franklin, *The Poems of Emily Dickinson* (Cambridge, MA, 1998), iii. 1333). Thomas H. Johnson's inaugural edition (Cambridge, MA, 1955) had 'upon'.

> Discovered what he was, and the hand—unswayed
> By the dictation of a single sense—
> Bodied the accurate and total knowledge
> In a calligraphy of present pleasure.

A poem on a painter, especially by a poet who is himself a visual artist, does well to invite us to consider these different ways of seeing and believing. In the apophthegmatic sequence 'what he saw | Discovered what he was', the simplest of reversals, *saw* into *was*, can effect the most complex of apprehensions, and this because of the refusal to be swayed 'By the dictation of a single sense'. Knowledge is at one with intuition and with happy accident; Tomlinson's quiet effect (there in the Conclusion of the line at 'saw') is both continuous with and crucially different from what William Blake effected when he set before our eyes and ears not an anagrammatic effect but a turn of a different kind: 'terrifid at the Shapes | Enslavd humanity put on he became what he beheld'.[18]

The instances that I shall now offer deserve more than their being reduced to instances, but my duty today is less to them than to Shakespeare. So, in brief, there is the art of Richard Morgan, who ends his *De Provinciis Consularibus*:

> The sleek roofs shine after the rain like keels
> In the rich sun which sometimes shines also on London.
> Men find it difficult not to hate this town.

I find it impossible not to love the fluidity (of water and of light) that slides with ease from 'sleek' to its reversal, in the Conclusion of the line, as 'keels'. Contemplating again a rainscape, I am moved by the very different dislocation in the Conclusion of Ted Hughes's *Heptonstall*:

> Life tries.
>
> Death tries.
>
> The stone tries.
>
> Only the rain never tires.

The double spacing is Hughes's, following upon three quatrains that were single-spaced. Such is the Conclusion of the poem, never tiring.

Fortunately, as Austin Clarke reminds us in *Martha Blake*, the anagram may repay prayer:

18. *Vala, or the Four Zoas: Night the Fourth.*

Afflicted by that love she turns
To multiply her praise,
Goes over all the foolish words
And finds they are the same;
But now she feels within her breast
Such calm that she is silent,
For soul can never be immodest
Where body may not listen.[19]

Here 'silent' is metamorphosed, with effortless felicity, in the
Conclusion, into 'listen'. The stanza's succession is a combination of
assonances (*turns / words, praise / same*), first with a rhyme where the
stress falls upon different syllables (*breast / immodest*) and then with
assonance likewise falling upon syllables differently stressed (*silent /
listen*) issuing furthermore in this simply miraculous anagram. (The
poem had earlier apprehended: 'The word is said, the Word sent down,
| The miracle is done'.) When 'silent' becomes 'listen' before our very
eyes, our ears may listen for ever to or for the silent intimation. There
is at this point in the poem no need for the clinching that a rhyme may
be, whereas at this turn in the preceding stanza (the sixth line into the
eighth), there had been the full rhyme *them / hem*, and in the stanza
before that, the full rhyme *tongue / sung*.

An anagram may assist a poem in its largest movements of mind but
then in its tender miniatures too. I think of the moment in Nabokov's
translation of *Eugene Onegin* when Tatiana is seen *not* to embroider:

Her delicate fingers
knew needles not; over the tambour bending,
with a silk pattern she
did not enliven linen.[20]

Agreed, there is a sound-link in 'enliven linen', but it would be misleading not to see another link (in the Conclusion); the word 'linen' is
glimpsed in 'enliven' in a way that is delightfully apt to the process of
embroidery. The tone is one of banter, not of barter—'enliven' is, after
all, a generous word, so that the shuffling of, and selection from, the
letters has its own dignity, and even has something of an eighteenth-
century mock-heroic manner:

19. I praised this irresistible achievement in *A Tribute to Austin Clarke on His Seventieth
    Birthday* (Dublin, 1966).
20. *Eugene Onegin*, ch. 2, stanza XXVI; tr. Vladimir Nabokov (London, 1964), i. 142.

> If DIAN at the Frame display'd her Power,
> And charg'd the Needle with the future Flower.[21]

The anagram may enliven poetry; there will always remain a proper
doubt as to whether it can, to the same degree or in anything like the
same way, enliven poetic drama. Yet Geoffrey Hill, in his masterly
translation of Ibsen's *Brand*, feels free to call not only upon off-rhyme
(*not / throat*) but upon the compounding of off-rhyme with a wrung
anagram (*groan / organ*):

> What have I made? Not music, not
> music! Cries wrung from music's throat!
> Splayed chords of discord, a groan
> rising in the place of praise, the organ
> stormed, faltered;[22]

Not music, in part because these cries are to be evoked by the mind's
eye as well as heard by the ear. Hill urged, in section 85 of his sequence
Speech! Speech!, 'Develop the anagram', and in section 97 he set before
our eyes

> millennial
> doom-mood, nihilism's palindrome,

—a palindrome that dislikes the doomster's complacency, even while it
manages—with its central *m-m*, confirmed by all those o/zeros—to
call up the millennium. There in sequence may be O O O O, for all
the world as though we were hearing again that Shakespeherian Rag.

There will always hang about the conversion that is anagram the
possibility of something perverse, but then again it is Hill who in *The
Orchards of Syon* XXV has said broodingly 'Perverse | to persever'. Not
persevere, but the good old form, perséver, ever-lasting. John Kerrigan,
in his edition of Shakespeare's sonnets, invited us to remember, though
not apropos of anagrams, that 'In our own time, the work of Geoffrey
Hill strikes the same troubled note.'[23]

21. Phanuel Bacon, *The Kite* (1722), Canto I.
22. *Brand: A Version for the Stage* (1978; third edn, Penguin, 1996), Act V, p. 123. Forming
    half of Hill's *Peer Gynt and Brand: Verse Translations by Geoffrey Hill* (Penguin, 2016).
23. *The Sonnets and A Lover's Complaint* (Harmondsworth, 1986), 29.

II

The gravity accorded to the anagram, as a historical phenomenon within the Renaissance, may be both seen and heard in George Chapman's dedication of *The Iliad*:

An Anagram of the Name of our dread Prince,
 my most gracious and sacred Mæcaenas:
  Henrye Prince of Wales
  Ovr Sunn, Heyr, Peace, Life

Be to us as thy great Name doth import,
  (Prince of the people;) nor suppose it vaine,
That in this secret, and prophetique sort,
  Thy Name and Noblest Title doth containe
So much right to us; and as great a good.
  Nature doth nothing vainly; much lesse Art
Perfecting Nature. No spirit in our blood,
  But in our soules discourses beares a part.
What Nature gives at random in the one,
  In th'other, orderd, our divine part serves.
Thou art not HEYR then, to our state alone;
  But SUNN, PEACE, LIFE. And what thy powre deserves
Of us, and our good, in thy utmost strife;
  Shall make thee to thy selfe, HEYR, SUNN, PEACE, LIFE.

With, the anagram not only at the head but, as so often, in the Conclusion.

For Matthew Arnold, this dedication by Chapman was immitigably unHomeric:

All the Middle Age, with its grotesqueness, its conceits, its irrationality, is still in these opening pages; they by themselves are sufficient to indicate to us what a gulf divides Chapman from the 'clearest-souled' of poets, from Homer; almost as great a gulf as that which divides him from Voltaire.[24]

There is a certain comedy, given the anagrammatism by Chapman, in Arnold's mentioning Voltaire here, Voltaire who chose his name as an approximate anagram of his surname at birth, Arouet.

Religion or its sibling superstition is everywhere to be found in the onomastic divination that constituted so much of the Renaissance

---

24. *On Translating Homer I; On the Classical Tradition*, ed. R. H. Super (Ann Arbor, MI, 1960), 113.

fervour for anagrams. James Stuart: a just master. Marie Stuvarte (Mary Stuart): Sa vertue m'attire; Tu as eu martire. It was pointed out by H. B. Wheatley that anagrams were common on tombs, 'as if the character or the fortunes of the person were providentially hidden in the name'.[25] There is the cry that one would like to think is apocryphal:

> What needs an anagram
> Since that her very name is Anna Grame?[26]

Or there is the preposterous inextricability of Crashaw and his friend Car:

CRASHAWE
THE
ANAGRAMME.
HE WAS CAR.

> Was CAR then Crashawe; or WAS Crashawe CAR,
> Since both within one name combined are?
> Yes, Car's Crashawe, he Car; t'is loue alone
> Which melts two harts, of both composing one.
> So Crashawe's still the same: so much desired
> By strongest witts; so honor'd so admired.
> CAR WAS but HE that enter'd as a friend

—and so for another forty lines or ad infinitum. Still, nil desperandum, for comic relief is at hand, in Wheatley's adducing

one of the most delightful anagrams on record. It contains all the requisites of a perfect one, every word is appropriate, and all must be charmed to find the qualities displayed in the name of such an honour to human nature as Miss Nightingale:
Flit on, cheering angel[27]

It is by no means certain that the Lady of the Lamp was one to flit; rather a heavy tread, fortunately, I'd have said. But what is clear is that the complimentary anagram has always liked the company of the satirical one, the opposite of a compliment though often with an element of reluctant admiration, especially for the natty turncoat.

> Harold Wilson: Lord Loinwash
> Tony Blair, MP: I'm Tory Plan B

---

25. H. B. Wheatley, *Of Anagrams* (1862), 122.   26. Ibid. 110.   27. Ibid. 138.

Arnold's belief that between the world of Homer and that of Chapman there loomed a great gulf, and that the anagram can represent this, might have to be modified if the classical world were not that of Homer but of Lucretius. For it is a long time ago that Paul Friedländer wrote on 'Pattern of Sound and Atomistic Theory in Lucretius',[28] demonstrating that what had been thought to be jingles in Lucretius were anagrammatic effects that derived from the congruence of atoms and letters within *elementa*. Of such a turn as *Ennius / perenni*, he argued that 'Ennius *is* an eternal poet. A similar chance joined the atoms into the shape of this poet and the atoms of language into his name expressing his eternity.'[29] Friedländer's arguments persuaded the Oxford editor of Lucretius, Cyril Bailey: 'a permutation of the letters changes the meaning, just as a rearrangement of the atoms in wood may produce fire'; 'The atomism which the Epicureans found in matter, time, and space, is extended also to language.'[30] Etymology is on good terms with atomology.

The linguistic theory of the last hundred years has been drawn into this. Cratylism became execrated.[31] The poets, or some of them, remonstrated, especially when it came to onomatopoeia and the linguists' claim to have shown (they have done no such thing) that, even if onomatopoeia existed, it would constitute nothing more than a peripheral or trivial objection to their dissociation of words from meanings. Claudel averred:

I know only too well the objections philologians could raise. Their arguments would be even more crushing as regards the symbolical value of written signs than that of phonetic signs. And yet, no proof would convince a poet that there is no rapport between the sound and the meaning of a word, for if there were none, he might as well give up his trade straight away. And is it really so absurd to believe that the alphabet is the epitome and image of all acts, all gestures, all attitudes, and in consequence, all feelings of humanity in the midst of the vast creation which surrounds us?

28. *American Journal of Philology*, 62 (1941), 16–35.
29. Similarly, *mater / terram* and *ligna / ignis*.
30. *De Rerum Natura*, ed. Cyril Bailey (1947), i. 158–9.
31. See Michel Pierssens, *La tour de Babil* (Paris, 1976), perversely translated as *The Power of Babel* (1980), which studies Plato's Cratylus, and Saussure, Mallarmé, and onomatopoeia. Also Josué V. Harari (ed.), *Textual Strategies* (Ithaca, NY, 1979). The outstanding essay on the ancient argument is by Hans Aarsleff, 'Locke on Leibniz on Language' (1964), collected in his *From Locke to Saussure* (Minneapolis, 1982).

Should one believe that between phonetic movement and written sign, between expression and that which is expressed, throughout linguistic history, the rapport is purely arbitrary?[32]

Saussure notoriously pursued anagrams.[33] In pursuing Saussure, Charles Rosen was moved to elicit explicitly what Valéry had been realizing within his poetic art:

To conceal a word phonetically within a set of different words is a legitimate poetic effect; there is a famous example in Valéry's *Cimetière Marin*:

> La mer, la mer, toujours recommencée
> O récompense après une pensée
> Qu'un long regard sur le calme des dieux.

The second line literally illustrates the preceding word *recommencée* by hiding it and expanding it over the entire line, like a larger wave that builds itself up and breaks after a moment's tension, broadening the faster and more regular rhythm that preceded it.[34]

This is exquisitely noticed. One might add that 'recommencée' does then itself inaugurate a recommencing; that wittily this word is positioned not at a commencing but in the Conclusion of the line; that the calm of the gods is Lucretian in a way that might be apt to atomology; and that Rosen's word 'phonetically', though true, does less than justice to the element that is graphic, the intimation to the eye that— giving weight to 'literally' as of the letters, and to 'illustrates' as for the eye—'literally illustrates the preceding word *recommencée* by hiding it and expanding it'.

Rosen moves on to make two general points, both strong although the first need not, I continue to believe, narrow itself to a *phonetic* pattern:

The significance of Saussure's ninety-nine notebooks is to show the intimate relationship between poetry and the processes of language and, above all, to demonstrate the power of a phonetic pattern to demand a meaning, the right to exist as a truly functioning part of language.
Saussure thought he was investigating not an attribute of language, but an esoteric technique of poetry. Ironically, what he found was an attribute of language which is a necessary condition for the existence of poetry.[35]

32. Quoted in Massin, *Letter and Image* (London, 1970), 127.
33. See Jean Starobinski, *Les Mots sous les mots: Les Anagrammes de Ferdinand de Saussure* (Paris, 1971); perversely translated as *Words upon Words* in 1980.
34. 'Concealed Structures' (1971), in *Romantic Poets, Critics, and Other Madmen* (Cambridge, MA, 1998), 196.
35. Ibid. 197–8.

The poets, no less than the linguists, have a way of havering. Valéry avers that 'There is no relationship whatsoever between the sound and the meaning of a word.' But this thoroughgoing insistence is modified, irreparably albeit evasively, when Valéry also claims: 'We realize that there is hardly an instance in which the connection between our ideas and the groups of sounds that suggest them each in turn is anything more than arbitrary or purely fortuitous.'[36] 'Hardly an instance' is easily said. But I should return from this controversy, ancient and modern, to the historical phenomenon and the Shakespearean moment. For the much mentioning of the anagram, both occult and overt, is a phenomenon of the half century that begins by nursing Shakespeare and his art. The *Oxford English Dictionary* (*OED*) can be seen to concentrate the word *anagram* and its cognates.

1589	anagram	Puttenham
c.1590	anagrammatized	Marlowe
1591	anagrammatize	Nashe
1605	anagrammatical	
	anagrammatically	
	anagrammatism	Camden, all three words
1613	anagrammatist	Gamage
	anagrammist	Hoby
1630	anagram [verb]	Taylor
1636	anagramize	Sampson

There is an intense topicality, then, attending upon the anagrams of this period; one might comparably imagine the annotation that, in times to come, will be needed by a future reader who stares blankly at a cartoon that shows a man in front of a computer screen and the words Waiting for Godot.com.

Moreover, this concentration is furthered if one adds to it, from these same years, the nouns *transposition* (especially of letters in a word, 1582) and *transpose* (1589, Puttenham). It is Puttenham who in *The Arte of English Poesie* (1589), the second book, chapter XII, writes at some length 'Of the Anagrame, or Posie transposed':

One other pretie conceit we will impart vnto you and then trouble you with no more, and is also borrowed primitiuely of the Poet, or courtly maker we may terme him, the *posie transposed*, or in one word a *transpose*, a thing if it be done for pastime and exercise of the wit without superstition commendable

36. Both quoted by Gérard Genette, *Textual Strategies* (London, 1980), 369–70.

inough and a meete study for Ladies, neither bringing them any great gayne
nor any great losse, vnlesse it be of idle time. They that vse it for pleasure is to
breed one word out of another, not altering any letter nor the number of
them, but onely transposing of the same, wherupon many times is produced
some gratefull newes or matter to them for whose pleasure and seruice it was
intended: and bicause there is much difficultie in it, and altogether standeth
upon hap hazard, it is compted for a courtly conceit.

Puttenham inadvertently bears witness to the wrangle as to whether
the anagram is pastime or providence. This paragraph may limit its
pleasure in the anagram to 'pastime and exercise of the wit without
superstition commendable inough and a meete study for Ladies, neither bringing them any great gayne nor any great losse, vnlesse it be of
idle time'. Yet in no time Puttenham himself is marvelling at the div-
inations of which he was the conduit, manifest in the anagrams in
Latin with which he honoured Queen Elizabeth:

> Both which resultes falling out vpon the very first marshalling of the letters,
> without any darknesse or difficultie, and so sensibly and well appropriat to her
> Maiesties person and estate, and finally so effectually to mine own wish
> (which is a matter of much moment in such cases), I took them both for a
> good boding, and very fatallitie to her Maiestie appointed by Gods proui-
> dence for all our comfortes. Also I imputed it for no litle good luck and glorie
> to my selfe to have pronounced to her so good and prosperous a fortune · · ·[37]

'Gods prouidence' is promptly and prudently seconded by 'no litle
good luck', a playing of both sides of the Street which is called Straight
such as is worthy of Benjamin Jowett's famous sermon in Balliol
Chapel in 1874: 'We owe this to Providence, and a series of happy
accidents.'[38]

To Puttenham in these years should be added William Camden,
likewise on onomastic 'Anagrammes', where again there is a reluctance
either to credit or to discredit the religious and superstitious claims:

> The onely *Quint-essence* that hitherto the *Alchimy* of wit coulde draw out of
> names, is *Anagrammatisme*, or *Metagrammatisme*, which is a dissolution of a
> Name truly written into his Letters, as his Elements, and a new connexion of
> it by artificiall transposition, without addition, substraction, or change of any
> letter into different words, making some perfect sence appliable to the person
> named.

---

37. *Elizabethan Critical Essays*, ed. G. Gregory Smith (Oxford, 1904), ii. 112, 114–15.
38. *Geoffrey Madan's Notebooks*, ed. J. A. Gere and John Sparrow (Oxford, 1981), 114.

But some of the sower sort will say it is nothing but a troublous toy, and because they cannot attaine to it, will condemne it, lest by commending it, they should discommend themselves. Others more milde will grant it to be a daintie devise and disport of wit not without pleasure, if it be not wrested out of the name to the reproach of the person. And such will not deny, but that as good names may be ominous, so also good *Anagrammes*, with a delightfull comfort and pleasant motion in honest mindes, in no point yeelding to many vaine pleasures of the body.[39]

III

The contrast between the anagram as a religious intimation and as a secular device may be seen if one sets Herbert beside Donne. Herbert, as everyone knows, has several poems that incorporate such effects, whether as a diagonal italicizing ('*My* words & thoughts do both expresse this notion'), as an echo-poem (*Paradise*, GROW / ROW / ow), or as a spelling-out ('JESU', *I ease you*). But one poem of his can be seen to turn entirely upon an anagram.

$$Ana\text{-}\left\{\begin{array}{c}\text{M A R Y}\\\text{A R M Y}\end{array}\right\}gram.$$

How well her name an *Army* doth present,
In whom the *Lord of Hosts* did pitch his tent!

The title in 1633 divides *Ana* from *gram*, these then enfolding the anagram *Mary* / *Army* within curled brackets as though pregnant with its incarnation, miraculously pregnant.[40] The name *Mary* does not appear in

---

39. Camden, 'Anagrammes', *Remains Concerning Britain* (1605), ed. R. D. Dunn (Toronto, 1984), 142–3; 'will condemne it, lest by commending it' has something of the ana-grammatic about it. Drummond of Hawthornden begins his 'Character of a perfect *Anagram*' with '*Anagrams* are Names turned', and he reports: 'One will say, it is a friv-olous Art and difficult' (*Works*, 230–1).

40. Randall McLeod, writing as Random Cloud, comments: 'when Herbert constructs a title like

$$Ana\text{-}\left\{\begin{array}{c}\text{M A R Y}\\\text{A R M Y}\end{array}\right\}gram.$$

he throws together different spacial modes. This uneasy combination resists our accus-tomed strategies of reading. Do we read "*Anagram*" and then the contents of the brackets, which sunder it? And do we read "ARMY" then "MARY", or "MARY" then "ARMY"?' ('Enter Reader', in *The Editorial Gaze: Mediating Texts in Literature and the Arts*, ed. Paul Eggert and Margaret Sankey (New York, 1998), 5–6.)

the poem itself; it is known and is to be divined.[41] In the title, the palindrome *ana* is consummated, in due course, by *gram*, which does have much of the look of *mary* spelt backwards (a lower-case y is all but a g). It is odd, and to me a disappointment, that Herbert's great editor F. E. Hutchinson says nothing at all about anagrams in this period (but then he has no notes at all to the poem, other than textual variants); the providential compliment that was so often the *raison d'être* of the anagram would seem worth adducing, as would the recency of the vogue or cult in English poetry. But Rosemond Tuve did much to rectify Hutchinson's neglect, and her account of Herbert's poem is a *locus classicus* not only for this but for many such contextualizings:

Two traditional associations made this poem both less startling and more enjoyable to its writer and its first readers than to us. The first is the image of an army with banners for the Virgin Mary, in biblical commentary, in the liturgy of many of her feasts, and in the motets which a person knowledgeable about church-music would know.

The anagrammatic point, possible only in English, is (to my knowledge) Herbert's own; but it would not be easy for even an ill-read seventeenth-century Anglican cleric to avoid thinking of Mary and Army as belonging together, and, moreover, to think of that Army as 'The Church Militant' *as well as* Mary. I wish I knew how many of my readers had caught on first reading the whole new spread of meaning which this double operation of the metaphor gives to a poem that is not so tiny after all—Herbert is constantly preoccupied with how the Lord of Hosts has 'pitched his tent' in the heart of his *familia*, and Mary is the great allegory of that descent and union. The last line is not only, in other words, a reference to the event of the Incarnation, but to the Incarnation as itself a great metaphor.

It is also, of course, a reference to the Incarnation as an event, and in most conventional terms, novel and witty as they may seem to us. They are wittier than we see. 'Pitched his *tent*' has for us various unsuitable reverberations; for Herbert it held pretty certainly the different and much deeper implications of some common Vulgate phrase like 'extendit *tabernaculum* suum,' which it translates. 'Pitched his *tent* in' appears a dozen times as the King James translation of '...tabernaculum'. Durandus explicitly glosses *tabernaculum* as 'tent' or 'womb of Mary'.[42]

41. A very different not-naming from Herbert's has been adduced in *The Triumph of King James and his August Descendants*, where—writing as Ana Mary Armygram—Randall McLeod comments on a detail in Willem de Passe's engraving of the family of King James, where the revisions to the plate brought about some strange substitutions as to names and faces: 'In life, her name was Henrietta Maria' (*Shakespeare Studies*, 28 (2000), 184–8).

42. *A Reading of George Herbert* (Chicago, 1952), 138–40.

To this ample account, what might be added? First, I should desire a fuller context for the anagram, and in particular for the anagram that divines a providential truth within a name. There is more to be furnished than simply 'The anagrammatic point, possible only in English, is (to my knowledge) Herbert's own.' Second, the contrast of the Church Militant with the Prince of Peace and with peace upon the face of the earth. Third, the extraordinary wealth of the noun *presentation* and of the verb *to present*, its presenting so many aspects that are germane to the poem's contrasts and to the one far-off divine effect from which the whole creation moved. These, from the *OED*, are apt aspects devout, humble, generous, clerical, and military.

presentation 1a. The formal bringing or presenting of a person before God, as a religious act. Specifically, the *Presentation of Christ in the Temple*, as recorded in Luke ii. 22–39, and *Presentation of the Virgin Mary*, as a child, narrated in the Apocryphal Gospels. 1400. [including] The Book of Common Prayer (1662) The Presentation of Christ in the Temple, commonly called, the Purification of Saint Mary the Virgin.

present 1a. To bring or place (a person) before, into the presence of, or under the notice of another.. *spec.* to introduce at court, or before a sovereign or other superior, *c.*1290

1b. To bring before or into the presence of God; to dedicate by so bringing. 1387

5b. To offer (battle or the like). 1600

9a. To point (a weapon, esp. a fire-arm) at something; to hold (it) out in the position of taking aim, so as to be ready to fire immediately. 1579

11 To bring or place (a thing) before or into the presence of a person... give (usually in a formal or ceremonious manner). With various connotations: as (*a*) to offer or give as a gift; (*b*) to offer as an act of worship, as a sacrifice; (*c*) to offer or hand something in ministration, service, or courtesy; (*d*) to deliver or hand a letter; (*e*) to offer a book or literary work to readers.

11c. To deliver, convey, give (something non-material. esp. a message, greeting, or the like). 1385

12 To give, make presentation of (a benefice) *to* a clergyman. 1390

All of these senses of the verb, variously and proportionately alive to and in the poem, come together with yet one more, one that gravitates to this earthly birth:

9b. *Obstetrics.* Of the fœtus: To direct (a particular part) towards the *os uteri* during labour. Usually *intr.* for *refl.* said of the part so directed, or of the fœtus in relation to its position during labour.

1597 Followinge the naturall Childebirth, the childe allways præsenteth first
his heade.

There remains perhaps one further play within Herbert's succinct
success. For a poem that both is and announces an anagram, and that
begins 'How well her name...', may wish us to see that not only the
name *Mary* but the word *name* may present an anagram: *amen*. Several
filaments could be plaited together to strengthen this. First, the
sequence of sound in 'her name an *Army*', with '*Army*' setting out as
though it might issue in *Amen*. Second, the fact that the phrase 'Army
doth present' contains, in sequence, the letters a m e n. Third, that if we
bear in mind that Herbert's poem invokes the Church Militant, it may
be worth pondering the one occasion on which the word 'Amen' is
invoked in a poem of his (and this in the Conclusion, at the end of a
line and of a sentence): in, of all poems, *The Church Militant* (53–6):

> Plato and Aristotle were at a losse,
> And wheel'd about again to spell Christ-Crosse.
> Prayers chas'd syllogismes into their den,
> And Ergo was transform'd into Amen.

Spelling is succeeded, not by a spell, but by a miracle, the language of
pagan philosophy transformed into that of the Christian religion: 'And
Ergo was transform'd into *Amen*.' Now that is what you might call a
miracle. The third line—'Prayers chas'd syllogismes into their den'—
contains within itself, in sequence, a m e n, from the first word to the last
(or, if you prefer a slightly later *a*, from the second word, 'chas'd', to the
last). But no amount of anagrammatic ingenuity could have transformed
Ergo into Amen. That asked a miracle.[43] 'Name' into 'Amen' is a different
story. It may well be that one heartfelt response to Herbert's poem—

> How well her name an Army doth present,
> In whom the Lord of Hosts did pitch his tent!

—would be the subtle simplicity of *Amen to that*.[44]

---

43. Frances Whistler has brought home to me the further anagrammatic teasing in these
lines: the *Plato / Aristotle* overlap, and *risto* taken up within *Christ-Crosse*. To spell
Christ-Crosse was to rehearse the alphabet.
44. Mary was the beneficiary of the best-known religious palindrome, the angel's salutation
to her as the second Eve: *Ave / Eva*. Robert Southwell, *The Virgins salutation*, opens:

> Spell Eva backe and Ave shall you finde,
> The first began, the last reverst our harmes,
> An Angels witching wordes did Eva blinde,

The anagram, then, may lend itself to deep and haunting suggestiveness. There is the explicit question and the implicit answer that (in the spirit of Herbert though not by him) sees within Pilate's scepticism, *Quid est veritas?*, the profoundest faith: *Est vir qui adest*—'It is the man who is in your presence.'[45] It is not for Christ to reply to Pilate's 'What is truth?', with anything of pride or vanity ('*I* am', or 'Me, actually'). Or even to tap His finger upon His chest. Rather, there is alive within Pilate's question, if only Pilate had ears to hear, the tacit answer itself. How finely the anagram has Christ speak of himself, not only in the third person (as in Herbert's line, with its turn from 'I' to the 'he' who is both Son and Father: 'Why, he that built the world can do much more'),[46] but as a man: *vir*. To me it would be a wanton prejudice for anyone to deny imaginative power to such a feat of inspired simplicity as *Quid est veritas? Est vir qui adest.*

It is not Herbert but Donne whose ways with the anagrammatic are securely secular. The practice of dubbing *The Anagram* what was in Donne's posthumous volume of 1633 *Elegie II* is ill-judged for two reasons. First, neither 1633 nor any of the manuscripts can lend authority to 'The Anagram' as title.[47] Second, the titular announcement 'The Anagram' reduces to predictable anticlimax what ought to be the sudden surprise of the cruel crux in mid-poem:

———

> An Angels *Ave* disinchants the charmes,
> Death first by womans weakenes entred in,
> In womans vertue life doth now begin.

'In womans vertue' there is, in sequence, a v e.

45. The *OED* has this under 'anagrammatically', from Chambers, *Cycl.*, 1751. The feat feels medieval. H. B. Wheatley, *Of Anagrams* (1862), 87, uses the word Lucretian 'elements' in duly marvelling: 'When Pilate asked the question, "What is truth?" Jesus returned him no answer, but, strange to say, the words themselves contained the elements of the best and most appropriate reply: *Quid est veritas? / Est vir qui adest.*' A triumph for the Latin Vulgate, not for the Greek.

46.   Some said, that I the Temple to the floore
        In three days raz'd, and raised as before.
        Why, he that built the world can do much more:
        Was ever grief like mine?

        (*The Sacrifice*, 65–8)

47. So I have to dissent from the titular decision in the magnificent achievement that *is The Variorum Edition of the Poetry of John Donne,* vol. 2: *The Elegies,* ed. Gary A. Stringer, Ted-Larry Pebworth, Ernest W. Sullivan, John R. Roberts, Diana Trevio Benet, Theodore J. Sherman, and Dennis Flynn (Bloomington, IN, 2000): 'we have supplied the heading popular in the poem's printed sources (*The Anagram*).' Not in the printed source that is the most important of them all, 1633.

> Though all her parts be not in th'usuall place,
> She'hath yet an Anagram of a good face.[48]
> If we might put the letters but one way,
> In the leane dearth of words, what could wee say?

Donne himself likes to counteract the lean dearth of words with the help of a thread that leads to the adipose comedy which the anagrammatic can tickle. As in *Loves diet*:

> To what a combersome unwieldinesse
> And burdenous corpulence my love had growne,
> But that I did, to make it lesse,
> And keepe it in proportion,
> Give it a diet, made it feed upon
> That which love worst endures, *discretion*.

Here 'corpulence', 'had growne', and 'feed upon' are set against 'to make it lesse'—and what better way could there be of feeding this contrarious process than by having *diet* grow corpulently into *discretion*? In the Conclusion, too, of line, sentence, and stanza.

But let me do no more than point to this kind of life in Donne from word to word. In *Elegie VIII: The Comparison*, the 'beauty-keeping chest' is constituted not only of the lodging of *urne* within *fortunes* but of *best* within *brest* (in the Conclusion):

> Like Proserpines white beauty-keeping chest,
> Or Joues best fortunes urne, is her faire brest.

In *Elegy XII: His parting from her*, the impossibility that you and I might ever be sundered is manifest in the way in which *Rend us* is reconstituted as *sunder*, and this in the immediate vicinity not only of 'canst not divide' rhyming with 'ty'd', but of a quiet pun on 'letters' and a hint of the anagrammatic in the word 'shifts':

> Rend us in sunder, thou canst not divide
> Our bodies so, but that our souls are ty'd,
> And we can love by letters still and gifts,
> And thoughts and dreams; Love never wanteth shifts.

Elsewhere, still preoccupied with 'thoughts', Donne relishes the idea that an honest lover's thoughts need never fear their being transparent

48. The editions of Donne have seen, or mis-seen, no need to tell us anything about the vogue or passion for anagrams at the time (with its possible relevance to dating this Elegy), whether the editor be Herbert Grierson, Helen Gardner, A. J. Smith, C. A. Patrides, John Shawcross, or, most crucially, those of the Variorum edition of the Elegies.

to others. The interaction is between his loved word for the transparent, 'through-shine', and the thought:

> This, as an Amber drop enwraps a Bee,
> Covering discovers your quicke Soule; that we
> May in your through-shine front your hearts thoughts see.
>
> *(To the Countesse of Bedford)*

There 'through-shine front' can help us to see, without misgiving, 'thoughts'. In *The first Anniversary: A Funerall Elegie* we meet again an enwrapping, a covering and a discovering, a rejection of disguise when it contemplates a body's honest relation to thought and to mind.

> One, whose clear body was so pure and thinne,
> Because it need disguise no thought within.
> 'Twas but a through-light scarfe, her minde to' inroule;

—where 'thought' is duly inrouled within 'through-light'. Expansion and contraction alternate happily. In *Elegie XIX: Going to Bed, far fairer* enacts its comparative before our very eyes and ears, with its diffusion (set paradoxically against the girdle, the zone, the incompassing) enacted doubly, as *far* first is expanded into *fair* and then, incompassing the whole happy sigh, yet again into *fairer.*

> Off with that girdle, like heavens Zone glittering,
> But a far fairer world incompassing.

In *To the Countesse of Salisbury*, there is not dilation but contraction, there in the rhyme that makes abridgement and that draws to less:

> All trying by a love of littlenesse
> To make abridgments, and to draw to lesse,

It was Geoffrey Hartman who did so much to create the terms of such elicitings, when he appreciated the opening of *A Hymne to Christ, at the Authors last going into Germany.*

The qualified hope, the precarious finality of Donne's poetry is also that of religious hope. How to 'cross-over'—or the dangers of passage—is the central theme:

> In what torn ship soever I embark
> That ship shall be my emblem of thy ark.

'Whatsoever' opens and swallows 'torn ship' as the poet severs the grammatical bond to interject his fear. But 'embark' also opens to let a saving rhyme 'emb(lem) ark,'...emerge as the poet converts fear into hope by further prolepsis.[49]

Hartman is lastingly effective in his apprehension of Donne's effects here, and my only furthering would be, first, to evoke yet again Drummond's 'in the Conclusion', and second, to mention the increment that comes with old spelling as against Hartman's modernized text.

> In what torne ship soever I embarke,
> That ship shall be my embleme of thy Arke.
> What sea soever swallow mee, that flood
> Shall be to mee an embleme of thy blood;

In setting *I, my, mee, mee,* in subjection to *thy* and *thy,* these lines in their old spelling give salience to the *me* that is in *embarke* and that is reiterated in *embleme,* itself reiterated.

Helen Vendler has said of Shakespeare's Sonnet 107: '*Rime* even contains *me,* so that "*I'll* live in this poor ri*me*" becomes a self-guaranteeing statement.' This may well be so, and yet to think of those four lines of Donne is to have a more insistent instance before us. The same is true of Donne's play with *I* and *me,* as against *her* and *her,* in *Elegy XVII: Variety:*

> The last I saw in all extreames is faire,
> And holds me in the Sun-beames of her haire;
> Her nymph-like features such agreements have

—lines which tempt a critic to underline what he sees as held before him in agreements:

> The last I saw in all extrea*me*s is faire,
> And holds *me* in the Sun-bea*me*s of her haire;
> Her nymph-like features such agree*me*nts have

IV

> Creating euery bad a perfect best
> As fast as obiects to his beames assemble: (Sonnet 114)

49. 'The Voice of the Shuttle', *The Review of Metaphysics,* 23 (2) (December, 1969); *Beyond Formalism* (New Haven, CT, 1970), 345.

How conclusively *assemble* assembles those *beames*.[50] Shakespeare is like
Donne, not like Herbert: the anagram is not God's providence but is a
provision; not providential, but provisional. The editors of the sonnets
have been right *not* to draw attention to anagrams or to anagrammatic
effects, clusters of letters of which the repetition does not amount to
a sheer anagram. This abstention by the sonnets' editors is a good
decision, not because there are no such things in the sonnets, but
because an editor should not do a reader's work of this kind, any more
than an editor, *qua* editor, should draw attention to alliteration or
internal rhyme. Except in cases where there is information that we
lack as readers (as happens when it comes to the overt invoking of
the anagram by Donne and by Herbert), we should be left by editors
to do our own noticing even while we all stand in need of help
from critics—who are distinguishable from editors, though not distinct
from them.

   So I judge it well-judged of editors to have been silent here-abouts:
John Kerrigan, *The Sonnets and A Lover's Complaint* (1986); Katherine
Duncan-Jones, *Shakespeare's Sonnets* (1997); and Colin Burrow,
Complete Sonnets and Poems (2002). The position of Stephen Booth is
somewhat different, for in his unremittingly imaginative edition of the
sonnets ('Edited with an analytic commentary', 1977), Booth does find
room for just about everything that might ever enter anyone's head
when it comes to a word's interactions with other words. So, given this
capaciousness of his, it is surprising that he has no interest in the anagrammatic. Helen Vendler, on the other hand, who gives us not an
edition but a commentary (along with the sonnets both modernized
and in their 1609 text), makes effects of this kind the central contention and solicitation of her book, *The Art of Shakespeare's Sonnets*.[51]

---

50. Kerrigan: 'as quickly as things seen take shape in its (the *eye's*) gaze. Alluding, again, to
   the idea that the *eye* creates the *beams* by which it sees.'
51. For witty scepticism about some aspects of Vendler, see William Logan, *Parnassus*, 24
   (1999), 268–9: 'she's all too eager to find "hidden" anagrams, like a dotty Scrabble player:
   "The *mira* of *miracle* may have appealed to Shakespeare as an anagram of *rima* (rhyme)".'
   (This is Vendler on Sonnet 65.) Logan: 'More than one line, like "Devouring time blunt
   thou the Lyons pawes" (19.1) or "And from the forlorne world his visage hide" (33.7),
   contains the scrambled letters h-e-l-e-n v-e-n-d-l-e-r, the latter even conceals the letters h-e-l-e-n v-e-n-d-I-e-r h-i-d t-h-i-s. Shakespeare played language games, but
   perhaps not these games.' For my part, though I dissent from a good many of Vendler's
   suggestions, I cannot—as will already be clear—agree with Logan that 'Such cryptograms, even if real, wouldn't tell us much', given moreover that for me the effects are
   not any such cryptograms.

Keats wrote to John Hamilton Reynolds, 22 November 1817:[52]

One of the three Books I have with me is Shakespear's Poems: I neer found
so many beauties in the sonnets—they seem to be full of fine things said unintentionally—in the intensity of working out conceits—Is this to be borne?
Hark ye!

> When lofty trees I see barren of leaves
> Which erst from heat did canopy the herd,
> And Summer's green all girded up in sheaves,
> Borne on the bier with white and bristly beard.

Keats's own language is itself full of fine things said unintentionally, if by
this we mean without conscious intention perhaps—the move from
'unintentionally' to 'intensity', for instance, or the awe at Shakespeare's
power, scarcely endurable for a fellow-poet, 'Is this to be borne?', when
the Shakespearean power is to be adduced in 'Borne on the bier'. If we
restore the 1609 spelling to the lines from Sonnet 12, even more may
be glimpsed in the Conclusion:

> And Sommers greene all girded vp in sheaues
> Borne on the beare with white and bristly beard:[53]

Kerrigan remarks the double sense of 'bier' ('barrow for carrying har-
vested hay and grain', and 'stand upon which a corpse rests or is carried'),
and speaks of 'a kind of fruitful corpse'.[54] The paradox—which is the
one that James Joyce girded up in his anagrammatic spelling *cropse*, 'on
the bunk of our breadwinning lies the cropse of our seedfather'—might
then be compounded by the old spelling 'beare' (as against 'bier'), since
this has affiliations not only with 'Borne' ('Borne on the beare') but
with its homophone 'Born'.[55] ('Thou met'st with things dying, I with
things new borne'.) A fruitful corpse, then, because *not* barren even if
the trees are now 'barren of leaues'. Vendler points out that 'the
Quarto spelling, *beare*, so resembles the anthropomorphic *beard*', the
one word resembling the other both to the eye and the ear.[56]

---

52. *The Letters of John Keats*, ed. Hyder Edward Rollins (Cambridge, 1958), i. 188–9.
53. 'beare' = bier, and 'beard' off-rhymes with 'herd', though no one knows exactly with
      what sound.
54. Introduction to *The Sonnets and A Lover's Complaint*, 38.
55. Burrow: 'The combination of senses [of "bier"] turns harvest into a funeral, as the
      friend turns opportunities for reproduction into self-love.' With reproduction then
      into born, perhaps.
56. Contrast elsewhere the disconcerting discrepancy of eye and ear, of sight and sound,
      'in the Conclusion' of the line, in Sonnet 89: 'knowing thy wil, | I will acquaintance

The complex interplay within 'Borne on the beare with white and bristly beard' might be contrasted with the simplicity of movement in Sonnet 15:

> Then the conceit of this inconstant stay,
> Sets you most rich in youth before my sight,

Vendler demonstrates the sheer candour of this: '*Sets YOU most rich in YOUTH before my sight*. As tru-th is true-ness and streng-th is strongness, so you-th is you-ness, in this adoring pun.' This is itself adorable, and it tacitly appreciates the entire identity of sound and sight ('before my sight') in the relation of *you* to *youth*. The full and equable accommodation of the one word within the other makes the effect less of a transpose and more of a transport. This happy ease should be contrasted with the sense of mild strain that bears witness to the complication of feelings in Sonnet 22, where *youth / thou* is not, and should not be, felt to be quite the same as the earlier *you / youth*.

> My glasse shall not perswade me I am ould,
> So long as youth and thou are of one date,
> But when in thee times forrwes I behould,
> Then look I death my daies should expiate.[57]

Both 'behould' and 'look I' do something to set the poem before not only our ears but our eyes. And the same is true of 'truly write' in Sonnet 21:

> and all things rare,
> That heauens ayre in this huge rondure hems,

---

strangle and looke strange'. How it looks is different from how it sounds, the hard g against the soft. Shakespeare's intimations through discrepancy must modify, for me, one of Vendler's delighted observations, on Sonnet 29:

> Yet in these thoughts my selfe almost despising,
> Haplye I thinke on thee, and then my state,
> (Like to the Larke at breake of daye arising)
> From sullen earth sings himns at Heauens gate,

'In the most joyous play of the poem, the disgruntled present participles—*wishing, desiring*, with their "wrong" arrangement of letters—suddenly give rise to new present participles where the letters are arranged "right": *despising, arising*, and then the verb *sing*.' This of Vendler's is lovely, and yet it ought to acknowledge the different *s* to be heard in *sing* as against the participles where it is sounded as *z*. There is not a perfect fit of eye to ear, or of ear to ear, and this protects the lines against their being too gratifying, 'too consolatory to console' (a fine phrase from Frank Kermode, elsewhere).

57. *forrwes*: furrows, though the frequency of the long *s* in the vicinity may also invite sorrwes, sorrows.

> O let me true in loue but truly write,
> And then beleeue me, my loue is as faire,
> As any mothers childe, though not so bright
> As those gould candells fixt in heauens ayer:
> Let them say more that like of heare-say well,
> I will not prayse that purpose not to sell.

The word 'heare-say' in the sonnet's penultimate line has perplexed editors. Booth: 'The word is curiously weak and flat here; its choice was probably dictated by Shakespeare's desire to include the idea that other poets write (say) only what they have heard, i.e. stock phrases.' As will be expected, I resist the equating within 'write (say)', since the sonnets seem to me alive to the difference. Hear + say, as against writing and reading. (Burrow on *hearsay*: 'oral testimony rather than truth, making an implicit opposition between the private "writing" of Shakespeare and the public report of the imagined other poets'.) But I can lend a sympathetic ear to Booth's subsequent cockings of his:

Shakespeare may also have been attracted to the word *hearsay* by its potential for play on 'heresy', 'here-say', 'air-say' (see *heaven's air* in line 12), and possibly 'her-say' or 'hare-say'; the evidence of Elizabethan puns and rhymes is not definitive, but the words we spell 'her', 'here', 'hear', 'hair', 'hare', 'heir', and— since initial *h* was ordinarily silent in common words—'ear' and 'air', all apparently sounded enough alike to be confusable.

Vendler, along her lines (which are for me among the right ones), looks for the anagrammatic: 'It is impossible for me not to find *heare-say* (the Quarto) a derivation from *reherse* [in line 4] (also Quarto spelling), thereby accounting for the rather odd presence of *heare-say* in line 12 [*read* 13].' Vendler's is a point that would be not forfeited but fortified if to 'reherse' there were added the phrase, 'heauens ayre', returning as 'heauens ayer' just before 'heare-say' and anagrammatically to be found hemmed in its rondure.

Anagrammatizing, then, may be germane to emendation. There is the inspired double (and related) error in the Conclusion of Sonnet 23:

> O learne to read what silent loue hath writ,
> To heare wit eies belongs to loues fine wiht.

Booth: 'The Q spelling, "wit," probably reflects only the printer's inclination or carelessness, but, whatever the spelling, Shakespeare and his readers probably heard some kind of likeness between contemporary pronunciations of *with* and *wit*, the last word of the poem.' Vendler:

'The faulty Quarto spelling in line 14 (*wit* for *with*, and *wiht* for *wit*)
suggests that even the compositor's eye was distracted by the play of
with and *wit* in the one line.' When Burrow agrees that 'Q's compositor
was thrown by the play on *with* and *wit*', his anticipating Vendler's word
play might call up the contrast upon which the whole sonnet turns, the
contrast of play with poem, of stage with page, that nevertheless is well
aware that we watch the stage (not the same as reading, and yet...) and
that we hear in our heads the words on the page (not the same as the
stage, and yet):

> As an vnperfect actor on the stage,
> Who with his feare is put besides his part,
> Or some fierce thing repleat with too much rage,
> Whose strengths abondance weakens his owne heart;
> So I for feare of trust, forget to say,
> The perfect ceremony of loues right,
> And in mine owne loues strength seeme to decay,
> Ore-charg'd with burthen of mine owne loues might:
> O let my books be then the eloquence,
> And domb presagers of my speaking brest,
> Who pleade for loue, and look for recompence,
> More then that tonge that more hath more exprest.
> O learne to read what silent loue hath writ,
> To heare wit eies belongs to loues fine wiht.

The contrast of page and stage strikes me differently from how it
strikes Vendler, particularly in its relation to the anagrammatic. Apropos
of this sonnet, she says

Silent reading carried in Shakespeare's day a powerful reminiscence of oral
reading (to oneself or an audience), and the number of auditory puns in the
Sonnets testifies to Shakespeare's own ever-active ear, trained, of course, by his
constant writing for oral delivery on the stage. Given Shakespeare's stage
labors, it is even surprising that the *Sonnets* retain so many visual effects (e.g.
the anagrams in 7 or the plays on *w* in 9).

For me, the argument runs the other way, and the sonnets depend upon
ceaseless realizations of the way in which the eye's reading is other than
oral reception. So I should put differently her final point there, and
should rather say: Given Shakespeare's stage labours, and his awareness
of how the stage is not the page, it is not surprising that the sonnets
retain so many visual effects (e.g. the anagrams). Again, Vendler maintains that 'Precisely because he was a dramatist by temperament and by

training, Shakespeare could, in the 1609 Quarto, turn the external dramatic enactment we see here into the interior meditative drama of lyric.'[58] It is true that the sonnets are, among other things, interior dramas that owe much to Shakespeare's sense of dramatic enactments, but the sonnets should not be assimilated to the plays with complete equanimity, not least because the sonnets avail themselves of resources not amenable to the stage. Vendler is right to insist that 'Shakespeare's insistence on the eye as the chief sexual organ is everywhere present in the *Sonnets*, as in the plays',[59] but this is in danger of ignoring the way in which—on her own anagrammatic showing—the sonnets are open to the eye's especial aptitudes. She is on surer ground, that of the page (though I think that 'no interest' overstates), when she says of Sonnet 11:

> Whether the foregrounding of *seale* is remembered when one encounters *that beauty which you hold in lease* in 13 perhaps depends on whether the reader shares with Shakespeare the Renaissance fascination with the way words look when printed. A purely oral poetry can have no interest in anagrams; but Shakespeare belongs to the world of print, a world in which anagrams were recognized and enjoyed.

Relatedly, I believe that although Burrow is right to say that Shakespeare's poems and sonnets 'should not be consigned to the ghetto of "the non-dramatic verse"', I should want to qualify any implication that the sonnets, as against the narrative poems perhaps, possess 'a manner which is distinctively that of a dramatist'.[60] Distinguishing a sonnet's manner from a drama's is what distinguishes the sonnets, and one aspect of this distinction is the verbal device which can be so promptly and exactly seized by the eye in reading: the anagram or cognate effect. Sonnet 26:

> To thee I send this written ambassage
> To witnesse duty, not to shew my wit.

Sonnet 32:

> But since he died and Poets better proue,
> Theirs for their stile ile read, his for his loue.

The interplay of the written and the spoken, of different powers, is clear in the 'powrefull rime' that is Sonnet 55, which Kerrigan sees as contrasting 'The liuing record of your memory' with 'the written bias

58. *The Art of Shakespeare's Sonnets*, 7.   59. Ibid. 15.
60. *Complete Sonnets and Poems*, 5.

of this *record*'. The intimacy of the written is contrasted with at least
the possibility of the anagrammatic:

> When wastefull warre shall *Statues* ouer-turne,
> And broiles roote out the worke of masonry,
> Nor *Mars* his sword, nor warres quick fire shall burne:
> The liuing record of your memory.

Am I imagining things, or was—more valuably—Shakespeare doing
so, with a turn upon 'ouer-turne', when he had 'the worke of masonry'
(there in the Conclusion of the line) succeeded at once by two words
that are the rubble of masonry: 'Nor *Mars*'? There comes to my mind
the pleasure that Donne might have felt if, in *An hymne to the Saints*,
he glimpsed that the rubble of *Monasteries* might be reduced—again in
the Conclusion—to heaps of stone:

> So fell our *Monasteries,* in one instant growne
> Not to lesse houses, but, to heapes of stone;

There is something to be seen at these moments, as in Sonnet 64 when
it reiterates 'When I haue seene by times fell hand defaced... | When
sometimes loftie towers I see downe rased... | When I haue seene the
hungry Ocean gaine | Aduantage on the Kingdome of the shoare'—
and then arrives at this:

> When I haue seene such interchange of state,
> Or state it selfe confounded, to decay,
> Ruine hath taught me thus to ruminate
> That Time will come and take my loue away.

Booth urges: 'Note the phonetic play of *Ruin* and *ruminate*', yet we
should note too what is not phonetic but graphic, in the expansion of
the old-spelling *Ruine* in its undamaged entirety into *ruminate*, an effect
which is weakened if we modernize as Booth does with 'Ruin'.[61] The
contrast might be with an effect that is phonetic alone, and none the
worse for that but differently effective, in Sonnet 10: 'Seeking that
beautious roofe to ruinate'.[62]

The same increment from what is graphic may augment the loveli-
ness of Sonnet 116 and its asseveration about love:

---

61. Similarly with Burrow: 'the fact that the letters which make up *ruin* are hidden within
    ruminate'.
62. Vendler says of Sonnet 64: 'by our almost instinctive deletion of *m*, *ruminate* comes to
    contain *ruinate*.' I am suspicious of 'almost instinctive', but not of her point.

> Lou's not Times foole, though rosie lips and cheeks
> Within his bending sickles compasse come,

Kerrigan comments: 'The *sickle* seems to encompass the sonnet's *rosy lips and cheeks*, with cruel conviction, as we read'; yes indeed, and with the curve of the syntax—not 'Come within his bending sickles compasse' but 'Within his bending sickles compasse come'—confirmed at once by the immediacy with which *compasse* is heard to pass at once to *come*, in the Conclusion. But the concurrence of sound and syntax, with sound and sight at one, is then further confirmed by the old spelling— as it is not by the modernized 'compass', for it is only if we grant *compasse* its final 'e' that the words can perfectly encompass expansion and contraction, an extraordinary *Within*. So that Kerrigan's phrase, 'as we read', will accrue a fuller rightness if we appreciate this detail that can be seen but not heard. The stoical resilience of this moment in Sonnet 116 may be the clearer if it is set against the deliberately ungainly conglomeration as the sonnet's opening line turns into its second line:

> Let me not to the marriage of true mindes
> Admit impediments, loue is not loue
> Which alters when it alteration findes,

The word *impediments* accretes so much of what has just constituted *mindes Admit*. The clutter of letters, of dissonant consonants that nevertheless have so much in common, is one form that alteration may take. Impediments indeed.

Time, always not only the subject but the element of the sonnets, commands many gaits. The sun-dial takes its time, and its incremental indeflectibility is there for us to see in the anagrammatic sequence 'thy dyals shady stealth' (Sonnet 77), following as it does upon so much that asks that we be aware that we are reading, not hearing:

> The vacant leaues thy mindes imprint will beare,
> And of this booke, this learning maist thou taste.
>
> . . .
>
> Thou by thy dyals shady stealth maist know,
> Times theeuish progresse to eternitie.
> Looke what thy memorie cannot containe,
> Commit to these waste blanks,[63] and thou shalt finde

---

63. The editors follow Theobald's conjecture, which became Malone's emendation, reading 'blanks' for 1609's 'blacks'.

Those children nurst, deliuerd from thy braine,
To take a new acquaintance of thy minde.
These offices, so oft as thou wilt looke,
Shall profit thee, and much inrich thy booke.[64]

For all his acumen, Booth—because of his indifference to the ana-grammatic—does something less than justice to the central moment when he reduces a phrase of four words to three words, dropping *thy* from the progress and modernizing *dyals* into 'dial's':

> Thou by thy dyals shady stealth maist know,
> Times theeuish progresse to eternitie.

The ultimate effect of the careful imprecision of *dial's shady stealth* is to give the phrase, the three words, the capability the sentence attributes to what the three words describe: *dial's shady stealth* in line 7 anticipates, lets a reader know, *Time's thievish progress* in line 8.

Though an editor should not, in my judgement, point out felicities to us, there are occasions when an anagrammatic possibility might affect a textual decision. I am thinking of the most famous, the least ignorable, crux in the sonnets, the opening of Sonnet 146:

> Poor soule the center of my sinfull earth,
> My sinfull earth these rebbell powres that thee array,

Kerrigan represents the second line simply by

> [   ] these rebel powers that thee array,

He notes that 'Scores of emendations have been proposed for the phrase repeated from line 1', and he lists many though not all of them:

---

64. Pertinent to the anagram is Colin Burrow's commentary on Sonnet 77.

On the face of it this poem offers much to materialistic critics: memory must be written down and needs a material record. As critics are coming to recognise, the ways in which writers from this period recorded their thoughts in the physical form of a commonplace book have a profound effect on how they shaped their learning as they wrote, and on the ways in which they conceptualised the workings of their minds. But we should also notice here that when memory *is* written down in a material form it becomes some-thing more than mere matter; it becomes alive, something, or even someone, that one has to meet anew, like a new friend. In the imagery of the Sonnets memory more often accompanies the language of life than that of dead material; and as a result the poems imply that there is something more vital to memory than script, print, or matter. ('Life and Work in Shakespeare's Poems'; Chatterton Lecture (1997), *Proceedings of the British Academy*, 97 (1998), 25–6.)

Foiled by; Spoiled by; Soiled by; Swayed by; Starved by; Thrall to; Yoked to; Prey to; Fooled by; Bound by; Grieved by; Galled by; Vexed by; Pressed with; Served by; Ruled by; Feeding; Hemmed with; Leagued with.[65]

It might be noted, as giving perhaps some support to Kinnear's conjecture (1883), 'Thrall to', that *Thrall* would take up *ll earth* in the Conclusion of the previous line. Or, still attending to anagrammatic possibility, that a construction parallel to 'center of', *Heart of*, would immediately represent *earth* and would anticipate *dearth* in the next line.[66]

Vendler persuasively sees the sonnets as alive to *live / evil / vile*, so I was reminded of the shifts to which I was once reduced when, forbidden to quote the Trinity manuscripts of Tennyson, I wished to make clear that in 1913 Hallam Tennyson had mistranscribed the opening of *Semele*:

> I wish'd to see Him. Who may feel
> His light and love? He comes.

'Love' is an error; the manuscript clearly reads: 'Who may feel | His light and...'—but the correct reading may not be quoted. Since apparently no other manuscript of 'Semele' survives, an editor has either to perpetuate the error 'love', or to amend it without being able to cite his authority. In the circumstances, one is tempted to go in for crossword-clues: this is an evil setback.[67]

But I should end, not with Tennyson but with Camden and with Goldsmith's *Retaliation*:

65. *Complete Sonnets and Poems, 378, 439.*
66. Quentin Skinner wrote to me after the lecture, and has generously allowed me to make public his support of the intriguing conjecture, 'Trick'd by'. (It was proposed by Latham Davis in 1905; see the Variorum edition of the sonnets.) Professor Skinner started by seeing, as I had not, that 'thee array' is an almost exact anagram of 'treachery' (a word that Shakespeare uses 26 times in the plays). 'Trick'd by' (which is along the lines of the conjectures 'Gull'd by' and 'Fool'd by') would have dealings not only with the overt 'rebbell powres' but also with the covert treachery that may lurk within 'thee array'. Moreover, the soul, two lines later, is addressed as 'Painting thy outward walls so costlie gay'. To trick is also *OED* 5, 'to dress, array' ('these rebbell powres that thee array'), and the verb did not in the sixteenth and seventeenth century need to be strengthened, as it now might, with *out*; there is the violent pastiche of the speech for the players, *Hamlet*, II. ii: 'horridly Trick'd | With blood of Fathers'. 'Trick'd by': arrayed as well as tricked in the other standard sixteenth-century sense, with treachery being the main or worst way in which we can be tricked. Booth quotes Clifford Leech's conjectural paraphrase, 'feigning to deceive by brave shows'. What better word, then, than 'Trick'd'? C. J. Sisson called this 'the prize crux of the Sonnets', in which case Quentin Skinner, seconding Latham Davis, has a strong claim to the prize.
67. Chatterton Lecture (1966), 'Tennyson's Methods of Composition'; *Proceedings of the British Academy*, 52 (1968), 210.

But heere it is time to stay, for some of the sowre sort beginne to laugh at these, whenas yet they have no better insight in Anagrammes than wise Sieur *Gaulard*, who when he heard a Gentleman report that he was at a supper, where they had not onely good company and good cheare, but also savory Epigrammes, and fine Anagrammes; he returning home, rated and belowted his Cooke as an ignorant scullion that never dressed or served up to him, either Epigrammes or Anagrams.[68]

'And thought of convincing, while they thought of dining.'

68. *Remains Concerning Britain*, ed. Dunn, 151.

3

Dryden's Heroic Triplets

Dryden was sovereign of the line, 'the *English* Verse, which we call Heroique'.[1]

But first a note on why it is better to call it, not the 'iambic pentameter', but the English heroic line. For *iambic pentameter* too much classicizes, submitting the English language and English versification to the practices and nomenclature of those quite other languages and versifications, Latin and Greek. English poets have for centuries argued about and repeatedly resisted this assimilation, this imperial validation. ('Feet', my foot.) As for *iambic*...

Dr Johnson's instances of an iamb are 'aloft' and 'create', *less-stressed > more-stressed*. (To characterize an iamb as *unstressed > stressed* is to suggest that there could be an altogether unstressed syllable.) It is very seldom that iambs constitute a whole line, or even the main tissue of a line, in the blank verse of a Shakespeare play, in *Paradise Lost* or *The Prelude*, or in the heroic couplets of Dryden and Pope. In Shakespeare, an authentically iambic pentameter—'Of hand, of foote, of lip, of eye, of brow' (Sonnet 106)—is exceptionally rare, this line asking recognition as especially telling in its clarity and rarity. King Lear's lamentation, 'Never, never, never, never, never', is indeed likewise a pentameter, having manifestly five stresses, and it is strikingly regular, but it has not a single iamb since it consists entirely of trochees, *more-stressed > less-stressed* (Johnson's instances of a trochee are 'holy' and 'lofty').

> Of Mans First Disobedience, and the Fruit
> Of that Forbidden Tree, whose mortal tast
> Brought Death into the World, and all our woe,
>
> (*Paradise Lost*, i. 1–3)

---

1. His 'Discourse concerning the Original and Progress of Satire' (1693).

Take heed of what is brought and wrought by the spondees, *more-stressed* > *more-stressed* ('Brought Death'), and on again, three stresses running ('Mans First Dis ···', 'all our woe'), supported not so much by iambs as by anapaests, *less-* > *less-* > *more-stressed* ('and the Fruit'). There is a scholarly move that speaks of these as 'substitutions' for iambs, but this rigs the argument, and the point soon comes when there are so many substitutions as to turn the iambs from being the fictive norm into being simply one among the many sequences of less- and more-stress.

If we are to define the heroic line, it should be definition not as a strict roster of necessary and sufficient conditions, but as the 'family resemblances' that Wittgenstein thought apt to definitions in these matters. So the definition of, say, a game may list half a dozen things that games, or most games, have in common, things like rules, the pleasure of play, a feeling for stylized competition, the consciousness that there may be a spectator- (though not only a spectator-) sport. Less a definition than a characterization, and certainly not a hard-and-fast identification.

The good thing about the term 'heroic line' is its acknowledging and welcoming flexibility, elusiveness, and variety, as against the schematic quasi-precision (and the classroom air) of 'iambic pentameter'. In this spirit, the greatness of the conclusion to Siegfried Sassoon's *Founder's Feast* can be seen to be its displaying to us (for the first and last time in its nineteen heroic lines, all bent upon pseudo-heroism, and ending in a heroic couplet) a conclusive iambic, all right, pentameter, all right:

> But on the Provost's left, in gold and blue,
> Sat ... O my God! ... great Major-General Bluff ...
> Enough enough enough enough enough!

But enough. The adjective 'heroic', when used 'of verse or metre', has the straightforward meaning, 'Used in heroic poetry'. The *OED* then reminds us that in Greek and Latin poetry this was the hexameter; in English, German, and Italian, the iambic of five feet or ten syllables; in French, the Alexandrine of twelve syllables. At which point, things have become less straightforward, with the arrival of 'iambic'. The roughly-five-foot and roughly-ten-syllable line used to be known, in the Augustan Age and after, by the term that Dr Johnson inherited and bequeathed: *the English heroic line*. Johnson wrote of 'the musick of the English heroick line', and he himself wittily turned the term at the turn of the line in one of his heroic couplets:

> For now no more we trace in ev'ry Line
> Heroic Worth, Benevolence Divine:
>
> *(The Vanity of Human Wishes, 87–8)*

'Which we call Heroique', its weight still in touch with Dryden's sense of heroic song and then with Johnson's sense of this, the heroic poem as 'reciting the acts of heroes'. The heroic couplet is recognized as both the favoured means and a characteristic flavour of Dryden's art, keen as he was to pursue and to outdo the instrumental skill developed during the 1640s by Edmund Waller and by Sir John Denham. But the heroic triplet? The development from couplet into triplet, the terms at least, may be simple enough in the *OED*. *Couplet*: a pair of successive lines of verse, *esp.* when rhyming together and of the same length. (This, from 1580.) *Triplet*: three successive lines of verse, *esp.* when rhyming together and of the same length. (This, not until 1656.) Mark Van Doren, whose book on Dryden was so influential not only, though *esp.*, because T. S. Eliot commended it, felt obliged to set limits to his praise for two aspects of Dryden's craft that are complementary and that distinguish his measures or numbers from those of his successor, Alexander Pope: the triplet and the alexandrine.

George Saintsbury, whose historical criticism of English prosody has often been contested but never superseded, thought that the impulse to use the triplet and the alexandrine began with the wish for elbow-room ('The original persuasive to both is, of course, clear enough—it is simply a case of too narrow room in the ten or twenty syllables'), but he soon complicated this *simply* of his, by picking up his own word 'persuasive' and then turning it to the thought of being unable to persuade, not others, but himself:

I have never been able to persuade myself that the giving up of them was not one of those rather unreasonable, though it would seem quite inevitable, 'tightenings up' of rule which have spoilt almost all games at one time or another. The triplet has no doubt a slight tendency to burlesque, and, if used often, throws the general effect out of character; but then it is the poet's business to guard against these results. Both in descriptive and argumentative verse it is of great importance, and has something of the effect of a parenthesis—that figure hated by the vulgar, and beloved by the elect.[2]

Van Doren, despite deprecating the triplets, valued this particular effect, 'the supplying of a colloquial first-hand tone', adding that 'The

---

2. *A History of English Prosody* (London, 1908; 2nd edn, 1923), ii. 389–90.

third line of a triplet in Dryden frequently represents a lowering of the voice to the level of parenthesis or innuendo'.[3] Such an effect is there for the hearing, a heightening that is aware of the low, a comic compounding when a triplet avails itself not only of the vocal level of a parenthesis but of a parenthesis proper (or faintly improper):

> *Hippomenes*, who ran with Noble strife
> To win his Lady, or to loose his Life,
> (What shift some men will make to get a Wife?)
> Threw down a Golden Apple in her way, · · ·
>
> (*Amaryllis, or the Third Idyllium of Theocritus, Paraphrased*, 91–4)

The energy of Hippomenes throws that Golden Apple so that it sails sheer through space, its arc open to the wry shift constituted by an entirely parenthetical line of inquiry.[4]

But of triplets more widely? The best canter round the field is still the one mounted in 1965 by Conrad A. Balliet.[5] Mark Van Doren in 1920 had been mildly grudging, judging that Dryden 'did not always succeed in rendering them organic to his verse structure; often they were excrescences'. Yet, as it aptly happens, an excrescence is just what the triplet can valuably be, not only in the *OED*'s sense of 'Something that grows out; a natural outgrowth or appendage', but (growing out of this) in the further sense of 'An abnormal, morbid, or disfiguring outgrowth; a disfiguring protuberance or swelling'. Dr Johnson, after defining the word in his *Dictionary* as 'Somewhat growing out of another without use, and contrary to the common order of production; preternatural production', naturally produced as his first citation the words of Dryden: 'All beyond this is monstrous, 'tis out of nature, 'tis an *excrescence, and not a living part of poetry'. The movement of

---

3. *The Poetry of Dryden* (New York, 1920), 101.
4. Though Dryden's interrogative 'What · · ·?' sounds like an echo, the effect is intriguingly different within Milton's blank verse: 'Thir song was partial, but the harmony | (What could it less when Spirits immortal sing?) | Suspended Hell, and took with ravishment | The thronging audience' (*Paradise Lost*, ii. 552–5).
5. 'The History and Rhetoric of the Triplet', *PMLA*, vol. 80 (1965), which incorporates this thoughtful listing: 'Poets adapted or created numerous techniques: a progression in the meaning of the three rhyming words; a shift of the caesura within the triplet; an expansion of the third pentameter to an Alexandrine; the placing of triplets at the end of poems, or parts of poems, or speeches (in plays) to emphasise the conclusion; the use of an epigram in the last line; an increase of the intensity and emphasis of the triplet by a more extensive use of such rhetorical devices as alliteration, balance, antithesis, turns, onomatopoeia, colloquial speech, repetition, and chiasmus.'

mind there from 'excrescence' to 'poetry' is the work of a poet for whom the triplet was certainly not 'without use'.

For the disfigured figure of the Earl of Shaftesbury precipitates the protuberant triplet that succeeds the run of seventy-seven consecutive couplets that opens *Absalom and Achitophel*.[6] There is conjured up—as more than a detail within the portrait of Shaftesbury in all his damaged and damaging energy—a corporeality that lives at first as a couplet but then swells to a triplet.

> A fiery Soul, which working out its way, ⎫
> Fretted the Pigmy Body to decay: ⎬
> And o'r inform'd the Tenement of Clay. ⎭   (156–8)

Dryden's triplet animates not only a 'soul' but a body, and then, through the body of the verse itself, it works out that of which it speaks. For the soul of the lines can be heard and felt to be working out its way, out through the acknowledged restraint, fretting to decay the body of the couplet and o'er-informing the tenement that is the couplet-form itself.

Such a realization of what the triplet can effect, by way here of irruption and disruption, is a powerful reminder of one form that power may take. In Shaftesbury there is felt the power of passionate ambition to break the social bonds of convention or tradition, this and the fierce power to break free from an oppressed body. Very small of stature, he possessed a pigmy body. But 'the Pigmy Body': this turn of phrase is not to be limited to him alone, for the body is a pigmy thing compared to the soul. Like Milton's Satan, to whom *Absalom and Achitophel* often likens him, Shaftesbury is to be excoriated and defied, but he is not to be condescended to or slighted or bantered. Fear of the Lord is the beginning of wisdom; the next pillar of wisdom may be fear of the Devil. The Duke of Monmouth staggers within Shaftesbury's coils of temptation: 'Him Staggering so when Hells dire Agent found' (373). The o'er-inform'd verse-form, from couplet into teeming ruptive triplet, is one of the means by which these counter-currents of judgement upon Shaftesbury are contained.

Dryden's triplets are at once conspicuous and little attended to. There is, for instance, nothing about the triplets of *Absalom and Achitophel* in Earl Miner's magisterially ample work, *Dryden's Poetry* (1967). The great satire contains, within its one thousand and thirty-one

---

6. The run of seventy-seven couplets is at one point abruptly heckled by a broken-off half-line that brandishes a right: 'And theirs the Native right—' (87).

lines, eight triplets. None of them is an excrescence, even while they
mimic and mock excrescency. All of them succeed in being organic in
their relation both to the tissue of the verse and to the issue of the
poem: the outcome that is awaiting the illegitimate issue that is, or
rather *who* is, the King's bastard son: the Duke of Monmouth, with his
claims to succeed. Dryden's indictment not only of Monmouth
(Absalom) but of his pernicious backer, Shaftesbury (Achitophel),
widens from Shaftesbury's body to the greater body politic, larger even
than England. For there ensues almost immediately the next triplet,
one that celebrates the Triple Bond: the 1668 Alliance between
England, the States General, and Sweden—celebrates it while execrat-
ing Shaftesbury's part in severing the Alliance, Shaftesbury who was
'Resolv'd to Ruine or to Rule the State':

> To Compass this the Triple Bond he broke;⎫
> The Pillars of the publick Safety shook: ⎬
> And fitted *Israel* for a Foreign Yoke.   ⎭   (175–7)

This triplet is meant to be heard, as the speaker's voice rises in volume
and vehemence, accusation after accusation. Duplicity exceeds duplicity into mendacity, just as the triplet exceeds couplet into outrage. The
triplet expands the couplet's compass, being fitted to a different yoke
from that of the couplet, a yoke foreign to the usual public safety—
safety as confidence of prediction (or succession) covenanted to the
verse-movement of the heroic couplet itself. The *English* heroic verse,
as against the French heroic verse? This triplet is in its way a tribute to
the Triple Bond, rhyme itself being by nature a bond, one that may
choose to embrace or to resist bondage. For Milton, *Paradise Lost* was to
stand as a Heroic Poem because it stood by the English heroic line,
constituting a political and social achievement as well as an artistic one:

This neglect then of Rime so little is to be taken for a defect, though it may
seem so perhaps to vulgar Readers, that it is rather to be esteem'd an example
set, the first in *English*, of ancient liberty recover'd to Heroic Poem from the
troublesom and modern bondage of Rimeing.

('The Verse', 1668—the year, as it happened, of the Triple Bond)

To Dryden, in this intensely Miltonic poem of his, it was now the
heroic couplet that might manifest an ancient liberty recovered to the
Heroic Poem—a liberty, moreover, asserted late, against Milton's deni-
gration of 'the troublesom and modern bondage of Rimeing', namely,
the rhyming couplet, delivered now in the refuge of the mock-heroic.

In lethal earnest, the great age of the heroic couplet is the great age of mock-heroic, from *MacFlecknoe* (1682) to *The Rape of the Lock* (1712–17) and *The Dunciad* (1728–42).

It is the imaginative aptness of particular triplets in Dryden, their being so variously germane, that makes good the apprehension of the triplet as much more than a convenience to the poet, much more than the lenient granting of an extension that owes its existence merely to the artist's having failed to compact into a couplet his thoughts and feelings. Take the measure of Shaftesbury's seduction of Monmouth in assuring him that the King's popularity is in decline. Twenty years ago, there had been a Restoration, but now the King's fortunes are, with any luck, beyond restoration. 'He is not now · · ·'—whereupon the couplet will have to amplify its memory of the fulsome welcome (painful for the King's enemies at the time, but now an occasion for gloating) that had overflowed, once upon a time:

> He is not now, as when on *Jordan's* Sand
> The Joyfull People throng'd to see him Land,
> Cov'ring the *Beach*, and blackning all the *Strand*:   (270–2)

Over and above the call of duty had been the people's joy, and therefore over and above anything that the dutiful couplet could accommodate. The 'full' in 'Joyfull' proceeds to fill the couplet so that it has to spill over (Dryden repeatedly relishes having some form of *full* or *-ful* within a triplet, the couplet turning out to be full and then some). The couplet is itself 'throng'd' to the point at which adulation spills over to a third line, brimming with participles, 'Cov'ring the *Beach*, and blackning all the *Strand*'.[7] The Strand as both ancient seashore and London thoroughfare.[8]

7. A. W. Verrall, *Lectures on Dryden* (Cambridge, 1914), 68–9: 'The reception of Charles at Dover in May 1660 is described in the triplet, 270 ff., a variation of the couplet rarely used in this poem. Some effect is here certainly both felt and meant; for note also the unique rhythm in the last line due to the two trisyllabic words "covering," "blackening," and compare with this the effect of the single trisyllabic "lengthening" in *v.* 269:—'The shadows *lengthening* as the vapours rise."What is the effect intended in the triplet? Is not the picture meant to be disagreeable?— "*Covering* the beach and *blackening* all the strand."What does it call up to us? Beetles?'
8. Johnson, in *Imitation of the Third Satire of Juvenal*, imitates Dryden, and asks, with some rolery (given his feelings as to Scotland versus London), 'For who would leave, unbrib'd, *Hibernia's* Land, | Or change the Rocks of *Scotland* for the *Strand?*' (*London*, 1718, 9–10). *The Poems of Samuel Johnson*, ed. David Nichol Smith and Edward L. McAdam, 2nd edn (Oxford, 1974).

Such an expansive welcome, as though with more than full-handed plaudits and with more than usually open arms, no longer greets the King, Shaftesbury dourly and delightedly reports. Soon Monmouth is heard to stir up the fickle populace with the help of rhetorical arts that he has learned from Shaftesbury. Among these arts is the triplet, which Monmouth trades upon (the King has taken liberties—worse, has taken away your liberties).

> Now all your Liberties a spoil are made; ⎫
> *Ægypt* and *Tyrus* intercept your Trade, ⎬
> And *Jebusites* your Sacred Rites invade. ⎭ (704–6)

Is nothing sacred? Not even the rite of the heroic couplet?

In Dryden, as in Milton, rites and liberties—including those of literary art itself—constitute an axis, not a direction. A particular device may be happy to lend itself to vice or to virtue; it may be open not only to the high-minded and highest bidder but to the lowest. The very same turn that could deplore, by means of a triple bond, the destruction of the Triple Bond, or that can take the liberty of a couplet to reprimand the taking of liberties, is one that can on a different occasion practise the art not of sinking but of raising or rising. *Absalom and Achitophel* is supreme as satire because not only its author personally but the poem impersonally can be trusted to value panegyric aright. A great age of satire stands in need of a great age of panegyric. (Which is one reason why the way we live now is not conducive to any substantiated art of satire as against lampoon or burlesque.) Dryden goes, not out of his way, but truly by means of his way, when he incorporates within his poem a tribute, rising to a triplet, devoted to the eldest son of the Duke of Ormond, a loyal son (unlike Monmouth), a son too soon dead:

>   always Mourn'd,
> And always honour'd, snatcht in Manhoods prime
> By' unequal Fates, and Providences crime:
> Yet not before the Goal of Honour won, ⎫
> All parts fulfill'd of Subject and of Son; ⎬
> Swift was the Race, but short the Time to run. ⎭ (832–7)

Unequal Fates are one thing, but to attribute to Providence a *crime*: heroically this risks blasphemy while preserving decorum in that the sudden daring is pinioned by 'honour'd' and by 'Honour'. It is only with 'All parts fulfill'd' (*ful-* and *fill* again) that the couplet permits itself to enter upon the ritual elaboration into a triplet. The further solemnization then itself embodies a paradox, in touch with the shock of 'Providences crime'. For the added observation—'Swift was the Race, but short the Time to run' (a famously favourite figure of speech and of thought for Dryden, fulfilled most memorably in *To the Memory of Mr. Oldham*)[9]—makes the run of the lines *less* swift and *less* short than would have been the case had the eulogy fulfilled itself with a couplet at the close: 'All parts fulfill'd of Subject and of Son'. The alliteration and assonance of Subject and Son suggest that these duties are perfectly at one.

The triplet that is positive, then, in owning virtue, as against disowning vice, is an indispensable counterthrust, a feat that is more than technical but never less than technically accomplished. So it is that Dryden's 'small but faithful Band' (-*ful* again signalling the onset of a triplet) grows before our very eyes and ears in size and consequence. A heroic stand deserves and commands a heroic tripling.

> These were the chief, a small but faithful Band
> Of Worthies, in the Breach who dar'd to stand,
> And tempt th' united Fury of the Land. (914–16)[10]

The breaching of the couplet is the condition of a larger way of being united (in faith, with daring 'in the Breach') than fury can be possessed by.

The last of the eight triplets in the poem (though not the last to be pondered here, since one of them is being reserved for its moment) comes within the King's ample speech that closes the poem (closes it, save only for six lines of narrative that both praise and predict). The King laments that it is his duty not to turn a blind eye to his son's rebellious misconduct.

> Oh that my Power to Saving were confin'd:
> Why am I forc'd, like Heaven, against my mind,
> To make Examples of another Kind? (999–1001)

The movement of mind is doubly of another kind. First, in that, by being a triplet, it is an example of another kind than has constituted the poem's main manoeuvre, and is itself less confined.[11] Second, in

9. 'To the same Goal did both our Studies drive, | The last set out the soonest did arrive. | Thus Nisus fell upon the slippery place, | While his young Friend perform'd and won the Race.'
10. For a triplet *stand / Band / Command* in praise of heroic loyalty, see p. 75 below.
11. Dryden enjoys placing 'confin'd' and 'unconfin'd' within the less narrow confinement that is the triplet. *The First Book of Ovid's Metamorphoses*, 125–7.

that of all the triplets, this, the conclusive one (more in sorrow than in anger, but in anger), is the only instance of there being an unremitting impetus from the second line into the third. Bring to mind again this triplet's predecessors.

> A fiery Soul, which working out its way,⎫
> Fretted the Pigmy Body to decay: ⎬
> And o'r inform'd the Tenement of Clay. ⎭

There, the second line (the completer of a couplet) is end-stopped, syntactically complete, and the move into the couplet's needing to become a triplet is signalled by a beginning again: 'And · · ·' The same goes for the second, fourth, and sixth triplets in the poem.

> To Compass this the Triple Bond he broke;⎫
> The Pillars of the publick Safety shook: ⎬
> And fitted *Israel* for a Foreign Yoke. ⎭

> ★ ★ ★

> Now all your Liberties a spoil are made;⎫
> *Ægypt* and *Tyrus* intercept your Trade, ⎬
> And *Jebusites* your Sacred Rites invade. ⎭

> ★ ★ ★

> These were the chief, a small but faithful Band⎫
> Of Worthies, in the Breach who dar'd to stand,⎬
> And tempt th' united Fury of the Land. ⎭

Two of the other triplets are not furnished with an 'And' (with which to re-commence) in introducing their third line, but the couplet that con-stitutes the first two lines does similarly conclude the sense, or a sense:

> He is not now, as when on *Jordan*'s Sand ⎫
> The Joyfull People throng'd to see him Land, ⎬
> Cov'ring the *Beach*, and blackning all the *Strand*:⎭

> ★ ★ ★

> Yet not before the Goal of Honour won, ⎫
> All parts fulfill'd of Subject and of Son; ⎬
> Swift was the Race, but short the Time to run. ⎭

It is solely the final triplet, the King's lament, that precludes any such pause or hesitation, any sense even of temporary or tentative completion, since the impetus of 'Why am I forc'd · · · | To · · ·' incarnates

> E're Sails were spread, new Oceans to explore:⎫
> And happy Mortals, unconcern'd for more, ⎬
> Confin'd their Wishes to their Native Shoar. ⎭

an overriding duty, one that has no choice but to override the
couplet:

> Oh that my Power to Saving were confin'd: ⎫
> Why am I forc'd, like Heaven, against my mind, ⎬
> To make Examples of another Kind? ⎭

The one remaining triplet in *Absalom and Achitophel* is in some ways
the most capacious and captivating of them all. Its compacted ingenuity and congruity should widen the terms of appreciation. It has a
different timbre.

> For *Shimei*, though not prodigal of pelf,
> Yet lov'd his wicked Neighbour as himself:
> When two or three were gather'd to declaim ⎫
> Against the Monarch of *Jerusalem*,   ⎬
> *Shimei* was always in the midst of them: ⎭   (599–603)

'For where two or three are gathered together in my name, there am
I in the midst of them' (Matthew 18:20). Is it sacrilege, or blasphemy,
or good clean fun, for Dryden so to compromise Christ's promise?
T. S. Eliot once said that it was impossible to imagine George Bernard
Shaw's blaspheming. There are worse things than blasphemy, in other
words, since blasphemy is possible only to one who is at least in some
part a believer. Eliot: 'I repeat that I am not defending blasphemy; I am
reproaching a world in which blasphemy is impossible.'[12] Reproaching
a world has its heroic side. (There must have been heroics or the heroic
in Margaret Fuller's avowal, 'I accept the universe.') Shaw in 1906 did,
as it happens, make play with the same biblical allusion as Dryden:

Weariness of the theatre is the prevailing note of London criticism. Only the
best critics believe that the theatre is really important: in my time none of
them would claim for it, as I claimed for it, that it is as important as the
Church was in the Middle Ages and much more important than the Church
was in London in the years under review [the 1890s]. A theatre to me is a
place 'where two or three are gathered together.' The apostolic succession
from Eschylus to myself is as serious and as continuously inspired as that
younger institution, the apostolic succession of the Christian Church.[13]

More was at stake for Dryden hereabouts than for Shaw. But it is the
sheer exuberance of Dryden's ways with Christ's words, the range of

---

12. *After Strange Gods* (London, 1934), 52.
13. 'The Author's Apology' (1906), in *Our Theatres in the Nineties* (London, 1932).

the concentration within his triplet, the prodigious prodigality of it all, that constitutes the poet's justification for risking blasphemy, justification by works in which we can justifiably have faith.

There is, for example, the dynamism, unparalleled in the other triplets of *Absalom and Achitophel* (their energies are different), by which, in the Shimei triplet, the first line of the-couplet-that-is-to-become-a-triplet is impelled into the second line, and this then into the third. (The Father, the Son, *and the Holy Ghost*...?) Next, there is the deliciously impertinent pertinence that has 'When two or three···' be the opening of a two-some that will evolve into a three-some. Next, there is the fact that the first twenty-two verses of this chapter of St Matthew do not just gather into themselves Christ's words about 'where two or three', but rather have the entire tissue be an elaboration of numbers, not the Book of Numbers but the chapter of them. In their sequence:

- one such little child
- one of these little ones [thrice]
- two hands or two feet
- one eye, rather than having two eyes
- an hundred sheep, and one of them be gone astray
- the ninety and nine [twice]
- take with you one or two more, that in the mouth of two or three witnesses
- if two of you

It is only after this thoroughly patient enumeration that Christ is moved to say 'For where two or three are gathered together in my name, there am I in the midst of them.' Then immediately, by an extraordinary vaulting into the very next verses, there comes one of the most intense of all the New Testament's numberings:

Then came Peter to him, and said, Lord, how oft shall my brother sin against me, and I forgive him? till seven times? Jesus saith unto him, I say not unto thee, Until seven times: but, Until seventy times seven.

Yet all these are only part of what Dryden gathers into his triplet. What prompted Dryden's auditory imagination (*declaim / Jerusalem / them*) was a partial echo, assisted by the timing of punctuation, within Christ's words in the King James Bible (*name / them*): 'For where two or three are gathered together in my name, there am I in the midst of them'.

When two or three were gather'd to declaim ⎫
Against the Monarch of *Jerusalem*,   ⎬
Shimei was always in the midst of them: ⎭

Then again the two Testaments are gathered. For not only does Christ gather with Shimei, but the very sounds reach to the New from the Old:

And when King David came to Bahurim, behold, there came out a man of the family of the house of Saul, whose name was Shimei, the son of Gera: he came forth, and cursed still as he came. (2 Samuel 16:5)

What is the sound that we hear declaimed by these two or three lines? The word *came*, three times, of Shimei.[14] Four times if you add 'King David came' (and five times if you register a rhyme in 'name'). When two or three...? Even 'forth' might find itself figuring: 'he came forth'.

Dryden is not one to play emptily with 'two or three' when introducing a triplet within a poem that is in couplets. Each of the eight triplets in *Absalom and Achitophel* has within it something that bears upon the couplet/triplet dynamic and upon what, at each particular point, the poem is engaging with. 'When two or three···': Dryden often has recourse to 'two or three', with its genially staunch approximation. 'To conclude, if in two or three places I have deserted all the Commentators, 'tis because I thought they first deserted my Author.'[15] There is something amiably offhand about 'two or three', or not so amiably when the idiom commands the tone that dismissiveness would take. Boileau tartly deplores the thousand-line poems of which only two or three lines are free of faults ('deux ou trois entre mille'); Dryden, translating Boileau, enjoys the exact comedy of rhyming on 'three' in a couplet.

A hundred Scribling Authors, without ground
Believe they have this only Phœnix found:

14. An old tradition tolls *came* three times.

Night came, but unattended with repose,   ⎫
Alone she came, no sleep their eyes to close,   ⎬
Alone, and black she came, no friendly stars arose. ⎭
(*The Hind and the Panther: The Third Part*, 607–9)

15. *Argument of the First Satyr of Juvenal*. Similarly, Explanatory Notes on *The Sixth Satyr of Persius* (note 4): 'And since he and *Lucan* were so great Friends, I know not but *Lucan* might help him, in two or three of these Verses.' Marcia Karp drew my attention to the erratum, correcting 'three' to 'two', in the first edition of Dryden's *Aeneis*, VI: 1131: 'the two devoted *Decij*.'

When yet th' exactest scarce have two or three
Among whole Tomes, from Faults and Censure free.

(The Art of Poetry, 321–4)

On one occasion, Dryden introduces a 'two or three' that is not to be
found in the original that he is translating:

PERSIUS How anxious are our Cares; and yet how vain
The best of our desires!
FRIEND   Thy Spleen contain;
For none will read thy Satyrs.
PERSIUS   This to Me?
FRIEND None; or what's next to none; but two or three.

(The First Satyr of Persius, 1–4)

It is a pleasing thought, that 'what's next to none' is not one 'but two or
three'. This touch of lugubrious comedy is not in the Latin, which has
a different inconsequence: nemo · · · nemo? Vel duo, vel nemo. Literally,
either two or none. Such comedy starts to add up when the idiom 'two
or three' occurs within a couplet that unearths a triplet.

I have already Buried two or three
That stood betwixt a fair Estate and me,
And, Doctor, I may live to Bury thee.

(The Third Satyr of Persius, 192–4)

Dryden's energy is happy to mount a succession of vivid displays, where
(on one occasion) five consecutive triplets enact, in various ways, that of
which they speak. Such is the momentum of a torrent of misbehavings. In
The Hind and the Panther: The First Part (361–75), an orderly sequence of
twenty couplets abruptly irrupts into riotous acts in triplicate:

The fruit proclaims the plant; a lawless Prince
By luxury reform'd incontinence,
By ruins, charity; by riots, abstinence.[16]
Confessions, fasts and penance set aside;
Oh with what ease we follow such a guide!
Where souls are starv'd, and senses gratify'd.
Where marr'age pleasures, midnight pray'r supply,
And mattin bells (a melancholy cry)
Are tun'd to merrier notes, encrease and multiply.

16. The California edition explains: 'The four vices of Henry VIII which are named
reform'd the Catholic vice, incontinence, and quelled the virtues of charity and abstinence,
along with three aspects of the sacrament of penance (Confessions, fasts and penance).'

> Religion shows a Rosie colour'd face;
> Not hatter'd out with drudging works of grace;
> A down-hill Reformation rolls apace.
> What flesh and bloud wou'd croud the narrow gate,
> Or, till they waste their pamper'd paunches, wait?
> All wou'd be happy at the cheapest rate.

Every one of these triplets makes a piercing point of what it is to have
to encrease, to excresce to a triplet, because of incontinence, say, or
because of a misguiding guide, or because of the urging to multiply, or
to roll downhill, or to crowd the narrow gate.

The comedy of numbers (poetic numbers as well as the simple
arithmetic) can add—to the two-or-three of couplet or triplet—a further sly comedy by which the triplet can accommodate within its
threesome the twofold thing that we somehow naturally expect *balance*
to be, alongside two worlds and two possibilities.

> Paint *Europe's* Balance in his steady hand,
> Whilst the two Worlds in expectation stand
> Of Peace or War, that wait on his Command?

(*The Art of Poetry*, 1064–6)

Among the expectations might well have been the expectation of a
couplet. Then the twofold balance often finds itself revealed by
Dryden within the threefold triplet (but then, three-legs can balance
better than two, stool-wise). Dryden everywhere rings changes on this
two-three-one effect. Or rather, *these* two-three-one effects, since
there is great variety in their tones and functions. The telling third line
may tell very different stories, 'I told you so' or 'I grant you that' or 'We
agree, perhaps?' or 'What I tell you three times is true'.

> Let all Records of *Will reveal'd* be shown;
> With *Scripture*, all in equal ballance thrown,
> And *our one Sacred Book* will be *That one.*

(*Religio Laici*, 123–5)

> If such a one you find, let truth prevail:
> Till when your weights will in the balance fail:
> A church unprincipl'd kicks up the scale.

(*The Hind and the Panther: The Second Part*, 622–4)

'What flesh and bloud wou'd croud the narrow gate?': Dryden's
heroic couplet may be a narrow gate, but it was wide enough to let in

Samuel Johnson, who fashioned—thanks to Dryden (and to Swift)—
the line 'Unnumber'd Suppliants croud Preferment's Gate'.[17] Johnson
is the poet-critic whose observation, with extensive view, surveyed the
busy scenes of Augustan verse, heroic and mock-heroic. In his life of
Dryden he is careful, not to set down the law, but to set out the
considerations:

> The Triplet and Alexandrine are not universally approved. Swift always cen-
> sured them, and wrote some lines to ridicule them. In examining their propri-
> ety, it is to be considered that the essence of verse is regularity, and its ornament
> is variety.

Johnson then undertakes his characteristically wise practice of adum-
brating a strong case from which, in the end, he withdraws some of his
support. Triplets are intrinsically unsatisfactory in breaching regularity,
the essence of verse. Yes, and yet not altogether so—for triplets may
be judged less unsatisfactory than would be their plain banishment.
The movements of mind are these:

> ···the English Alexandrine breaks the lawful bounds, and surprises the reader
> with two syllables more than he expected.
> The effect of the Triplet is the same: the ear has been accustomed to expect
> a new rhyme in every couplet; but is on a sudden surprized with three rhymes
> together, to which the reader could not accommodate his voice, did he not
> obtain notice of the change from the braces of the margins. Surely there is
> something unskilful in the necessity of such mechanical direction.
> Considering the metrical art simply as a science, and consequently exclud-
> ing all casualty,[18] we must allow that Triplets and Alexandrines, inserted by
> caprice, are interruptions of that constancy to which science aspires. And
> though the variety which they produce may very justly be desired, yet to make
> our poetry exact, there ought to be some stated mode of admitting them.
> But till some such regulation can be formed, I wish them still to be retained
> in their present state. They are sometimes grateful to the reader, and some-
> times convenient to the poet. *Fenton* was of opinion that Dryden was too
> liberal and Pope too sparing in their use.[19]

Yet there is occasion for respectful dissent from Johnson. First, the
lawful bounds of a verse-form are exactly what is in contention.

17. *The Vanity of Human Wishes*, 73, and Swift, *To Doctor Delany, on the Libels Writ against
    him*, 93.
18. Johnson's *Dictionary*, sense 1: 'Accident; a thing happening by chance, not design'; both
    citations speak of 'mere casualty'.
19. Elijah Fenton (1683–1730) translated four books of the *Odyssey* for Pope. *The Lives of
    the Poets* (ed. Lonsdale), ii. 154.

Second, there is nothing intrinsically inartistic or unavailing about *surprise*, twice invoked (predictably) by Johnson. Next, the braces within the margin are not a necessity, only a signal convention that may be of service, resembling such a stage direction as [*Aside*, of which Johnson avails himself in *Irene*.[20]

Further, for Johnson to consider the metrical art simply as a science is simply inapposite, since no such art can be a science, even when one allows for the different colouring of those words in 1779. It is a lapse in Johnson to be even tempted by the thought of the metrical art as consequently excluding all casualty, since it is he of all critics who most truly appreciates the 'felicities' of artistic accomplishment, felicities being exactly such effects as happily befall by benign casualty. Johnson praised Pope's epitaph on Simon Harcourt:

> This epitaph is principally remarkable for the artful introduction of the name, which is inserted with a peculiar felicity, to which chance must concur with genius, which no man can hope to attain twice, and which cannot be copied but with servile imitation.[21]

Why then is the metrical art an aspect of the poetical art that cannot benefit from such a concurrence of chance with genius?

20. A tragedy in the most blank of verse, but with each Act ending with a pair of heroic couplets, *Irene*'s only accomplished poetry and insufficiently esteemed.

> When ev'ry Storm in my Domain shall roar,
> When ev'ry wave shall beat a *Turkish* Shore,
> Then, CALI, shall the Toils of Battle cease,
> Then dream of Prayer, and Pilgrimage, and Peace.   (Act I)
>
> To deck these Bow'rs each Region shall combine,
> And ev'n our Prophet's Gardens envy thine:
> Empire and Love shall share the blissful Day,
> And varied Life steal unperceiv'd away.   (Act II)
>
> Reproach not, *Greece*, a Lover's fond Delays,
> Nor think thy Cause neglected while I gaze,
> New Force, new Courage, from each Glance I gain,
> And find our Passions not infus'd in vain.   (Act III)
>
> Profuse of Wealth, or bounteous of Success,
> When Heav'n bestows the Privilege to bless,
> Let no weak Doubt the gen'rous Hand restrain,
> For when was Pow'r beneficent in vain?   (Act IV)
>
> When haughty Guilt exults with impious Joy,
> Mistake shall blast, or Accident destroy;
> Weak Man with erring Rage may throw the Dart,
> But Heav'n shall guide it to the guilty Heart.   (Act V)

21. *The Lives of the Poets*, iv. 85.

Finally, when Johnson presses upon us that 'we must allow that Triplets and Alexandrines, inserted by caprice, are interruptions of that constancy to which science aspires', we should dissent from this move of his. Not only because the aspirations of 'science' may not minister to the aspirations of art, but because of the injustice of *caprice*: 'Freak; fancy; whim', in Johnson's *Dictionary*. It is not by caprice (as the instances from *Absalom and Achitophel* show) that Dryden inserted a triplet, and 'inserted' is coercive too. Moreover, Dryden does not limit himself to adducing, he educes a triplet, and most educative the process is. What better way could there be to see the Three Unities than under the aspect of a triplet, one that will then incorporate the word 'tripled'?

> Time, Action, Place, are so preserv'd by thee ⎫
> That even *Corneille*, might with envy see   ⎬
> Th' Alliance of his tripled Unity.   ⎭

> (*To my Friend, the Author* [Peter Motteux], 1698, 33–5)

What had been valued in the political world of 1668 as a Triple Alliance returns in the critical world of 1698 as the Alliance of a tripled Unity.

'The braces of the margins', deprecated by Johnson as unskilful and mechanical direction to the reader, are themselves oddly suggestive when it comes to being, not at sixes and sevens, but at twos and threes. The OED defines this sense of *brace* as 'a sign used in printing or writing, chiefly for the purpose of uniting together two or more lines, words, staves of music, etc.' (from 1656), but when we come to the lines of Augustan verse, the brace is at the service not of 'two or more lines', but invariably of three. A brace in the margin is the mark of a triplet.

But the very next definition in the OED is a reminder that (despite the marginal brace's being for a threesome) on other occasions a brace is 'two things taken together; a pair, a couple. Often a mere synonym for *two.*' It is in this sense, of a pair, that Dryden himself uses the word 'brace' in his poetry. The couplet meets the triplet (into which it expands) there in the word and in the sign 'brace'. The linguistic anomaly may contribute to the triplet's expert use, short in historical span but wide in imaginative aptness, in making a case for its existence.

Of triplets and alexandrines: 'Dryden was too liberal and Pope too sparing in their use.' It is imaginatively magnanimous of Johnson that, when he came to praise Dryden, it should have been by courtesy of the particular tribute that Pope had fashioned for his predecessor, a tribute that takes the apt form of a triplet concluding in an alexandrine.

What can be said of his versification, will be little more than a dilatation of the praise given it by Pope:[22]

> Waller was smooth; but Dryden taught to join ⎫
> The varying verse, the full-resounding line, ⎬
> The long majestic march, and energy divine.[23] ⎭

Pope honours Dryden by assuming the form that energy delightingly took in Dryden. The wit of Pope's triplet is manifest, first, in the way in which *full-* (biding a moment for the fulfilment of its hyphen in *-resounding*) then prompts the overflowing into the next line; next by the extension intimated in 'The long···'; and then in the sequences that come to constitute an alternation of twos and threes. Yet not an alternation exactly. For this interplay takes one of the shapes in which Augustan verse delighted, a b b a, *chiasmus*[24]—a shaping that is in tension, perfectly happily, with the shape of couplets themselves, the paired planks that build the platform that is so firm under foot: aa, bb, cc, dd... This, with 'varying verse' and 'energy divine' as the pairs that open and close the sentiment, and with 'full-resounding line' and 'long majestick march' as the triplicities that resound at the heart of the lines.

If we ask what form, for both Dryden and Pope, the 'energy divine' supremely took, the answer is the Trinity. The words 'energy divine' here conclude Pope's threefold verse-form, and Pope, in paying this tribute to his predecessor (Dryden dead but still living through his art and his faith), may be recalling how Dryden himself used the triplet to incarnate the Trinity:

> Good life be now my task: my doubts are done,
> (What more could fright my faith, than Three in One?)
> Can I believe eternal God could lye ⎫
> Disguis'd in mortal mold and infancy? ⎬
> That the great maker of the world could dye? ⎭

(The Hind and the Panther: The First Part, 78–82)

---

22. *The Lives of the Poets*, ii. 153. The form *dilatation* has its pertinence on an occasion when a couplet is finding itself dilated into a triplet. *OED*: 'the etymologically correct formation', still common in the eighteenth century although *dilation* is to be found in 1598 in Florio (where the word was corrected to its expansion, its dilatation, in 1621).
23. *The First Epistle of the Second Book of Horace Imitated*, 267–9. (17th- and 18th-century pronunciation of 'join', the vowel as in 'line'.)
24. *OED*: 'A grammatical figure by which the order of words in one of two parallel clauses is inverted in the other.' Widened, then, to larger patterns of *a b b a*.

The majestic march, then, may honour not only kings but the King of Kings. Pope's phrase certainly honours Dryden, not least in that the word 'Majesty' is the one that Dryden had selected to celebrate the consummation of a triplet by an alexandrine ('the Pindarick Line') in the artistic decision for his heroic translation of the heroic *Aeneid*:

When I mention'd the Pindarick Line, I should have added, that I take another License in my Verses: for I frequently make use of Triplet Rhymes, and for the same Reason: Because they bound the Sense.[25] And therefore will I generally join these two Licenses together: and make the last Verse of the Triplet a Pindarique: For besides the Majesty which it gives, it confines the sense within the barriers of three Lines, which wou'd languish if it were lengthen'd into four. ('Dedication')

Dryden seizes an initiative in advancing that the triplet, far from being a lax couplet, may be two couplets economized.

Johnson was to sum up the case of Milton and 'the English heroick verse without rhyme': 'But, whatever be the advantage of rhyme, I cannot prevail on myself to wish that Milton had been a rhymer; for I cannot wish his work to be other than it is; yet, like other heroes, he is to be admired rather than imitated.'[26] It is always a fine thing when someone as strong-minded as Johnson admits to being in two minds. Similarly, he declared of triplets that 'to make our poetry exact, there ought to be some stated mode of admitting them', yet he proceeded again to *But*: 'But till some such regulation can be formed, I wish them still to be retained in their present state.' Finding himself unable to characterize, let alone to

25. For 'bound' within triplets, there is *The Medall*, 239–41:

> On utmost bounds of Loyalty they stand;
> And grin and whet like a Croatian Band,
> That waits impatient for the last Command.

To Sir Godfrey Kneller, 147–9:

> Thy Genius bounded by the Times like mine,
> Drudges on petty Draughts, nor dare design
> A more exalted Work, and more Divine.

The triplet may intimate the Divine. For the special *sound* of the triplet, after invoking the triplicity that is Heaven, Earth, and Skies there is *The Twelfth Book of Ovid His Metamorphoses*, 56–60:

> Full in the midst of this Created Space,
> Betwixt Heav'n, Earth and Skies, there stands a Place,
> Confining on all three; with triple Bound;
> Whence all Things, though remote, are view'd around;
> And thither bring their Undulating Sound.

26. *The Lives of the Poets*, i. 293–4.

establish, any such mode, Johnson in his mature poems did without triplets. But there is a charm in recalling that the young Johnson had shown a shrewd sense of what might be done with them. For one thing, there is the good old play of 'two' against three—this, in the mode of Dryden—alongside the hint of something 'perverse' and 'careless' (and 'grown'), and with a principled anxiety as to whether the arrival of a triplet might not stand in need of being somehow 'foreshown' or 'foretold':

> This scarce I lead, who left on yonder rock
> Two tender kids, the hopes of all the flock.
> Had we not been perverse and careless grown,
> This dire event by omens was foreshown;
> Our trees were blasted by the Thunder stroke, ⎫
> And left-hand crows, from an old hollow oak, ⎬
> Foretold the coming evil by their dismal croak. ⎭
>
> *(Translation of Virgil, Pastoral I, 19–25)*

Alert again to the critical questions prompted by the triplet, the young Johnson supplied such intimations as 'retards' and 'surprise' (the older Johnson remarking that the reader 'is on a sudden surprized with three rhymes together'):

> Part turn their Backs, part seiz'd with wild surprise
> Utter sad groans and lamentable cries.
> Impending death they strive to 'scape in vain ⎫
> For fear retards their flight, the cruell Crane ⎬
> Scatters their breathless bodies o'er the plain.[27] ⎭
>
> *(Translation of Addison's 'Battle of the Pygmies and the Cranes', 28–33)*

It was thanks to the triplet that Dryden received, and donated, particular insights and pleasures; Pope, less so; Johnson, not really, once

---

27. The hint in 'retards' resembles those in 'Form', 'Shewn', and 'improve' when the young Johnson showed how to improve the couplet-form into a triplet:

> With his own Form acquaint the forward Fool,
> Shewn in the faithful Glass of Ridicule;
> Teach mimick Censure her own faults to find, ⎫
> No more let Coquets to themselves be blind, ⎬
> So shall Belinda's Charms improve Mankind. ⎭
>
> *(To a Young Lady on her Birth-day, 15–19)*

There is musical play when the couplet's reign will prolong the chain:

> But when your Musick sooths the raging pain, ⎫
> We bid propitious Heav'n prolong your reign, ⎬
> We bless the Tyrant, and we hug the Chain. ⎭
>
> *(To Miss Hickman playing on the Spinet, 6–8)*

he came into his own. It was to the heroic couplet and its potentialities
that Johnson remained steadfast, and he hailed the most gifted successor in the tradition, George Crabbe (1754–1832), and the art of *The
Village.*

DR. JOHNSON TO SIR JOSHUA REYNOLDS
March 4, 1783

Sir:
I have sent You back Mr. Crabb's poem which I read with great delight. It
is original, vigorous, and elegant.
   The alterations which I have made, I do not require him to adopt, for my
lines are perhaps not often better [than] his own, but he may take mine and
his own together, and perhaps between them produce something better
than either⋯I do not doubt of Mr. Crabbe's success.[28]

~I do not doubt of Mr. Crabbe's success~

A heroic line.
   From the start Crabbe believed not only in the couplet but the
heroic triplet. In his poems of the eighteenth century, he had the triplet announced, 'foreshown', 'foretold'. *The Village* (1783), *The Parish
Register* (1807), and *The Borough* (1810) display the brace; but *Tales*
(1812) and *Tales of the Hall* (1819) do not. 'Surely', Dr Johnson had said
(the infirm word), 'Surely there is something unskilful in the necessity
of such mechanical direction.' For Crabbe, there might be a somewhat
better chance of resisting mechanical direction if we faced without
surprise, and with great skill, a clock's everyday peremptoriness:

> Above her head, all gorgeous to behold,
> A time-piece stood on feet of burnish'd gold;
> A stag's head crest adorn'd the picture'd case,
> Through the pure chrystal shone th' enamell'd face;
> And, while on brilliants mov'd the hands of steel,
> It click'd from pray'r to pray'r, from meal to meal.

(Procrastination; Tale IV, 174–9)

Crabbe was devout, and devoted to many things: his calling as a clergyman, his vocation as a poet, his zeal as a geologist, his responsibilities as
a father.[29] His world, which is the world of all of us (without being the
whole world and nothing but the world), is alive with his unwincing

---

28. *The Letters of Samuel Johnson,* ed. Bruce Redford (Princeton, 1992–4), iv. 116–17.
   Prominent in *The Life of George Crabbe by His Son* (1834), ch.V.
29. *The Life of George Crabbe by His Son* bears witness.

contemplation of all those abstract nouns that decline to be calmatively abstract. Stubborn abstract nouns within such titles for the *Tales* (1812) as *Resentment, The Struggles of Conscience, Delay Has Danger*. His couplets are at their deepest when the triplet is there for them to operate with, within passages that decline to pass, their life confined by such repetitions as are laced with infinitesimal changes infinitely dispiriting because they change nothing. Endurance is the thing that endures, the recognition of induration and its strata. 'Poetry makes nothing happen'? This poetry makes *nothing* happen.

In *The Poor of the Borough: Peter Grimes*, the rhyme of 'tide' and 'glide' swells so fully, not only because a rhyme-word takes up 'the Tide's delay', 'the Tides', 'the Tide', and 'Tides', as inexorably repetitive as the tides, but because it swells the couplet to a triplet—and sets (with the fixity of 'sets') before us the cruel and cruelly suffering figure of Peter Grimes tied to his dread monotony of tidescape.[30]

> Thus by himself compell'd to live each day,
> To wait for certain hours the Tide's delay;
> At the same times the same dull views to see,
> The bounding Marsh-bank and the blighted Tree;
> The Water only, when the Tides were high,
> When low, the Mud half-cover'd and half-dry;
> The Sun-burnt Tar that blisters on the Planks,
> And Bank-side Stakes in their uneven ranks;
> Heaps of entangled Weeds that slowly float,
> As the Tide rolls by the impeded Boat.
>
> When Tides were neap, and, in the sultry day,
> Through the tall bounding Mud-banks made their way,
> Which on each side rose swelling, and below
> The dark warm Flood ran silently and slow;
> There anchoring, *Peter* chose from Man to hide, ⎤
> There hang his Head, and view the lazy Tide ⎬
> In its hot slimy Channel slowly glide;   ⎦
> Where the small Eels that left the deeper way
> For the warm Shore, within the Shallows play;
> Where gaping Muscles, left upon the Mud,
> Slope their slow passage to the fallen Flood;—
> Here dull and hopeless he'll lie down and trace

---

30. From an essay of mine, 'George Crabbe's Thoughts of Confinement', *Essays in Appreciation* (Oxford, 1996), 67–89. Crabbe, like Dryden, apprehends that confinement may be more fully—yet unexpectedly—realized with the aid of the triplet.

How sidelong Crabs had scrawl'd their crooked race;
Or sadly listen to the tuneless cry
Of fishing *Gull* or clanging *Golden-eye*;
What time the Sea-birds to the Marsh would come, ⎫
And the loud *Bittern*, from the Bull-rush home, ⎬
Gave from the Salt-ditch side the bellowing boom:[31] ⎭

The previous twenty-five lines are the tracing of full true rhymes, whereas the triplet's three rhymes are all at odds, and they sound this out.

The triplet can be the instrument of tragedy, of torment, of a trap. By the same token, its axis can intimate escape. Escape, say, from falsity of feeling, from the poeticalities that are among the potent opponents of true poetry. Once upon a time, a highly compacted poem by Sir Henry Wotton (1568–1639) had told a touching truth.

Upon the death of Sir Albert Morton's Wife

He first deceas'd; she for a little tri'd
To live without him: lik'd it not, and di'd.

The two lines, he and she, are in the third person; there is no third person; there is a single couplet to honour a married couple.

In the fullness of time, or rather in the great emptying of Time's wallet, the sentiment of Wotton's poem had become open to sentimentalities; not Wotton's fault, but realism was now called for.

George, born to fortune, though of moderate kind,
Was not in haste his road through life to find:
His father early lost, his mother tried
To live without him, liked it not—and sigh'd
When, for her widow'd hand, an amorous youth appli'd:
She still was young, and felt that she could share
A lover's passion, and an husband's care · · ·

(*Tales of the Hall*, 1819; Book II, *The Brothers*, 71–7)

Quite at home, in its way, the triplet taking the hand of its alexandrine there. But Wotton's poem survives any due scepticism or undue cynicism, or so I judged in gracing with it the *Oxford Book of English Verse* (1999).

---

31. *The Borough*, Letter XXII, *The Poor of the Borough: Peter Grimes* (1810) 171–98. *The Complete Poetical Works*, ed. Norma Dalrymple-Champneys and Arthur Pollard (Oxford, 1988).

It is characteristic of Crabbe's judgements that they permit of caveats, with the triplet being the steely instrument. As when mother and eldest daughter are perfectly and disconcertingly matched:

> They were companions meet, with equal mind,
> Bless'd with one love, and to one point inclin'd;
> Beauty to keep, adorn, increase, and guard,
> Was their sole care, and had its full reward:
> In rising splendour with the one it reign'd,
> And in the other was by care sustain'd,
> The Daughter's charms increas'd, the Parent's yet remain'd.
>
> (*The Mother*; Tale VIII, 79–85)[32]

The couplet incarnates companionship, there in all that is equal, one love, one point, their sole care. The reward of these lines is then increased by that which is sustained, having remained: the rhyming that reigned as the concluding triplet with its alexandrine, where the marked caesura embodies the way in which Daughter and Parent curtsey to one another in complacency's courtesy, an elegant and unlovely equipollence. *Égoisme à deux*.

Crabbe participated in the traditional English sport of ribbing the French, and he was aware of the part that the heroic couplet could play. So this present tour of the triplet moves now finally towards an epilogue by Dryden, via Crabbe, each wise in his own eyes as to the French.

The Earl of Roscommon, in *An Essay on Translated Verse* (1684–5), had asked and answered his own rhetorical question:

> But who did ever in *French Authors* see
> The Comprehensive, *English Energy*?
> The weighty *Bullion* of *One Sterling Line*,
> Drawn to *French Wire*, would through whole *Pages* Shine.
> I speak my *Private*, but *Impartial sense*,
> With *Freedom*, and (I hope) without *offence*:

---

32. The triplet's charge in Crabbe's word 'remain'd' was varied (but remained) later in *Tales*:

> But the good Parent was so pleas'd, so kind,
> So pressing *Colin*, she so much inclin'd,
> That night advanc'd; and then so long detain'd,
> No wishes to depart she felt, or feign'd;
> Yet long in doubt she stood, and then perforce remain'd.
>
> (*Jesse and Colin*, Tale XIII, 502–6)

> For I'le Recant, when *France* can shew me *Wit*
> As strong as *Ours*, and as *succinctly Writ*.

One sterling line—*a fortiori*, two such, fashioned as the weapon of a couplet. *Touché*. The international duel, for Crabbe and for his contemporaries, could not but be political. In *The Dumb Orators*, the rebuke from the patriotic throat was what it has always been: if you don't like this country, how about your going to live in the country that you (deludedly) &c.?

> 'Let them to *France*, their darling country, haste,
> And all the comforts of a Frenchman taste;
> Let them his safety, freedom, pleasure know,
> Feel all their rulers on the land bestow;
> And be at length dismiss'd by one unerring blow;
> Not hack'd and hew'd by one afraid to strike,
> But shorn by that which shears all men alike;
> Nor, as in *Britain*, let them curse delay
> Of law, but borne without a form away—
> Suspected, tried, condemn'd, and carted in a day;
> Oh! let them taste what they so much approve,
> These strong fierce freedoms of the land they love.'[33]

Those heroic couplets, understood by their author to be lashing out and yet not wide of the mark, urge that freedom is something very different from 'freedoms'. This conviction can be enforced because the couplet itself incarnates the right freedom, in necessitating discipline, in entering into a willing bond, and in fortifying an enduring precedent. Enjoying, too, the right, on occasion, to depart respectfully from the 'form' of the couplet (there is the deference to Pope),[34] in order to proceed to a triplet. Twice, in those dozen lines, with each of the triplets calling upon an alexandrine to consummate its insistence.

The alexandrine has long been a surprising ally of the English heroic line. Since the alexandrine is the French heroic line, it might be an adversary. But when Johnson declared that 'the English Alexandrine breaks the lawful bounds, and surprises the reader', he did so in an English Alexandrine, twelve syllables assisted by the break that is a caesura:

~The English Alexandrine   breaks the lawful bounds~

---

33. *The Dumb Orators; or, The Benefit of Society; Tales* (1812); Tale I, 253–64.
34. He had struck at Addison as one who was willing to wound, and yet 'afraid to strike', *An Epistle to Dr. Arbuthnot*, 203.

English poetry, instead of spurning the alexandrine, colonized it, and often used it to develop our heroic couplet into a heroic triplet—this in the face of France's disavowal of triplets.[35] The French alexandrine is 'turned' by the English spy-mastery so that it becomes a double agent.[36]

But national security may have to be alerted. Dryden's *Prologue spoken at the Opening of the New House*, although it musters four sets of triplets, does not once avail itself of the French machine that is the alexandrine. 'While Troops of famisht *Frenchmen* hither drive' (38), our gulled compatriots fall into a French intonation for the English cadence (*cadénce*? come now):

> Mark, when they Play, how our fine Fops advance⎫
> The mighty Merits of these Men of *France*,   ⎬
> Keep Time, cry *Ben*, and humour the Cadence:[37] ⎭
> Well, please your selves, but sure 'tis understood,
> That *French* Machines have ne'r done *England* good: (44–8)

Comedy attended no less upon Dryden's decision as to how then to end his ensuing *Epilogue*. It was with two triplets that the *Epilogue* had opened its sense that an Opening was ending:

> Though what our Prologue said was sadly true,⎫
> Yet, Gentlemen, our homely House is new,   ⎬
> A Charm that seldom fails with, wicked, You. ⎭
> A Country Lip may have the Velvet touch,   ⎫
> Tho' She's no Lady, you may think her such, ⎬
> A strong imagination may do much.   ⎭

A strong imagination will sometimes be one that cannot rest satisfied with a couplet but needs an ampler field for the new. So this *Epilogue* was to end, even as it began, with two triplets. Between opening and closing, it had enjoyed itself with more than a dozen couplets, before reaching its *sotto voce* finale:

---

35. Conrad A. Balliet, *PMLA* 1965, on 'the French hexameter couplet': 'no significant writer of French heroic verse would have considered using triplets—it would have been too sharp a variation from the rules. The triplet is an English phenomenon.'
36. For the terrifyingly real thing, within the treacherous tragedy of espionage, see the reference to the Double-Cross System, p. 287 below.
37. They cry *bien*, and they stress—as the English do not—the second syllable of 'cadence', an advance from France.

> The best which they reserv'd they now will Play,[38] ⎤
> For, like kind Cuckolds, tho' we have not the way ⎬
> To please, we'l find you Abler Men who may.   ⎦
> If they shou'd fail, for last recruits we breed   ⎤
> A Troop of frisking Monsieurs to succeed: ⎬
> (You know the *French* sure cards at time of need.) ⎦   (135–40)

The final triplet makes a mock of French breeding, while thinking twice about what it means to succeed—always a crucial consideration in this poet who so much pondered successes and successions. But at the moment when the *Epilogue* shares its confidences, wise to this public occasion it lowers its voice.

Of its own accord, a triplet will invite a third party to join the couple ('Like kind Cuckolds'). No need, then, for an alexandrine, although as it happens the etymology of the word would have provided a happy touch, 'some deriving it, according to Ménage, from the name of Alexandre Paris, an old [Old, surely?] French poet who used this verse' (*OED*). 'According to Ménage' invites the thought that, in so often consummating the triplet, an alexandrine might constitute a *ménage à trois*. A strong imagination may do much.

38. The California editors explain this cryptic line: 'The best wit (plays) from the older period, their exclusive property, and hitherto unproduced in these times, the management at this theatre will now proceed to revive for your delectation, as a more than sufficient offset to the empty magnificence which is the best the other house has to offer.'

4

T. S. Eliot and 'Wrong'd Othello'

The individual talent—genius, rather—of T. S. Eliot threw down a gauntlet to challenge a tradition when in 1927 he wrote of how and why he set such very different store by Othello's magnificence, there in the astonishing speech of the final Act mounting to self-slaughter. 'This heavy Act', in the last scene's last line. For Eliot, Othello was not so much heroic as taking a heroic line. This, the better to hide from himself what he had done.

What had long been admired in both the character of Othello and in Shakespeare's characterization of him had been the hero's so rising to his occasion. For Eliot, though, what had been occasioned, staged, was, on the contrary, Othello's sinking to a nadir. A sinking of which we all are all too capable.

In due course—thanks to whirligig revenges—Eliot's own page of criticism, which for some of us has always been a high point of his critical imagination, has found itself reprimanded as a low point, a low move. A return now to Eliot's lecture, 'Shakespeare and the Stoicism of Seneca' (1927) is in the conviction that Eliot's radical proposal ought to have remained unignorable in its chastening attention to all that Othello himself—to the bitter end—was tragically successful in ignoring.[1]

★ ★ ★

I have always felt that I have never read a more terrible exposure of human weakness—of universal human weakness—than the last great speech of Othello. (I am ignorant whether anyone else has ever adopted this view, and it may appear subjective and fantastic in the extreme.) It is usually taken on its face value; as expressing the greatness in defeat of a noble but erring nature.

---

1. *Decisions and Revisions in T. S. Eliot* (London, 2002) accommodated my first engagement with Eliot on Othello.

Soft you; a word or two before you go.
I have done the state some service, and they know 't,
No more of that. I pray you, in your letters,
When you shall these unlucky deeds relate,
Speak of me as I am; nothing extenuate,
Nor set down aught in malice; then must you speak
Of one that loved not wisely but too well;
Of one not easily jealous, but, being wrought,
Perplex'd in the extreme; of one whose hand,
Like the base Indian, threw a pearl away
Richer than all his tribe; of one whose subdued eyes,
Albeit unused to the melting mood,
Drop tears as fast as the Arabian trees
Their medicinal gum. Set you down this;
And say, besides, that in Aleppo once,
Where a malignant and a turban'd Turk
Beat a Venetian and traduced the state,
I took by the throat the circumcised dog,
And smote him, thus.[2]

What Othello seems to me to be doing in making this speech is *cheering himself up*. He is endeavouring to escape reality; he has ceased to think about

2. *The Folio:*

> Soft you; a word or two before you goe:
> I haue done the State some seruice, and they know't:
> No more of that. I pray you in your Letters,
> When you shall these vnluckie deeds relate,
> Speake of me, as I am: Nothing extenuate,   5
> Nor set downe ought in malice.
> Then must you speake,
> Of one that lou'd not wisely, but too well:
> Of one, not easily Iealious, but being wrought,
> Perplexed in the extreame: Of one, whose hand   10
> (Like the base Iudean) threw a Pearle away
> Richer then all his Tribe: Of one, whose subdu'd Eyes,
> Albeit vn-vsed to the melting moode,
> Drops teares as fast as the Arabian Trees
> Their Medicinable gumme. Set you downe this: 15
> And say besides, that in *Aleppo* once,
> Where a malignant, and a Turbond-Turke
> Beate a Venetian, and traduc'd the State,
> I tooke by th'throat the circumcised Dogge,
> And smoate him, thus.   20

Quarto variants of wording 1 before you goe:] *not in* Q * 5 me, as I am] them as they are Q * 10 Perplexed] Perplext Q * 11 Iudean] Indian Q * 14 Drops] Drop Q2 * 15 Medicinable] medicinall Q

Desdemona, and is thinking about himself. Humility is the most difficult of all virtues to achieve; nothing dies harder than the desire to think well of oneself. Othello succeeds in turning himself into a pathetic figure, by adopting an *aesthetic* rather than a moral attitude, dramatizing himself against his environment. He takes in the spectator, but the human motive is primarily to take in himself. I do not believe that any writer has ever exposed this *bovarysme*, the human will to see things as they are not, more clearly than Shakespeare.[3]

★ ★ ★

It is excruciating that Eliot speaks not simply or solely of Othello's weakness but 'of human weakness—of universal human weakness'. Irrespective of whether Eliot takes the measure of Othello's nature, those who slight these observations of Eliot's have been perfunctory as to what exactly he was maintaining.

'The human will to see things as they are not': in '"Rhetoric" and Poetic Drama' (1919), Eliot had already been bent upon seeing for himself, inclining to italics to have us, too, *see* something:

The really fine rhetoric of Shakespeare occurs in situations where a character in the play *sees himself* in a dramatic light:

OTHELLO.   *And say, besides,—that in Aleppo once...*[4]

From '*sees*' into '*say*': it is, in Eliot's phrase, 'tragic intensity' that drove such pivotings as Othello's from 'turban'd Turk' to 'took by the throat'. (Eliot, who truly listened to Othello, was to proceed to take up an extension of this very turn: 'He takes in the spectator, but the human motive is primarily to take in himself.') The climax of Othello's performative utterings was a further and conclusive rotation in sound-effectiveness, his biding our time in order then to swoop from *Set you down this* to *And smote him, thus*.

'Contemplating the spectacle of himself,' attested F. R. Leavis,[5] 'Othello is overcome with the pathos of it. But this is not the part to die in: drawing himself proudly up, he speaks his last words as the stern soldier who recalls, and re-enacts, his supreme moment of deliberate courage.' (Drawing himself up, and cheering himself up?) 'It is a superb *coup de théâtre.*'

But those are not 'his last words'. Nor is it clear that killing the Turk was an act of deliberate courage: there is not said to have been more

3. *Selected Essays* (London, 1932; 3rd edn, 1951), 130–1.   4. Ibid. 39.
5. 'Diabolic Intellect and the Noble Hero' (1937), in *The Common Pursuit* (London, 1952), 152.

than one of him, he is not glimpsed as the better-armed (or even as armed? 'but thought he had no weapon', said of Othello at the end), and, for all we know, he may have been taken not only by the throat but by surprise, even as Othello now needed to surprise his standers-by. The killing in Aleppo was no Shakespearean duel of honour or dishonour. (I am ignorant whether anyone else has ever adopted this view, and it may appear subjective and fantastic in the extreme.)

From 'Set you down this' to 'And smote him, thus'. But Othello's *this* is not to be cancelled by his *thus*. He was to need *this* again, for his encore within the finishing end, his positively (and, he hopes, positive) last appearance. What Eliot carefully called Othello's 'last great speech' was indeed great of scale but it stands as his famous-all-but-last-words, and it knew to yield to the very different scale of a couplet, having recourse (for the final clinch—or finale) to the word *this*, now set pre-ciously within a full rhyme (thus, this time, not an off-rhyme), a full rhyme moreover that draws upon a further sound-effect, *kist / kill'd*, as well as upon the tradition by which rhyme itself is seen and felt under the aspect of a kiss.[6] Othello sought to have the very last words:

> I kist thee, ere I kill'd thee: No way but this,
> Killing my self, to dye upon a kisse.[7]

A *heroic* couplet, it intimates. Yet what of the coupled lovers them-selves? Are *I* and *thee* accorded equipollent intensity when seen in this dramatic light? *I . . . thee . . . I . . . thee . . . my self.*

Such seeing himself in a certain light, to and for the very end, has need of limelight (a dangerous substance, and not only physically as inflammable). Granted, we the audience then 'have this necessary advantage of a new clue to the character, in noting the angle from which he views himself.' *But.* 'But when a character *in* a play makes a direct appeal to us, we are either the victims of our own sentiment, or we are in the presence of a vicious rhetoric.'[8]

6. Keats: 'So said, his erewhile timid lips grew bold, | And poesied with hers in dewy rhyme' (*Isabella*, IX). The kiss is a rhyme because it rhymes their lips and doubly so because the upper and lower lips already rhyme with each other.

7. The most moving moment, for me, in any production of *Othello* came within Desdemona's cry when Othello strikes her (IV. i): 'I have not deserv'd this', the stress not upon *deserv'd* but upon *this*. Marie Kohler, in a Harvard production of the early 1970s, was yearning to be able to concede—bewildered as to how this could possibly be—that she must have done something that deserved *something*, but not *this*.

8. *Selected Essays*, 40.

The propensity to dramatize oneself, like a vicious rhetoric, is inescapable but not irresistible. Eliot himself came to dramatize this in his last great poem:

> And last, the rending pain of re-enactment
> Of all that you have done, and been; the shame
> Of motives late revealed, and the awareness
> Of things ill done and done to others' harm
> Which once you took for exercise of virtue.
> Then fools' approval stings, and honour stains.

(Little Gidding, II)

Eliot dramatized one word of this for John Hayward: 'I want to preserve the association of "enact"—to take the part of oneself on a stage for oneself as the audience.'[9] Eliot was always returning to such cases. What in 1927 he was identifying—both anew to himself and newly to others—was Shakespeare's recognition of 'the attitude of self-dramatization assumed by some of Shakespeare's heroes at moments of tragic intensity'. That Othello is the particular tragedy singled out for Eliot's dramatic realization may have been compounded by its being the only one of the tragedies that summons tragic, a loading we can scarcely bear to look on: 'Look on the tragic loading of this bed'. Tragic intensity then proves to harbour a hiding place of its power (and of its understanding of what Othello is hiding from himself) in the quietude with which Eliot's way of putting it will find itself calling upon Othello's. Not to be ignored is this:

Eliot: fantastic in the extreme

Othello: Perplex'd in the extreme

Far from distancing himself from Othello (as Othello himself does when casting himself repeatedly as 'One who···'), Eliot has his being in the same mortal moral and spiritual world as Othello. In the extreme. In extremis.

It is, at first, those 'moments of tragic intensity' that impel Eliot to build up such a persistent continuity as that of Othello's verse-music with his own unportentous prose. The weight of this accumulating accommodation may be felt if we simply set Eliot's gravity (and gravamen) alongside George Bernard Shaw's levity, bent upon an actor with a 'reputation which carried him over parts he could not play at all,

9. 22 September 1942; The Poems of T. S. Eliot, ed. Ricks and McCue, i. 667.

such as Othello, through which he walked as if the only line in the play
that conveyed any idea to him was the description of Othello as "perplexed in the extreme"'.[10]
The convergences deepen to a ground-swell.

Eliot: Humility is the most difficult of all virtues to achieve; nothing dies
harder than the desire to think well of oneself.[11]

> then must you speak
> Of one that loved not wisely but too well;
> Of one not easily jealous,

Eliot: see things as they are not

> Speake of them as they are [Quarto; Folio '· · · me as I am'][12]

One asseveration had stood forth earlier in Eliot's speech:

I am *not* under the delusion that Shakespeare resembles myself, either as I am
or as I should like to imagine myself

> Speak of me as I am

Eliot's syntax ('I am not') continues into the later stylized modesty:
'(I am ignorant whether anyone else has ever adopted this view, and it
may appear subjective and fantastic in the extreme.)' It was in post-
publication revision that Eliot added the round brackets or lunulae—
there were none here in the published lecture—upping his downplaying
with lunulae's particular power to suggest that they are containing at
once a crux and an aside. (Emilia in this scene, V. ii, calls Othello 'As
ignorant as durt'.)

Eliot chose not to limit his catchment-area to Othello's own music-
wording (though the traffic brought the initiating energy for this
achievement of Eliot's in combining the compassionate with the
dispassionate). He needed to summon the play *Othello* as well as the
character Othello. But to agree in any way with (say) Iago is, in some
eyes, to be damnable—

---

10. *Our Theatres in the Nineties*, iii. 286, 14 December 1895, of Barry Sullivan.
11. Othello being about to die by his own hand. Perhaps 'harder' is touched not only by
    Eliot's 'most difficult' and Othello's 'not easily' but by 'Soft you'. Eliot feels for
    Othello's self-stationing at the brink of death. ('I cannot say that it is Shakespeare's
    "philosophy". Yet many people have lived by it'; *Selected Essays*, 129.)
12. Laurence Olivier chose, not the Folio reading, but the Quarto's 'Speake of them as
    they are'.

Iago, for whom the Moor's richly ornamented language amounts to nothing more than 'a bombast circumstance | Horribly stuffed with epithets of war' (I. i. 12–13). Iago's judgement is uncomfortably mirrored in the dismissive responses of such twentieth-century critics as T. S. Eliot, with his infamous assertion that Othello in his last great aria is merely 'cheering himself up'.[13]

It may be judged unseemly these days to wish upon a responder to a Shakespearean tragedy anything at all 'uncomfortable'. But the greatest Shakespearean critics have always acknowledged that among the greatest of Shakespeare's powers of perception is his understanding of how percipient those bad people, even evil people, often prove to be. It may be uncomfortable, but it is an uncomfortable truth (a salutary discomfiture), that the judgements passed by bad men and woman are not debarred—on occasion or in certain respects—from being markedly *sound*. Acumen, discernment, imagination, and intense attentiveness are among the characteristics of flawed royalty, Lear, Richard III, Macbeth, Claudius, and Hamlet (both King and Prince); the soldier-politicians, Coriolanus and Antony; the administrator, Angelo; alongside family-members, Edmund, Goneril, Iachimo, and Lady Macbeth. We had better not wince from the fact that we good people are often imperceptive, or from the fact that bad people often are not.

'I have always felt that I have never read a more terrible exposure of human weakness—of universal human weakness—than the last great speech of Othello': Eliot's tone and proceeding are nothing like the prurient gloating that Michael Neill and Robert Cushman enjoy attributing to Eliot: Othello as 'an egotist who deserves even more than he gets'.[14]

Eliot listens more sustainedly to Othello than to Iago, but nobody's evidence is to be deemed inadmissible. (William Empson: 'all the characters are on trial in any civilized narrative'.[15]) Though it is hateful of Iago to say to Othello 'Ay, there's the point', it would be irresponsible to have it that Iago never has a point.

13. *Othello*, ed. Michael Neill (The Oxford Shakespeare, 2006), 74. This particular *merely* is not Eliot's.
14. Brandished twice in *Othello*, ed. Neill, 60, 92. In presenting 'Othello's last big speech' as a return to 'studied self-display', 'such attitudinizing', Neill (pp. 134–5) is more patronizing than Eliot.
15. *Milton's God* (1961), 94.

Eliot: a noble but erring nature

IAGO   *I would not have your free, and Noble Nature*
              Out of selfe-bounty, be abus'd;

                        ⋆ ⋆ ⋆

OTHELLO   *And yet how Nature erring from it selfe—*
IAGO   *Ay. there's the point* (III iii)[16]

Eliot: subjective and fantastic

IAGO   *bragging, and telling her fantasticall lies* (II. i)

Even Eliot's threefold toying with the everyday word *think* was (I think) alive to Iago's heinous genius.

He [Othello] has ceased to think about Desdemona, and is thinking about himself.[17] . . . nothing dies harder than the desire to think well of oneself.

OTHELLO   *What do'st thou thinke?*
IAGO   *Thinke, my Lord?*
OTHELLO   *Thinke, my Lord? Alas, thou eccho'st me*
              As if there were some Monster in thy thought
              Too hideous to be shewne.

                        ⋆ ⋆ ⋆

OTHELLO   *Shew me thy thought.*
IAGO   *My Lord, you know I love you.*
OTHELLO   *I thinke thou do'st:*

                        ⋆ ⋆ ⋆

IAGO   *For Michael Cassio,*
              I dare be sworne, I thinke that he is honest.
OTHELLO   *I think so too.*

                        ⋆ ⋆ ⋆

IAGO   *Why then I thinke Cassio's an honest man.*
OTHELLO   *Nay, yet there's more in this?*
              I prythee speake to me, as to thy thinkings (III. iii)

Perhaps such parallels, given that they may be (to those who are not jealous) 'trifles light as air', should be demoted to coincidences, taken on no more than their face value.

---

16. Othello tragically seconds Brabantio who had exclaimed (of Desdemona's choosing Othello) 'For Nature, so prepostrously to erre · · · so could erre | Against all rules of Nature' (I. ii).

17. 'Killing my self, to dye upon a kisse.'

Eliot: It is usually taken on its face value, as expressing the greatness in defeat of a noble but erring nature.

> DESDEMONA   *For if he be not one, that truly loves you* · · ·
> *I have no judgement in an honest face*
> (III. iii, to Othello, of Cassio)
>
> OTHELLO   *begrim'd and blacke*
> *As mine owne face* (III. iii)

Any deep literary criticism by Eliot apprehends and comprehends a current towards his own poems. *Speak to me, as to thy thinkings.* When Eliot echoed Othello (and Iago), his twinings of *think* (and *speak*) were in touch with another marital monster of thought, that of *The Waste Land*.

> 'Speak to me. Why do you never speak. Speak.
> 'What are you thinking of? What thinking? What?
> 'I never know what you are thinking. Think.'
>
> I think we are in rats' alley
> Where the dead men lost their bones.

That Eliot is in deadly earnest in his disconcerting lack of awe in the face of Othello's flights (universal weakness and its tragic intensity being for Eliot the immitigable facts) is corroborated by his need to move from English to French, from drama to novel, and from the seventeenth century to the nineteenth—and the twentieth—century: 'I do not believe that any writer has ever exposed this *bovarysme*, the human will to see things as they are not, more clearly than Shakespeare.'

Eliot prefers to the Anglicizing form (bovarism) the latter of the *OED*'s further alternatives bovarysm(e): *bovarysme*, from the name of the principal character in Flaubert's novel *Madame Bovary* (1857).

(Domination by) a romantic or unreal conception of oneself. [1902 J. DE GAULTIER (*title*) Le Bovarysme.]

At which point the *OED* (Second Edition) slips a little, in that it provides as its first English citation Aldous Huxley (1929) quoting Jules de Gaultier. Eliot's clarion does follow in the Dictionary, but it ought to precede, not follow, Huxley, since it belongs to 1927, not (the *OED*'s dating) to 1934.[18] It is Eliot, not Huxley, who first grasps the import of

---

18. *Elizabethan Essays*, which was not even Eliot's first collecting of 'Shakespeare and the Stoicism of Seneca' (this had been *Selected Essays*, 1932).

bovarysme, and it is Eliot's understanding—'the human will to see things as they are not'—that we should adopt rather than Huxley's wishful amelioration in 1936: 'the power granted to man to conceive himself as other than he is'. (This misguidingly makes it sound like a markedly good thing.) The power that had been granted to Eliot was the power to grant Flaubert's greatness while yet proclaiming, in a supreme tribute, that even Flaubert did not apprehend *bovarysme* as profoundly as Shakespeare: 'I do not believe that any writer has ever exposed this *bovarysme*, the human will to see things as they are not, more clearly than Shakespeare.'

Yet tragic intensity is manifestly not the whole of it, since Eliot came up with an unexpected locution that was patently intended to tease his readers (listeners, rather, in the first place): 'What Othello seems to me to be doing in making this speech is *cheering himself up*.' Then, of Stoicism: 'It is the permanent substratum of a number of versions of cheering oneself up. Nietzsche is the most conspicuous modern instance of cheering oneself up.' This, played from a wicked pack of cards. It was not tragic intensity but comic downplaying that then prompted the anger against Eliot and 'his infamous assertion'.

One of those who was not repelled by the phrase *cheering himself up* was William Empson. On the matter of 'convention' when it comes to judgements, he wrote, 'I think that the answer was given by Mr. Eliot in his lecture on the influence of Seneca, in which he said that Othello's last speech was a repulsive attempt to cheer himself up and ignore the realities of what he had done.'[19] And Empson's judgement might well carry more weight in that there is some distance between his and Eliot's feeling for, say, self-dramatizing rhetoric. Empson dissociates himself from 'the heroics of Othello' but not from the conviction that Henry the Fifth is 'meant to have a command of forthright self-praise'. Empson believes that, although Othello is culpably self-skilled at ignoring what he has done, there is often something to be said for being able to ignore: 'a good deal of firm ignoring of the facts around one may be positively heroic, or agreeably spirited'.[20] True, the ignorable facts when you come to brass tacks do well not to include one's having murdered one's innocent wife. But even hereabouts, Empson issues a wide reminder: 'That there is usually a tension between a Shakespearean

19. 'Honest in Othello', in *The Structure of Complex Words* (London, 1951), 239–40.
20. 'Theories of Value', ibid. 423.

character (as judged by his speech-rhythms and so on) and his actions no one need be anxious to deny.'

Another who did not recoil from the words *cheering himself up* was Herbert Grierson, who wrote to Eliot (2 October 1927):

You say Othello is 'cheering himself up', 'has ceased to think about Desdemona'. In a way he has. He has said his last word over Desdemona ··· It is quite natural that he shd in the reaction turn to consider himself & those who judge him: we can't escape from the thought of ourselves & our social environment. But if he is 'cheering himself up' it is in preparation for executing justice upon himself. He says as it were 'You are not the people to condemn me. I have served you well. It is I who condemn & slay myself.'

To which Eliot replied with equal courtesy, moved to conclude his thought with an exquisite English heroic line, *the imperfections of humanity*:

Thank you very much for taking so much notice of my short address on Shakespeare. Like most delivered addresses, it seems to me rather thin on re-reading it in type. I am glad, however, to have so much of your approval as you have given me. What you say about *Othello* is very likely more just than what I said myself, but it does not cheer me up any better than I cheered up *Othello*. Your interpretation seems to me to make the whole business even more immoral than mine. But perhaps I am very old fashioned in my attitude to some of the Shakespearian heroes. At any rate what I said was certainly not intended to reflect upon Shakespeare but merely to attribute to Shakespeare a profound knowledge of the imperfections of humanity.[21]

—*merely!*

cheer up. *trans.* To raise the spirits of (anyone) by cheering words; to brighten up.

It is not exactly the *OED* entry in itself that can defend Eliot against the flushed charge of having been frivolous, even flippant, in enlisting *cheering himself up*. Or rather, it is only a clue within the first two *OED* citations that can bring home to us how it was that Eliot was able to combine, in this demotic turn, a comic light with a tragic shadow. For in judging deeply a play by Shakespeare, Eliot seized upon an aspect of Shakespearean English in which *cheering up* gravitated to the immediate vicinity of death (Othello's case, and not *his* death alone). For the first two *OED* citations are from Shakespeare, yours in the face of death: 'My Sovereign Lord, cheer up yourself, look up' (*2 Henry IV*, IV.

21. 5 October 1927. *The Letters of T. S. Eliot, vol. 3: 1926–1927*, ed. Valerie Eliot and John Haffenden (London, 2012), 737–8.

iv), prompted by the King's cry: 'O me, come near me, now I am much ill'. And the three Witches: 'Come Sisters, cheer we up his sprights' (*Macbeth*, IV. i), Macbeth having exclaimed: 'For the blood-bolter'd Banquo smiles upon me'. Within Shakespeare's world, cheering yourself up, or someone else, is especially—as Eliot had it be for Othello—for when the pressure of death is not only immanent (universal, human and more than human) but imminent. For soldiers like those whose darkened plight it is, as on the eve of the battle of Bosworth Field.

> Thomas the Earle of Surrey, and himselfe,
> Much about Cockshut time, from Troope to Troope
> Went through the Army, chearing up the Souldiers.
>
> (*Richard III*, V. iii)[22]

22. Further instances of the death-gravity of Shakespeare's *cheering up*:

> Like soldiers when their captain once doth yeeld,
> They basely flie, and dare not stay the field.

> Thus stands she in a trembling extasie,
> Till cheering up her senses all dismayd,
> She tels them tis a causlesse fantasie,
> And childish error that they are affrayd,
>   Bids them leave quaking, bids them feare no more,
>   And with that word, she spide the hunted boare.
>
> (*Venus and Adonis*, 894–900)

> He cryes aloud; Tarry my Cosin Suffolke,
> My soule shall thine keepe company to heaven:
> Tarry (sweet soule) for mine, then flye a-brest:
> As in this glorious and well-foughten field
> We kept together in our Chivalrie.
> Upon these words I came, and cheer'd him up,
> He smil'd me in the face, raught me his hand,
>
> ...
>
> And so espous'd to death, with blood he seal'd
> A Testament of Noble-ending-love: (*Henry V*, IV. vi)

> Whereat the great Lord of Northumberland,
> Whose Warlike eares could never brooke retreat,
> Chear'd up the drouping Army, and himself,
> Lord Clifford and Lord Stafford all a-brest
> Charg'd our maine Battailes Front: and breaking in,
> Were by the Swords of common Souldiers slaine. (*3 Henry VI*, I. i)

> I cheer'd them up with justice of our Cause,
> With promise of high pay, and great Rewards:
> But all in vaine, they had no heart to fight (*3 Henry VI*, II. i)

> Must you with hot Irons, burne out both mine eyes?
>
> ...
>
> Have you the heart? When your head did but ake,

'The attitude of self-dramatization assumed by some of Shakespeare's heroes at moments of tragic intensity': such intensity is palpitatingly alive as Othello nears death. As Eliot has it in his pendant publication of the same year: 'The ethic of Seneca is a matter of postures. The posture which gives the greatest opportunity for effect, hence for the Senecan morality, is the posture of dying.'[23] But Eliot ventures to counterpoint tragedy, to complement it, thanks to the comic intensity of the phrase *cheering himself up*. Then, by a last twist of the knife, cheering oneself up (or others) turns out to have a knife-edge to it, particularly within Shakespearean usage. In any event, self-dramatization is as fond of moments of *comic* intensity (often breathing an air of indifference, making light of intensity) as of tragic, and Eliot had dexterously staged himself so for his delivery of 'Shakespeare and the Stoicism of Seneca' to the Shakespeare Association in 1927. One of his best performances, this had proffered itself as comic self-dramatization, a matter of medium, the lecturer playing badinage with his audience.[24]

As uttered, and as first published at two shillings, it cast itself at once in a dramatic comic light:

Desiring to make the most of the opportunity which had been given me of addressing the inmost circle of Shakespeare experts, I cast about, as any other mere journalist would do in the circumstances, for some subject in treating which I could best display my agility and conceal my ignorance of all the knowledge of which everyone present is master. I abandoned several interesting topics on which I might hope to impress almost any other audience— such as the development of dramatic blank verse or the relation of Shakespeare to Marlowe—in favour of one which, if I am in disagreement with anybody, I shall be in disagreement with persons whose opinions will be regarded as suspiciously by the Shakespeare Association as are my own. I am a timid person, easily overawed by authority; in what I have to say I hope that authority is at least as likely to be of my opinion as not.

The last few years have witnessed a number of recrudescences of Shakespeare ···

I knit my hand-kercher about your browes

···

Still and anon cheer'd up the heavy time;
Saying, what lacke you? and where lies your greefe?   (*King John*, IV. i)

23. 'Seneca in Elizabethan Translation' (Introduction to *Seneca His Tenne Tragedies*, ed. Charles Whibley, 1927); *Selected Essays*, 72.
24. I expand a few pages from the Panizzi Lectures. On the medium (not just genre) of the lecture, see Erving Goffman, *Forms of Talk* (1981).

As the revised text in *Selected Essays* has it, 'Shakespeare and the Stoicism of Seneca' opens in vigorous immediacy with that last sentence, swift and deft and relishing the sound as well as the thought of 'recrudescences'. But something of value did vanish when those preamblings were excised. For they have their own delicious disconcertings, their feints and velleities and stylizations, this speaking of 'Shakespeare experts' (as though an 'expert' in literature were not suspect to the point of indictment—and 'the inmost circle of Shakespeare experts'? Where exactly is the inmost circle of Dante experts going to end up?), this gravelling listeners by affecting to grovel ('as any other mere journalist would do'), this speaking of how best to display not ability but 'agility', while not concealing the wish to 'conceal my ignorance of all the knowledge of which everyone present is master'. (What, *everyone*? This is masterly.) 'I am a timid person, easily overawed by authority'—but not, I can assure me, easily gulled by self-styled authorities, gullible though the 'experts' are when it comes to such flattery as is laid on with a vengeance.

The pleasantries were integral to a dramatizing that distinguishes the lecture 'Shakespeare and the Stoicism of Seneca' from its pendant preface to another's scholarship, 'Seneca in Elizabethan Translation'. Three paragraphs after the excised preamble, there begins a rueful autobiographical account by the poet of how critics get things wrong, an account that functions not just differently but less effectively once it has become deprived of the herald who had figured earlier in the social occasion. A loss was entailed when the preamble rightly went (now an essay, no longer a lecture with an audience to be availed of), and the loss goes beyond that of Eliot's maintenance of his felicitous way of speaking. For the core of his argument is anticipated by the preamble in which Eliot had staged himself to such effect in affecting the abashed or the bashful. Eliot's evocation of *Othello* is no longer exactly the same once it figures without the lecture's curtain-raising. When Eliot said of Othello that 'He takes in the spectator, but the human motive is primarily to take in himself', we were to take in Eliot's words about his own self-presentation and his having had spectators, including his subsequently having come to exclude 'those preambular remarks and incidental pleasantries which, having been intended to seduce the listener, might merely irritate the reader'. What Eliot had grasped as his original point of entry had been powerfully at one with his succeeding advance, 'Shakespeare's instinctive recognition of something of theatrical utility'. For 'the attitude of self-dramatization assumed by some of Shakespeare's heroes' had been assumed by Eliot at his opening moment of unheroic comic intensity, when Eliot (like Othello while so unlike him) had been 'dramatizing himself against his environment'.

The year 1927 is a record of Eliot's refusal, inability (an odd thought), to leave these matters alone, his occupation by such self-stagings, self-sightings, self-occupations including Othello's occupation.[25] The lecture on 'Shakespeare and the Stoicism of Seneca', starring Othello, was delivered on 18 March 1927 (published 22 September).[26] In May 1927 there were Eliot's words on Baudelaire, a lacerating account of the terror of escaping all laceration: 'Experience, as a sequence of outward events, is nothing in itself; it is possible to pass through the most terrible experiences protected by histrionic vanity.'[27] The *Times Literary Supplement* of 16 June 1927 carried (unsigned) his 'Nicolo Machiavelli': 'It is easy to admire Machiavelli in a sentimental way. It is only one of the sentimental and histrionic poses of human nature—and human nature is incorrigibly histrionic—to pose as a "realist".' Charging sentimentalists with 'a form of self-satisfaction and self-deception', Eliot wrote of Machiavelli: 'He had none of the instinct to pose.' Pose is then understood to collude with posture: 'The ethic of Seneca is a matter of postures' ('Seneca in Elizabethan Translation', September 1927).

These insistences in 1927 may have had something to do with the dedications of himself at the time, dedications that Eliot needed to distinguish from dramatizations. In early 1927 he consulted the Reverend William Force Stead about being received into the Church of England ('for the moment, it concerns me alone, & not the public— not even those nearest me'), and in June he was baptized by Stead.[28] In May, he had let it be known in the Press that he would seek British citizenship, and in October he mentioned to his brother Henry that

---

25. *Othello* inculcates wariness as to both 'selfe-charitie' (II. iii) and 'selfe-Bounty' (III. iii).
26. Eliot had the year catch the light: 'in this year 1927', and six lines later 'as we feel and think in 1927', these words of the lecture then being revised to 'as we felt and thought in 1927'. *Selected Essays*, 126–7.
27. 'Baudelaire in Our Time', in *The Dial*, May 1927, a review of Arthur Symons, *Baudelaire: Prose and Poetry*; to be distinguished from Eliot's 'Baudelaire' (1930), in *Selected Essays*.
28. My debt here, and elsewhere, is to John Haffenden for his lucid and highly knowledgeable year-by-year account of Eliot; this, under 1927.

he had applied for naturalization: 'If this shocks you, I will present you my reasons; in any case don't tell mother.' To Charles Whibley (10 November) he staged himself along comic lines:

I was only disappointed to find the oath of allegiance a very disappointing inferior ceremony. I expected to be summoned to the Home Office at least, if not before the Throne. Instead I merely had to swear an ordinary oath before an ordinary commissioner, just as one does in ordinary life.

It was left to *Time* magazine 1927 (28 November) to treat history histrionically, dramatizing Eliot comically, even comedically, against his environments, plural:

Last week a sleek, brilliant citizen of the U. S. became a subject of His Britannic Majesty King George V. He is Thomas Stearns Eliot, relative of the late Charles William Eliot, President Emeritus of Harvard University. Poet and critic, he is the author of *The Waste Land*, a poem which won the Dial prize for 1922, and *The Sacred Wood*, a volume of critical works. Mr. Eliot, now 39 years old, was born in St. Louis. His education was wrought at Harvard, the Sorbonne, the Harvard Graduate School, Merton College, Oxford. During the War, he functioned as assistant editor of *The Egoist*, recherché London magazine. Today he is editor of *The Criterion*, a neoteric quarterly of pronounced modernist tendencies. Although Burton Rascoe thought his *The Waste Land* a 'thing of bitterness and beauty,' a nameless London editor pronounced it 'an obscure but amusing poem.' The reader must judge for himself. But of his brilliance as a critic there can be little doubt, however much his taste may be in dispute. His many adverse critics, in no wise surprised by his change of nationality, hint that a certain superciliousness in his attitude toward U. S. letters caused him to feel more at home in England, where neo-literary figures abound profuse as the autumnal leaves.

(England as Vallombrosa, the valley of the shadow of death, its *mise en scène* by Milton, with neo-literary figures as fallen angels.)

Meanwhile, to the perils of publicity attending upon state or church were added, continuing through 1927, those perils that attended upon and that emanated from Vivien Eliot. She had written to her husband on 5 January 1926: 'I appeal to you once more. Will you protect me, or will you not?'[29] Eliot was to protect himself against her and against his own sense of guilt, not with histrionic vanity but with skilled chill (and with brother-in-lawfulness, the backing of her brother Maurice Haigh-Wood); he wrote to his brother Henry, 30 August 1927:

29. *The Letters of T. S. Eliot*, vol. 3, 3.

no doctor will commit anyone to an asylum unless they have either manifestly tried to commit suicide or committed a criminal assault upon someone else. So there is no likelihood of getting Vivien into a Home at present. We must therefore wait until she either annoys people in the public street (which I am always expecting) or tries to take her own life, before I can do anything about it. Meanwhile I feel that I must not leave her, even for a night, as this sort of thing might happen at any time.[30]

—*this sort of thing?* Annoying people in the public street, and taking her own life?

ENOBARBUS	I saw her once
	Hop forty Paces through the publicke streete,
	And having lost her breath, she spoke, and panted,
	That she did make defect, perfection,
	And breathless power breathe forth.
MECENAS	Now Antony must leave her utterly.

(*Antony & Cleopatra*, II. ii)[31]

I must not leave her, even for a night. (A heroic line, tragic in its cadence.) Now Eliot must leave her utterly.

He could not, in 1927, leave either Othello's taking of his own life after he took that of his wife, or the dismaying display of universal human weakness on stage. Poems that Eliot publishes in 1927 lace Othello's 'last great speech' with something that chastens or even chastises his speech acts. *Journey of the Magi*, published as an Ariel Poem on 23 August 1927, has long been known to remember not only Othello's 'Nor set down aught in malice ··· Set you down this', but this: 'Secondly, set down this; that to find where He is, we must learn of these to ask where He is', from Lancelot Andrewes' Christmas Sermon 1622:

> All this was a long time ago, I remember,
> And I would do it again, but set down
> This set down
> This: were we led all that way for
> Birth or Death?

But there was many a setting down. One might summon a further one from Shakespeare (it has been broached above):

---

30. *The Letters of T. S. Eliot*, Vol. 3, 674.
31. The words 'having lost her breath' and 'breathless ··· breathe' become presentiments within the play.

RATCLIFFE   Thomas the Earle of Surrey, and himselfe,
              Much about Cockshut time, from Troope to Troope
              Went through the Army, chearing up the Souldiers.
RICHARD   So, I am satisfied: Give me a Bowle of Wine,
              I have not that Alacrity of Spirit,
              Nor cheere of mind that I was wont to have.
              Set it downe. Is Inke and Paper ready?

(Richard III, V. iii)

Set it down as both the bowl of wine and—with the help of 'Inke and
Paper'—as intimating a historical record. (Othello: 'in your Letters, |
When you shall these unluckie deeds relate'.)

Whereupon the scene from *Richard III* can be seen to traffic with
the Othello scene to which Eliot brought that infamous turn of phrase
of his, *cheering himself up*: 'chearing up the Souldiers' (and Richard's
'cheere of mind', all in the face of death, most of them as the fate of
soldiers, even as was Othello).

At which point there enter the claims of *Fragment of an Agon*, which
in January 1927 was published in *The Criterion*.[32] When we edited *The
Poems of T. S. Eliot*, Jim McCue and I were aware that the Commentary
on *Fragment of an Agon* needed to be, in its way, a commentary on
'Shakespeare and the Stoicism of Seneca'.[33]

SWEENEY   I knew a man once did a girl in—

Sweeney twice says so.

SWEENEY   I knew a man once did a girl in
            Any man[34] might do a girl in
            Any man has to, needs to, wants to
            Once in a lifetime, do a girl in.

SWARTS   What did he do?
            All that time, what did he do?
SWEENEY   What did he do! what did he do?
            That don't apply.

32. To become the second half of *Sweeney Agonistes* when this was published in 1932.
33. *The Poems of T. S. Eliot*, i. 813–14, the Commentary to lines 104–31 of *Fragment of an
    Agon*.
34. Wielded by IAGO (IV. i): 'But if I give my wife a Handkerchiefe—' OTHELLO 'What
    then?' IAGO 'Why then 'tis hers (my Lord); and being hers, | She may (I thinke)
    bestow't on any man.' (Iago had spoken to Cassio of 'You; or any man living', II. iii.)

> Talk to live men about what they do.
> He used to come and see me sometimes
> I'd give him a drink and cheer him up.

DORIS   Cheer him up?
DUSTY   Cheer him up?
SWEENEY   Well here again that don't apply

Do a girl in. Instances of *do in* that are unequivocally extreme ('often, to murder, kill') tend to be on the prowl for female victims, perhaps because of what it is—or was—to do a girl.

'Dear Sir John' (the Duchess had scrawled)—I am not murdered—'done in' I think is the local expression.[35]

The local expression, but not simply a local phenomenon ('Any man · · ·'). For Eliot's expressing of all this in relation to Vivien Eliot ('Must I kill her or kill myself?'[36]), see the Commentary in *The Poems of T. S. Eliot.* And *doing in?* 'What Othello seems to me to be doing in making this speech is *cheering himself up*.' Well here again that might apply. In the words of Henry James, he 'had done in the girl he was engaged to'.[37]

'I have always felt that I have never read a more terrible exposure of human weakness—of universal human weakness—than the last great speech of Othello.' It is a hard saying. In some respects, it was a less hard saying in Leavis's formulation of such a judgement. For Leavis's characterizing of Othello, though more harsh than Eliot's in one way (in that for Eliot what is at issue is not an individual failing but 'the imperfections of humanity', the race of man), was respectful of Othello's being who he is and promulgating himself as he does.

For even, or rather especially, in that magnificent last speech of his Othello does tend to sentimentalize,* though to say that and no more would convey a false impression, for the speech conveys something like the full complexity of Othello's simple nature, and in the total effect the simplicity is tragic and grand.

* There is, I find, an admirable note on this speech in Mr T. S. Eliot's essay, 'Shakespeare and the Stoicism of Seneca.'[38]

35. 1917 citation, *OED.*
36. To J. Middleton Murry, probably April 1925; *The Letters of T. S. Eliot, vol. 2: 1923–1925,* ed. Valerie Eliot and Hugh Haughton (London, 2009), 628.
37. 'He saw more even than I had done in the girl he was engaged to; as time went on · · ·' (*The Next Time;* see p. 183 below).
38. 'Diabolic Intellect and the Noble Hero', in *The Common Pursuit,* 152–3.

Admirable in Leavis's eyes, in that Eliot's two pages were not admiring of Othello when it came to self-knowledge and self-dramatization. Othello found ways to set to one side, or even ignore, what he had done; Leavis did not bring himself to ignore Eliot's essay, though the asterisked mention of it is so laconic as to intimate a limiting judgement ('to say that and no more would convey a false impression'?). Yet there is in Leavis's rendering of Othello a certain magnanimity of concession that will not let itself be altogether quenched by a necessary *but*.

He really is, beyond any question, the nobly massive man of action, the captain of men, he sees himself as being, but he does very much see himself· · · Othello really is, we cannot doubt, the stoic-captain whose few words know their full sufficiency; up to this point, we cannot say he dramatizes himself, he simply is.

For the tragedy of Othello is alive not only to but within Leavis, he knows—and sympathizes—from experience.

And Othello is not merely a glamorous man of action who dominates all companies, he is (as we have all been) cruelly and tragically wronged—a victim of relentless intrigue, and, while remaining noble and heroic, is allowed to appreciate the pathos of his own fate. He has, in fact, all the advantages of that last speech, where the invitation to identify oneself with him is indeed hardly resistible. Who does not (in some moments) readily see himself as the hero of such a *coup de théâtre*?

Leavis's 'cruelly and tragically wronged' is a profound divination, for *Othello* has at its heart what it is *to wrong*: 'To do wrong or injury to (a person); to treat with injustice, prejudice, or harshness; to deal unfairly with, withhold some act of justice from (some one)'[39] (*OED* 1). Othello and Iago are quick to interchange the word. Othello to Iago:

> Thou do'st conspire against thy Friend (Iago)
> If thou but think'st him wrong'd, and mak'st his eare
> A stranger to thy Thoughts.   (III. iii)

Then Iago to Othello:

> That Cuckold lives in blisse,
> Who certaine of his Fate, loves not his wronger:

---

39. The language no longer has, as the symmetrical antithesis *to right* in this sense, 'To do justice or make reparation to (a person); to redress the injuries of; to avenge' (*OED*). *Othello* has the cognate noun, Iago urging Roderigo to the murder of Cassio: 'if you dare do your selfe a profit, and a right'.

But oh, what damned minutes tels he ore,
Who dotes, yet doubts: Suspects, yet soundly loves?

★ ★ ★

Witnesse that heere *Iago* doth give up
The execution of his wit, hands, heart,
To wrong'd Othello's Service.   (again, III. iii)[40]

How poignant, in the wish for detachment and in the admission that nothing will quite secure this, are Leavis's round brackets, the lunulae: 'he is (as we have all been) cruelly and tragically wronged'. 'Who does not (in some moments) readily see himself as the hero of such a coup de théâtre?'

On days when we judge all this to be too hard, we should have recourse to William Empson, and should apply to Othello his closing words about another of Shakespeare's heroes—and about all of us ('as we have all been . . .').[41] This, in the light of what had moved Eliot to confront Othello in the first place: Shakespeare's 'profound knowledge of the imperfections of humanity'. Empson:

The eventual question is whether you can put up with the final Hamlet, a person who frequently appears in the modern world under various disguises, whether by Shakespeare's fault or no. I would always sympathise with anyone who says, like Hugh Kingsmill, that he can't put up with Hamlet at all. But I am afraid it is within hail of the more painful question whether you can put up with yourself and the race of man.

There remains the possibility of turning to—returning to—the mounting means by which Dr Johnson found himself moved to pity Othello.

The fiery openness of Othello, magnanimous, artless, and credulous, boundless in his confidence, ardent in his affection, inflexible in his resolution, and obdurate in his revenge; the cool malignity of Iago, silent in his resentment, subtle in his designs, and studious at once of his interest and his vengeance; the soft simplicity of Desdemona, confident of merit, and conscious of innocence, her artless perseverance in her suit, and her slowness to suspect that she can be suspected, are such proofs of Shakespeare's skill in human nature, as, I suppose, it is vain to seek in any modern writer. The gradual progress which Iago makes in the Moor's conviction, and the circumstances which he employs to inflame him, are so artfully natural, that, though it will perhaps not be said of him as he says of himself, that he is 'a man not easily jealous,' yet we cannot but pity him when at last we find him 'perplexed in the extreme.'[42]

40. Iago had practised this (while practising upon Othello), at Cassio's drunken quarrel: 'Yet I perswade my selfe, to speake the truth | Shall nothing wrong him' (II. iii).
41. '"Hamlet" When New' (1953, revised), in *Essays on Shakespeare*, ed. David Pirie (Cambridge, 1986), 118.
42. *Johnson on Shakespeare*, ed. Arthur Sherbo, Yale Edition of the Works of Samuel Johnson, viii (New Haven, CT, 1968), 1047.

Johnson catches as no other critic has so compactly done the contrariety not only within Othello but within our responses to him. It is *cannot but* which effects the responsible reluctance here: 'yet we cannot but pity him'. For this concedes, not without pain, how much there is about Othello that we might loathe and are loath to pity. And 'perhaps' holds its ground: 'though it will perhaps not be said of him as he says of himself···'

'I cannot but hope that···'. 'I cannot but think that···'. 'I cannot but regret that···'. 'I cannot help thinking that···'. This daily knot within Johnson's letters is not an idle mannerism, it has the full force of both concession and stubbornness, as Johnson himself so fortifyingly had. The syntax is that of probity's declining to yield either to the softhearted or the hard-nosed. Johnson:

If I were to visit Italy, my curiosity would be more attracted by convents than by palaces; though I am afraid that I should find expectation in both places equally disappointed, and life in both places supported with impatience, and quitted with reluctance. That it must be so soon quitted, is a powerful remedy against impatience; but what shall free us from reluctance? Those who have endeavoured to teach us to die well, have taught few to die willingly; yet I cannot but hope that a good life might end at last in a contented death.[43]

~Might end at last in a contented death~

The heroic line.

'To die well': just so. Responsible recalcitrance is arching itself against compassionate concession: *I cannot but hope.* As had been the case in the pained unjust hope of Desdemona's father that his daughter's love-match might yet be overruled by Venice's rulers (I. ii). For Johnson's way of speaking of the play, as with Eliot, is touched by how the tragedy itself has come to speak:

> Mine's not an idle Cause. The Duke himselfe,
> Or any of my Brothers of the State,
> Cannot but feele this wrong, as 'twere their owne.

Universal human weakness, yet then also sporadic human strength: these might move us to something other than an idle cause, set down where we cannot but feel Othello's pain as though it were our own.

43. To Giuseppe Baretti, 10 June 1761; *The Letters of Samuel Johnson,* ed. Redford, i. 200.

5

Congratulations

A congratulation? Rather, congratulations. For the word belongs among *pluralia tantum*, nouns that—in some given sense—occur only in the plural. There the word is, in the company of thanks, regards, credentials, auspices, and, it must be admitted, amends.

Among the things for which one might have to make amends is self-congratulation, the unlovely possibility that hangs around any offering of congratulations. To be invited to join in honouring: this is, after all though not above all, an honour. Happy to pay tribute to the life's work of John Barnard (literary scholar-critic), we who were invited to be contributors to his Festschrift all hastened with pleasure to celebrate him.[1] But eluding the self-pleasuring that is self-congratulation, this asked—as it always does in honouring anyone—both tact and luck.

The poet Yeats had his heroes, and was keen to provide portraits of their portraits in *The Municipal Gallery Revisited*. Particularly anxious, though, to give credit where credit is due, namely to himself, he ended his grand tour roundly:

> You that would judge me, do not judge alone
> This book or that, come to this hallowed place
> Where my friends' portraits hang and look thereon;
> Ireland's history in their lineaments trace;
> Think where man's glory most begins and ends,
> And say my glory was I had such friends.

Is this really what friends are for?

But then what is so bad about self-congratulation? Several *self*-prefixed words manage to preserve the possibility that they are not

---

1. *Re-Constructing the Book: Literary Texts in Transmission*, ed. Maureen Bell and others (Aldershot, 2003).

simply self-serving. Although it is a charge against Malvolio that he is 'sick of self-love', had he been a man of good will, not of ill will, then his self-love might have been of a good kind. You are to love your neighbour as yourself, not not-love yourself. Milton was aware that pride can come not only before a fall but before a right rising. Self-esteem likewise. Yet:

> weigh with her thy self;
> Then value: Oft times nothing profits more
> Then self-esteem, grounded on just and right
> Well manag'd; of that skill the more thou know'st
> The more she will acknowledge thee her Head · · ·
>
> *(Paradise Lost*, VIII. 566–70)

Disapproval of the male chauvinism that frames these admonitions from Raphael to Adam ought not to move us to disown what is here of profit, just and right, well managed, and alive with skill. Not, 'Nothing profits more | Then self-esteem'; rather, that 'Oft times' this is so, but only provided that the self-esteem is 'grounded on just and right'—and that even this is not enough, for round the corner there is a further warning sign:

> grounded on just and right
> Well manag'd;

Even the old-world 'then' as accommodating 'than' makes its modest contribution. The move from the consecutive 'Then' to the other one (its sense being 'Than') is a scruple of cautioning, there at the head of successive lines:

> Then value: Oft times nothing profits more
> Then self-esteem, grounded on just and right

Why then should self-congratulation be intrinsically any more obnoxious than self-esteem, on occasion estimable? Because of what ought to be the honourably stubborn prefix 'con-'. For congratulation is, from the start, from its being the start, a 'together with another'.

congratulate [*con-* together + *gratulare* to manifest or express one's joy]
+1. *intr.* To rejoice along *with* another; to express to a person one's pleasure or gratification at his good fortune, success, or happiness.
+2. *trans.* To express sympathetic joy on the occasion of;
    b. to celebrate *with*.

4. To address (a person) with expressions of joy or satisfaction on an occasion considered fortunate; 'to compliment upon any happy event' (Johnson); to felicitate.

When we say 'to express to a person' or 'To address (a person)', do we really have in mind that the addresser may be the addressee as well? Granted, people do talk to themselves. But that way madness lies. Again, when the OED includes within the definition of 'congratulation' 'the expressing to anybody in a complimentary way gratification at his success, fortune, or happiness', does 'anybody' there really include oneself, as against 'the expressing to somebody else'? The dictionary cites Thomas Fowler in 1887: 'To the act of "rejoicing with others" there is no single term appropriated. The outward expression of the feeling is, however, known as *congratulation*.'[2] A good point, and one that rests on specifying 'rejoicing with others'.

Yet it might seem that '*congratulation* 3 (*Obs.*)', 'on one's own behalf', is evidence that long ago 'congratulation' had slipped free of others. Yet how could there be '*Grateful* and glad acknowledgement on one's own behalf' except by the acknowledgement of something or someone other? Self-gratitude would be a teaser.

But then self-congratulation is a teaser, a perplexity. Its *con-* (together *with another*, not just with, not just the *con-* of, say, 'confidence') is paradoxical at root; yet the reflexive use is ancient and should warn us against waxing politico-moralistic about a modern degeneration. So OED '4b. *refl.*' presents a challenge: 'To call or account oneself happy or *fortunate* in relation to some matter'. Yet the citations, though, particularly the early ones, are wary. Henry More in 1664, in *A Modest Enquiry into the Mysteries of Iniquity*: 'To congratulate our selves that we are neither Turks nor Papists' (*OED*). It is not themselves whom Christians should congratulate that they are neither Turks nor Papists. 'The Pharisee stood and prayed thus with himself, God, I thank thee, that I am not as other men are, extortioners, unjust, adulterers, or even as this publican.' Or even as those Turks or Papists. But then 'not as other men are' admits the other.

For the reflexive 'congratulate' was promptly averse to what was spotted, as when it is the disgusting Gulosulus whom Johnson catches:

as he thought no folly greater than that of losing a dinner for any other gratification, he often congratulated himself, that he had none of that disgusting

---

2. A convention of the OED, to use two dots (..) for an OED ellipsis within a citation.

excellence which impresses awe upon greatness, and condemns its possessors to the society of those who are wise or brave and indigent as themselves. (*The Rambler*, no. 206, 7 March 1752)

Conversely but complimentarily, when we find in Dr Burney's *Memoirs of Metastasio* in 1796 (this, too, cited in the *OED*) the words 'Congratulating myself for the good fortune which has procured me such valuable friends', it is the thanks to fortune, which is not of one's own making, that may make 'congratulating myself' something other than self-contradictory folly.

One way to get your mind round a word is to muster its opposite, or rather its opposites. One opposite of taking pleasure in people's happiness is taking pleasure in their unhappiness—or at any rate discomfiture. English-speakers are reluctant to admit that English has any truck with such nastiness, falling back upon the unEnglish Schadenfreude (German, literally *harm* + *joy*). Richard Chenevix Trench legendarily schuddered:

What a fearful thing it is that any language should have a word expressive of the pleasure which men feel at the calamities of others, for the existence of the word bears testimony to the existence of the thing. And yet in more than one such a word is found.[3]

In more than one language, but not, thank somebody, in ours. Trust Carlyle to take a different tack, one (moreover) for which there is something, albeit not really enough, to be said: 'Have not I a kind of secret satisfaction, of the malicious or even of the judiciary kind (*schadenfreude*, "mischief-joy", the Germans call it, but really it is *justice*-joy withal).'[4]

The faithful antithesis of congratulation is the one that Samuel Beckett summoned:

' "Nelly is in heat", she said, without the least trace of affectation, in a voice both proud and sad, and paused for Murphy to congratulate or

3. *On the Study of Words* (1852), ii. 29, the first citation in the *OED*. The *TLS* review (21, 28 December 2018) of Tiffany Watt Smith, *Schadenfreude: The Joy of Another's Misfortune*, moved Mark Forsyth to remonstrate (25 January 2019): 'Kathryn Hughes repeats the venerable line that there is no English word for *Schadenfreude*. We do have such a word. It is gloating.' *Touché?* But the thrilled and thrilling definition of *gloat* in the *OED* brings out that this won't quite do: 'To gaze with intense or passionate satisfaction (usually implying a lustful, avaricious or malignant pleasure) ··· to feast one's eyes upon, to contemplate, think of, or dwell upon with fierce or unholy glee.'
4. *Shooting Niagara* (1867), the second *OED* citation for *schadenfreude*.

condole, according to his lights.'⁵ How unaffectedly 'heat' arrives in the end at 'lights'. There could be lights without heat. Beckett's French for 'congratulate or condole', in due course, was 'ses condoléances ou de ses félicitations'. In that order, partly for rhythmical reasons. The French 'félicitations' escapes the difficulties that lurk within the English 'con-'. Littré, *Dictionnaire* (1873):

congratuler On dit *féliciter* ou *complimenter*, sauf quand il y a une nuance de plaisanterie, cas où congratuler est employé; il n'est pas rare en français qu'un mot qui vieillit se dégrade et passe dans la catégorie du langue de plaisanterie.⁶

Beckett has an eye for our congratulating ourselves. There is a chastening instance in *Murphy*:

Miss Counihan congratulated herself on having closed her eyes when she did. With closed eyes, she said to herself, one cannot go far wrong. Unless one is absolutely alone. Then it is not necessary to—er—blink at such a rate.⁷

In *Molloy*:

I went out. But as with delicate steps, almost mincing, congratulating myself as usual on the resilience of my Wilton, I followed the corridor towards my room, I was struck by a thought which made me go back to my son's room.⁸

And in *Malone Dies*:

There are rabbits that die before they are killed, from sheer fright ··· And you congratulate yourself on having succeeded with the first blow, and not caused unnecessary suffering, whereas in reality you have taken all that trouble for nothing.⁹

In all these cases, *se féliciter* strikes a different chill.

It is 'condole' that is the complementary opposite of congratulate. For its formations make clear that *con-* must call up other people or other things.

condole To grieve *with*; to express sympathy *with* another in his affliction. (The only extant use.)

condolement The expressing of sympathy with another on account of loss, bereavement, or other grief.

condolence Outward expression of sympathy with the grief of others.

5. *Murphy* (New York, 1938), ch. 5, p. 98.
6. 'We say *felicitate* or *compliment*, except when there is a nuance of pleasantry, in which case 'congratulate' is used; it is not unusual in French for a word to degenerate as it becomes an old usage and for it to pass into the language of pleasantry.'
7. Ch. 10, p. 227.   8. *Molloy* (New York, 1955), 149.
9. *Malone Dies* (New York, 1956), 40.

Self-congratulation ought to announce itself as no less contortionist than would be self-condolence. (Self-pity is something else.) The *OED* does not contain, to my eyes, any formation parallel to 'self-congratulation', *self-* followed by *co-*, *con-*, or *com-* in the sense of together with another. Such self-co-operation, say, would baffle the mind. The language does not permit of self-commiseration, commiseration being the other candidate for a complementary opposite of congratulation.

commiserate
2. To express sympathy, condole with.
3. *intr.* To sympathize or express sympathy *with*. (The only current usage.)

commiseration the expression of feelings of pity or sorrow for the affliction or distress of another.

There was once a noun 'miseration', though no verb. You used to be able to dole, but not to miserate.

The awkwardness of congratulation, both the giving and the receiving of it, remains. There is the notorious difficulty of congratulating someone on having gained an honour that you yourself already enjoy; a careful letter is called for. Unease was already audible a century ago, in the slang forms. '**congrats** colloq. abbrev. of *congratulations*, usu. as *int*.' An interjection which, as the first three instances in the *OED* make clear, quivered with class distinctions.

1884 Received . . congrats on Ernest's appointment to the Royal Yacht.
1894 'A.HOPE' *Dolly Dialogues* So you've brought it off. Hearty congrats.
1908 *Punch* Lord and Lady Knightsbridge . . were simply *loaded* with congrats about their brilliant son's success.

The same goes for the elongated braying of '**congratters** colloq. abbrev. of *congratulations*, usu. as *int*.'

1906 R.BROOKE Congratters on Cambridge's political enlightenment.
1914 'I.HAY' *Lighter Side School Life* 'Congratters!' said Blake awkwardly.
1930 D.SAYERS Tremendous congratters and all that.
1960 O.NORTON The Brig lifted his glass. 'Congratters my dear. Good show.'

'Congratters!' said Blake awkwardly. And so say all of us.

In self-congratulation the self is split, is both itself and another (else, why con-? 'Je est un autre'), which is not at all the same as seeing yourself as others see you. Self-congratulation may enjoy a divided self. And this, not with such self-knowledge as ruefully acknowledges that one's present self falls short of one's past self. Self-congratulation would not

be the right word for Jonathan Swift in age, apocryphally chastened by
A Tale of a Tub: 'Good God! What a genius I had when I wrote that
book.' But the attempt by Samuel Rogers to protect 'self-congratulation'
against self-contradiction was a failure. He meant only to tell us how
pleased he was, but the rhythm of his heroic lines issues in the complacent
climactic conclusion that is self-congratulation:

> Am I in ITALY? Is this the Mincius?
> Are those the distant turrets of Verona?
> And shall I sup where JULIET at the masque
> Saw her beloved MONTAGUE, and now sleeps by him?
> Such questions hourly do I ask myself;
> And not a stone, in a cross-way, inscribed
> 'To Mantua'—'To Ferrara'—but excites
> Surprise, and doubt, and self-congratulation.
>
> *(Italy*, 1822, 1828, IX. 1–8)

The doubt in question should have been whether Rogers could protect self-congratulation against its propensities.

But it may be too easy to smirk when the first instance of 'self-
congratulation' in the *OED* turns out to be from Joseph Addison, the
man who summoned to his deathbed his stepson Lord Warwick so as
to vouchsafe the words 'See in what peace a Christian can die'.

The transmission of this famous or notorious announcement has its
own cross-currents. We famously owe the reported utterance to
Edward Young's *Conjectures on Original Composition* (1759). Addison's
thoroughgoing biographer Peter Smithers distrusts those who have
distrusted the scene; he is sure that 'The words uttered would be sincere', and after a tour of the evidence concludes: 'All of these considerations seem to point to the likelihood of the famous story being true
and I entertain no doubt upon the point.'[10] C. S. Lewis left judgement
to the All-Judging:

> The story that he summoned Lord Warwick to his deathbed *to see how a
> Christian can die* is ambiguous; it can be taken either as evidence of his
> Christianity or as a very brimstone proof of the reverse. I give no vote: my
> concern is with books.[11]

But Lewis's concern was not perhaps with the original book, since
there are differences not only of rhythm but of substance between 'to

10. *The Life of Addison* (Oxford, 1954), 448n.
11. 'Addison' (1945), in *Selected Literary Essays*, ed. Walter Hooper (Cambridge, 1969), 157.

see how a Christian can die' and 'See in what peace a Christian can die'—the heroic line! I have some sympathy with the early editions of the *Oxford Dictionary of Quotations*, which were so good as to sink the upper-case 'Christian' to the lower-case 'christian': 'See in what peace a christian can die'. This would claim less by way of successful *Imitatio Christi*. Edward Young reports of Addison that 'he softly said' the words, but Young does capitalize in the story.

Yet Addison comes better out of all this matter of self-congratulation when his use of the word ('How many self-congratulations naturally rise in the mind', *OED*; read 'arise') is accorded its full context. For his rejoicing does make explicit how much the self owes to all that is not self, and this means that self-congratulation is alive to and with gratitude.

A Man, who uses his best Endeavours to live according to the Dictates of Virtue and right Reason has two perpetual Sources of Chearfulness; In the Consideration of his own Nature, and of that Being on whom he has a Dependance. If he looks into himself, he cannot but rejoice in that Existence, which is so lately bestowed upon him, and which, after Millions of Ages, will be still new, and still in its beginning. How many Self-Congratulations naturally arise in the Mind, when it reflects on this its Entrance into Eternity. (*The Spectator*, no. 381, 17 May 1712)

~ He cannot but rejoice in that Existence ~

Alive in the heroic line, the gist is not the personal complacency, the cadency, of Addison but the way in which he understands his own words, his new way of putting it. He senses that *con-* should be heeded. In this he inaugurates some finely redeemed uses of the paradoxical compound as it comes to the nineteenth century.

Addison sought the possibility of a proper self-congratulation, something asking that others or another be acknowledged as having played their part. This is differently valuable from the more usual warning against self-congratulation *tout court*, as when Cowper moves within a dozen lines from 'self-reproaching conscience' to its opposite, 'self-congratulating pride' (*The Task*, v. 622). The redemption of the self-congratulation is a greater challenge.

Jane Welsh Carlyle rose to it. She evokes 'honest self-congratulation'. The phrase comes in the very first letter in *Letters and Memorials of Jane Welsh Carlyle* (prepared for publication by Thomas Carlyle, edited by James Anthony Froude, 1883). It is to her mother in Scotsbrig, from Chelsea, 1 September 1834. Thomas Carlyle comments, in his pages introducing the letter: 'From birth upwards, she had lived in opulence; and now, for my sake, had become poor—so nobly poor. Truly, her pretty little brag (in this letter) was well founded.' (How free her own prose is from condescension can be felt in the contrast with Thomas Carlyle's affectionate diminutivery.)

Our little household has been set up again at a quite moderate expense of money and trouble; wherein I cannot help thinking, with a *chastened vanity*, that the superior shiftiness and thriftiness of the Scotch character has strikingly manifested itself··· To see how they live and waste here, it is a wonder the whole city does not 'bankrape, and go out o' sicht';—flinging platefuls of what they are pleased to denominate 'crusts' (that is what I consider all the best of the bread) into the ashpits! I often say, with honest self-congratulation, 'In Scotland we have no such thing as "crusts"'. On the whole, though the English ladies seem to have their wits more at their finger-ends, and have a great advantage over me in that respect, I never cease to be glad that I was born on the other side of the Tweed, and those who are nearest and dearest to me are Scotch.

~ In Scotland we have no such thing as 'crusts'
To have their wits more at their finger-ends ~

What makes an honest woman of such self-congratulation is the acknowledgement that the self is not one's singular creation: 'In Scotland we have no such thing as "crusts"'. The gladness, the rejoicing, has to be (in its way) with others, since 'I never cease to be glad that I was born on the other side of the Tweed'. Self-congratulation does not expand into the fatuous fantasy of giving birth to oneself.

The faithful text of this letter is even better, in details germane to self-congratulation and to honesty.[12] For J.W.C. did not put within quotation marks her words to herself: not

I often say, with honest self-congratulation, 'In Scotland we have no such thing as "crusts"'

but (without those mincing commas, too)

I often say with honest self-congratulation in Scotland we have no such thing as '*crusts*'.

She did not put the idiom within quotation marks or proffer one of the flavoured spellings: not 'it is a wonder the whole city does not

---

12. *The Collected Letters of Thomas and Jane Welsh Carlyle*, ed. Charles Richard Sanders and Kenneth J. Fielding, vol. 7 (Durham, NC, 1977), 88.

"bankrape, and go out o' sicht"', but 'it is a wonder the whole City does not bankrape and go out o sight—'. She did not have the exclamation mark, crowing, after 'ashpits' ('into the ashpits!'). She is briskly idiomatic: not 'glad that I was born on the other side of the Tweed' but '···the other side the Tweed'. Last but not least, it is a felicity, not an indifference, that has 'nearest' rising endearingly to 'Dearest': not 'glad that···those who are nearest and dearest to me are Scotch', but that 'those who are nearest and Dearest to me are Scotch'.

Jane Welsh Carlyle rescues self-congratulation from dishonesty, which is exactly what she does with 'shiftiness', for 'the superior shiftiness and thriftiness of the Scotch character', with its pawky rhyme, is a tribute to the national character that she was so lucky as to be born to: OED 'shifty'—'well able to shift for oneself'—includes 1859: 'The canny, shifty, far-seeing Scot', and, again in a Scottish context, 1888, 'shifty and business-like'. In the matter of self-congratulation, and the possibility of an honest form of it, Jane Welsh Carlyle is truly shifty.

Walter Scott, too, had the imaginative skill to invoke an honest self-reflection. He wrote to Joanna Baillie, 23 November 1810.

But planting and pruning trees I could work at from morning till night and if my poetical revenues enable me to have a few acres of my own that is one of the principal pleasures I look forward to. There is too a sort of self-congratulation a little tickling self-flattery in the idea that while you are pleasing and amusing yourself you are really seriously contributing to the future wellfare of the country and that your very acorn may send its ribs of oack to future victories like Trafalgar.[13]

A heroic line there at the close, provided that we hear the honoured name pronounced as they then heard the heroic battle:

~ To future victories like Tráfalgár ~[14]

The easy running-on by Scott is incompatible with pomposity: 'There is too a sort of self-congratulation a little tickling of self-flattery in the idea that···'There is a little tickling going on, nipping along, as there is the miniature roundness of 'your very acorn'. It all has its own sly

13. *The Letters of Sir Walter Scott 1808–1811*, ed. Grierson (London, 1932), 402–3.
14. As is metrically clear from *Nelson and His World*, online, citing Branwell Brontë: 'They see where fell the "thunderbolt of war" | On the storm-swollen waves of Trafalgar', and George Meredith: 'Uprose the soul of him a star | On that brave day of Ocean days: | It rolled the smoke of Trafalgar | To darken Austerlitz ablaze'.

saltiness. And if your trees grow, well and good, but this is not exactly your doing, that you should grow too ripely self-congratulatory.

Too ripe, on any occasion when the word and the name Hero tempt too easy a move: 'In emulation of Leander and Don Juan, he swam, I hear, to the opposite shores the other day, or some world-shaking feat of the sort, himself the Hero whom he went to meet' (*The Ordeal of Richard Feverel*, chapter XXXV). The pun on Hero and the swell heroic line

~ Himself the Hero whom he went to meet ~

so plump out the reflexive image as to make it seem that it is not Richard Feverel, about whom those words are penned in a letter, or even Adrian Harley, who pens them, but the author of them, George Meredith, who really breathes the air of self-congratulation.

The poet who most deeply set himself to speak of self-congratulation without yielding to it was Wordsworth. True, he had his lapses. Nothing protects self-congratulation or its poet in the heroic couplets of *Lines written on a blank leaf in a copy of the author's poem 'The Excursion', upon hearing of the death of the late Vicar of Kendal*:

> To public notice, with reluctance strong,
> Did I deliver this unfinished Song;
> Yet for one happy issue;—and I look
> With self-congratulation on the Book
> Which pious, learned MURFITT saw and read;—
> Upon my thoughts his saintly Spirit fed;
> He conn'd the new-born Lay with grateful heart;
> Foreboding not how soon he must depart,
> Unweeting that to him the joy was given
> Which good Men take with them from Earth to Heaven.

This is itself insufficiently weeting. Murfitt's gratitude to Wordsworth is too patently a gratification, and is not held in balance with any gratitude from Wordsworth for anything or to anybody. 'Which good Men take···': the poet pats his chest and himself on the back. But then it is characteristic of Wordsworth to mishandle opportunities that elsewhere he delicately takes in hand. 'Self-congratulation' is finely ensconced within the felicities of *The Old Cumberland Beggar* and its humane insinuations as to all that the beggar unweetingly effects:

> The easy man
> Who sits at his own door,—and, like the pear

>That overhangs his head from the green wall,
>Feeds in the sunshine; the robust and young,
>The prosperous and unthinking, they who live
>Sheltered, and flourish in a little grove
>Of their own kindred;—all behold in him
>A silent monitor, which on their minds
>Must needs impress a transitory thought
>Of self-congratulation, to the heart
>Of each revealing his peculiar boons,
>His charters and exemptions; and, perchance,
>Though he to no one give the fortitude
>And circumspection needful to preserve
>His present blessings, and to husband up
>The respite of the season, he, at least,
>And 'tis no vulgar service, makes them felt.   (116–32)

This, in its own circumspection, is itself a monitor. It makes its blessings felt. For the thought of self-congratulation is valuable in proportion as it is transitory. Those who are not beggars are blessed to move in kindness beyond their own kindred. The source of their happiness is found outside self, outside them, and this with the double impress of 'must needs'. Each such person appreciates, thanks to the figure who moves among them, his peculiar boons; the passage speaks both of boons and of blessings, aware that these ask thanks and do not emanate from the self who may enjoy for a while a principled self-congratulation.

We are invited by such lines to revise our sense of what self-congratulation must needs be. The revision of *The Prelude* did not ask of Wordsworth any second thoughts as to the central contention, the redemption of self-congratulation.

>I spare to speak, my friend, of what ensued:
>The admiration and the love, the life
>In common things—the endless store of things
>Rare, or at least so seeming, every day
>Found all about me in one neighbourhood—
>The self-congratulation, the complete
>Composure, and the happiness entire.
>
>(*The Prelude*, 1805, i. 116–22)

>I spare to tell of what ensued, the life
>In common things—the endless store of things,
>Rare, or at least so seeming, every day

> Found all about me in one neighbourhood—
> The self-congratulation, and, from morn
> To night, unbroken cheerfulness serene.
>
> (*The Prelude*, 1850, i. 108–13)

As always with Wordsworthian revision, the gains and losses would ask patience on a Wordsworthian scale. 'The admiration' of 1805 disappears, perhaps as having put 'self-congratulation' at the old risk, yet with some sense of retreating from a boldness. The delicate line-ending—

> the complete
> Composure,

—with 'complete' waiting for its unhurried and untroubled and unprecarious completion—was at one with the deep Wordsworthian alignment of composure, including self-composure, and composition. And how deftly the 1805 lines become entire only with the conclusive word 'entire', the adjective following its noun but in no way tardy. The 1850 lines gain in some ways by not explicitly mentioning love—'that much-mentioned brilliance, love', in the words of Philip Larkin, who said that 'Deprivation is for me what daffodils were for Wordsworth'.[15] And 'serene' has its own calmative finality. As for 1850's 'cheerfulness', we may remember that this was explicitly the subject of that essay in the *Spectator* which brought forward the first, and the proper, self-congratulation: 'two perpetual sources of Cheerfulness · · · How many Self-Congratulations naturally arise in the Mind.'

It matters to congratulation, and to the bizarrerie that is self-congratulation, that there were once the words 'gratulation' and 'gratulate' (expressing or manifesting joy). Wordsworth, like Milton and Cowper, was enabled to be vigilant about self-congratulation by courtesy of 'gratulate', a word that all these poets rightly valued. Scott respected the word, which is one reason not only why he could be wise about self-congratulation but why Crabbe, expressing gratitude to Sir Walter (21 December 1812), hit not only the right tone but the right word, repeatedly:

so my want of Communication with & even of Knowledge of the Men of Genius in our Days renders the opening of an Intercourse with you highly pleasant & a motive for much Self-Gratulation and I do accordingly gratulate

15. *Love Songs in Age*, and 'An Interview with the "Observer"' (1979), in *Required Writing* (London, 1983), 47.

myself and reflect on my Acquisition with the Spirit of a Man growing rich: I have a new Source of Satisfaction.[16]

With characteristic modesty and firmness, Christina G. Rossetti (6 June 1853) likewise knew how to minister to a proper pleasure, not in and for herself but in and for another:

My dear Mrs Heimann,
It would be asking too much of boys to require them to prefer study to play: so if your young friends display no worse taste than this, I think you have cause for self gratulation.[17]

Cause for 'self-gratulation': and how then to give effect to the cause? Fortunately we have great exemplars. There was William Empson's remonstration, aware that he would be charged with self-congratulation. Accused of perpetrating a jeering joke upon his readers (*The Structure of Complex Words* as hoax), Empson rose to the occasion:

What I feel about the book, if there is any doubt, is easily told. I think it is wonderful; I think it goes up like a great aeroplane. A certain amount of noisy taxi-ing round the field at the start may be admitted, and the landing at the end is bumpy though I think without causing damage; but the power of the thing and the view during its flight I consider magnificent.[18]

Empson knew that 'This is disagreeably like writing an advertisement for myself'. But the alternative would have been his colluding in the demeaning of something that both was and was not himself: this book that he believed in. Together with something other, namely the book itself.

A different challenge once confronted James Joyce. 'Is this the great James Joyce?' asked Sylvia Beach, admiring. It was a difficult question for him to answer. 'No' would have been harsh. 'Don't know', winsome. 'Not for me to say', cadging. 'Yes', self-congratulatory. 'James Joyce', he granted, extending his hand and his imagination.

16. *Selected Letters and Journals of George Crabbe*, ed. Thomas C. Faulkner with Rhonda L. Blair (Oxford, 1985), 94.
17. *The Letters of Christina Rossetti*, ed. Antony H. Harrison, i (Charlottesville, VA, 1997) 67.
18. *Mandrake* (Autumn and Winter 1955–6); *Selected Letters of William Empson*, ed. John Haffenden (Oxford, 2006), 247–9.

6

The Novelist as Critic

It was in Ezra Pound's 1922 review of *Ulysses*, the-novel-to-end-Victorian-novels, that he issued one of his many remarkable insistences:

The best criticism of any work, to my mind the only criticism of any work of art that is of any permanent or even moderately durable value, comes from the creative writer or artist who does the next job; and *not*, not ever from the young gentlemen who make generalities about the creator.[1]

Pound, who was 15 when Queen Victoria died, never meant to be a gentleman, young or old, nor was meant to be. He knew—as a Victorian novel might have set itself to demonstrate—that it takes three generations to make a gentleman. Meanwhile, his ear, pricked, told him that gentlemen make generalities. As was his practice, he particularized at once: 'Laforgue's *Salomé* is the real criticism of *Salammbô*; Joyce and perhaps Henry James are critics of Flaubert.'[2]

The real and durable form that criticism takes, then, is *the next job*, creation at once subsequent and consequent. Creation is itself the highest, widest, and deepest form of criticism. This, whether or not the artistic medium or the literary kind happen to stay the same. The poems of Baudelaire, no less than his 'Le Peintre de la Vie Moderne', are critiques of connoisseurship and of its arts. T. S. Eliot's *Portrait of a Lady* canvases not only Edwardian portraiture and Winthrop Mackworth Praed's benign light verse, *Portrait of a Lady*, but James's novel too, *The Portrait of a Lady* with its connoisseur of weighty malignity. Gilbert Osmond is soulless and sterile, but the novelist who imagined him into existence was the soul of creativity.

---

1. *The Dial*, lxxii, June 1922; in *Literary Essays*, ed. T. S. Eliot (London, 1954), 406.
2. *Salomé* (1887); Flaubert's *Salammbô* (1862).

Our echoes roll from soul to soul,
And grow for ever and for ever.

(The splendour falls on castle walls)

When Tennyson wrote *The Princess* (1847), his medley of political education, he knew himself to be the heir to Machiavelli's *The Prince*. Likewise with James's *The Princess Casamassima* (1886) in relation to both of those predecessors. *The Portrait of a Lady* (1881) would echo and roll and grow, being a living apprehension of a recent half-dead novel by George Eliot.

Henry James wrote to his brother William James in 1876: 'Daniel Deronda (Dan'l. himself) is indeed a dead, though amiable failure. But the book is a large affair; I shall write an article of some sort about it.'[3] Write an article of some sort about it, James did. Reprint this article as the appendix to a critical study of the Victorian novel, Dr F. R. Leavis did.

The Great Tradition found itself in straitened circumstances: George Eliot, Henry James, and Joseph Conrad had only Jane Austen to look briefly back upon, and D. H. Lawrence (reserved by Leavis for a later occasion) to look forward to. But the process of retrospect and prospect that *The Great Tradition* illuminated was simultaneously creative and critical. James's article of some sort,' "Daniel Deronda": A Conversation', staged the shrewd reflections of Theodora, Pulcheria, and Constantius on the new George Eliot novel that the three of them had been (by and large) enjoying. James had issued an interim report, a holding operation of a page or so, on the first instalment of *Daniel Deronda*, but it was to be the eighteen-page Conversation in which, a few months later, he invested himself.[4] Yet James's greatest investment in *Daniel Deronda*, with compound interest, was the novel that he floated the next year, 1877, and launched in 1881. *The Portrait of a Lady* does not exactly observe George Eliot's conventions, but its acumen is an observation of her aims and accomplishments. It is also, with the right peculiar gratitude, an observation of the misjudgements and infelicities in *Daniel Deronda*.

3. To William James, 29 July 1876; *Letters*, vol. ii *1875–1883*, ed. Leon Edel (Cambridge, MA, 1980), 59. The period concluding *Dan'l.* is supplied from *The Correspondence of William James*, vol. 1: *William and Henry: 1861–1884*, ed. Ignas K. Skrupskelis and Elizabeth M. Berkeley (Charlottesville, VA, 1992), 271.
4. *Nation*, 24 February 1876; in *Essays on Literature: American Writers: English Writers*, ed. Leon Edel and Mark Wilson (New York, 1984), 973–4. *Atlantic Monthly*, December 1876; reprinted in *Partial Portraits* (1888); in *Essays on Literature: American Writers: English Writers*, 974–92.

Much first-rate criticism has derived from Leavis's demonstration (more widely than in just this one case, too) that 'It is not derivativeness that is in question, but the relation between two original geniuses'. Thanks to the imaginary Conversation, 'it can be shown, with a conclusiveness rarely possible in these matters, that James did actually go to school to George Eliot'.[5] *The Portrait of a Lady*, like any novel that *succeeds*, owes its achievement not only to what a predecessor had achieved but also to that which she or he had not achieved. Perhaps the predecessor had left something unattempted, still to be done. Or perhaps some part of the enterprise had been ill-essayed, as with the whole half, so to speak, of *Daniel Deronda* that Leavis lopped: 'It will be best to get the bad half out of the way first.' You know, Dan'l. himself, Judaism, Zionism, and so on and so forth. Which leaves '*Gwendolen Harleth* (as I shall call the good part of *Daniel Deronda*)'.[6]

Leavis argued; often he argued that a critical conversation naturally took the form of *Yes, but*... If there were not some kind of agreement, some sort of *Yes*, conversation stalled at once; but if there were no *but*, it was forestalled at once. What, then, might a *Yes, but*... sound like, in reply to his account of James's engagement with George Eliot? It need not primarily (however disputable the judgement) be Leavis's assurance that James is much the lesser genius. Though the presence of George Eliot's novel, a presence that amounts to inspiration, is convincingly substantiated by Leavis, not so much substantiated as asserted is James's falling short of her achievement in her '*Gwendolen Harleth*', especially his being held to do so in every single respect. For Leavis's word *subtilized* is far from a compliment: 'The moral substance of George Eliot's theme is subtilized into something going with the value James sets on "high civilization"; her study of conscience has disappeared.'[7]

Leavis's reservations about *The Portrait of a Lady* are telling, especially as to Isabel Archer and James's estimation of her, his esteem for her. Leavis: 'The differences, however, as I see them are fairly suggested by saying that Isabel Archer is Gwendolen Harleth seen by a man.' There is much there that invites a *Yes, but*... and that would

5. *The Great Tradition* (London, 1948), 14, 16.
6. Ibid. 80, 85. *Daniel Deronda*: 'As things are, there is, lost under that damning title, an actual great novel to be extricated' (p. 122). But then Leavis has his unwinning titles: *English Literature in Our Time and the University* (1969), and *Nor Shall My Sword* (1972), inviting a sequel, *Sleep in My Hand*.
7. *The Great Tradition*, 15.

require a reply that is patiently attentive (for Leavis is more patient in these pages than was his wont). 'It isn't that George Eliot shows any animus towards Gwendolen; simply, as a very intelligent woman she is able, unlimited by masculine partiality of vision, and only the more perceptive because a woman, to achieve a much *completer* present-ment of her subject than James of his.'[8] Leavis's recourse to *simply* betrays a simple coercion. After all, an intermittent animus towards— *against*—some of her women characters has often been glimpsed or plausibly imagined, and this by critics respectful and responsible. But the more immediate matter is the way in which this account of James might accommodate Pound's emphasis. On this occasion, *the next job* turned out to be a bit of a botched job. James 'largely mistakes the nature of his inspiration, which is not so much from life as he sup-posed', with the result that 'he fails to produce the fable that gives inevitability and moral significance. He can remain unaware of this failure because he is so largely occupied (a point that can be illus-trated in detail) in transposing George Eliot, whose power is due to the profound psychological truth of her conception, and the consist-ency with which she develops it.' By contrast, James's *in*consistency 'partly empties the theme of *The Portrait of a Lady* of moral substance'.[9] Not that, when it comes to *the next job*, Pound's position would require Pound to deny such a possibility. The situation would be (though it would not *simply* be) that, should the next job prove botched, this next creation could not rise to constituting the best criticism of its predecessor.

The limits of James's achievement in or with *The Portrait of a Lady* may be as Leavis maintains. But in what respects might James's novel be held to be, not only a novel that went to school to George Eliot, but a critique of her novel?

Foremost is James's sense (a creative understanding that anticipates Leavis's critical understanding) of how fatal to her venture it had been for her to embark upon the heavily-freighted, religiously-rigged half of *Daniel Deronda*. The germane tribute to James was voiced by the author of *Portrait of a Lady*, T. S. Eliot: 'James's critical genius comes out most tellingly in his mastery over, his baffling escape from, Ideas; a mastery and an escape which are perhaps the last test of a superior intelligence.

8. *The Great Tradition*, 86–7.   9. Ibid. III.

He had a mind so fine that no idea could violate it.'[10] James had seen
that the objection to the ideas in *Daniel Deronda* is that they are Ideas,
and that the objection to George Eliot is that she permits her mind to
be violated by them. Alerted and even warned by George Eliot's mis-
judgement, James is fortified in his determination that *The Portrait of a
Lady* escape all such servitudes and grandeurs. There is less to the
Judaism in the many many pages of *Daniel Deronda* than there is in a
single moment in *Our Mutual Friend*. Not, as it happens, the figure
itself of the good Jew, Mr Riah, which has something of George Eliot's
well-meaning ill-judgement (and is even by way of being a reparation
by the fashioner of Fagin), 'CHARACTERS' being identified by Dickens
at the head of the book: 'Mr. Riah, a venerable Jew, of noble and generous nature'. No, the great Dickens is not to be found in Mr Riah, who
is not a Character but an Idea; rather, the great Dickens flashes out in
a remark cast at Mr Riah, dubbing him with a name that is not his
name but the badge of all his tribe, despatching Mr Riah at the moment
of despatching the chapter (Book the Third, chapter XII, 'Meaning
Mischief'):

'Do I go, sir?'
'Do you go?' sneered Fledgeby. 'Yes, you do go. Toddle, Judah!'

Those are the authentic accents not only of Fascination Fledgeby but
of Fascination Dickens.

  The gait (*Toddle!*) is just one of the many gaits observed within the
movements of compassion and dispassion. We contemplate with dignity and sympathy a certain kind of heroism (however unsympathetic
its bearer), a bearing:

And now, among the knot of servants dressed in mourning, and the weeping
women, Mr. Dombey passes through the hall to the other carriage that is waiting to receive him. He is not 'brought down,' these observers think, by sorrow
and distress of mind. His walk is as erect, his bearing is as stiff as ever it has
been. He hides his face behind no handkerchief, and looks before him. But
that his face is something sunk and rigid, and is pale, it bears the same expression as of old. He takes his place within the carriage, and three other gentlemen follow. Then the grand funeral moves slowly down the street. The feathers
are yet nodding in the distance, when the juggler has the basin spinning on a
cane, and has the same crowd to admire it. But the juggler's wife is less alert
than usual with the money-box, for a child's burial has set her thinking that

10. *Little Review*, v (1918), 46; also *The Egoist*, January 1918.

perhaps the baby underneath her shabby shawl may not grow up to be a man, and wear a sky-blue fillet round his head, and salmon-coloured worsted drawers, and tumble in the mud. (*Dombey and Son*, chapter XVIII, 'Father and Daughter')

~Among the knot of servants dressed in mourning
He hides his face behind no handkerchief
But that his face is something sunk and rigid
It bears the same expression as of old
The grand funeral moves slowly down the street
The feathers are yet nodding in the distance
The juggler's wife is less alert than usual
To be a man and wear a sky-blue fillet~

Such is the genius that inspired the critical insight of Edward FitzGerald, alert to this novel:

The intended Pathos is, as usual, missed: but just turn to little Dombey's Funeral, where the Acrobat in the Street suspends his performance till the Funeral has passed, and his Wife wonders if the little Acrobat in her Arms will so far outlive the little Boy in the Hearse as to wear a Ribbon through his hair, following his Father's Calling. It is in such Side-touches, you know, that Dickens is inspired to Create like a little God Almighty.[11]

~The intended Pathos is, as usual, missed
Just turn to little Dombey's Funeral
As to wear a Ribbon through his hair~

This is masterly criticism in the tradition of Samuel Johnson, without envious malignity or superstitious veneration. Fitz has no pleasure in finding the pathos to be a failure, though he takes a quiet pleasure in how the various things that *missed* might hit. How lovingly *suspends* catches both the acrobat and the juggler. How understated is the word *passed* in the procession of a funeral (picking up but not just repeating, and certainly not pastiching, Dickens's own touch, 'Mr. Dombey passes through the hall'). How deftly the little Acrobat proceeds to a little God almighty. How entirely without condescension or sarcasm is the word *calling*, for the baby's relation to the juggler's livelihood: 'following his Father's Calling'. (Fitz is following Dickens's steps: 'He takes his place within the carriage, and three other gentlemen follow.') And

11. To Fanny Kemble, 3 February 1880; *The Letters of Edward FitzGerald*, ed. A. McK. Terhune and A. B. Terhune (Princeton, 1980), iv. 288; included in *Charles Dickens*, ed. Stephen Wall (Penguin Critical Anthologies, 1970), 211.

how central in its understanding of Dickens is the touch that gives us not only *Side-touches* but the assurance, the re-assurance, the *it-is-so-isn't- it?* in which Leavis would sometimes unexpectedly delight, of *you know*: 'It is in such Side-touches, you know, that Dickens is inspired to Create like a little God Almighty.' We know all right, we really do. The continuity of Fitz's criticism with Dickens's creation is itself creative, and is true criticism. Not only is Dickens's art proved upon our pulses, so is the critic's art. I am thinking of Keats's praise of Wordsworth: 'we find what he says true as far as we have experienced and we can judge no further but by larger experience—or axioms in philosophy are not axioms until they are proved upon our pulses: We read fine—things but never feel them to the full until we have gone exactly same steps as the Author.'[12] ('His walk is as erect · · ·') If this is true of philosophy, it cannot be less true of the art of a poet or novelist. Not Ideas about the thing but the thing itself.

W. B. Yeats was to begin his account of the philosophy of Shelley (1900) with a section headed 'His Ruling Ideas', the trouble being that Ruling Shelley is what his Ideas did. As for T. S. Eliot and 'the last test of superior intelligence', it was in his journal, *The Criterion*, that William Empson characterized (not defined) intelligence in a reflection on Aristotle, Copernicus, and the parallax: 'I find this a pleasing historical fact because it shows that both these great men were more intelligent (less at the mercy of their own notions) than Mr Burtt wishes to think them.'[13] George Eliot in *Daniel Deronda* was no less at the mercy of her notions because they were not her notions alone. For his part, James skirts notions. To him, the role of notions, ideas, and (in ascending order) Ideas in the Victorian novel was all staged, high-minded to the point of loftiness, mounting aerially to the emptily didactic and the fully dictated. Take John Henry Newman's novel of ideas, *Loss and Gain*, 1848, the year of quite some novels: *Dombey and Son*, for one, *Mary Barton*, *Vanity Fair*, and *The Tenant of Wildfell Hall*, for some others. *Loss and Gain*? As art, a dead loss. 'The Story of a Convert' is not converted into a novel. The story of Charles Reding does not make for charismatic reading. This is not a novel of ideas, it is Newman's Idea of a Novel.

12. Keats, to John Hamilton Reynolds, 3 May 1818; *Letters*, ed. Hyder Edward Rollins (Cambridge, MA, 1958), i. 279.
13. Review of E. A. Burtt, *The Metaphysical Foundations of Modern Science*, in *The Criterion*, October 1930; in *Argufying*, ed. John Haffenden (London, 1987), 531–2.

There is a second respect in which *The Portrait of a Lady* may be seen as a critique of *Daniel Deronda*, allied with Leavis's 'limiting judgments' about James. For Leavis, it is unremittingly the case, in this comparison with George Eliot, that James's presentment is 'partial in both senses of the word—controlled, that is, by a vision that is both incomplete and indulgent', one that 'entailed much excluding and simplifying': 'The difference between James and George Eliot is largely a matter of what James leaves out.' It is true that Leavis immediately hastens to a concession—'The leaving out, of course, is a very positive art that offers the compensation.'[14] But the concession is empty (*of course* is the mere twaddle of graciousness), since the 'compensation' that so abruptly breaks off Leavis's sentence never gets actually specified or substantiated. So I should like to turn the argument through 180 degrees, along the same axis but in the opposite direction, in the matter of Isabel's hideous mismarriage, as against Gwendolen's. For Gwendolen's mis-decision was the product of economic necessity and pressure. This pressure is a condition of George Eliot's deep sympathy with Gwendolen's plight, the novelist's unsentimental compassion enabling her to give fully realized life to one of her most firm and most famous beliefs: 'Pity and fairness—two little words which, carried out, would embrace the utmost delicacies of the moral life.'[15]

But what, then, is made artistically available to James once he decides to do otherwise and to grant an ample freedom from financial pressures to his mismarrier, Isabel Archer, when she gives to Gilbert Osmond not only her hand but—unless she is careful, or perhaps even if she is—her soul? (Freedom from financial pressures, thanks to Ralph Touchett's munificence.) The answer is one form that artistic freedom may take in its turn, a freedom from one perilous need or impulse, to *explain*. To Gwendolen, there did belong the tragedy and the pathos that attend upon a decision's being explicable, explainable, humanly on the cards even if the card is the Queen of Spades. But James holds his cards very close to his chest, and sometimes declines, wisely, to play them at all. And so to Isabel, on the losing hand, there belong the tragedy and pathos that attend upon a decision's remaining obdurately beyond explanation. The gap between what she chooses and any guess

14. *The Great Tradition*, 86, 91, 110.
15. To Mrs H. F. Ponsonby, 17 October 1877; *The George Eliot Letters*, ed. Gordon S. Haight, vi (New Haven, CT, 1955) 407.

as to why she chooses it will remain a constant abyss in the world of a novel in which constancy is itself dark and mysterious. What is the first thing that the Wife of Bath needs to say?

> Experience, thogh noon auctoritee
> Were in this world, is right inogh for me
> To speke of wo that is in mariage.

The prologue to marriage is a wedding. (Is a wedding assuredly a weal and not a woe, or a weal as against a *weal*?) The prologue to a wedding is a plighting. (Is this assuredly a plighting, as against a plight?) It is not so much a refusal in James to explain Isabel's acceding to Osmond's proposal, as a refusal by James to be held to be in the explaining business. Osmond can explain, and he expends some glacially laconic energy in doing so; and we can to some extent explain the desirability to him of her. Her money, for a start. She herself remains distant from certain kinds of comprehension or certain ambitions that comprehension, in us or in novelists, may nurse; naturally we are allowed and even invited to presume some psychological likelihoods, but on the understanding that we waive any claim to a full understanding, to comprehension's presumption. Far from indulging Isabel Archer in any such respect, *The Portrait of a Lady* is declining to indulge the reader. It conveys that it may be childish to keep asking *Why?*

Leavis gives a summing-up as to Isabel: 'She is merely to make a wrong choice, the wrongness of which is a matter of an error in judgment involving no guilt on her part, though it involves tragic consequences for her.'[16] It is the word *merely* that is the error in judgement by the critic here. The words that Leavis rightly uses in praise of George Eliot, 'inevitability' and 'consistency', are indeed the conditions of her art, but the conditions of James's art include an immitigable scepticism as to inevitability and consistency whether in life or in art. Scepticism, not cynicism, because James dislikes cynicism's pleasure at the thought of its own omniscience. James does not play what we misleadingly call the omniscient narrator. As to *the omniscient narrator*, all we usually mean is that the narrator is alone in knowing certain things, particularly thoughts. This, God knows, is a far cry from omniscience. It was from Kenneth Graham that we learned that it was as long ago as 1894 that Sir Walter Raleigh characterized such a narrator with this inordinate extension: 'He is invisible and omniscient.'[17]

16. *The Great Tradition*, 98.
17. *English Criticism of the Novel, 1865–1900* (Oxford, 1965), 121.

It is a complicated matter, the Jamesian claim in the matter of knowing, with the knots of its *not*s. In *What Maisie Knew*, 'I may not even answer for it that Maisie was not aware of how, in this, Mrs. Beale failed to share his all but insurmountable distaste for their allowing their little charge to breathe the air of their gross irregularity.'[18] What is the price that is paid for James's withholdings? Leavis had a way of immediately following one question with another, not staying for an answer, prosecutorially. 'Isn't there, in fact, something evasive about James's inexplicitness; something equivocal about his indirectness and the subtlety of implication with which he pursues his aim of excluding all but the "essential"? What, we ask, thinking by contrast of the fullness with which · · ·' etc.[19] Insufficiently permitting of response, and using the phrase *in fact* of what is not a fact but a judgement, this does nevertheless identify the charge to which James is often open and of which he is sometimes guilty. For Empson was not out of court when he remarked, of a Milton/James contrast adduced by T. S. Eliot, 'It seems to me that Mr Eliot does not know when Milton is good, and I certainly do not know when Henry James is good; I always feel sure he is jabbering like that only to make the reader as helplessly confused about the rights and wrongs of the case as he is himself.'[20] The rights and wrongs of the case: the wrong charge against James was the one made, as it happens, by T. S. Eliot himself in judging *Roderick Hudson*: James 'too much identifies himself with Rowland, does not see thorough the solemnity he has created in that character, commits the cardinal sin of failing to "detect" one of his own characters'.[21] What is wrong with this is T. S. Eliot's twofold confidence, that there is such a thing as 'the cardinal sin' for a novelist and that failing to detect one of his or her characters is it.

Conversely, the rights and wrongs of the case when it comes to George Eliot have to do with the limits within which Leavis's values of inevitability and consistency should themselves be valued. George Eliot's determination to understand, and to fashion a plot (a *fable*, Leavis is happy to call it) such as to ensure understanding and explanation, makes visible some truths while it occludes some others. It cannot but prompt on occasion the charge to which she in her turn is often open and of which she is sometimes guilty. Guilt is the nub.

18. *What Maisie Knew* (1897), ch. XX, p. 171.   19. *The Great Tradition*, 110.
20. *Milton's God* (1961), 27.   21. *Little Review*, August 1918.

(Leavis deprecated James for supposing that his Isabel could be both believable and guiltless.) The prosecution of George Eliot in this matter is led by W. B. Yeats, who calls Balzac to witness against her:

> In *La Peau de chagrin* Balzac spends many pages in describing a coquette, who seems the image of heartlessness, and then invents an improbable incident that her chief victim may discover how beautifully she can sing. Nobody had ever heard her sing, and yet in her singing, and in her chatter with her maid, Balzac tells us, was her true self. He would have us understand that behind the momentary self, which acts and lives in the world, and is subject to the judgment of the world, there is that which cannot be called before any mortal judgment seat, even though a great poet, or novelist, or philosopher be sitting upon it. Great literature has always been written in a like spirit, and is, indeed, the Forgiveness of Sin, and when we find it becoming the Accusation of Sin, as in George Eliot, who plucks her Tito [in *Romola*] in pieces with as much assurance as if he had been clockwork, literature has begun to change into something else. George Eliot had a fierceness hardly to be found but in a woman turned argumentative, but the habit of mind her fierceness gave its life to was characteristic of her century, and is the habit of mind of the Shakespearian critics.[22]

We should oppose much of this: the capital letters with which Yeats heightens Forgiveness, Accusation, and Sin; the injustice to George Eliot's Tito Melema, who is indeed inspected but not as clockwork, rather as a geological specimen, the strata of his indurated habituated selfishness; the injustice to so much else of George Eliot; the exultant misogyny of Yeats, and its confidence of applause: all these raise resistance. Yet the comparison with Balzac, including the admission of his imperfection as a novelist ('invents an improbable incident'), is on to something, and it has its bearing on whether the determination to *understand* does not preclude some forms or channels that sympathetic imagination may take. Inevitability can harden the heart, and it is the opposite of what T. S. Eliot valued in James: his power to *escape*.

The succeeding novelist achieves an imaginative critique of his or her predecessors. But to the critique of a predecessor must immediately be added self-criticism, the novelist as self-critic. For Pound's declaration asks to be understood as complemented by inward self-criticism, such as might be devoted either to one's previous work (predecessor not *of*

22. 'At Stratford-on-Avon' (1901); in *Selected Criticism*, ed. A. Norman Jeffares (London, 1964), 9–8. In an essay for the centenary (1980) of George Eliot's death ('She Was Still Young'), I remarked Yeats's wielding one of her loved words, *argumentative* ('Victorian Lives', in *Christopher Ricks, Essays in Appreciation* (Oxford, 1996), 229).

but *by* oneself), or to the work in progress, the here and now. John Keats, a superb reviser, was eloquent in the belief that creation itself has to be unremittingly critical:

'My judgment, (he says,) is as active while I am actually writing as my imagination. In fact all my faculties are strongly excited & in their full play— And shall I afterwards, when my imagination is idle, & the heat in which I wrote, has gone off, sit down coldly to criticise when in Possession of only one faculty, what I have written, when almost inspired.'[23]

Dickens's imagination was never idle and he never sat down, let alone coldly. His revisions are strongly excited criticism. They are therefore themselves open to criticism, not always appreciative. Happily, the evidence that was mounted a while ago (1957) as *Dickens at Work*, a succinct precise study by John Butt and Kathleen Tillotson that has been augmented but not superseded, mostly bears witness to Dickens as a superb novelist–self-critic. This may be a matter of a particular crystallization, as when the entertained title *Nobody's Fault* found itself improved into *Little Dorrit*.

It seems likely that Little Dorrit was not at first intended to be so important a character; indeed, in manuscript, proofs and letters we can trace the way she grew in importance, and even see her acquiring her name. She was introduced in the third chapter, merely as an unknown girl seen in Mrs Clennam's room and inquired about by Arthur Clennam. In the manuscript her name does not appear; Affery only says 'Oh! *She's* nothing; she's a whim of hers.' Her name is added in proof as 'Dorrit', which is then altered in a different coloured ink to 'Little Dorrit.'[24]

Whereupon Butt and Tillotson identify, with affectionate respect, not only the process by which the name established itself for Dickens as entitled to the novel, but the grounds for believing that the title that duly found itself replaced, *Nobody's Fault*, would have been slighter, belittling.

Other revisions by Dickens have proved enduringly controversial, most famously or most notoriously his changing the end of *Great Expectations*. The account of the matter that I have found both the clearest and the fullest is that of Edgar Rosenberg in his excellent Norton Critical Edition of the novel (1999). Occupying thirty pages,

---

23. No question-mark to complete 'And shall I · · · ' (there is no question as to the answer); recorded by Richard Woodhouse, July (?) 1820. *The Keats Circle*, ed. Hyder Edward Rollins (Cambridge, MA, 1965), i. 128–9. Woodhouse's revisions are omitted above.
24. *Dickens at Work* (1957), 231.

'Putting an End to "Great Expectations"' sets out the facts crisply before scrupulously adjudicating the understandable disputes that the textual history has occasioned.

Great Expectations, as we now meet it, closes with expectations that are still opening for Pip and Estella, even as the heroic poem *Paradise Lost* closes with the prospect of what Adam and Eve may yet come to find, intimated by the cadence of heroic elegy: 'They hand in hand with wandring steps and slow ···'.

'Glad to part again, Estella? To me parting is a painful thing. To me, the remembrance of our last parting has been ever mournful and painful.'

'But you said to me,' returned Estella, very earnestly, '"God bless you, God forgive you!" And if you could say that to me then, you will not hesitate to say that to me now—now, when suffering has been stronger than all other teaching, and has taught me to understand what your heart used to be. I have been bent and broken, but—I hope—into a better shape. Be as considerate and good to me as you were, and tell me we are friends.'

'We are friends,' said I, rising and bending over her, as she rose from the bench.

'And will continue friends apart,' said Estella.

I took her hand in mine, and we went out of the ruined place; and, as the morning mists had risen long ago when I first left the forge, so the evening mists were rising now, and in all the broad expanse of tranquil light they showed to me, I saw no shadow of another parting from her.[25]

~Not hesitate to say that to me now
To understand what your heart used to be
I took her hand in mine, and we went out
The morning mists had risen long ago
In all the broad expanse of tranquil light
No shadow of another parting from her~

But at the proof stage for the volume publication of 1862, the ending had been significantly other. Pip is in London, with 'little Pip', Joe Gargery's child, and they meet Estella; her first, brutal, husband having died, she has married again.

I was in England again—in London, and walking along Piccadilly with little Pip—when a servant came running after me to ask would I step back to a lady in a carriage who wished to speak to me. It was a little pony carriage, which the lady was driving; and the lady and I looked sadly enough on one another.

25. Previously, ~I saw the shadow of no parting from her~. This is the reading in 'all texts earlier than 1862 (the serial versions, first edition [1861], and early American editions based on *All the Year Round*)', *Great Expectations*, ed. Edgar Rosenberg (New York, 1999), 501.

'I am greatly changed, I know, but I thought you would like to shake hands with Estella too, Pip. Lift up that pretty child and let me kiss it!' (She supposed the child, I think, to be my child.)

I was very glad afterwards to have had the interview; for, in her face and in her voice, and in her touch, she gave me the assurance, that suffering had been stronger than Miss Havisham's teaching, and had given her a heart to understand what my heart used to be.

~Lift up that pretty child and let me kiss it!
Supposed the child, I think, to be my child
In her face and in her voice, and in her touch
To understand what my heart used to be~

This ending first saw the tranquil light of day within the third volume of John Forster's *Life of Charles Dickens* in 1874. It has come to be characterized as the unhappy ending. (Not that this would be an easy or simple judgement.) The so-called happy ending (likewise) had replaced it for publication in 1862. Dickens wrote to Forster on 1 July 1861, crediting or debiting Edward Bulwer-Lytton:

You will be surprised to hear that I have changed the end of *Great Expectations* from and after Pip's return to Joe's, and finding his little likeness there. Bulwer, who has been, as I think you know, extraordinarily taken by the book, so strongly urged it upon me, after reading the proofs, and supported his views with such good reasons, that I resolved to make the change. You shall have it when you come back to town. I have put in as pretty a little piece of writing as I could, and I have no doubt the story will be more acceptable through the alteration.[26]

Ominous, the blithe invoking there of the 'more acceptable' and of 'as pretty a little piece of writing as I could'. Whose novel is it anyway? Before setting about Dickens's novel, Bulwer-Lytton had entitled one of his own *My Novel*.

~Had given her a heart to understand
To understand what my heart used to be~

Ever since Forster's revelation of the earlier ending, the hearts of readers have had to engage with what Dickens's novel used to be.

Do I know how I feel? Do I know what I think?
Let me take ink and paper, let me take pen and ink...[27]

26. *The Letters of Charles Dickens*, ed. Graham Storey, vol. ix (Oxford, 1997), 432–3.
27. T. S. Eliot's ellipsis; *The Poems of T. S. Eliot* (ed. Ricks and Jim McCue), i. 269. Eliot briefly thought himself entitled to *He do the police in different voices* for *The Waste Land*;

T. S. Eliot thought about 'intelligence, of which an important function is the discernment of exactly what, and how much, we feel in any given situation'.[28] All the more taxing when we find ourselves not in a given situation but in two different situations given by a novelist of genius.

Constituting creative self-criticism on the most ample scale is the entire re-fashioning of an enterprise. This, which never comes easily to any creator, is sometimes precipitated by effective criticism from others. One of the most effective forms of criticism may of course be censorship, or worse; one recalls Shelley on *Paradise Lost*:

Milton gives the Devil all imaginable advantage; and the arguments with which he exposes the injustice and impotent weakness of his adversary are such as, had they been printed distinct from the shelter of any dramatic order, would have been answered by the most conclusive of syllogisms—persecution.[29]

A differently effective form of criticism is the rejection slip. Yet this may then turn out to be something that posterity will have cause to welcome. For had not the publishers in 1932 rejected *Dream of Fair to Middling Women*, we should never have had Beckett's *More Pricks than Kicks* (1934), a supremely successful conversion of chaos into cosmos.[30] Had not *The Professor* been repeatedly rejected, we should never have had what is for some of us a novel greater even than *Jane Eyre*, Charlotte Brontë's *Villette* (1853). The editors of the Oxford edition (1987) of *The Professor*, Margaret Smith and Herbert Rosengarten, record that on 15 July 1847, after the manuscript had suffered its sixth rejection, Charlotte Brontë sent it to the London firm of Smith, Elder. They add that, writing as *he* (Currer Bell), she described the publisher's response in the *Biographical Notice* of 1850:

Ere long, in a much shorter space than that on which experience had taught him to calculate—there came a letter, which he opened in the dreary expectation of finding two hard hopeless lines, intimating that Messrs. Smith, Elder and Co. 'were not disposed to publish the MS.,' and, instead, he took out of the envelope a letter of two pages. He read it trembling. It declined, indeed, to

---

he had an uncertain respect for Dickens ('the terribly serious, even savage comic humour, the humour which spent its last breath in the decadent genius of Dickens'; 'Christopher Marlowe', 1919; in *Selected Essays* (1932; 1951), 123).

28. *The Egoist*, November 1917.
29. 'Essay on the Devil and Devils'; in *Shelley's Prose*, ed. D. L. Clark (Albuquerque, 1954), 267.
30. *Dream of Fair to Middling Women*, ed. Eoin O'Brien and Edith Fournier, published by the Black Cat Press in 1992 and by John Calder in 1993.

publish that tale, for business reasons, but it discussed its merits and demerits so courteously, so considerately, in a spirit so rational, with a discrimination so enlightened, that this very refusal cheered the author better than a vulgarly-expressed acceptance would have done.[31]

Jane Eyre being published in October 1847, within two months Charlotte Brontë returned to the novel that had been rejected:

A few days since I looked over 'the Professor.' I found the beginning very feeble, the whole narrative deficient in incident and in general attractiveness; yet the middle and latter portion of the work, all that relates to Brussels, the Belgian school &c. is as good as I can write; it contains more pith, more substance, more reality, in my judgment, than much of 'Jane Eyre.' It gives, I think, a new view of a grade, an occupation, and a class of characters—all very common-place, very insignificant in themselves, but not more so than the materials composing that portion of 'Jane Eyre' which seems to please most generally—.

My wish is to recast 'the Professor,' add as well as I can, what is deficient, retrench some parts, develop others—and make of it a 3-vol. work; no easy task, I know, yet I trust not an impracticable one.[32]

~More pith, more substance, more reality~

'Much of the Brussels material would reappear, though greatly transformed, in *Villette*.' It was in 1855 that Charlotte Brontë's first and deepest biographer,[33] E. C. Gaskell, was told by the widower, Mr A. Nicholls, that 'he had the manuscript of *The Professor* in his possession; but he would not let Mrs. Gaskell see it, "saying that whole pages of it had been embodied in *Villette*"'.[34] Two years later, *The Professor* was published, with a preface by Nicholls. *The Professor* is alive with things to be grateful for, but we should be even more grateful to the publishers who rejected it and who thereby made possible *Villette*, the work of genius, genius that, prompted by criticism from without, duly profited by criticism from within, the novelist as self-critic.

Those of us who engage in literary studies have come to adopt the term *poet-critic* in paying homage to a noble line within English and American literature. To turn now from the novelist as critic to the

31. *The Professor*, ed. Margaret Smith and Herbert Rosengarten (Oxford, 1987), p. xvii.
32. To W. S. Williams, 14 December 1847; *Selected Letters of Charlotte Brontë*, ed. Margaret Smith (Oxford, 2007), 93.
33. The artistic achievement that is Gaskell's *Life of Charlotte Brontë* (1857) should not have suffered condescension of late; see *Essays in Appreciation* (1996), 118–45.
34. pp. xxiv–xxv.

poet-critic is in hope of instancing touchstones of the kind that Arnold proposed, but not from poetry, from criticism. Tennyson is here the poet, Arnold the critic:

> Yet all experience is an arch wherethrough
> Gleams that untravell'd world, whose margin fades
> For ever and for ever when I move.   (*Ulysses*)

It is no blame to the thought of those lines, which belongs to another order of ideas than Homer's, but it is true, that Homer would certainly have said of them, 'It is to consider too curiously to consider so.' It is no blame to their rhythm, which belongs to another order of movement than Homer's, but it is true that these three lines by themselves take up nearly as much time as a whole book of the *Iliad*.[35]

Arnold here achieves something no less remarkable than 'What oft was *Thought*, but ne'er so well *Exprest*', for he expresses, with succinct simplicity, something (something mysterious, moreover) that I for one had not thought, would not have been capable of thinking, but can now never *not* have in mind—while no longer needing *consciously* to have it there—whenever I read these lines from one of Tennyson's greatest poems or the many other lines in Tennyson that evince this haunting quality, this extraordinary disposition towards time. Arnold's characterization of the Tennyson lines is neither blame nor acclaim; it is an appeal, pure and simple, from a sensibility to other sensibilities, that is accompanied by a surge of explanatory power. It is itself a touchstone. It is curiously yet aptly tinged with comedy, in the asseveration that Homer would certainly have said some words that would come to be said in an age between Homer's and Tennyson's, the words not of Homer but ('to consider too curiously') of Horatio in *Hamlet*. In no way a digression from Arnold's central question—in what verse-form might it be best to translate Homer?—the critical demonstration is persuasively at one with the account elsewhere in Arnold of a principle creative and critical: 'The superior character of truth and seriousness, in the matter and substance of the best poetry, is inseparable from the superiority of diction and movement marking its style and manner. The two superiorities are closely related, and are in steadfast proportion

---

35. *On Translating Homer*, III (1861); in *On the Classical Tradition*, ed. R. H. Super (Ann Arbor, MI, 1960), 147. Yet the commentator on Homer nods, misquoting five words of Tennyson's three lines (as 'For all', 'whose distance', and 'as we gaze').

one to the other.'³⁶ Exactly valuable, this, in its not permitting *inseparable* to slide into the distortive sentimentality of *indistinguishable*. The two superiorities are distinguishable though not distinct.

Again Tennyson, but this time with Hopkins the critic. Again, a classic achievement of criticism, with a principle that precipitates an instance that then itself flowers into a further principle.

Great men, poets I mean, have each their own dialect as it were of Parnassian, formed generally as they go on writing, and at last,—this is the point to be marked,—they can see things in this Parnassian way and describe them in this Parnassian tongue, without further effort of inspiration. In a poet's particular kind of Parnassian lies most of his style, of his manner, of his mannerism if you like. But I must not go farther without giving you instances of Parnassian. I shall take one from Tennyson, and from *Enoch Arden*, from a passage much quoted already and which will be no doubt often quoted, the description of Enoch's tropical island.

> The mountain wooded to the peak, the lawns
> And winding glades high up like ways to Heaven,
> The slender coco's drooping crown of plumes,
> The lightning flash of insect and of bird,
> The lustre of the long convolvuluses
> That coil'd around the stately stems, and ran
> Ev'n to the limit of the land, the glows
> And glories of the broad belt of the world,
> All these he saw.

Now it is a mark of Parnassian that one could conceive oneself writing it if one were the poet. Do not say that *if* you were Shakespear you can imagine yourself writing Hamlet, because that is just what I think you can*not* conceive.³⁷

The contrast of Parnassian with inspiration is itself inspired, markedly in the last leap. For it is a mark of Hopkins's genius that though I could, I suppose, conceive of myself coming up with some distinction between the inspired and the not inspired, I cannot conceive of myself creating the penetrating terms of this principle itself. Do not say that *if*

---

36. 'The Study of Poetry' (1880); in *English Literature and Irish Politics*, ed. R. H. Super (Ann Arbor, MI, 1973), 171.
37. To A. W. M. Baillie, 10 September 1864 (*Enoch Arden* had been published the previous month); *Further Letters of Gerard Manley Hopkins*, ed. Claude Colleer Abbott, 2nd edn (London, 1956), 216–17.

you were Hopkins you can imagine yourself writing these sentences, because that is just what I think you can*not* conceive.[38]

Criticism by poet-critics as humanely penetrating as Arnold on Tennyson, or Hopkins on Tennyson, is admittedly of rare value—and rare. Tennyson himself was no such poet-critic. Although he exercised fine critical judgement in helping F. T. Palgrave to create a great anthology of English verse, *The Golden Treasury* (1861),[39] and although his off-the-cuff remarks were felicitous, especially as to infelicities (Shelley seems to go up and burst, Wordsworth is thick-ankled, and Jonson, in his comedies, appears to move in a wide sea of glue), Tennyson did not write criticism, and neither he nor we should repine at this. Or take Browning. An uninspired essay on Shelley, or rather on Shelley's letters. Or Hardy. His love of William Barnes did triumph over his disinclination to set his pen to critical paper, but no more, and there is no denying that there have always been poets who are *not* critics, and that it is the Victorian age where this is manifestly the case.

The term *critic-poet* (used by Herbert Read in 1938) yielded to *poet-critic*, the provenance being the learned journals: *Essays in Criticism* (1956), 'Poet-critics as dissimilar as Arthur Symons and Mr. Eliot', and *English Studies* (1964), 'Of course a poet-critic may be allowed to speak in images' (*OED*). The *poet-critic* is not complemented by *novelist-critic*, or *critic-novelist*, although *critic-dramatist* is recorded in the *Westminster Gazette*, 1906.[40] The compounded compliment *novelist-critic* would recognize, as *poet-critic* often does, genius doubly manifested. We seldom feel the need for the term *novelist-critic* because the phenomenon was not a frequent one. Granted, each of the great Victorian novelists incarnates the crucial element of the novelist as critic: creation as itself

38. Drawing on 'Literary Principles as against Theory', in *Essays in Appreciation* (1996), 329. Similarly, the Introduction to *The Oxford Book of English Verse* (1999), for the great poet-critics.
39. For the collaboration, see *The Golden Treasury* (ed. Ricks, Penguin, 1991).
40. Leavis dubs Henry James 'poet-novelist' (*The Great Tradition*, 12), which is a different story, though not a convincing one as characterized by Leavis: 'It was the profundity of the pondering that I had in mind when I referred to him as a "poet-novelist"' (p. 128). Aware of the unthinking disparagement of the novel, Leavis sought to raise the standing of novels by calling them dramatic poems ('The Novel as Dramatic Poem', a series in *Scrutiny*), but there was a price to be paid in the misleading implication that poetry is inherently better than prose and that a truly great novel attains poemhood. Such condescension to prose was the subject of my inaugural lecture as Professor of Poetry at Oxford (*Times Literary Supplement*, 25 February 2005), included here as Chapter 1, pp. 1–18.

criticism, whether of others' art or of one's own. But what of the further, the discursive, activity, valuable and indispensable in its way? Criticism is the art of noticing things that the rest of us may well not have noticed for ourselves and might never have noticed. It asks tact, of itself and of its readers, for it must neither state nor neglect the obvious. Whether something is obvious may not be obvious. At its best, criticism participates in the higher reaches of art itself: noticing relations between the things that it notices. But so far as criticism goes, the attending is primarily to art, more than to all the other things which together with art make up the world. Criticism is not a service industry but a service art, one that begins with the asking of crucial questions, a necessary (not a sufficient) condition of seizing crucial answers.

It is not difficult to adduce criticism of the novel, by Victorian novelists of genius, for which one can be grateful. But the gratitude is for the serviceable, the shrewd, the apt, and the historically pertinent, all fine in their way but all falling short of the penetrative surprise that characterizes criticism that is, in both senses, *of genius*, and that can then constitute a touchstone of the critical art.

For instance, George Eliot's essay 'Silly Novels by Lady Novelists' (*Westminster Review*, October 1856) is never other than markedly intelligent, and it is—as her modern editor says—'of special interest as a record of George Eliot's thoughts about the writing of fiction made just at the time when she began her first story'.[41] It has the value that attends upon any critical enterprise that is essentially hygienic, given that the fashionable novels that George Eliot deplores, of 'the *maid-and-millinery* species', are deplorable. But silly novels by lady novelists cannot precipitate the greatest criticism, any more than a silly play can elicit the greatest acting. *The Natural History of German Life*, three months earlier in the *Westminster Review* (July 1856), can briefly breathe a larger air because of the spirit of Dickens: 'We have one great novelist who is gifted with the utmost power of rendering the external traits of our town population; and if he could give us their psychological character—their conceptions of life, and their emotions—with the same truth as their idiom and manners, his books would be the greatest contribution Art has ever made to the awakening of social sympathies.'[42] (Yes, the next word is *But*.) Not self-evidently true, this characterization of Dickens's genius, but self-evidently worth thinking about. Yet it

41. Thomas Pinney, *Essays of George Eliot* (New York, 1963), 300–1.   42. Ibid. 271.

does not acknowledge any critical problems. Dickens has truth to idiom and manners, we are assured; are these, then, so assuredly separable from truth of psychological character, of emotions, and of conceptions of life? Do not idioms and manners often prove to be character in action?

The gratitude we may feel for such criticism is of a lesser order than that which George Eliot's novels elicit. The notable critic W. W. Robson used to say in class, when something from Victorian literature was found wanting, 'Well, yes, of course, but better than you or I could do.' Agreed, as to George Eliot on Dickens. But this would fall short of the tribute that Hopkins not only paid but earned: 'Now it is a mark of Parnassian that one could conceive oneself writing it if one were the poet. Do not say that *if* you were Shakespear you can imagine yourself writing Hamlet, because that is just what I think you can*not* conceive.'

For to read the Victorian novelists on the Victorian novel may entail concluding, regretfully and respectfully, that they mostly duck wholehearted critical engagement. Trollope offered advice to George Eliot: 'Do not fire too much over the heads of your readers.'[43] It was in this spirit that he himself penned 'On English Prose Fiction as a Rational Amusement' (1870), which, although it may now have its historical interest, offers as criticism nothing more than rational amusement.

If we call to mind the many volumes in the *Critical Heritage* series, responsibly representative as they are, and duly eager to muster distinctive criticism, it is remarkable how seldom the novelists themselves achieve criticism that is remarkable, anything that moves beyond summary, the under-described, the unimpinging. *Needless to say*, one finds oneself saying to oneself. Needless to say, the patent and patient exception is Henry James, the novelist-critic *par excellence*.

It is not that Dickens forbore to write criticism, for his energies are there in *Household Words* and *All the Year Round*, journals of his that are not exactly alive with criticism but are on occasion alive to it, and there are the letters and the prefaces to the novels. But he never remarkably noticed something about anyone else's novel, as against his having a genius for noticing things within his own novels; at least, there is not the cogent extravagance with which he registered, for instance, the art of pantomime.

43. 28 June 1862. *The Letters of Anthony Trollope*, ed. N. John Hall (Stanford, CA, 1983), i. 187.

How came I, it may be asked, on the day after Christmas Day, of all days in the year, to be hovering outside Saint Luke's [Hospital for the Insane], after dark, when I might have betaken myself to that jocund world of Pantomime, where there is no affliction or calamity that leaves the least impression; where a man may tumble into the broken ice, or dive into the kitchen fire, and only be the droller for the accident; where babies may be knocked about and sat upon, or choked with gravy spoons, in the process of feeding, and yet no Coroner be wanted, nor anybody made uncomfortable; where workmen may fall from the top of a house to the bottom, or even from the bottom of a house to the top, and sustain no injury to the brain, need no hospital, leave no young children; where every one, in short, is so superior to the accidents of life, though encountering them at every turn, that I suspect it to be the secret (though many persons may not present it to themselves) of the general enjoyment which an audience of vulnerable spectators, liable to pain and sorrow, find in this class of entertainment.[44]

It is *or even from the bottom of a house to the top* that does it, a feat not just of acrobatic wording but of critical acumen, soaring into the ways of the imagination within this class not just of entertainment but of art. Everyday heroism may consist of being 'superior to the accidents of life, though encountering them at every turn'. The leap is from a Hospital for the Insane to what, wrongly considered, might be taken for the insanity of the goings-on in the jocund world of Pantomime, a world that understands the therapeutic as finely as does the world of the circus.

Sometimes it will be anger's freeing power that liberates critical writing from the conventional, the craven, or the pious.[45] So it is that Charlotte Brontë's low estimate of Jane Austen rises above stormy Sisterhood.

I have likewise read one of Miss Austen's works 'Emma'—read it with interest and with just the degree of admiration which Miss Austen herself would have thought sensible and suitable—anything like warmth or enthusiasm; anything energetic, poignant, heart-felt, is utterly out of place in commending these works: all such demonstration the authoress would have met with a well-bred sneer, would have calmly scorned as outré and extravagant. She does her business of delineating the surface of the lives of genteel English people curiously

---

44. 'A Curious Dance Round a Curious Tree' (*Household Words*, 17 January 1852, with W. H. Wills); in *The Uncollected Writings of Charles Dickens: Household Words, 1850–1859*, ed. Harry Stone (Bloomington, IN, 1968), ii. 383-4.

45. Stevie Smith's poem about a raven, *Anger's Freeing Power*, ends: 'Anger it was that won him hence | As only Anger taught him sense. | | Often my tears fall in a shower | Because of Anger's freeing power.'

well; there is a Chinese fidelity, a miniature delicacy in the painting: she ruffles
her reader by nothing vehement, disturbs him by nothing profound: the
Passions are perfectly unknown to her; she rejects even a speaking acquaintance with that stormy Sisterhood; even to the Feelings she vouchsafes no
more than an occasional graceful but distant recognition; too frequent con-
verse with them would ruffle the smooth elegance of her progress. Her business is not half so much with the human heart as with the human eyes, mouth,
hands and feet; what sees keenly, speaks aptly, moves flexibly, it suits her to
study, but what throbs fast and full, though hidden, what the blood rushes
through, what is the unseen seat of Life and the sentient target of Death—this
Miss Austen ignores; she no more, with her mind's eye, beholds the heart of
her race than each man, with bodily vision sees the heart in his heaving breast.
Jane Austen was a complete and most sensible lady, but a very incomplete, and
rather insensible (not senseless) woman; if this is heresy—I cannot help it. If
I said it to some people (Lewes for instance) they would directly accuse me of
advocating exaggerated heroics; but I am not afraid of your falling into any
such vulgar error.

> Believe me
> Yours sincerely
> C. Brontë[46]

Believe her, sincerely. We are in the presence not of 'heroics' but of an
unwavering staunchness. Here I stand, I can do no other. *If this is heresy—
I cannot help it.* If this be error, and upon me proved...

   Charlotte Brontë on Jane Austen is a classic statement of a critical
judgement, stringent and astringent, that must not be waived, particularly by those who would contest it; itself deserving at least the compliment of rational opposition; and at one point, in its imaginative
depth, achieving the power of a critical touchstone: 'what throbs fast
and full, though hidden, what the blood rushes through, what is the
unseen seat of Life and the sentient target of Death'.

   Yet when she confronted a novel that did comprehend 'the unseen
seat of Life and the sentient target of Death', she could not but vacillate.

---

46. To W. S. Williams, 12 April 1850; *Selected Letters of Charlotte Brontë*, 161–2. (Retaining
the edition's underlining, not converting to italics.) A similar vein had been opened in
a letter to G. H. Lewes, 12 January 1848: 'I had not seen "Pride & Prejudice" till I read
that sentence of yours, and then I got the book and studied it. And what did I find?
An accurate daguerreotyped portrait of a common-place face; a carefully-fenced,
highly cultivated garden with neat borders and delicate flowers—but no glance of a
bright vivid physiognomy—no open country—no blue hill—no bonny beck.
I should hardly like to live with her ladies and gentlemen in their elegant but confined
houses. These observations will probably irritate you, but I shall run the risk.' *Selected
Letters*, 99. ~And then I got the book and studied it~

Writing the Editor's Preface to the New Edition of her sister's
Wuthering Heights (1850), she half-acknowledges 'what are termed (and,
perhaps, really are) its faults'; she adduces Austen-type readers (men
and woman 'naturally very calm, and with feelings moderate in
degree'), understandingly enough though not without condescension;
and she is concessive to the point of all-but-surrender: 'Whether it is
right or advisable to create beings like Heathcliff, I do not know:
I scarcely think it is.'

~I do not know: I scarcely think it is~

(*Advisable*: such a word belongs rather to the world of Jane Austen.)
She continues: 'But this I know; the writer who possesses the creative
gift owns something of which he is not always master—something
that at times strangely wills and works for itself.' She concludes: 'If the
result be attractive the world will praise you, who little deserve praise;
if it be repulsive, the same world will blame you, who almost as little
deserve blame.'[47]

Repulsive: it is in such terms that Matthew Arnold blames *Villette*:

Miss Brontë has written a hideous undelightful convulsed constricted novel—
what does Thackeray say to it. It is one of the most utterly disagreeable books
I ever read—and having seen her makes it more so. She is so entirely—what
Margaret Fuller was partially—a fire without aliment—one of the most distressing barren sights one can witness. Religion or devotion or whatever it is
to be called may be impossible for such people now: but they have at any rate
not found a substitute for it and it was better for the world when they comforted themselves with it.[48]

~One of the most distressing barren sights~

Why is Villette disagreeable? Because the writer's mind contains nothing but
hunger rebellion and rage—and therefore that is all she can in fact put into
her book. No fine writing can hide this thoroughly—and it will be fatal to her
in the long run.[49]

Such writing is itself convulsed, constricted, and disagreeable—
particularly from a critic who justly prided himself on urbanity. But
Arnold has manifestly seized upon *something* that a reader needs to
reckon with, not as a matter of the authority attaching to Arnold but

47. Included in *Emily Brontë*, ed. Jean-Pierre Petit (Harmondsworth, 1973).
48. To Clough, 21 March 1853; *The Letters of Matthew Arnold*, ed. Cecil Y. Lang, vol. i
    (Charlottesville, VA, 1996), 258.
49. To his sister Jane ('K'), 14 April 1853; *The Letters of Matthew Arnold*, i. 262.

as inviting attention not only to 'spilt religion'[50] and its acids, but to how a work of art may indeed *contain* (a pregnant word), and not merely vent, the satanic trinity of hunger, rebellion, and rage. A caveat: that it is a marked feature of such throbbing criticism as Brontë on Austen, or Arnold on Brontë, that it is to be found in personal letters, which have their own responsibilities to discretion.

If, then, the Victorian novelists of genius seldom show themselves to be novelist-critics of genius, where might the most illuminating criticism of the novel be found? In the guild that constitutes one of the accomplishments of the age: *man of letters*, a man of learning, a scholar; now usually, a man of the literary profession, an author.[51]

The term 'woman of letters' did not establish itself, despite the achievements of (among others) Jane Welsh Carlyle, Julia Wedgwood, Margaret Oliphant, and Vernon Lee. For me, a particular honour attaches to one whose quarry was the novel's sister-art, the drama: Frances Anne Kemble. One route to her may proceed from F. R. Leavis. When he set down his convictions as to Shakespearean drama, he dissociated such drama—and what it asked by way of imaginative attention—from the reductiveness often visited upon the plots and characterization of novels. It was *à propos* of *The Winter's Tale* that Leavis made his point with admirable succinctness:

if our preconceptions don't prevent our being adverted by imagery, rhythm, and the developing hints of symbolism—by the subtle devices of the poetry and the very absence of 'psychology'—we quickly see that what we have in front of us is nothing in the nature of a novel dramatically transcribed.[52]

Victorian tributes to Kemble's acting make clear that she did not transcribe, she transformed. As did her words, remarkable not only for the versatile vivacities of her diaries and letters but for the compassion that fulfilled its tragic duty in her *Journal of a Residence on a Georgian Plantation* (the residence 1838–9, the publication 1863). It was her imaginative powers on the stage that animated her critical trenchancy, manifest in her *Notes upon Some of Shakespeare's Plays*. Her theatre-criticism may act as a reminder that it will sometimes be from the boards that we learn how psychological acumen is at one with quick-witted apprehension

50. T. E. Hulme: 'Romanticism then, and this is the best definition I can give of it, is spilt religion' ('Romanticism and Classicism', 1911–1912?, in *Speculations*, 1924; *The Collected Writings of T. E. Hulme*, ed. Karen Csengeri (Oxford, 1994), 62).
51. OED; 1811 is apparently the first citation in this sense.
52. *The Common Pursuit*, 175.

of, yes, imagery, rhythm, symbolism and poetry—but not 'the very absence of "psychology"', rather the true presence of it. When Kemble calls up Lady Macbeth 'urging her husband to the King's murder', the urgency is active in the syntax and its momentum:

She has her end to gain by talking, and she talks till she does gain it; and in those moments of mortal agony, when his terrors threaten with annihilation the fabric of their fortunes—that fearful fabric based on such infinite depths of guilt, cemented with such costly blood—when she sees him rushing upon inevitable ruin, and losing every consciousness but that of his own crimes, she, like the rider whose horse, maddened with fear, is imperilling his own and that rider's existence, drives the rowels of her piercing irony into him and with a hand of iron guides and urges, and *lifts* him over the danger. But, except in those supreme instants, where her purpose is to lash and goad him past the obstruction of his own terrors, her habitual tone, from beginning to end, is of a sort of contemptuous compassion towards the husband whose moral superiority of nature she perceives and despises.[53]

~The rowels of her piercing irony
And with a hand of iron guides and urges~

What guides and urges this is a deep aptness of the kind often to be found in the poet-critic but seldom in the Victorian novelist-critic, and which in this woman of letters who is an actor lifts her to the narrative-imagery of three successive scenes of the play itself.

MESSENGER   ···our *Thane* is comming:
One of my fellowes had the speed of him;
Who almost dead for breath, had scarcely more
Then would make up his Message.   (*Macbeth*, I. v)

★ ★ ★

KING   Where's the Thane of Cawdor?
We courst him at the heeles, and had a purpose
To be his Purveyor: But he rides well,
And his great Love (sharpe as his Spurre) hath holp him
To his home before us...   (*Macbeth*, I. vi)

★ ★ ★

MACBETH   I have no Spurre
To pricke the sides of my intent, but onely

Vaulting Ambition, which ore-leapes it selfe,
And falles on th'other.   (*Macbeth*, I. vii)

It is in the men and women of letters that we encounter Victorian criticism that delights us with its power to notice and to make us feel and think. Take Walter Bagehot on Thackeray and his thinking:

He could gauge a man's reality as well as any observer, and far better than most: his attainments were great, his perception of men instinctive, his knowledge of casual matters enormous; but he had a greater difficulty than other men in relying only upon his own judgment. 'What the footman—what Mr. Yellowplush Jeames would think and say,' could not but occur to his mind, and would modify, not his settled judgment, but his transient and casual opinion of the poet or philosopher. By the constitution of his mind he thought much of social distinctions, and yet he was in his writings too severe on those who, in cruder and baser ways, showed that they also were thinking much.[54]

Or the studied flexibility with which Bagehot compares the English novel to the French.

We pay our writers to be moral, and they are moral. But the French have no such custom; on the contrary, a French novelist is rather expected to be immoral. Among the purchasers of such works, probably the majority would feel *hurt* if they contained no scenes which English morals would forbid, and which English women would shrink from. A mere infraction of the marriage vow is too trifling a peccadillo, if indeed it is even a peccadillo, to be the subject of an exciting narrative. Dumas *fils* has indeed contrived to render it proper for modern art. His '*Roman d'une Femme*' entirely turns on such an event; but he escaped the vice of commonplace by making the wife love her husband, and *not* love her lover all the while that she is guilty of adultery with her lover; and thus contrived to make the situation sufficiently *piquant*.[55]

~Scenes which English morals would forbid
A mere infraction of the marriage vow~

It is delicious that the word is not piquant but *piquant*, and that the word is in audible touch with that repeated 'peccadillo'. Such acknowledgement of titillation plays its sly part within the national distinction that the critic is drawing and drawing upon.

54. 'Sterne and Thackeray' (*National Review*, April 1864); in *Literary Essays*, ed. Norman St John Stevas (London, 1965), ii. 309–10.
55. From a review of *La Griffe Rose* (by Armand Renaud) in *The Spectator*, 13 September 1862; the attribution to Bagehot, proposed by W. D. Paden, is credited by Stevas, *Literary Essays*, 263–4.

Bagehot has his apt levity. With Ruskin it is gravity, his deep dismay at the death-dealing world of Dickens, which Ruskin challenges in the conviction that this both is and is not the world, for it is the world sensationalized and indurated.

The monotony of life in the central streets of any great modern city, but especially in those of London, where every emotion intended to be derived by men from the sight of nature, or the sense of art, is forbidden for ever, leaves the craving of the heart for a sincere, yet changeful, interest to be fed from one source only.

~The sight of nature, or the sense of art~

Ruskin's convictions and indictments inhabit the tragic city-world (that had been Tennyson's *Maud*, and would be Baudelaire's and T. S. Eliot's all-too-real cities).

It might have been thought by any other than a sternly tentative philosopher, that the denial of their natural food to human feelings would have provoked a reactionary desire for it; and that the dreariness of the street would have been gilded by dreams of a pastoral felicity. Experience has shown the fact to be otherwise; the thoroughly trained Londoner can enjoy no more excitement than that to which he has been accustomed, but asks for *that* in continually more ardent or more virulent concentration; and the ultimate power of fiction to entertain is by varying to his fancy the modes, and defining for his dullness the horrors, of Death. In the single novel of *Bleak House* there are nine deaths (or left for deaths, in the drop scene[56]) carefully wrought out or led up to, either by way of pleasing surprise, as the baby's at the brickmaker's, or finished in their threatenings and sufferings, with as much enjoyment as can be contrived in the anticipation, and as much pathology as can be concentrated in the description. Under the following varieties of method:

One by assassination	Mr Tulkinghorn
One by starvation, with phthisis	Joe
One by chagrin	Richard
One by spontaneous combustion	Mr Krook
One by sorrow	Lady Dedlock's lover
One by remorse	Lady Dedlock
One by insanity	Miss Flite
One by paralysis	Sir Leicester

56. The final scene (as of a play).

Besides the baby, by fever, and a lively young French woman left to be hanged.[57]

It is the grim comedy of *One by chagrin*, of *Besides the baby*, and of *lively*, that brings this home. Ruskin has assuredly seized upon something, and in such criticism we experience what Empson admired in pastoral: 'the sense of richness (readiness for argument not pursued)'.[58]

But waiting in the wings throughout these pages there has been the exception, unignorable because of what he gave that is unignorable: Henry James, the Victorian and Edwardian novelist of genius who is the novelist-critic of genius, the first such (*first* in both senses). As the reviewer of Dickens and *Our Mutual Friend* ('it is one of the chief conditions of his genius not to see beneath the surface of things'); of George Eliot and *Middlemarch* ('If we write novels so, how shall we write History?'); of Trollope and *Can You Forgive Her?* ('The question is, Can we forgive Miss Vavasor? Of course we can, and forget her, too, for that matter'); of Hardy and *Far from the Madding Crowd* ('Everything human in the book strikes us as factitious and insubstantial; the only things we believe in are the sheep and the dogs'): these become touchstones not only because of their memorability but because they are points not scored or made but raised in the service of authentic criticism.[59] The same goes for James's critical commentaries on his own novels, for instance the Preface (1908) to *What Maisie Knew*, in the New York Edition:

To live with all intensity and perplexity and felicity in its terribly mixed little world would thus be the part of my interesting small mortal; bringing people together who would be at least more correctly separate; keeping people separate who would be at least more correctly together; flourishing, to a degree, at the cost of many conventions and proprieties, even decencies; really keeping the torch of virtue alive in an air tending infinitely to smother it; really in short making confusion worse confounded by drawing some stray fragrance of an ideal across the scent of selfishness, by sowing on barren strands, through the mere fact of presence, the seed of the moral life.[60]

---

57. 'Fiction, Fair and Foul' (*Nineteenth Century*, June 1880); included in *Charles Dickens*, ed. Wall, 211–15.
58. 'Marvell's Garden', in *Some Versions of Pastoral* (London, 1935), 145.
59. *Essays on Literature: American Writers: English Writers*, 856, 965–6, 1318, 1048.
60. *Literary Criticism: French Writers: Other European Writers: The Prefaces to the New York Edition*, ed. Leon Edel and Mark Wilson (New York, 1984), 1158–9.

This is the real thing. See the felicity, and surprise, of the word *felicity* there. Here is a genuinely imaginative attention to the ways of the imagination, James's but not James's alone. The same is true of his engagement with *the novel*, as against a particular novel by himself or by another. 'The Art of Fiction' demonstrates the art of criticism. When James says, in 1884, that such-and-such is still the case, we need to acknowledge that it still remains the case and moreover needs to do so, since these are the contentions and the contentiousness that are at stake and that we must not make the mistake of wishing away:

> It is still expected, though perhaps people are ashamed to say it, that a production which is after all only a 'make-believe' (for what else is a 'story'?) shall be in some degree apologetic—shall renounce the pretension of attempting really to represent life. This, of course, any sensible, wide-awake story declines to do, for it quickly perceives that the tolerance granted to it on such a condition is only an attempt to stifle it disguised in the form of generosity. The old evangelical hostility to the novel, which was as explicit as it was narrow, and which regarded it as little less favourable to our immortal part than a stage-play, was in reality far less insulting.[61]

~Only an attempt to stifle it
Disguised in the form of generosity~

It is in large part thanks to James and his generosity that what in due course succeeded the Victorian novelists' relative unsuccess when it came to illuminating the novel with enduring criticism (as against the far more valuable thing, their writing enduringly illuminating novels) was the extraordinary burst of critical energy in Edwardian and Georgian times: the deep appreciation of the novel and of novels, by the novelists themselves. Henry James still. Or E. M. Forster on Proust:

> His book is the product of a double curiosity. The initial curiosity was social; he went to all those awful parties and had those barren relationships and expensive illnesses, and knew in his own person what it is to be a snob, a jealous lover, an orphan, and an invalid with a red nose. And then came the second curiosity, the artistic. He recollected the parties, and robbed them of their stings; they hurt him no longer, and were for the first time useful.[62]

Or D. H. Lawrence on Nathaniel Hawthorne:[63]

61. *Essays on Literature: American Writers: English Writers*, 45.
62. 'Proust' (1929), in *Abinger Harvest* (London, 1936), 101–2.
63. *Studies in Classic American Literature* (1923). *The Forest Lovers*: a chivalric romance by Maurice Hewlett (1898).

Nathaniel Hawthorne writes romance.

And what's romance? Usually, a nice little tale where you have everything As You Like It, where rain never wets your jacket and gnats never bite your nose and it's always daisy-time. *As You Like It* and *Forest Lovers*, etc. *Morte D'Arthur*.

Hawthorne obviously isn't this kind of romanticist: though nobody has muddy boots in *The Scarlet Letter*, either.

But there is more to it. *The Scarlet Letter* isn't a pleasant, pretty romance. It is a sort of parable, an earthly story with a hellish meaning.

All the time there is this split in the American art and art-consciousness. On the top it is as nice as pie, goody-goody and lovey-dovey. Like Hawthorne being such a blue-eyed darling, in life, and Longfellow and the rest such sucking-doves. Hawthorne's wife said she 'never saw him in time', which doesn't mean she saw him too late. But always in the 'frail effulgence of eternity'.

~The 'frail effulgence of eternity'~

7

Henry James and the
Hero of the Story

'The free spirit, always much tormented, and by no means always
triumphant, is heroic, ironic, pathetic or whatever.' So says the
Master, himself heroic, ironic, pathetic or whatever. He adds that the
free spirit is '"successful" only through having remained free.'[1] The writers
within two Henry James stories, *The Modern Warning* and *The Next Time*,
may be judged 'successful', provided that this admits those quotation-
marks. Sir Rufus Chasemore penned—did not quite publish—a polemic
against the United States of America, *The Modern Warning*, he being a
Member of Parliament and in the eyes of his American brother-
in-law 'plainly an agent of the British government, the head of some
kind of department or sub-department'. As for *The Next Time*, its trio
of writers accommodates 'beautiful talents the exercise of which yet is
n't lucrative', where James and his publishers knew the importance of
differentiating not only *is n't* from *isn't* but *yet is n't* from *is n't yet*.[2]

James exercised his beautiful talents in his Address to the graduating
class at Bryn Mawr College, Pennsylvania, on 8 June 1905. In 'The
Question of Our Speech', he spoke as a man of letters, as a novelist
who is truly an artist, and as the most high of journalists. He urged the
young women to value aright the Answer of Our Speech and to
understand why this will ask heroism of them: 'I am asking you to take
that truth well home and hold it close to your hearts, setting your
backs to the wall to defend it, heroically, when need may be.'

1. Preface to *The Spoils of Poynton* in the New York Edition, vol. x (1908), p. xv.
2. 'Is *that* Mr. Bousefield's idea of literature?' 'No, but he says it 's the public's': the spacing
   convention, differentiating an apostrophe that means an elision from one that does not,
   is at once useful and minute in the New York Edition (this instance is from *The Next
   Time*, vol. xv (1909), 200).

'Heroically' then asked of James that he himself hear, and bring home to those that had ears to hear, the cadence of the English heroic line. When he first turns explicitly to put words not only into the ears but into the mouths of his young listeners, it is this varying cadence that he intimates: 'You would say if you thought about the point at all: "Why, of course we speak in happy forms".'

~Why, of course we speak in happy forms~

And when he brings this little imagined speech of theirs to an end, it fulfils the arc:

~Comfortably and agreeably understood~

as a cadence itself does well to be. Often the lines so shaped have a way of involving some allusion to such rhythms themselves. The burden, say, that might be that of a song:

~The whole of the burden of a care for tone~

Or the intimations of rivalry:

~Sounds of a mysterious intrinsic frankness
Sounds of a mysterious intrinsic meanness~

Or a list that feels listless:

~The confused, the ugly, the flat, the thin, the mean~

as against there bringing to mind ~all the inveterate amenities of life~

~What has become of the principle of taste
Has passed into our conduct and our life
Has become, as we say, a second nature
These truths, you see, are incontestable
The way we say a thing, or fail to say it
To find our way among noted sounds
Left to run wild and lose their way together
The voice plus the way it is employed
Begin to work round to the notion of
For that is indissolubly involved~

In the final sentence of the Address, James's cadences became indissolubly involved with those of Milton. The vista is of 'the wide fair country · · · in which perhaps, at last, *then*, "in solemn troops and sweet societies," you may, sounding the clearer notes of intercourse as only women can, become yourselves models and missionaries, perhaps a little even martyrs, of the good cause'.

I. The Modern Warning

A word of warning: *The Modern Warning* (1888) was not included by Henry James, twenty years later, in his New York Edition. But then of his 112 tales, only 59 did gain admission there. Many considerations weighed with and upon James. On the one hand, he 'had always relished, up to a point, the prospects of a chance "to quietly disown a few things by not thus supremely adopting them" (as he had written on 6 June 1905)'.[3] It was in this spirit, two months later, that he characterized the vast revisionary enterprise:

> Its *raison d'être* (the edition's) is in its being selective as well as collective, and by the mere fact of leaving out certain things (I have tried to read over *Washington Square* and I *can't*, and I fear it must go!) I exercise a control, a discrimination, I treat certain portions of my work as unhappy accidents— (many portions of many—of all—men's work are).

On the other hand, as his foremost commentator Philip Horne then points out, 'The length limit, set by Scribner at 120,000 words and somehow mistaken by the amplifying James as 150,000 words per volume, was one restriction on his freedom to include what he wanted.'

By 6 August [1908], the temporary mislaying of a page of 'Brooksmith' prompted James to give voice again to his pangs: 'if I do have to omit "Brooksmith", it won't be alas the only valuable item our limits of space compel me greatly to regret!' The exclusion of a work from the New York Edition, then, does not prove James wished to 'quietly disown' it.

But how valuable an item is *The Modern Warning*? Among the disquieted disowners is Leon Edel ('a piece of hackwork when compared with the sharpness and vigour of *The Patagonia*').[4] Confronting Edel, there is the author of an essay on 'James, Trollope and the American-English Confrontation', Q. D. Leavis. For her, *The Modern Warning* is a work

in which there is no superfluous word or ambiguous sentence, the tone is throughout profoundly serious, nothing is shirked or undervalued, and complete impartiality is maintained throughout. It seems to me to be the finest

3. Philip Horne, *Henry James and Revision: The New York Edition* (Oxford, 1990), 13–14.
4. Introduction to *The Complete Tales of Henry James*, vol. 7 (London, 1963), 9.

expression of the deepest realization of the insoluble difficulties of the member of the James family who was in spite of his disabilities a major novelist, making his art out of those difficulties and knowing any solution of them must be illusory or dishonest.[5]

In the Notebooks, James had arrived at an acknowledgement that what he drily summed up as 'internationalism, etc.' did present him with some difficulties, not least in seeming easy and usual. But by the time his three-hundred-word entry conceded as much, he had already made manifest his engagement with the imagined situation, and then, immediately following his caveat, there comes his characteristic conclusion, an underlining of the *author*.

July 9th, 1884. This idea has been suggested to me by reading Sir Lepel Griffin's book about America. Type of the conservative, fastidious, exclusive Englishman (in public life, clever, etc.), who hates the U.S.A. and thinks them a contamination to England, a source of *funeste* warning, etc., and an odious country socially. He falls in love with an American Girl and she with him—this of course to be made natural if possible. He lets her know, frankly, that he loathes her country as much as he adores her personally, and he begs her to marry him. She is patriotic in a high degree—a genuine little American—and she has the sentiment of her native land. But she is in love with the Englishman, and though she resists on patriotic grounds she yields at last, accepts him and marries him. She must have a near relation—a brother, say—who is violently American, an *anglophobiste* (in public life in the U.S.A.); and of whom she is very fond. He deplores her marriage, entreats her to keep out of it, etc. He and the Englishman *loathe* each other. After the marriage the Englishman's hostility to the U.S. increases, fostered by the invasion of Americans, etc. State of mind of the wife. Depression, melancholy, remorse and shame at having married an enemy of her country. Suicide? There is a certain interest in the situation—the difficulty of choice and resignation on her part—the resentment of a rupture with the brother, etc. Of course internationalism, etc., may be found overdone, threadbare. That is to a certain extent a reason against the subject; but a weak, not a strong one. It is always enough if the *author* sees substance in it.[6]

5. *Collected Essays,* vol. 2: *The American Novel and Reflections on the European Novel,* ed. G. Singh (Cambridge. 1985), 141.
6. *The Complete Notebooks of Henry James,* ed. Leon Edel and Lyall H. Powers (New York, 1987), 29–30. 'Sir Lepel Griffin's book about America': *The Great Republic* (1884); not identified by Edel and Powers although Griffin is: '(1840–1908), travel writer and historian'. James takes up the phrase that was Griffin's title: 'it was not very easy to say how Macarthy would have preferred that a stranger, or that Sir Rufus in particular, should take the great republic'. But then for Sir Rufus, the great republic (to him, 'the misbegotten republic') *is* the modern warning. (Note James's plural 'them', a usage that would now be held to slight *United*: 'who hates the U.S.A. and

~He falls in love with an American Girl
She has the sentiment of her native land
She yields at last, accepts him and marries him
He and the Englishman loathe each other
Having married an enemy of her country
The resentment of a rupture with the brother~

The author of the tale *The Modern Warning*, James is a consummate author. His imagined Englishman is not altogether such, since his full-scale book, *The Modern Warning*, remains unconsummated.

The Notebook initiation has its sombre pleasures, for instance in speaking of 'a source of *funeste* warning'. (Could the story have borne *The Funeste Warning?*) Then there is a lighter lurking: 'He falls in love with an American Girl and she with him—this of course to be made natural if possible.' One knows what he means. As with that sly gallicizing of the American Girl's all-American anti-English brother as 'an *anglophobiste*'.

At this stage, the tale bore no title. When first published in *Harper's New Monthly Magazine* (June 1888), it was *Two Countries*, opening more widely than had *A Tale of Two Cities*.[7] James's tale opens in Italy, with the catchment proving to be of more than two countries, in that it addresses Two Continents. A Grand Tour, in its way, with some sense of 'the Hero' or the mock-hero, 'the young Aeneas':

> Intrepid then, o'er seas and lands he flew,
> Europe he saw, and Europe saw him too
>
> (*The Dunciad*, iv. 289, 293–4, 335)

To T. S. Eliot, writing in the wake of James's death ('In Memory'), 'It is the final perfection, the consummation of an American to become, not an Englishman, but a European—something which no born European, no person of any European nationality, can become.'[8] The American author of *The American* (1879), who was also the European author of *The Europeans* (1878), published *Italian Hours* but not *The Italian*, and *A Little Tour of France* but not *The Frenchman*. As for *The Englishman* . . .

—————

thinks them a con tamination'. Below: 'Sir Rufus personally did not like the United States: he did not like them yet he made an immense effort to behave as if he did.')

7. As *The Modern Warning*, it appeared, later in 1888, in the company of *The Aspern Papers*.
8. *The Egoist* (January 1918).

The word 'modern' has for ages acted by way of a warning, as in the Augustan satires by Soame Jenyns, *The Modern Fine Gentleman* (1746) and *The Modern Fine Lady* (1751), and the Victorian sonnet-sequence by Meredith, *Modern Love* (1862). As for 'warning', the immediate question to put to James's tale is 'Warning against what, exactly?' Not only is this the first question, it continues, throughout the story, to be the foremost one. The very title functions both for the tale and within it. *The Modern Warning* tells of the writing by the Englishman of a book that excoriates America: *The Modern Warning*. The warning is not single but manifold. For one thing it is a warning against supposing that there is only one thing that needs to be warned against. But then the immediate feeling that the title is biding its time before becoming actively fissiparous is there in the simple dual fact that a modern warning might be our being warned by the modern or warned against it. James enjoys all such discomfiture.

Here is a possible proliferation:

A warning against the modern. [Or against the ancient.]

Against the United States of America. [Or against England, come to that. Or Europe.]

Against democracy. [Or against aristocracy as against plutocracy.]

Against expatriation. [Or against there being No place like home.]

Against credulity about expatriation. [Or against cynicism about it.]

Against marrying someone of a different nationality. [Or against national inbreeding.]

Against marrying a writer. [Or against a writer's marrying.]

Against brothers. [Or siblings. Or against gullibility about the brotherhood of man. Or the sisterhood of woman.]

Against supposing you could always go back. [Or never. Or against others' supposing either of these.]

Against marrying an Englishman. [Or an American, come again to that. Or against marrying at all.]

Obituaries used to say, darkly: *He never married.* This would include such as Henry James. On the other hands, an obituary of the Cambridge man of letters, Hugh Sykes Davies, said of him that he had several wives, *some of them his own.* It was left to Saul Bellow to grant that he was a serial marrier.

Then there is the possibility of a warning against the mistake that most men most make, or against the one that most women most make. The tendency is for a man to be happy in the thought that the woman should not change and fortunately will not, and a woman in the thought that the man should change and fortunately will.

It matters that the word 'warning' lurks (twice in the story) before being given as the title of Sir Rufus's book, though from the first the context is national prejudice or preconception. Agatha is politic about Sir Rufus's prejudice (as is James, with his sequence 'she could make him like the people' suggesting for a split second a conceivable-albeit-impossible similitude, assimilation, and then at once moving on to mere amiability):[9]

Somehow, by showing him how nice she was herself she could make him like the people better with whom she had so much in common, and as he admitted that his observation of them had after all been very restricted she would also make him know them better. This prospect drew her on till suddenly her brother sounded the note of warning. When it came she understood it perfectly; she could not pretend that she did not. If she were not careful she would give her country away: in the privacy of her own room she had coloured up to her hair at the thought.

~By showing him how nice she was herself
She would also make him know them better~

In giving her hand, being given away in marriage, would she be giving her country away, in the double sense that *betray* can similarly possess?[10] 'That was the only fashion, as yet, in which Lady Chasemore had given away her brother to her husband.'

~Had given away her brother to her husband~

Sir Rufus, too, had sounded—plumbed—the note of warning:

He looked at her as if he saw some warning in her face and continued: 'Excuse my going so far. In this last month that we have spent together so happily for me I had almost forgotten that you are one of them.'
Lady Chasemore said nothing—she did not deny that she was one of them.

9. Robert Lowell ('Cal' to his intimates) asks in *Caligula*: 'Tell me what I saw | to make me like you'. His expatriation and his marriages constitute something of a post-modern warning.
10. 'The Question of Our Speech', 40: 'What we least desire to do with these things is to give them, in our happy phrase, "away;" and we must allow that if this be none the less what has really happened in our case the reason for the disaster resides in the seemingly overwhelming (for the time at least) forces of betrayal.'

~As if he saw some warning in her face
Almost forgotten that you are one of them~

Yet, does not her having become the very non-American thing, un-
American thing even, Lady Chasemore, signal that she is no longer
altogether one of them?

These two instances of 'warning' may take up the title of James's
story but they precede any mention of Sir Rufus's book. A later sounding—
of the cognate form, to *warn her off*—occurs at the sight of the proofs
of the book, lying there. 'On the table, in their neat little packet, they
seemed half to solicit her, half to warn her off.' Not only the modern
warning then, but a modern solicitation.

~Half to solicit her, half to warn her off~

James's *The Modern Warning* does not concur with Sir Rufus's *The
Modern Warning*, for the story establishes that even while James (the
author, twenty years later, of *The American Scene*) knows what Sir Rufus
means, there is a great deal wrong with the pleasure that Sir Rufus
takes in repudiation, in his flourishing 'a vivid warning', and in his having the word *master* be only a word away from the word *subject*, 'master
the subject', not innocuously at all:[11]

It turned out that the opinion he had formed of the order of society in the
United States was even less favourable than she had had reason to fear. There
were not many things it would have occurred to him to commend, and
the few exceptions related to the matters that were not most characteristic of
the country—not idiosyncrasies of American life. The idiosyncrasies he had
held to be one and all detestable. The whole spectacle was a vivid warning, a
consummate illustration of the horrors of democracy. The only thing that had
saved the misbegotten republic as yet was its margin, its geographical vastness;
but that was now discounted and exhausted. For the rest every democratic
vice was in the ascendant and could be studied there *sur le vif*; he could not be
too thankful that he had not delayed longer to go over and master the subject.
He had come back with a head full of lessons and a heart fired with the

---

11. Within Agatha's exchange with her brother, *slave* is followed by *master*.

To this Agatha replied:

'Ah, you see, Englishmen are like that. They expect women to be so much honoured by their wanting them to do anything. And it must always be what *they* like, of
course.'

'What the men like? Well, that's all right, only they mustn't be Englishmen,' said
Macarthy Grice.

'Oh, if one is going to be a slave I don't know that the nationality of one's master
matters!' his sister exclaimed.

resolve to enforce them upon his own people, who, as Agatha knew, had begun to move in the same lamentable direction.

~The whole spectacle was a vivid warning~

Thinking of her brother, Agatha knew that what was at issue was not exactly his reading the book. 'He would never read *The Modern Warning* but he would hear all about it.' Judge then of her relief when Sir Rufus thinks better of the whole business. Or does at any rate capitulate:

He remarked to her that clearly he must simply give way to her opposition. If she were going to suffer so inordinately it settled the question. The book should not be published and they would say no more about it. He would put it away, he would burn it up and *The Modern Warning* should be as if it had never been. Amen! amen!

~He would put it away, he would burn it up~

He would not suffer the book to be published if it would make her suffer so inordinately. In an oratorio, *Amen! amen!* may be truly (albeit repetitively) conclusive, but *so inordinately* does keep ordinately in play Sir Rufus's opposition to her opposition. She finds that her very gratitude to him becomes her undoing, and his, not least because she craves his being grateful to her.

She had been in love with Sir Rufus from the day he sought her hand at Cadenabbia, but she was never so much in love with him as during the weeks that immediately followed his withdrawal of his book. It was agreed between them that neither of them would speak of the circumstance again, but she at least, in private, devoted an immense deal of meditation to it. It gave her a tremendous reprieve, lifted a nightmare off her breast, and that in turn gave her freedom to reflect that probably few men would have made such a graceful surrender. She wanted him to understand, or at any rate she wanted to understand herself, that in all its particulars too she thoroughly appreciated it; if he really was unable to conceive how she could feel as she did, it was all the more generous of him to comply blindly, to take her at her word, little as he could make of it. It did not become less obvious to Lady Chasemore, but quite the contrary, as the weeks went on, that *The Modern Warning* would have been a masterpiece of its class.

~Would have been a masterpiece of its class~

But a visit to London from New York by her brother is imminent.

Suddenly, illogically, fantastically, she could not have told why, at that moment and in that place, for she had had no such intention when she came into the room, she broke out: 'My own darling, do you know what has come over me?

I have changed entirely—I see it differently; I want you to publish that grand thing.' And she stood there smiling at him, expressing the transformation of her feeling so well that he might have been forgiven for not doubting it.

Nevertheless he did doubt it, especially at first. But she repeated, she pressed, she insisted; once she had spoken in this sense she abounded and overflowed. It went on for several days (he had begun by refusing to listen to her, for even in touching the question she had violated his express command), and by the end of a week she persuaded him that she had really come round. She was extremely ingenious and plausible in tracing the process by which she had done so, and she drew from him the confession (they kissed a great deal after it was made) that the manuscript of *The Modern Warning* had not been destroyed at all, but was safely locked up in a cabinet, together with the interrupted proofs.

~Do you know what has come over me?
(They kissed a great deal after it was made)
Safely locked up in a cabinet
Together with the interrupted proofs~

Confessionally intimate, the kisses are tucked up in passing within their little lip-like moons (their *lunulae*, Erasmus's word for round brackets—but are these decrescent or crescent, waning or waxing?) The whole story lives along these lines of punctuational precision, and James always makes great play, grim play, with any such moment as occurs midway through a sentence whose parentheses establish it as double-dealing, having the air of an aside but the weight of a crux. Sir Rufus

was prepared to ask if she on her side recollected giving him notice that she should convert him into an admirer of transatlantic peculiarities. She had had an excellent opportunity, but she had not carried out her plan. He had been passive in her hands, she could have done what she liked with him (had he not offered, that night by the lake of Como, to throw up his career and go and live with her in some beastly American town? and he had really meant it—upon his honour he had!), so that if the conversion had not come off whose fault was it but hers?

There is all the difference in the world between James's sequence—'she could have done what she liked with him (had he not offered··· upon his honour he had!) so that if···'—and a feasible punctuation that would have signalled something markedly other, the gloves off, an ungentlemanly throwing down of the velvet glove from the iron hand: 'she could have done what she liked with him. Had he not offered, that night · · · upon his honour he had!' No, such a full stop before *Had he not*, with its pomp and circumstance, is not how Sir Rufus would have conducted his defence. James had earlier unfolded a sequence of such parentheses, a sequence that is more than a mere *tour de force* because it realizes so movingly the heroic efforts that Agatha makes:

For she had to make up her mind to this, that after all (it was vain to shut one's eyes to it) Sir Rufus personally did not like the United States: he did not like them yet he made an immense effort to behave as if he did. She was grateful to him for that; it assuaged her nervousness (she was afraid there might be 'scenes' if he should break out with some of his displeasures); so grateful that she almost forgot to be disappointed at the failure of her own original intent, to be distressed at seeing or rather at guessing (for he was reserved about it even to her), that a nearer view of American institutions had not had the effect which she once promised herself a nearer view should have. She had married him partly to bring him over to an admiration of her country (she had never told any one this, for she was too proud to make the confidence to an English person and if she had made it to an American the answer would have been so prompt, 'What on earth does it signify what he thinks of it?' no one, of course, being obliged to understand that it might signify to *her*); she had united herself to Sir Rufus in this missionary spirit and now not only did her proselyte prove unamenable but the vanity of her enterprise became a fact of secondary importance.

~(It was vain to shut one's eyes to it)
An immense effort to behave as if he did
(Understand that it might signify to her)~

It was not that the national prejudices had dawned on them only slowly. What further dawned, too late, was that the matter could not rest a source of banter, of badinage, as 'the Englishman' can for a while take it to be. Agatha had remonstrated, but she had been helpless against his drollery, his making light of any dark thoughts.

'You may laugh at me or you may despise me,' she said when she could speak, 'and I daresay my state of mind is deplorably narrow. But I couldn't be happy with you if you hated my country.'

'You would hate mine back and we should pass the liveliest, jolliest days!' returned the Englishman, gratified, softened, enchanted by her tears. 'My dear girl, what is a woman's country? It's her house and her garden, her children and her social world. You exaggerate immensely the difference which that part of the business makes. I assure you that if you were to marry me it would be the last thing you would find yourself thinking of. However, to prove how little I hate your country I am perfectly willing to go there and live with you.'

'Oh, Sir Rufus Chasemore!' murmured Agatha Grice, protestingly.

'You don't believe me?'

She believed him not a bit and yet to hear him make such an offer was sweet to her, for it gave her a sense of the reality of his passion. 'I shouldn't ask that—I shouldn't even like it,' she said; and then he wished to know what she would like.

~And we should pass the liveliest, jolliest days!
Gratified, softened, enchanted by her tears
My dear girl, what is a woman's country?
A sense of the reality of his passion
I shouldn't ask that—I shouldn't even like it
And then he wished to know what she would like~

In obdurately due course, the story *The Modern Warning* moves to its tragic end. His hating her country? 'I assure you that if you were to marry me it would be the last thing you would find yourself thinking of.' Such it would indeed prove to be, the last thing she would find herself thinking of as she killed herself.

Her brother would never read *The Modern Warning*. But then nor would the public, at any rate for the duration of this war, the duration of a story of which the pages close with this:

The Modern Warning has not yet been published, but it may still appear. This doubtless will depend upon whether, this time, the sheets have really been destroyed—buried in Lady Chasemore's grave or only put back into the cabinet.

~The Modern Warning has not yet been published~

In not yet having been published, *The Modern Warning* is not to be mistaken for *The Modern Warning*.

Agatha had colluded with Sir Rufus and his amiable protestations; we can and should sympathize with her but this should not melt into such sentimentality as would exclaim that in criticizing her we are *blaming the victim*. Victims are often blameworthy, in varying degrees and in ways quite other than the blame attaching to the victimizer. In any case, Agatha is not a woman of the kind that James was inclined to be solicitous of, for all his authentic sympathy.

What he had said about a woman's country being her husband and children, her house and garden and visiting list, was very considerably verified; for it was certain that her ladyship's new career gave her, though she had no children, plenty of occupation. Even if it had not however she would have found a good deal of work to her hand in loving her husband, which she continued to do with the most commendable zeal. He seemed to her a very magnificent person, bullying her not half so much as she expected. There were times when it even occurred to her that he really did not bully her enough, for she had always had an idea that it would be agreeable to be subjected to this probation by someone she should be very fond of.

The phrase 'commendable zeal' is not a sarcasm, for it does not mean merely the opposite of what it says; it is an irony and is the occasion for neither simple commendation nor simple condemnation.[12] She is genuinely to be commended for a certain generosity of spirit, after all. James knows how resourceful, in their contrariety of impulse, are the words *after all*:

and as he admitted that his observation of them had after all been very restricted she would also make him know them better.

He was very glad after all, because for several days he had been wanting to speak.

For she had to make up her mind to this, that after all (it was vain to shut one's eyes to it) Sir Rufus personally did not like the United States.

—that was an irregularity which was after all shut up in her own breast, where she could trust her dignity to get some way or other the upper hand of it.

But after all it was not very easy to say how Macarthy would have preferred that a stranger, or that Sir Rufus in particular, should take the great republic.

Even if a woman's country were her husband and children, her house and garden and visiting list, it remains the case that an Englishman's home is his castle. It is far from clear that an American woman's home is her castle even if she does come to live in a land where an Englishman's castle may be his home. At which point it is as well to remember the range of meanings that the verb *to expatriate* had long borne.

12. William Empson: 'An irony has no point unless it is true, in some degree, in both senses' (*Some Versions of Pastoral*, 56). As when James effects a great deal with the three words 'not altogether unjust', in contrasting Macarthy's English with that of the Englishman Sir Rufus: 'Macarthy, who spoke very slowly, with great distinctness and in general with great correctness, was annoyed not only by his companion's intonation but by the odd and, as it seemed to him, licentious application that he made of certain words. He struck him as wanting in reverence for the language, which Macarthy had an idea, not altogether unjust, that he himself deeply cherished.' Not altogether expected, this justice to Macarthy and to one branch of American English-speakers. Yet it is hearteningly consonant with James's own reverence for the language, in 'The Question of Our Speech'.

1. (trans.) To drive a person away from his native country; to banish.
2. (refl.) (rarely intrans. for refl.) To withdraw from one's native country; in the Law of Nations, to renounce one's citizenship or allegiance.

expatriation
1. The banishing of a person from his own country; the state of being banished; banishment, exile.
2. The action of leaving one's country for another; emigration. Also, in the Law of Nations, renunciation of one's country.

What now is the standard sense (the only current sense?) of the noun *expatriate* had to wait until the *OED*'s Supplement of 1972, where it was ineptly defined: 'In modern usage, a person who lives in a foreign country.' (Actually a great many people who are not expatriates live in a foreign country.) The pressure of the less modern senses is felt in James's nineteenth-century world, alive to the charge that accompanies banishment, exile, or the renunciation of one's citizenship or one's allegiance or one's country. Agatha, in the inflamed eyes of her brother, is in these darker ways an expatriate, an ex-patriot. It was to be a successor of James, an American turned Englishman (is that a coat that one hears being turned?), who wrote in 1931:

The American intellectual of to-day has almost no chance of continuous development upon his own soil and in the environment which his ancestors, however humble, helped to form. He must be an expatriate: either to languish in a provincial university, or abroad, or, the most complete expatriation of all, in New York. And he is merely a more manifest example of what *tends* to happen in all countries. (T. S. Eliot, *The Criterion*, April 1931)

Agatha had in a way been warned, and she had known this but had been powerless in the face of Sir Rufus's touching, not only her heart, but her face with his breath:

He was very glad after all, because for several days he had been wanting to speak. He loved her as he had never loved any woman and he besought her earnestly to believe it. What was this crude stuff about disliking the English and disliking the Americans? what had questions of nationality to do with it any more than questions of ornithology? It was a question simply of being his wife, and that was rather between themselves, was it not? He besought her to consider it, as *he* had been turning it over from almost the first hour he met her. It was not in Agatha's power to go her way now, because he had laid his hand upon her in a manner that kept her motionless, and while he talked to her in low, kind tones, touching her face with the breath of supplication, she stood there in the warm darkness, very pale, looking as if she were listening to a threat of injury rather than a declaration of love.

~He besought her earnestly to believe it
And while he talked to her in low, kind tones
Touching her face with the breath of supplication
She stood there in the warm darkness, very pale
Listening to a threat of injury~

Her brother's urging to her that 'the very breath of Sir Rufus's nostrils was the denial of human equality' proved no match for 'touching her face with the breath of supplication'. Meanwhile James is his precise self here within the sequence of three question-marks: since the first and second questions are indeflectibly cognate, the second one must not begin with a capital letter such as would slow down the impetus:

What was this crude stuff about disliking the English and disliking the Americans? what had questions of nationality to do with it any more than questions of ornithology? It was a question simply of being his wife, and that was rather between themselves, was it not?[13]

There she is, 'looking as if she were listening to a threat of injury rather than a declaration of love': and so she was, she was, with James aware that a declaration of love always carries within it the possibility of a threat of injury.

Her brother, who in these matters is all repugnance and oppugnancy, is the more hostile because, although his sister cannot but be special for him, she is by no means a special case. 'It was not unknown to Macarthy that the repugnance in question appeared to be confined to the American male, as was shown by a thousand international marriages, which had transplanted as many of his countrywomen to unnatural British homes.' Fortunately and unfortunately, Agatha is aware that there are unlovely and unloving impulses within Macarthy, even as James's story is aware of a long tradition that seeks to warn sisters against brothers, especially when it comes to marriage. Lady Chasemore, a distant relation of the Duchess of Malfi, says of her bachelor-brother:

'It sometimes seems to me as if he didn't marry on purpose to make me feel badly.'

---

13. Later, tragically, there are the cognate question-marks and the lower-case 'ah' in her cry: 'How could you? ah, how *could* you?'

That was the only fashion, as yet, in which Lady Chasemore had given away her brother to her husband. The words fell from her lips some five years after Macarthy's visit to the lake of Como—two years after her mother's death—a twelvemonth after her marriage. The same idea came into her mind—a trifle whimsically perhaps, only this time she forbore to express it—as she stood by her husband's side, on the deck of the steamer, half an hour before they reached the wharf at New York.

~The same idea came into her mind~

When they went ashore and drove home with Macarthy Agatha received exactly the impression she had expected: her brother's life struck her as bare, ungarnished, helpless, socially and domestically speaking. He had not the art of keeping house, naturally, and in New York, unless one were a good deal richer than he, it was very difficult to do that sort of thing by deputy. But Lady Chasemore made no further allusion to the idea that he remained single out of perversity. The situation was too serious for that or for any other flippant speech.

~Exactly the impression she had expected
The situation was too serious for that
Or for any other flippant speech~

There in New York, Macarthy is briefly pleased 'to see that she enjoyed her native air and her temporary reunion with some of her old familiars. This was a graceful inconsistency on his part: it showed that he had not completely given her up. Perhaps he thought Sir Rufus would die and that in this case she would come back and live in New York. She was careful not to tell him that such a calculation was baseless, that with or without Sir Rufus she should never be able to settle in her native city as Lady Chasemore.'

~To see that she enjoyed her native air~

It is not exactly that she should never be able to settle in her native city, as that she should never be able to do so *as Lady Chasemore*. 'She was well aware that there were many things in English life that she should not like, and she was never a more passionate American than the day she married Sir Rufus Chasemore.' But it never feels as though being her ladyship was one of the many things in English life that she did not like. To revert to being Agatha Grice would be out of the question. ('"Oh, Sir Rufus Chasemore!" murmured Agatha Grice, protestingly.') The ladyship is at once an inclusion and a precluding, as it will prove to be in *What Maisie Knew* when Ida Farange marries Sir Claude, titularly. Agatha even contemplates a promotion, an ascent to a higher order of ladyship, the wife of a lord. We are told of a promotion for Sir Rufus: 'This gave Lady Chasemore an opportunity to reflect that she might some day be a peeress · · · She was obliged to admit to herself that the reflection was unattended with any sense of horror; it exhilarated her indeed to the point of making her smile at the contingency of Macarthy's finding himself the brother of a member of the aristocracy'.

~Unattended with any sense of horror
A member of the aristocracy~

The narration is markedly even. ('He talked with no one, for the Americans seemed to him all taken up with each other and the English all taken up with themselves.') Neither of the Two Countries enjoys a monopoly of self-deception. One warning about Macarthy might question the authenticity of his political convictions.

Sir Rufus was plainly an agent of the British government, the head of some kind of department or sub-department. This did not make Macarthy like him any better. He was displeased with the idea of England's possessing colonies at all and considered that she had acquired them by force and fraud and held them by a frail and unnatural tenure. It appeared to him that any man who occupied a place in this unrighteous system must have false, detestable views.[14]

~England's possessing colonies at all~

It is then a shrewd stroke on James's part to have Sir Rufus reach for the terms of empire, imperial English because not native to the English, when he assures Agatha that he has done his best to placate Macarthy: 'I should like to show him I like him, and I have salaamed and kowtowed to him whenever I had a chance; but he won't let me get near him.'[15] But you don't get *liked* by salaaming and kowtowing. Anyway,

---

14. Rebekah Scott pointed out the cardinal echo of Hobbes, or of those who have echoed Hobbes: 'force, and fraud, are in war the two cardinal virtues' (*Leviathan*, part I, ch. 13).
15. Similarly within Sir Rufus's expostulation to Agatha: 'One tells a girl one adores her and she replies that she doesn't care so long as one doesn't adore her compatriots. What do you want me to do to them? What do you want me to say? I will say anything in the English language, or in the American, that you like. I'll say that they're the greatest of the great and have every charm and virtue under heaven. I'll go down on my stomach before them and remain there for ever. I can't do more than that!'

~I'll say that they're the greatest of the great
And have every charm and virtue under heaven~

Macarthy is not to be placated, is implacable. He would be right to judge that Sir Rufus's insouciance in the face of Macarthy's dislike is merely another form of insolence. Agatha may try to reassure Sir Rufus: "'It's not directed to you in particular, any dislike he may have. I have told you before that he doesn't like the English,"Agatha remarked.' But he: 'Bless me—no more do I! But my best friends have been among them.' As for Toryism:

> It gave Macarthy a kind of palpitation to think that his sister had been in danger of associating herself with such arrogant doctrines. Not that a woman's political creed mattered; but that of her husband did. He had an impression that he himself was a passionate democrat, an unshrinking radical.

~It gave Macarthy a kind of palpitation
A passionate democrat, an unshrinking radical~

Not that Agatha, for her part, is either deceived or self-deceived when confronted by her brother's insistences as to democracy.

> He hoped she had measured in advance the strain that might arise from the fact that in so many ways her good would be his evil, her white his black and *vice versâ*—the fact in a word that by birth, tradition, convictions, she was the product of a democratic society, while the very breath of Sir Rufus's nostrils was the denial of human equality. She had replied, 'Oh yes, I have thought of everything;' but in reality she had not thought that she was in any very aggressive manner a democrat or even that she had a representative function. She had not thought that Macarthy in his innermost soul was a democrat either; and she had even wondered what would happen if in regard to some of those levelling theories he had suddenly been taken at his word.

~So many ways her good would be his evil~[16]

But there remains a related warning, not only to Macarthy but to his sister, and it has to do with their playing the Irish race card (whereupon Sir Rufus will play such a card of his own, being of Ascendancy descent). She:

> 'I have told you before that we are of Irish descent, on my mother's side. Her mother was a Macarthy. We have kept up the name and we have kept up the feeling.'
> 'I see—so that even if the Yankee were to let me off the Paddy would come down! That's a most unholy combination. But you remember, I hope, what I have also told you—that I am quite as Irish as you can ever be. I had an Irish grandmother—a beauty of beauties, a certain Lady Laura Fitzgibbon.'

16. Michael Prince pointed out that 'Agatha' is etymologically 'good'.

~If the Yankee were to let me off
A most unholy combination
I am quite as Irish as you can ever be~

The future Lady Chasemore is not persuaded except in the sense that
she persuades herself that marriage to Sir Rufus will prove a most holy
combination. In time, this all becomes comically ugly, when she chooses
to excite herself and he chooses to lapse into bland condescension:

She was far from being a fanatic on this subject, as he knew; but when America
was made out to be an object of holy horror to virtuous England she could
not but remember that millions of her Celtic cousins had found refuge there
from the blessed English dispensation and be struck with his recklessness in
challenging comparisons which were better left to sleep.

When his wife began to represent herself as Irish Sir Rufus evidently
thought her 'off her head' indeed: it was the first he had heard of it since she
communicated the mystic fact to him on the lake of Como. Nevertheless he
argued with her for half an hour as if she were sane, and before they parted
he made her a liberal concession, such as only a perfectly lucid mind would
be able to appreciate.

Namely, 'The book should not be published and they would say no
more about it.'

It is infidelity that this story of married love most turns upon.
There is the matter of Lady Chasemore's dread both of being and of
seeming unfaithful to her country. In her sense of all this, she is not
her brother Macarthy by a long shot, but she is never out of range of
his outrage.

Fraternal tenderness in Macarthy's bosom followed a different logic. He was
so fond of his sister that he had a secret hope that she would never marry at
all. He had spoken otherwise to his mother, because that was the only way not
to seem offensively selfish; but the essence of his thought was that on the day
Agatha should marry she would throw him over. On the day she should marry
an Englishman she would not throw him over——she would betray him. That
is she would betray her country, and it came to the same thing. Macarthy's
patriotism was of so intense a hue that to his own sense the national life and
his own life flowed in an indistinguishable current.

~Hope that she would never marry at all
He had spoken otherwise to his mother
She would not throw him over—she would betray him~

Believing as he does 'that she had in a manner almost immoral deserted
him for the sake of an English title', Macarthy

regarded her marriage as an abjuration, an apostasy, a kind of moral treachery. It was of no use to say to him that she was doing nothing original or extraordinary, to ask him if he did not know that in England, at the point things had come to, American wives were as thick as blackberries, so that if she were doing wrong she was doing wrong with—well, almost the majority; for he had an answer to such cheap arguments, an answer according to which it appeared that the American girls who had done what she was about to do were notoriously poor specimens, the most frivolous and feather-headed young persons in the country.

~American wives were as thick as blackberries~

Even when it might briefly seem that Macarthy had 'accepted his sister's perfidious alliance', the very wording seethes, thick as thieves, with 'perfidious alliance' only just swerving from *perfidious Albion*.

Then there is the matter of Sir Rufus's infidelity, and whether, in yielding to his wife's susceptibilities, he is unfaithful not only to his political convictions but to his writerly duty. He is perturbed by this thought, and Agatha is more than perturbed by it, she is racked. For she comes to think of herself as a *femme fatale*, and her figure of speech cuts a sorry figure.

He was one more in the long list of those whom a woman had ruined, who had sold themselves, sold their honour and the commonwealth, for a fair face, a quiet life, a show of tears, a bribe of caresses. The vision of this smothered pain, which he tried to carry off as a gentleman should, only ministered to the love she had ever borne him—the love that had had the power originally to throw her into his arms in the face of an opposing force. As month followed month all her nature centred itself in this feeling; she loved him more than ever and yet she had been the cause of the most tormenting thing that had ever happened to him. This was a tragic contradiction, impossible to bear, and she sat staring at it with tears of rage.

~Sold their honour and the commonwealth~

(So convincing a surprise, the last word, above: *rage*.) Her thought of 'those whom a woman had ruined' is morbid and extravagant, and it abets his own figure of speech and its toying with an amatory story:

Sir Rufus was immensely taken up with the resumption of his task; the revision of his original pages went forward the more rapidly that in fact, though his wife was unaware of it, they had repeatedly been in his hands since he put them away. He had retouched and amended them, by the midnight lamp, disinterestedly, platonically, hypothetically; and the alterations and improvements which suggest themselves when valuable ideas are laid by to ripen, like a row of pears on a shelf, started into life and liberty. Sir Rufus was as happy as a man who after having been obliged for a long time to entertain a passion in secret finds it recognised and legitimated, finds that the obstacles are removed and he may conduct his beloved to the altar.

> ~To ripen, like a row of pears on a shelf
> Started into life and liberty
> He may conduct his beloved to the altar~

Such cadences do themselves entertain a passion in secret, as (surprisingly, given the delicacy) George Bernard Shaw heard when he attributed Shakespearean delineation of character to 'the turn of the line, which lets you into the secret of its utterer's mood and temperament, not by its commonplace meaning, but by some subtle exaltation, or stultification, or slyness, or delicacy, or hesitancy, or what not in the sound of it'.[17]

Sir Rufus loves his pages 'platonically', perhaps, but only perhaps, given such turns of phrase as 'though his wife was unaware of it', 'his hands', 'retouched', and his 'passion in secret'. This is the writer's itch, and it surreptitiously scratches the American constitutional enterprise in its sequence 'into life and liberty · · · as happy'. Is each of them, husband and wife, making a Declaration of Independence? 'Life, liberty and the pursuit of happiness.'[18]

It is the complementarity, or even the collusion, of Sir Rufus and Agatha that leads her to think of *The Modern Warning* in such terms on this same page: 'It was his affair altogether now.' Infidelity in love comes to stain the story, and this with the sad assistance of the great observers of jealousy and broken faith. Iago, among them.

> Trifles light as ayre,
> Are to the jealious, confirmations strong,
> As proofes of holy Writ.   (*Othello*, III. iii)

'She tried to teach herself that her suspicions were woven of air and were an offence to a just man's character.'

---

17. *Our Theatres in the Nineties*, i. 26 (2 February 1895).
18. The wording of the Declaration, from Jefferson on, had itself 'repeatedly' undergone 'revision' of its 'original pages · · · retouched and amended' with 'alterations and improvements which suggest themselves when valuable ideas are laid by to ripen'. In this, the Declaration of Independence evokes not only Sir Rufus's but James's own writings and their declarations of independence, including independence of earlier published authorized states.

She thought there had been no change, but now she suspected that there was at least a difference. She had read Tennyson and she knew the famous phrase about the little rift within the lute.

The allusion to *Merlin and Vivien* from *Idylls of the King* invites widening beyond the famous phrase.

> 'In Love, if Love be Love, if Love be ours,
> Faith and unfaith can ne'er be equal powers:
> Unfaith in aught is want of faith in all.
>
> 'It is the little rift within the lute
> That by and by will make the music mute,
> And ever widening slowly silence all.
>
> 'The little rift within the lover's lute
> Or little pitted speck in garner'd fruit,
> That rotting inward slowly moulders all.
>
> 'It is not worth the keeping: let it go:
> But shall it? answer, darling, answer, no.
> And trust me not at all or all in all.'

Laid by to ripen like a row of pears on a shelf, but now there is the little pitted speck in garner'd fruit.

Her pain when she reads the proofs of *The Modern Warning* (proofs that are a test, a probation, of the love of each of them and of both of them) is at one with the pain of a wife wronged by a husband's infidelity.

She stopped when he entered and stood there looking at him; she was in her dressing-gown, very pale, and she received him without a smile. He went up to her, kissed her, saw something strange in her eyes and asked with eagerness if she had been suffering.

'Yes, yes,' she said, 'but I have not been ill,' and the next moment flung herself upon his neck and buried her face there, sobbing yet at the same time stifling her sobs. Inarticulate words were mingled with them and it was not till after a moment he understood that she was saying, 'How could you? ah, how *could* you?' He failed to understand her allusion, and while he was still in the dark she recovered herself and broke away from him.

~'Yes, yes,' she said, 'but I have not been ill'
Yet at the same time stifling her sobs
She recovered herself and broke away from him~

He failed to understand her allusion because it sounded ('How could you? ah, how *could* you?') for all the world like an accusation of something quite other. ('He had by this time become aware that even though she had flung herself upon his breast his wife was animated by a spirit of the deepest reproach, an exquisite sense of injury.') As to any such form of infidelity as that, he had nothing with which to reproach himself. 'She took notice of two things: the first of which was that he had a perfectly good conscience and that no accusing eye that might have been turned upon him would have made him change colour. He had no sense that he had broken faith with her.'

~No sense that he had broken faith with her~

She poisons herself.

The concluding paragraph of the story insists on our hearing the doctor's voice which is careful only to intimate something (a bed*side* manner), not to accuse anyone.

Lady Chasemore had taken something—the doctor gave it a name—but it was not by mistake. In the hall, downstairs, he stood looking at Macarthy, kindly, soothingly, tentatively, with his hand on his shoulder. 'Had she—a— had she some domestic grief?' Macarthy heard him ask.

Yes, she had a domestic grief, but it was not of a divorce-court kind, and moreover it was more than domestic, it encompassed 'Two Countries'. Glimpsed from the closing words of the story, there remains the possibility of a further infidelity.

The Modern Warning has not yet been published, but it may still appear. This doubtless will depend upon whether, this time, the sheets have really been destroyed—buried in Lady Chasemore's grave or only put back into the cabinet.

Not that 'buried' would necessarily constitute having 'really been destroyed'. Dante Gabriel Rossetti changed his heart and then rifled the grave in which he had buried his poems.

On the night of 5 October 1869 Rossetti's friend Charles Augustus Howell and lawyer Henry Vertue Tebbs, with two hired workmen and medical witness Dr Williams, dug up the Rossetti family grave in the west section of Highgate Cemetery, opened the coffin of Gabriel's wife, and extracted the red-edged book of poems bound in rough grey calf tangled in her hair. She had been buried on 17 February 1862, after an inquest decided that her death by laudanum overdose (early on 11 February) was 'accidental', and not the suicide strongly suggested by Elizabeth having pinned a note to her gown (immediately destroyed).[19]

19. From Samantha Matthews, *Poetical Remains: Poets' Graves, Bodies, and Books in the Nineteenth Century* (Oxford, 2004), 20–1.

The Modern Warning is instinct with a warning that James came to issue to himself: he must not prove unfaithful either to America or to England. This self-addressed warning came home to him (after all, he was one of those on whom nothing is lost) when on 27 November 1894 he wrote to his French friend Urbain Mengin, who had been a French tutor in England, had now returned to France, and was teaching English at the Lycée d'Albi:[20]

This time you must keep well hold of your English—you must not give it up. You will find much to do with it—only you must *live* with it if you expect it to live with you. One's own language is one's mother, but the language one adopts, as a career, as a study, is one's wife, and it is with one's wife that *on se met en ménage*. English is a very faithful and well-conducted person, but she will expect you too not to commit infidelities. On these terms she will keep your house well.

Poor Macarthy had not had 'the art of keeping house, naturally', and 'it was very difficult to do that sort of thing by deputy'. True, the French language will always be happy to deputize on Henry James's behalf, and *on se met en ménage*. But not *en ménage à trois*. Not, please (once the mother has gone, she who had held family forces together and at bay), the freighted threesome of wife and brother and husband.

II. The Next Time

Henry James is known to account for his artistry both in prospect and in retrospect: the Notebooks can be looking forward, and in due course, the Prefaces to the New York Edition can look back. His story *The Next Time*, published in the *Yellow Book* in July 1895, is forecast in the Notebooks, though its author is as yet only 'SEMI-CONSCIENT' of the story's profound engagements:

January 26ᵗʰ, 1895. The idea of the poor man, the artist, the man of letters, who all his life is trying—if only to get a living—to do something *vulgar*, to take the measure of the huge, flat foot of the public: isn't there a little story in it, possibly, if one can animate it with an action; a little story that might perhaps be a mate to *The Death of the Lion*? It is suggested to me really by all the little backward memories of one's own frustrated ambition—in particular by its having just come back to me how, already 20 years ago, when I was in Paris writing letters to the *N.Y. Tribune*, Whitelaw Reid wrote to me to ask me virtually *that*—to make 'em baser and paltrier, to make them as vulgar as he could, to make them, as he called it, more 'personal.' Twenty years ago, and so it has been ever, till the other night, Jan. 5ᵗʰ, the *première* of *Guy Domville*. Trace the history of a charming little talent, charming artistic nature, that has been exactly the martyr and victim of that ineffectual effort, that long, vain study to take the measure above-mentioned, to 'meet' the vulgar need, to violate his intrinsic conditions, to make, as it were, a sow's ear out of a silk purse. He tries and he tries and he does what he thinks his coarsest and crudest. It's all of no use—it's always 'too subtle,' always too fine—never, never, vulgar enough. I had to write to Whitelaw Reid that the sort of thing I had already tried hard to do for the *Tribune* was the very worst I *could* do. I lost my place—my letters weren't wanted. A little drama, climax, a denouement, a small tragedy of the *vie littéraire*—mightn't one oppose to him some contrasted figure of another type—the creature who, dimly conscious of deep-seated vulgarity, is always trying to be refined, which doesn't in the least prevent him—or her—from succeeding. Say it's a woman. *She* succeeds—and she *thinks* she's fine! Mightn't *she* be the narrator, with a fine grotesque *inconscience*? So that the whole thing becomes a masterpiece of close and finished irony? There *may* be a difficulty in that—I seem to see it: so that the necessity may be for the narrator to be *conscient*, or SEMI-CONSCIENT, perhaps, to get the full force of certain efforts. The narrator at any rate, a person in the little drama who is trying bewilderedly the opposite line—working helplessly for fineness.[21]

~Trying bewilderedly the opposite line~

One remarks, first, the play upon *the poor man*[22] (pitied, and pitied specifically for needing the specie, the money); next, the six-times-repeated *little*, risking belittling. Then there is James's strong sense of being implicated in his story, his personal literary plight, urged as he had absurdly been by his editor to make his writings 'as vulgar as he [*not I*] could, to make them, as he called it, more "personal".' A personal involvement by our author, and yet James may be presumed to be putting some distance between his own powers and that charming little talent.

21. *The Complete Notebooks of Henry James*, 109–10. Robert B. Pippin seized 'the age of trash triumphant': 'The phrase is from the funniest account of his own failures as a popular writer and dramatist, "The Next Time," about James's own inability to write for the new reading public, to make a "sow's ear out of a silk purse"' (*Henry James and Modern Moral Life* (Cambridge, 2000), 33, 51).
22. The story has "poor' more than twenty times, with Limbert in the fore. Poor Ray Limbert, poor Limbert, poor Ralph, poor Ray, poor love, poor dear, poor duck, a poor man, as a poor man, poor man, 'The poor man'. The final 'poor': 'Poor Limbert in this long business always figured to me an undiscourageable parent to whom only girls kept being born.'

But as to the conscient, James's sketch was as yet inconscient of the fact that *The Next Time* is about rivalries not only literary but amatory, not unlike the combination within Shakespeare's sonnets. The two moments in the Notebooks that just might have intimated the amatory are concerned to do no such thing: *be a mate*, yes (but 'to *The Death of the Lion*'), and *frustrated*—here not thought of as erotic in the least. True, there will prove to be in the story a binary opposition: the literary vulgarian (a woman) whose books sell and are 'placed', oh dear yes, by James, is set against the man who fails to fail as an artist, and whose work proves incapable of being market-placed. [23] Yet the binary plot expands to the triangular: for there is the male narrator—a writer of a particular sort, a dark horse of another colour—up against those two further kinds of writer. And this triangle is paired with an eternal triangle: two men in competition for another woman. On this rivalry in love, the entry in the Notebooks is misleadingly silent. As is the later entry, 4 June 1895, which expatiates magnificently, over several pages, on the problems of just who the narrator should be and how he (no longer she?) might operate, all this without the faintest intimation that the narrator, if a he, might turn out to be an unsuccessful suitor, amorous of the woman while also being not only envious of his rival but cross-grainedly amorous of him too. [24] 'Our odd situation, that of the three of us.'

But then the same silence is later to be heard, so to speak, in the Preface. To jump from 1895 to 1908 is to find that the retrospective Preface, for all its air of the thoroughgoing, likewise limits itself to the plight of a writer unable to be vulgar enough, with the Preface actively disattending to the other story: the plight of two men in love with the same woman, with one of them enjoying—assuredly enjoying—the privilege of being the narrator of the other's story, personally telling it, first-personally, gloatingly, and with a double envy.

Like the Notebooks, the Preface pays no attention to this countervailing thrust within the story, and averts its eyes from half of this human fate. But then the Prefaces, bent upon the explanation of our writer's writing, must be expected to attend especially upon writers (as against lovers). James finds himself speaking of how some such plight

23. Within the story, there is Limbert's novel *The Major Key*: 'It converted readers into friends and friends into lovers; it placed the author, as the phrase is—placed him all too definitely; but it shrank to obscurity in the account of sales eventually rendered.'
24. *The Complete Notebooks of Henry James*, 123–5.

as Ray Limbert's 'had from far back insidiously beset the imagination of the author of "The Next Time"'.

One besetter of James's imagination in the stories and then in the Preface was a cadence:

Just so there are other talents that leave any fine appreciation mystified and gaping, and the active play of which may yet be observed to become on occasion a source of vast pecuniary profit. Nothing then is at moments more attaching··· to fix a bit exactly the point at which a beautiful talent, as I have called it, ceases, when imperilled by an empty pocket, to be a 'worldly' advantage···thus to become susceptible of much fine measurement···a straight dependence on the broad-backed public is a part of the issue···

> ~Appreciation mystified and gaping
> A source of vast pecuniary profit
> Nothing then is at moments more attaching
> A beautiful talent, as I have called it, ceases
> When imperilled by an empty pocket
> Susceptible of much fine measurement
> A straight dependence on the broad-backed public~

Much in the Preface is here for tears, but apparently nothing for tears such as lovers weep. The story, we are assured, 'is in essence a "story about the public"', not a story about the private too. Some of James's best critics have colluded with him in selling the story short.[25]

★ ★ ★

The story introduces us at once to the bestselling author: her name, Mrs Highmore, brings about the opening of the door, the narrator answering it: 'Mrs Highmore's errand this morning was odd enough to deserve commemoration: she came to ask me to write a notice of her great forthcoming work.' (There is not even the split-second wait of that supremely nominal Jamesian opening, 'She waited, Kate Croy, for her father to come in, but he kept her unconscionably···') Introduced as we immediately are to Mrs Highmore, and in no time to Ray Limbert—or rather to 'Poor Ray Limbert'—we are introduced more sustainedly to our narrator (whose name, in a story so alive with names, we are never to learn).[26] He is sardonic, precise, witty, happy to be

25. R. P. Blackmur, 'In the Country of the Blue' (1943), in *Studies in Henry James* (New York, 1983); quoted by Roger Gard in the volume he edited, *Henry James: The Critical Heritage* (1968), 540–1.
26. Some of the names: Minnie Meadows ('the new lady-humourist every one is talking about'); Mr Bousefield ('the proprietor of a "high-class monthly"'); Pat Moyle ——

disingenuous, and—when it comes to ways with words—expert. In short, he both is and is not Henry James. For a crucial element in the high art of this story is its constituting a manifestation not only of James's powers but of his further power to judge his own propensities and feats. The manner and movement of this first paragraph are delectable and insufferable, the very acumen acutely disconcerting in its being in both senses so superior.

Mrs Highmore's errand this morning was odd enough to deserve commemoration: she came to ask me to write a notice of her great forthcoming work. Her great works have come forth so frequently without my assistance that I was sufficiently entitled on this occasion to open my eyes; but what really made me stare was the ground on which her request reposed, and what leads me to record the incident is the train of memory lighted by that explanation. Poor Ray Limbert, while we talked, seemed to sit there between us: she reminded me that my acquaintance with him had begun, eighteen years ago, with her having come in precisely as she came in this morning to bespeak my charity for him. If she didn't know then how little my charity was worth she is at least enlightened about it to-day, and this is just the circumstance that makes the drollery of her visit. As I hold up the torch to the dusky years—by which I mean as I cipher up with a pen that stumbles and stops the figured column of my reminiscences—I see that Limbert's public hour, or at least my small apprehension of it, is rounded by those two occasions. It was *finis*, with a little moralising flourish, that Mrs Highmore seemed to trace to-day at the bottom of the page. 'One of the most voluminous writers of the time,' she has often repeated this sign; but never, I dare say, in spite of her professional command of appropriate emotion, with an equal sense of that mystery and that sadness of things which to people of imagination generally hover over the close of human histories. This romance at any rate is bracketed by her early and her late appeal; and when its melancholy protrusions had caught the declining light again from my half-hour's talk with her I took a private vow to recover while that light still lingers something of the delicate flush, to pick out with a brief patience the perplexing lesson.[27]

(a London correspondent: 'the problem offered to Ray Limbert was to try to be livelier than Pat Moyle'); 'poor Lady Robeck' (who 'secretly wrote for one of the papers)'; and of course Mrs Grundy.

27. *Embarrassments* (1896); text from *The Complete Tales of Henry James*, ed. Leon Edel, vol. 9 (London, 1964), 185–229. There were to be local revisions for the New York Edition (vol. xv 1909), a few of which are adduced here but none of which affects the present account—though Jamesians may enjoy the revision of 'I had made myself a little specialty of seeing nothing in certain celebrities ···', into 'I had cultivated the queer habit ···'. ('It's something else; one must find out *what* it is. Is it something awfully queer?—you blush!—something barely decent?')

~A notice of her great forthcoming work
What really made me stare was the ground
Memory lighted by that explanation
As I hold up the torch to the dusky years
Rounded by those two occasions
The most voluminous writers of the time
That mystery and that sadness of things
Over the close of human histories
With a brief patience the perplexing lesson~

The reader may well feel at once a chill and a burn. The fuse that runs from 'the *ground*' ('the singular ground', we are soon to learn is a matter of some heated feelings) to 'the *train* of memory *lighted* by that explanation' (with, later on, *the torch*) is one that refuses to let *lighted* remain solely a word of illumination, as against being touched with something more incendiary, heat as well as light. Memory, and particularly the memories of this doubly defeated rival of Limbert's, may be 'a line of gunpowder or other combustible substance laid so as to convey fire to a mine or charge for the purpose of exploding it'. *That explanation* of explosions, explodings (of reputation and of hopes), which lurk underground, just below the surface of this story about undermining. The Shakespearean funerary flourish of 'my small apprehension · · · rounded by those two occasions' ('and our little life | Is rounded with a sleep') is at once snug and smug, further rounded by the elegiac Virgilian satisfaction in 'that sadness of things'. Limbert, we divine, is dead, and is being mourned, in a way, in a way. Already, back then, the end is being intimated. (Geoffrey Madan, a great admirer of Henry James, was laconically allusive: 'The *Times* obituary department: emotion anticipated in tranquillity.'[28]) 'It was *finis*, with a little moralising flourish, that Mrs Highmore seemed to trace to-day at the bottom of the page.' Geoffrey Hill opened his poem 'The Imaginative Life' with the thought of such mortalities: 'Evasive souls, of whom the wise lose track, | Die in each night'. He finished the poem with dismay at all those easy bookish dismissals of the dead: 'As though the dead had *Finis* on their brows.'[29]

---

28. *Geoffrey Madan's Notebooks*, ed. J. A. Gere and John Sparrow (Oxford, 1981), 69. Wordsworth had written that poetry 'takes its origin from emotion recollected in tranquility'. (The author of the preface to *Lyrical Ballads* also wrote three *Essays upon Epitaphs*.)
29. A traditional figure of speech that had aspired to piety: 'for with two such names "in the forehead of the book" any edition must contain matter of value, whatever the shortcomings of the editor', C. H. Wilkinson, *The Poems of Richard Lovelace* (Oxford, 1925).

The arrival at the narrator's acknowledgement of the love-rivalry is effected by the dexterous transition, from the proem, to §I, where the story proper or improper may be not only held to begin but held to account. The proem had closed with pondering what was sure to be the latest bestseller from Jane Highmore (who is the sister of Maud, whom we are soon to meet): 'The book doesn't exist, and there's nothing in life to say about it. How can there be anything but the same old faithful rush for it?' At which point there succeeds—immediately and yet across the boundary signalled by the roman numeral for the ensuing section I—the answer not to this question but to a different one, about a different sense of the *faithful*:

This rush had already begun when, early in the seventies, in the interest of her prospective brother-in-law, she approached me on the singular ground of the unencouraged sentiment I had entertained for her sister. Pretty pink Maud had cast me out, but I appear to have passed in the flurried little circle for a magnanimous youth. Pretty pink Maud, so lovely then, before her troubles, that dusky Jane was gratefully conscious of all she made up for, Maud Stannace, very literary too, very languishing and extremely bullied by her mother, had yielded, invidiously as it might have struck me, to Ray Limbert's suit, which Mrs Stannace was not the woman to stomach.[30]

Our narrator half-reveals and half-conceals his own lacerations. There is the downplaying of his desire as 'the unencouraged sentiment I had entertained', and the downplaying of his desired one as 'Pretty pink Maud', at the head of two consecutive sentences, a turn of phrase to which he purringly returns yet again, for the third time in this one paragraph. He can caress (menace and caress) the cadence that envelops her, *taught to be flowerlike to every one*.[31] He will not lose composure, later in his telling, when he can call her by her maiden name, Maud Stannace, as life allows him to do for a while, but you can feel the queasy imbalance when he has to say '*The Major Key* in other words ran ever so long, and before it was half out Limbert and Maud had been married and the common household set up.' And the resentment

30. That strain again: ~which Mrs Stannace was not the woman to stomach~
31. Tennyson's *Maud*, with its rivalries in love, haunts James's story: 'and Maud looked pale and proud', as she had done in Tennyson. 'The deeper rose of Maud's little preparations' summons the rose cherished so often in the vicinity of Tennyson's Maud ('But the rose was awake all night for your sake'), even when she too is pale: 'a paleness, an hour's defect of the rose'. Tennyson's Maud, too, had been taught to be flowerlike to every one. (Her feet 'left the daisies rosy'; Tennyson: 'Because if you tread on the daisy, it turns up a rosy underside.')

becomes yet more palpable when he has to start acknowledging her as *Mrs Limbert*, with the gloating that is enviously audible in the moment that contemplates the household of the three of them, Limbert, Maud, and his mother-in-law:

Within doors and without Limbert's life was overhung by an awful region that figured in his conversation, comprehensively and with unpremeditated art, as Upstairs. It was Upstairs that the thunder gathered, that Mrs. Stannace kept her accounts and her state, that Mrs. Limbert had her babies and her head-aches, that the bells for ever jangled at the maids, that everything imperative in short took place—

> ~It was Upstairs that the thunder gathered
> That Mrs. Stannace kept her accounts and her state
> That Mrs. Limbert had her babies and her headaches
> That the bells for ever jangled at the maids
> That everything imperative in short
> Took place~

There is the nod to that unhappily-married romantic man, Shelley, with a premeditated use of his 'unpremeditated art' from *To a Skylark* —and so with a dark pun on 'strains': 'profuse strains'. No 'blithe Spirit!' here, and with Shelley's 'from Heaven or near it' replaced as the glowering 'Upstairs'. There is the doubled zeugma: Mrs Stannace keeping her accounts and her state, Mrs Limbert having her babies and her head-aches. Her babies and her headaches (mummy's headaches?): that, or those, will teach her, have taught her.[32] 'It struck me all the more that Mrs Limbert was flying her flag. As vivid as a page of her husband's prose, she had one of those flickers of freshness that are the miracle of her sex and one of those expensive dresses that are the miracle of ours.' There the narrator's own flicker is not of freshness but of the snake's tongue. ('The creature was even cleverer, as Maud Stannace said, than she had ventured to hope. Verily it was a good thing to have a dose of the wisdom of the serpent.' This last is said mockingly of Ray but is true—verily—of the narrator.) Later you can feel the relish in his mouth when he turns to the matters that he had to discuss (intimately)

---

32. There is malice as well as authorly comedy in the narrator's description of Limbert's novel *The Major Key*, 'when, in its lemon-coloured volumes, like a little dish of three custards, the book was at last served cold' (the lemon-coloured book, appearing first here in the *Yellow Book*); and there is the greater malice in the likelihood that the three custards, the last course, are to be brought into relation to Limbert and Maud, 'with three babies in due course'.

with Maud, the tremulous sympathy and antipathy that hover pruri-
ently around her intercourse with her husband, the admission that she
is 'Mrs Limbert' granted with a curl of his unstrenuous tongue:

There were likewise odder questions than this in the matter, phenomena more
curious and mysteries more puzzling, which often for sympathy if not for
illumination I intimately discussed with Mrs Limbert. She had her burdens,
dear lady: after the removal from London and a considerable interval she twice
again became a mother.

~For sympathy if not for illumination
I intimately discussed with Mrs Limbert~

The *dear lady* is not dear to him, for she has cost him—and continues
to cost him—dear. There will prove to be one occasion, and one only
(it comes later in this very paragraph), when he is able to bring himself
to speak of the couple (with perhaps their children?) as 'the Limberts'.
He assures the world of his compassion, as he wonders whether Mrs
Stannace would do the right thing and leave something substantial to
her daughter: 'My compassion for the Limberts led me to hover perhaps indiscreetly round that closing scene, to dream of some happy
time when such an accession of means would make up a little for their
present penury.'

~Indiscreetly round that closing scene~

Lavished upon legator and legatees, these are alligator's tears. For the
only happy time of which the unsuccessful suitor can dream is way in
the past, and is what was not to be.

But back to the opening of section I, 'Pretty pink Maud', and
what was our first meeting with her. There is 'the singular ground',
with its averted couple or coupling; there is the pleasure in intimating, with pseudo-sympathy, that Maud really has rather lost her
looks ('so lovely then, before her troubles'); and there are the half-
boastful, half-confessional, admissions within the mockery-modesty:
'but I appear to have passed in the flurried little circle for a magnanimous youth': all these come together in the thought of Maud's
having preferred his rival, 'invidiously as it might have struck me'—
might have?

What, after all, had Ralph Limbert (as Ray briefly becomes, seen in
a light that is both different and the same) to say for himself? 'Ralph
Limbert, who belonged to nobody and had done nothing—nothing

even at Cambridge—had only the uncanny spell he had cast upon her younger daughter to recommend him.'

~Belonged to nobody and had done nothing~

This does not *recommend him* to the speaker. The dextrous back of the hand that knows Cambridge like the back of its hand ('had done nothing—nothing even at Cambridge—') is followed by a rueful casting: 'the uncanny spell he had cast···'—*uncanny*, for how could she? Limbert may have 'belonged to nobody', but he and Maud did come to belong to one another.

'Pretty pink Maud' had charmed the narrator, a spell uttered three times; had in due course been condescended to, as he protects himself against her having slighted him; and was to suffer a hideous change, an Ovidian metamorphosis, into the most predatory wording that the serpentine narrator could swallow, as he imagines his competitor being swallowed, the wisdom of the serpent indeed:

His danger appeared to have acted upon him as the anaconda acts upon the rabbit; fascinated and paralysed, he had been engulfed in the long pink throat. When a week before, at my request, Limbert had let me possess for a day the complete manuscript, beautifully copied out by Maud Stannace, I had flushed with indignation at its having to be said of the author of such pages that he hadn't the common means to money.

~As the anaconda acts upon the rabbit
Had been engulfed in the long pink throat~

Pink Maud; in the long pink throat; Limbert not in the pink but in the red. The narrator's indignation on Limbert's behalf will be succeeded by a certain kind of solicitude on Maud Limbert's behalf. 'She had said to me once—only once, in a gloomy hour in London days when things were not going at all—that one really had to think him a very great man because if one didn't one would be rather ashamed of him. She had distinctly felt it at first—and in a very tender place—that almost every one passed him on the road.'

~Almost every one passed him on the road~

But the truth is, that while our vines and hers may have tender grapes, his have sour grapes:

He saw more even than I had done in the girl he was engaged to; as time went on I became conscious that we had both, properly enough, seen rather more than there was. Our odd situation, that of the three of us, became perfectly possible from the moment I observed that he had more patience with her than I should have had. I was happy at not having to supply this quantity, and she, on her side, found pleasure in being able to be impertinent to me without incurring the reproach of a bad wife.

~More patience with her than I should have had
Able to be impertinent to me
Incurring the reproach of a bad wife~

Happy at this? The gentleman doth protest too much, and anyway is not a gentleman. She would never have incurred the reproach of a bad wife. She had incurred the reproach of not being *his* wife.

Everything has been set for us to be told of the sympathetic role that our narrator, early on, had found himself called upon to play—told of this in words that preserve both the proprieties and the resentments:

The young couple, neither of whom had a penny, were now virtually engaged: the thing was subject to Ralph's putting his hand on some regular employment. People more enamoured couldn't be conceived, and Mrs Highmore, honest woman, who had moreover a professional sense for a love-story, was eager to take them under her wing. What was wanted was a decent opening for Limbert, which it had occurred to her I might assist her to find, though indeed I had not yet found any such matter for myself. But it was well known that I was too particular, whereas poor Ralph, with the easy manners of genius, was ready to accept almost anything.

The sequence of words, as elsewhere in the narration, has a way of looking as though it might be set to conclude differently, betrayingly, and then pulling itself together. Here there could have been the thought of 'Ralph's putting his hand on her'. ('People more enamoured couldn't be conceived.') But no: 'Ralph's putting his hand on some regular employment'. At an earlier moment, there might have been 'the unencouraged sentiment I had entertained for her'. But no: 'the unencouraged sentiment I had entertained for her sister'.

Again, the unsuccessful suitor remembers: 'I stood there blank, but not unaware in my blankness of how history repeats itself. There came to me across the years Maud's announcement of their'—their what? their engagement, Limbert's and hers? No, 'their ejection from the *Beacon*, and dimly, confusedly the same explanation was in the air' (the *Beacon* being the journal that had dispensed with Limbert's services). Not then their engagement, their ejection, but if the engagement were dimly, confusedly, in the air, *his* ejection. 'It rankled in me at first to see his reward'—not surprising that it rankled, given his having bettered you in two unforgettable ways. But no, 'It rankled in me at first to see his reward so meagre, his conquest so mean', an announcement that offers to do credit to our narrator, not mean at all, it seems.[33] Or there is his vexation at Ray Limbert: 'Now and then he made a hit that—it was stupid of me—brought the blood to my face. I hated him'—ah, at last an open acknowledgement of his hatred (amatory and literary). But no, what had opened the possibility of confession is to shut at once: 'I hated him to be so personal; but still, if it would make his fortune—!'

The teller of the tale has published his first volume, which he immediately doffs (deprecation soliciting a higher appreciation) as 'mere faded ink to-day, a little collection of literary impressions'. His friend Limbert publishes a piece in praise of it. As we all know, no such praise is ever sufficient, and something in the narrator smarts at it and at his being in need of such praise from Limbert. What did Limbert say? 'I remember his saying it wasn't literature.' Well, that would be enough to make anyone smart. And then the sentence resumes, with quite another destination in mind: 'I remember his saying it wasn't literature, the stuff, superficial stuff, he had to write about me.' Ah.

'Maud behaved well, I thought, to—': to whom? Not to me, to her mother.

Maud behaved well, I thought, to her mother, and well indeed for a girl who had mainly been taught to be flowerlike to every one. What she gave Ray Limbert her fine abundant needs made him then and ever pay for; but the gift was liberal, almost wonderful—an assertion I make even while remembering to how many clever women, early and late, his work had been dear.

Malice aforethought and an afterthought. What did she most crucially give Ray Limbert? Her hand. And how did the narrator spend the money that he earned from that little book of his that his friend had reviewed as an act of patronage? A review, not at all incidentally, that had cost Ray Limbert dear, it being the final reason for his editor's dismissing him : ' "But surely such a thing as his notice of my book—!" "It was your wretched book that was the last straw! He should have treated it superficially." "Well, if he didn't—!" I began. Then I checked myself.' Then I checked myself: that is our man.

33. These are dour counterparts to effects more blithe, such as the remark about Jane Highmore's bestsellers: 'The public *would* have her, as her husband used roguishly to remark.'

But remember what he did with what he got for that book of his: 'I sold the thing, I remember, for ten pounds, and with the money I bought in Vigo Street a quaint piece of old silver for Maud Stannace, which I carried to her with my own hand as a wedding gift.' My own hand, no word of hers, it being another man's.

Maud Limbert, née Stannace. The narrator, a born best man. Limbert, the better man. This pun hovers in the air when the narrator congratulates himself on a generosity towards Limbert in passing a literary employment on to him: 'I seem to recall that I got rid of it in Limbert's interest, persuaded the editor that he was much the better man. The better man was naturally the man who had pledged himself to support a charming wife. We were neither of us good, as the event proved, but he had a finer sort of badness.'[34]

~But he had a finer sort of badness~

Not so, my dear sir, it is you who must muster the finer sort of badness.

Maud exclaimed to the worsted suitor: 'But what on earth are we to marry on?' She can scarcely have meant to open here the maw of the pronoun *we* (you and I? No, Ray and I), but the narrator closes in on all such things. His answer to Maud's question is this: 'You're to marry on *The Major Key*.' Whereupon, with another of those immediate transitions of the master across a section of the story, into James's roman numeral II, we learn more of *The Major Key*, 'a consummation' that will make possible the marriage:

The Major Key was the new novel, and the great thing accordingly was to finish it; a consummation for which three months of the *Beacon* had in some degree prepared the way.

A consummation devoutly to be wished, by Ray and Maud, and one not altogether unwished-for by the narrator, whose mixed feelings do include some wish that he were not Malvolio and who does reluctantly respect Limbert's artistry, in some degree.

There is a brilliantly betraying moment when the narrator talks about log-rolling in reviewing, letting us know of Limbert's insistence upon 'such public patronage of my performances as he had occasionally been in a position to offer'. Limbert declines any such help in

---

34. In the New York Edition: 'to provide for a charming woman', and 'had the braver badness'.

return: 'it was always part of the bargain that I shouldn't make him a topic. "How can I successfully serve you if you do?" he used to ask: he was more afraid than I thought he ought to have been of the charge of tit for tat. I didn't care, for I never could distinguish tat from tit.'

~How can I successfully serve you if you do?
I never could distinguish tat from tit~

What is striking here is the narrator's use of *tit for tat* as an act of friendship, whereas we know, as does the *OED*, that it is 'One blow or stroke in return for another; an equivalent given in return (usually in the way of injury, rarely of benefit); retaliation'. Rarely of benefit, although the narrator does tacitly benefit from the fact that it is not *never* so, a move which permits at once an admission and a denial. It is not really that the narrator 'never could distinguish tat from tit', it is that he affects not to distinguish the sense that the phrase has, or to distinguish a blow from a benefit.

Did James know just what he was doing when he has his narrator admit 'I felt a prick'? Those words come hard upon 'more keyed up', 'suggestive', 'point to with pride',[35] 'stiff'.

'Oh, you're more keyed up than he! Mr Bousefield says that of course he wanted things that were suggestive and clever, things that he could point to with pride. But he contends that Ray didn't allow for human weakness. He gave everything in too stiff doses.'
Sensibly, I fear, to my neighbour I winced at her words; I felt a prick that made me meditate.

~He gave everything in too stiff doses
I felt a prick that made me meditate~

Wincing at words, and mincing them, remain among the narrator's habits.

'What was the matter with Ralph Limbert': this is seized to be pondered by the narrator. What is the matter with the narrator is weighed by us, by courtesy of James. In his Notebooks, the author had wondered about all this: '*I* become the narrator, either impersonally or in my unnamed, unspecified personality. Say I chose the latter line · · ·'[36] Fortunately, James did not become his narrator, though it is true that

---

35. Shakespeare, Sonnet 151: 'flesh staies no farther reason, | But rysing at thy name doth point out thee, | As his triumphant prize, proud of this pride, | He is contented thy poore drudge to be, | To stand in thy affaires, fall by thy side'.
36. *The Complete Notebooks of Henry James*, 123.

everything about the narrator that is both becoming and unbecoming is an act of judgement, sometimes of self-criticism, by the author. That James is in many ways like naive Limbert, this is manifest and is suggestive.[37] But a happy complication is that James is both like and blessedly unlike the suave narrator as well. A proverb, retorted, is voiced by the knowing narrator, going along (part of the way) with James:

We sat drawn up by the pavement, facing poor Limbert's future as I saw it. It relieved me in a manner to know the worst, and I prophesied with an assurance which as I look back upon it strikes me as rather remarkable. '*Que voulez-vous?*' I went on: 'you can't make a sow's ear of a silk purse!'

~Facing poor Limbert's future as I saw it~

James had written at the same place in the Notebooks: 'He wants to marry—he wants to do at least once something that will sell; BUT—do what he will—he *can't* make a sow's ear out of a silk purse.' To some degree, then, James is at one with his narrator. But there is no counterpart in James to the duplicity (it is rich) of 'It relieved me in a manner to know the worst', a duplicity one arm of which is genuine well-wishing, and the other, *Schadenfreude*.

Or there is the narrator's recalling 'a passage from our friend's last instalment. The passage—I couldn't for my life help reading it—was simply superb.' Superb: I couldn't for my life help admitting it... 'He couldn't trouble me, whatever he did, for I practically enjoyed him as much when he was worse as when he was better.' And that's true, too, twice over.

~I couldn't for my life help reading it~

---

37. Philip Horne, 'Henry James and the Economy of the Short Story', in *Modernist Writers and the Marketplace*, ed. Ian Willison, Warwick Gould, and Warren Chernaik (London, 1996), 1–35, on James's 'becoming notorious like his own Ray Limbert in "The Next Time" (1895) as a non-seller, even treated sometimes as a jinx on the publication that bore him by his too evidently artful intricacies and indirections. His earlier success and consequent acknowledged major status seem to have partly provoked and made socially tolerable a jocular or snide vein of mock-lament in literary circles about his increasing unintelligibility—with direct effects on his ability to take advantage of the growing market··· The "cachet" of being "unsaleable at any price", of course, can be exaggerated; but there is a businesslike, marketing wisdom for the "better" publisher or magazine editor in buying in some of the real thing (Art) when its reputation as Art is established; it ostentatiously puts a weight in the scale of cultural respectability which somehow has to be balanced against that of business expediency or the pursuit of profit.'

Limbert's final novel is *Derogation*. The derogatory narrator knows all about *Derogation*. His story, which is Limbert's story but also Maud's story (or rather Mrs Limbert's) as well—or as ill—as his own barren story, nears its end: 'He didn't describe it further, contrary to his common practice, and I only knew later, by Mrs Limbert, that he had begun *Derogation* and that he was completely full of his subject. It was a subject however that he was not to live to treat.'

~He was completely full of his subject~

Derogation: a subject of which the narrator is completely full, and that he, unlike Ray Limbert, lives not only to treat but to treat himself with. In the very end:

He stayed till death knocked at the gate, for the pen dropped from his hand only at the moment when from sudden failure of the heart his eyes, as he sank back in his chair, closed for ever. *Derogation* is a splendid fragment; it evidently would have been one of his high successes. I am not prepared to say it would have waked up the libraries.

It is *finis*, with a little moralizing flourish, that our narrator seems to trace today at the bottom of the page. This, along with the unremitting chilliness that plays the *eyes closed for ever* against *waked up*.

In James, it is often the women who come to wake up, whose eyes will not stay closed to what heroes and heroines and the heroic can get up to. James had urged the graduates of Bryn Mawr to value the truth that is incarnate in a respected language: 'I am asking you to take that truth well home and hold it close to your hearts, setting your backs to the wall to defend it, heroically, when need may be.' But the heroic has its temptations. Take what Isabel Archer thinks to herself. 'Sometimes she went so far as to wish that she might find herself some day in a difficult position, so that she should have the pleasure of being as heroic as the occasion demanded' (*The Portrait of a Lady*, chapter 6). Take what she finds herself thinking of Lord Warburton.

She found herself liking him extremely; the first impression he had made on her had had weight, but at the end of an evening spent in his society she scarce fell short of seeing him—though quite without luridity—as a hero of romance. (chapter 7)

Take her recourse when her benefactor Ralph Touchett tries to warn her against the man she has set herself to marry:

He wished to interrupt, to reassure her; for a moment he was absurdly incon-
sistent; he would have retracted what he had said. But she gave him no chance;
she went on, having caught a glimpse, as she thought, of the heroic line and
desiring to advance in that direction. (chapter 34)

The heroic line conveys ~desiring to advance in that direction~.
Madame Merle fulfils her desires and takes direction, when as the
mistress of Isabel's husband she says to her, 'Now don't be heroic, don't
be unreasonable, don't take offence.' And then: 'Ah then, you take it
heroically! I'm very sorry. Don't think, however, that I shall do so'
(chapter 49).

In *The Next Time*, 'the pen dropped from his hand only at the
moment when···'. Henry James might have recalled—in this story
that is about not only the hand that pens, but the hand that is given in
marriage ('a quaint piece of old silver for Maud Stannace, which I carried to her with my own hand as a wedding gift)'—the words of
Thackeray in *The Newcomes*: 'He might pretend surely to his kins-
woman's hand without derogation.' 'Derogation': 'The taking away (in
part) of the power or authority (*of* a person, etc.); lessening, weakening,
curtailing, or impairment of authority.' Here, the authority of authors,
as also of the heroes of stories.

8

John Jay Chapman
and a Vocation for Heroism

John Jay Chapman (1862–1933), American man of letters, had 'a vocation for heroism'.[1] A vocation is a calling, and whether it is right to answer the call must depend on who is doing the calling. 'The action on the part of God of calling a person to exercise some special function, especially of a spiritual nature' (*OED* 1); 'The particular function or station to which a person is called by God' (*OED* 2a): both of these are immensely weightier than 'One's ordinary occupation, business, or profession' (*OED* 2b). For Carlyle, the word belonged within *On Heroes, Hero-Worship and the Heroic in History*: 'Luther and Knox were by express vocation Priests.'[2]

But 'calling persons or mankind to a state of salvation' (*OED* 1b) should call to mind that other destination, damnation. Over a calling there may hang a fear of madness, of being possessed, of hearing voices. The Duke of Monmouth heard and followed Satan's calling ('Him Staggering so when Hells dire Agent found'), as did his co-conspirator, the Earl of Shaftesbury.

> Great Wits are sure to Madness near ally'd;
> And thin Partitions do their Bounds divide.[3]

Dryden understood the equanimity that such a balanced heroic couplet could embody. The different equanimity that index-entries maintain can help to establish a *cordon sanitaire* between us and Chapman when he is frenzied, 'mad Jack Chapman'[4] to his allies as well as to his adversaries.

1. William Arrowsmith, *Arion* (Spring–Fall 1992–3), 10.
2. 'The Hero as Prophet', in *On Heroes, Hero-Worship and the Heroic in History*; in *Works*, ed. H. D. Traill (London, 1896–1907), 116.
3. Dryden, *Absalom and Achitophel*, 373, 163–4.
4. *The Selected Writings of John Jay Chapman*, ed. Jacques Barzun (New York, 1957), p. ix.

The body of the life-and-letters itself plunges us in the immediate company of someone 'heroically mad'.[6]

Chapman, convinced that the happiness of Minna Timmins [a woman dear to him, whom he came to marry] was in peril through another man, took it upon himself, quite without her knowledge, to give this man a savage thrashing. Then in a sudden revulsion from what he had done, and in a frenzy of expiation, he thrust his hand into a fire, and burned it so severely that it had to be amputated.[7]

But then this, in its turn, is nothing like as obdurate as what Chapman himself set down in the 'Retrospections' of old age:

When the evening was half over, I invited the gentleman to whom I have referred to step on the lawn, and there I beat him with a stick—whence procured I don't know—about the head and shoulders···The next thing I remember is returning late at night to my room.··· There was a hard coal fire burning brightly. I took off my coat and waistcoat, wrapped a pair of suspenders tightly on my left forearm above the wrist, plunged the left hand deep in the blaze and held it down with my right hand for some minutes. When I took it out, the charred knuckles and finger bones were exposed. I said to myself, 'This will never do.' I took an old coat, wrapped it about my left hand and arm, slipped my right arm into an overcoat, held the coat about me and started for Boston in the horsecars. On arriving at the Massachusetts General Hospital I showed the trouble to a surgeon, was put under ether, and next morning waked up without the hand and very calm in my spirits.[8]

There is much that is heroic in this ('showed the trouble to a surgeon'), both then and thereafter. To his mother in New York, he was very calm when lying: 'Please don't be scared by telegram from hospital. I had my left hand run over yesterday and taken off. I am perfectly well and happy. Don't mind it a bit—it shall not make the least difference in my life.'[9] He enjoyed self-reliance ('a romantic and courageous appearance, greatly enhanced by the fact of my having only one hand'),[10] and he enjoyed being able to rely on such a friend as Mrs Endicott Peabody, especially when a coincidence infiltrated a holiday moment:

5. M. A. DeWolfe Howe, *John Jay Chapman and His Letters* (Boston, MA, 1937).
6. Dryden, once more; see p. 303.   7. January 1887. *Chapman and His Letters*, 59.
8. Ibid.   9. Ibid. (27 January 1887), 60.   10. Ibid. 69.

We then went on to Saint-Malo, where, as we were walking on the old walls, Jack caught sight of a bell with rope attached. His one hand was always busy, and with it he rang the bell feeling that something would happen; it did, and as this might get us all into trouble he turned and ran the other way, meeting the fire chief who told him he had committed a serious offence. However, it passed off.[11]

'The fire chief who told him he had committed a serious offence': this must have rung more than one bell.

'It shall not make the least difference in my life.' But could he forget, leave alone forgive himself? 'I have been and indeed am, laid up with a broken arm—luckily the left upper arm. Everytime I have an accident to that arm, it means—whatever it means. I have been exceedingly miserable—but this, it appears is common with broken arms.'[12] Self-considering, he was also considerate of others.

N.B. One ought not to wear anything that meets and occupies the subconscious attention of other people with problems. That's why I hate a false arm. People find it out by degrees and are worried all the time until they do—and then by that time—they can think of nothing else.[13]

Could he think of nothing else? Ten years after the *auto-da-fé* that had been a *felo-de-se*, and following the tragic death of his wife Minna after childbirth, he wrote to Elizabeth Chanler, whom he was soon to marry:

[*Enclosing clipping from a Memphis, Tennessee, newspaper about the loss of his hand.*]

April 6: 1897

ELIZABETH—I had just thrown this away, but I keep it. It is too interesting and unexpected—and on the whole very accurate. Like catching sight of oneself in the glass. First I was shocked—then I laughed, then I threw it away, then kept it. What eternal blazon unfit for ears of flesh and blood have I lived in till I don't even hear—and let's not hear it...[14]

'But this eternal blason must not be | To eares of flesh and bloud.' What was it that brought to Chapman's more-than-mind these cadences of Hamlet's father's ghost? What but this: 'Till the foule crimes done in my dayes of Nature | Are burnt and purg'd away' (I. v).

I threw it away, then kept it. In middle life, Chapman wrote his *Sonnet on Middle Life*:

11. *Chapman and His Letters*, 63.
12. Ibid., to William James (27 February 1909), 238.
13. Ibid., to Minna Timmins Chapman (9 December 1894), 102.
14. Ibid. (6 April 1897), 165.

> The Sibyl paused, her pen above the leaf···
> And next, the god inflamed her, and her hand
> In a poetic fury wrote amain—[15]

—'···inflamed her, and her hand'. In later life, it was a mercy that he lived to accommodate his inferno and his purgatorio to something that is, in its way and in the end, a paradiso:

About a year after his death a small card, never seen before, was found in his room, with *Te Deum Laudamus* beneath a Fra Angelico angel. On the back of it were the words, in Chapman's handwriting: 'Elizabeth came with a book in each hand. In her left hand she held the mind of the world and this book she gave first. In her right hand she held the heart of the world and that she gave me and the hand that held it.'[16]

> ~In her right hand she held the heart of the world
> And that she gave me and the hand that held it~

Lineated as the English heroic line, this would have about it something of the world of forgiveness that is Shakespeare's late plays. But it had been reproach, including self-reproach, that had characterized Chapman's attention when a heroic couplet by him was bent not upon Elizabeth's heart or the world's but upon his own:

> His own heart by his own heart criticized—
> The thing most worshipped seeming most disprized.[17]

For I am nothing, if not critical. (Iago relishes acerbic heroic couplets.) *Othello* had consumed Chapman.

I had come to see that she was in love with someone. It never occurred to me that she might be in love with me. An onlooker might have said, 'You loved her for the tragedies of her childhood and she loved you that you did pity them.'[18]

> She lov'd me for the dangers I had past,
> And I lov'd her, that she did pitty them.   (*Othello*, I. iii)

Chapman could never pass off or pass over the sequent dangers that he had been unable to let pass—rather, had plunged his hand deep into. This, in the madness of jealousy. *Othello* was 'the best picture of

15. 7 November 1918. *Chapman and His Letters*, 341.   16. Ibid. 462.
17. His Phi Beta Kappa poem on Harvard, 17 June 1912, of himself; *Chapman and His Letters*, 213.
18. Ibid. 59.

jealousy in literature', and Chapman writhes at it: 'If considered seriously, *Othello* is a plea for evil; but, properly taken, it is a sort of awful *jeu d'esprit*. An odious play it is.' He acknowledges his awe at the full-headedness of such art: Shakespeare 'gives me the impression that all the thoughts of all the characters are going on in his head all the time—and each one of these characters is apt to have as full a head as any one of us. In fact some of the characters who had broad-gauge natures like Othello are totally beyond our understanding even of themselves.'[19] Yet they are always filling our heads. Chapman's head was occupied by Professor G. L. Kittredge of Harvard, 'an iron man who could be seen stalking about Cambridge with a vicious looking small bag filled with burglar's tools and footnotes on Othello'.[20]

> I tooke by th'throat the circumcised Dogge,
> And smoate him, thus.   (*Othello*, V. ii)

'I get so violent··· Some men are to be taken by the throat, some jollied, some taken aside.'[21]

The self-inflicted ordeal by fire was Chapman's personal tragedy. Two dozen years later, in August 1911, this was compounded by a public tragedy at which Chapman could not but cry out. To commemorate the burning alive of a man, exactly a year after the protracted killing had been perpetrated, Chapman travelled to the scene of the crime, Coatesville, Pennsylvania. There, on 18 August 1912, he held a prayer-meeting at which he spoke. Spoke of dishonour, with honour.

We are met to commemorate the anniversary of one of the most dreadful crimes in history—not for the purpose of condemning it, but to repent of our share in it. We do not start any agitation with regard to that particular crime. I understand that an attempt to prosecute the chief criminals has been made, and has entirely failed; because the whole community, and in a sense our whole people, are really involved in the guilt. The failure of the prosecution in this case, in all such cases, is only a proof of the magnitude of the guilt, and of the awful fact that everyone shares in it.

I will tell you why I am here; I will tell you what happened to me. When I read in the newspapers of August 14, a year ago, about the burning alive of

19. 'Shakespeare' (1922), in *Selected Writings of Chapman*, 262. *Chapman and His Letters* (16 July 1896), 114.
20. 'I looked with a shudder on both Child and Kittredge', ibid. 194. (Professor F. J. Child.)
21. Ibid. 68.

a human being, and of how a few desperate fiend-minded men had been permitted to torture a man chained to an iron bedstead, burning alive, thrust back by pitchforks when he struggled out of it, while around about stood hundreds of well-dressed American citizens, both from the vicinity and from afar, coming on foot and in wagons, assembling on telephone call, as if by magic, silent, whether from terror or indifference, fascinated and impotent, hundreds of persons watching this awful sight and making no attempt to stay the wickedness, and no one man among them all who was inspired to risk his life in an attempt to stop it, no one man to name the name of Christ, of humanity, of government! As I read the newspaper accounts of the scene enacted in Coatesville a year ago, I seemed to get a glimpse into the soul of this country. I saw a seldom revealed picture of the American heart and of the American nature.···And I am here today chiefly that I may remember that vision. It seems fitting to come to this town where the crime occurred and hold a prayer-meeting···The act, to be sure, took place at Coatesville, and everyone looked to Coatesville to follow it up. Some months ago I asked a friend who lives not far from here something about this case, and about the expected prosecutions, and he replied to me: 'It wasn't in my county,' and that made me wonder whose county it was in. And it seemed to be in my county. I live on the Hudson River; but I knew that this great wickedness that happened in Coatesville is not the wickedness of Coatesville and of today. It is the wickedness of all America and of three hundred years—the wickedness of the slave trade.[22]

> ~Chained to an iron bedstead, burning alive
> Thrust back by pitchforks when he struggled out
> No one man to name the name of Christ
> The wickedness of all America~

Coatesville came to be a capital of Chapman county, his consciousness and conscience. 'If you should see a man being burned alive by respectable rate-payers, you would cry out—not you but something in you—would burst into agonized protest, accusing those rate-payers; and your language would be harsh.'[23] His own language, within his long-deferred 'Retrospections', was to fold and fold again the name *Coates*ville as he re-lived (not relieved) his agonizing expiation, back in 1887: 'There was a hard-coal fire burning brightly. I took off my coat and waist-coat···I took an old coat, wrapped it about my left hand and arm, slipped my right arm into an overcoat, held the coat about me and

---

22. For this 'outrage upon a black American', see *Chapman and His Letters*, 214–19, and *Selected Writings of Chapman*, pp. v–ix; what Chapman said at Coatesville in 1912 occupies pp. 255–8.
23. 'William Lloyd Garrison', ibid. 93.

started for Boston.'²⁴ Over the next few months of 1887 he wrote to Minna, knowing full well what he was writing. Of the books he had been reading during his twenty days of pain in hospital, 'There was fire in everything I touched.' 'I do think there was something promethean in it, in the capacity to yield.'²⁵

An individual madness of injustice was to come to meet a communal madness of injustice. Chapman took real risks in going to Coatesville and in speaking as he did. For many of us, there would be nothing exaggerated in calling it heroic of him, since a decent working characterization of the heroic might be its exhibiting a great deal more courage than you or I are likely to have been able to muster. Chapman himself did not like the word *heroic* to be lavished—on himself, among others, with the unusual plural 'heroisms' playing charmingly along. 'I tell you the kind of man I am thrives only in romance. In real life he does murders, loves, revenges, heroisms, and crimes.'²⁶ Or 'heroic' as ministering to, say, Arthur Balfour. 'Now Balfour was the most astute, practical parliamentarian of the century, but to the social world he was an heroic figure.'²⁷ Yet Chapman always showed respect for any neglected poignancy: 'the heroism of these men has been forgotten, the losing heroism of conservatism'.²⁸

Chapman apprehended why William Lloyd Garrison (1805–79), abolitionist, leader of the American Anti-Slavery Society, deserved high praise, and had insufficiently received it. 'We shall see Garrison as one of our greatest heroes.'²⁹ Chapman's preface to the second edition (1921) of his *William Lloyd Garrison* (1913) opens with an anecdote about Abraham Lincoln; shrewdly remarks that 'This anecdote shows how much easier it is to see a hero in the past than in the present'; and proceeds 'to explain why Garrison has never been adopted as a popular hero in America. He gave a purge to his countrymen, and the bitter taste of it remained in our mouths ever after.'³⁰

From Garrison's mouth there came *The Liberator*. The impassioned utterance of its first editorial (1 January 1831) incarnated liberation and

24. *Chapman and His Letters*, 59. 25. Ibid. 81, 82.
26. Ibid. (summer 1897), 149. 27. Ibid. ('Retrospections'), 41.
28. 'Emerson' (1898), in *Selected Writings of Chapman*, 152.
29. Chapman's 'We shall see' could, as a matter of family history, look back towards the sustaining of the past, *we have seen*, for (as Nuzhat Bukhari pointed out to me) Chapman's paternal grandmother Maria Weston Chapman was a heroic campaigner against slavery, working with Garrison on *The Liberator*.
30. *Selected Writings of Chapman*, 3.

the freedom that such prose can enjoy, especially when it is open to the
traditions that animate the heroic line. Chapman, in his book on
Garrison, has us listen to Garrison's courage in the vital prose of *The
Liberator*, where the fiery momentum accommodates with dignity the
cadences of such moments as these (plucked from the burning here, so
that they may be not only registered but heard and listened to):

~Afflicted but did not dishearten me
Defending the great cause of human rights
Timidity, injustice, and absurdity
To think, or speak, or write, with moderation
Hasten the resurrection of the dead
Enables me to disregard the fear
His truth in its simplicity and power~[31]

   Chapman himself knew the servitudes and grandeurs of hero-
worship, for Theodore Roosevelt had allured and lured.

When Roosevelt came back from Cuba, he came back as a hero. I shall never
forget the lustre that shone about him; for I went to see him at Montauk
Point, and my companion accused me of being in love with him, and indeed
I was. I never before nor since have felt that glorious touch of hero-worship
which solves life's problems by showing you a man.[32]

(Showing *a man* to you? Showing *you* to be a man?) The Teddy
Roosevelt myths, the magnifications and the military mendacities,
brought into the mind of a fellow-diner with Chapman at the Century
Club 'the old paradox, that it made no difference when once a hero
was established—whether he had been a hero or not. I contested this
on the ground that such a record on such facts deceived the young as
to the true nature of life.'[33]

31. *Selected Writings of Chapman*, 22–3.
32. Ibid. 142.
33. Chapman had led into this paradox by reporting a nested lie. 'You know, I suppose,
that R. [Roosevelt] went up the wrong hill—in disobedience of orders—and would
have been destroyed unless a regiment of Negroes had been sent to save him and his
Rough Riders. He never was on San Juan Hill. But he had a picture painted of himself
on horseback going up San Juan Hill. The military men wouldn't stand for this; and
laughed the picture into the cellar of the White House. As a matter of fact—no one
was on horseback at San J. It was so steep—they clawed up it on foot. Well the man
next me at table—a knowing sort of cuss—said that he knew from inside information
of a U.S. Department that an effort was now being made to rename the maps of the
battle ground so that the words San Juan hill should *cover Kettle Hill*—which Roosevelt
ran up—as if San Juan was a term that included Kettle.' *Chapman and His Letters*, to
Elizabeth Chanler Chapman (21 February 1929), 423–4.

Chapman was not pacific, and he was not a pacifist. He was an activ-
ist, the opposite of a passivist. He not only believed in practical agitation, he practised it. It is a strength of his conception of heroism that it
lives in such close affinity with action. Of William Lloyd Garrison: 'He
lived a life of heroism and of practical achievement'[34]—where it is *and*
which effects so much, in refusing to identify heroism with practical
achievement while equally refusing to dislink the two. In this matter,
Guesses at Truth, by the brothers Hare, retrieved something that is
enduring—they thank the Greeks for it—and something that is more
precise than a guess: 'Heroism is active genius; genius, contemplative
heroism. Heroism is the self-devotion of genius manifesting itself in
action.'[35]

Chapman was a man of letters; writing was the action that he was a
man of. By one of life's little ironies, likewise death's, the terms in
which Chapman wrote about Thomas Carlyle in 1923 might in our
day be retorted upon Chapman himself, John Jay Chapman being no
longer a name to conjure with, to adjure with, or to injure with.

This summer I wrote quite a ponderous essay upon Carlyle—to clear my
mind. He's a rabid chimera, *bombinans in vacuo*—and I can't be sure that I've
got him snap-shotted. He was once a popular writer, a being regarded by
contemporaries as a classic—that's the key to him somehow. Of course no one
cares a rap for him today– except perhaps a few gnarled veterans who can't get
over their youth. One would have to dig them out in order to knock them on
the head and say 'Ho! You there! I'm going to write about Carlyle.'[36]

Chapman never published his forty-page essay on Carlyle, but there
are three pages about it in Richard Hovey's *John Jay Chapman—An
American Mind* (1959):

A person with Chapman's interests, temperament, and vocation could hardly
ignore Thomas Carlyle. However the Scotsman differed from the American,
their points of affinity were unmistakable: both were wits and humorsome
characters; both were of a puritan heritage; both were self-tormentors; both
denounced their times with the rage of a Hebrew prophet; both employed a
style of unusual force.[37]

Chapman on Carlyle is disguised autobiography, 'for unconsciously
Chapman identified himself with Carlyle, whose inner conflicts he

34. *Selected Writings of Chapman*, 135.
35. *Guesses at Truth* by Two Brothers (J. C. and A. W. Hare, 1827).
36. *Chapman and His Letters*, to Robert Nichols (12 November 1923), 394.
37. Richard Hovey, *John Jay Chapman—An American Mind* (1959), 314.

probed as if to throw light on his own'. It is open to question whether one man exactly *identifies* himself—even 'unconsciously'—with another whom he sums up as 'a frenzied theologian, ambitious revivalist, tortured artist', but there is kinship all right, and Hovey quotes a magnificent image of Chapman's for Carlyle's non-movement of mind. Chapman's image is fraught with reluctant admiration (there is felt to be a kind of genius in Carlyle's effecting this grinding of the teeth's cogs), perhaps because the point is also true, often, of Chapman's own wrenched wisdom: 'We can understand from his own description why his thought shows no progression. He turns on the high power and at the same time throws all the brakes. The machine emits a most terrible racket, but, so far as the thought goes, it is standing still.' What is characteristic of Chapman is the tacit comedy of 'so far as the thought goes, it is standing still' (*far? goes?*). Seconded by his invoking (for Carlyle of all people) *the machine*. The Hero as Prophet had minced no words:[38]

What is the chief end of man here below? Mahomet has answered this question, in a way that might put some of *us* to shame! He does not, like a Bentham, a Paley, take Right and Wrong, and calculate the profit and loss, ultimate pleasure of the one and of the other; and summing all up by addition and subtraction into a net result, ask you, Whether on the whole the Right does not preponderate considerably? No; it is not *better* to do the one than the other; the one is to the other as life is to death,—as Heaven is to Hell. The one must in nowise be done, the other in nowise left undone. You shall not measure them; they are incommensurable: the one is death eternal to a man, the other is life eternal. Benthamee Utility, virtue by Profit and Loss; reducing this God's-world to a dead brute Steam-engine, the infinite celestial Soul of Man to a kind of Hay-balance for weighing hay and thistles on, pleasures and pains on · · ·

~The one is death eternal to a man~

Comedy, clearly, but tragedy too. 'He turns on the high power and at the same time throws all the brakes. The machine emits a most terrible racket, but, so far as the thought goes, it is standing still.' Whereupon there come back to haunt the mind, and not just the mind, some lines of Alexander Pope that combine the very different poignancies of a camera's still and a camera's footage:

---

38. 'The Hero as Prophet', in *On Heroes, Hero-Worship and the Heroic in History*; *Works*, ed. H. D. Traill (1896–1907), 75–6.

Still round and round the Ghosts of Beauty glide
And haunt the places where their Honour dy'd.
    See how the World its Veterans rewards!
A Youth of frolicks, an old Age of Cards,
Fair to no purpose, artful to no end,
Young without Lovers, old without a Friend.
A Fop their Passion, but their Prize a Sot,
Alive, ridiculous, and dead, forgot!

(*Epistle II. To a Lady: Of the Characters of Women*, 241–8)

William Empson apprehended the force of this: 'with a feverish anger, like the screws of a liner racing above water, Pope finds himself indeed hag-ridden by these poor creatures; they excite in him feelings irrelevantly powerful, of waste, of unavoidable futility, which no bullying of its object can satisfy.'[39] The heroic couplets have seen fit to welcome, however warily, the mock-heroic, artful to the end.

In Hovey's summary of Chapman's pages on Carlyle, nothing is said of *On Heroes, Hero-Worship, and the Heroic in History*, a masterpiece that is in some ways luridly maladroit but is in many ways profound. It is Carlyle who makes clear what it would be about Chapman's sense of the heroic that most entitles him to respect. For it is Carlyle who gives inimitable voice to the height of mind without which there will never be any depth of dignity. 'I am well aware that in these days', he said in 1840, 'Hero-worship, the thing I call Hero-worship, professes to have gone out, and finally ceased ··· Show our critics a great man, a Luther for example, they begin to what they call "account" for him; not to worship him, but take the dimensions of him,—and bring him out to be a little kind of man!'[40] Carlyle knows that any central human propensity that is thrown out of the front door will have a way of coming back in through the window or the back door. The conviction that Carlyle is not alone in honouring must for some people insist on being satisfied. 'It is a thing for ever changing, this of Hero-worship: different in each age, difficult to do well in any age. Indeed, the heart of the whole business of the age, one may say, is to do it well.'[41]

As always, with any idea or ideal, the strict sense (with its danger of becoming narrow) must be held in tension with the wide sense (with its danger of becoming slack). The faith in heroism must resist both

39. *Seven Types of Ambiguity* (London, 1930; rev. edn, 1947), 151.
40. 'The Hero as Divinity', in *On Heroes, Hero-Worship, and the Heroic in History*, 12.
41. 'The Hero as Prophet', ibid. 43.

the hardening which would speak as if heroism can take one form and one form only, and the relaxing which would speak as if greatness, or even any abstention from pusillanimity, constituted heroism. Carlyle's power was in his constituting six exemplars: the Hero as Divinity, as Prophet, as Poet, as Priest, finally as King—and, most penetratingly along his way, the Hero as Man of Letters. 'Few shapes of Heroism can be more unexpected.'

The Hero as *Man of Letters*, again, of which class we are to speak today, is altogether a product of these new ages; and so long as the wondrous art of *Writing*, or of Ready-writing which we call *Printing*, subsists, he may be expected to continue, as one of the main forms of Heroism for all future ages. He is, in various respects, a very singular phenomenon···Meanwhile, since it is the spiritual always that determines the material, this same Man-of-Letters Hero must be regarded as our most important modern person. He, such as he may be, is the soul of all. What he teaches, the whole world will do and make. The world's manner of dealing with him is the most significant feature of the world's general position.[42]

Whereupon Carlyle turned to his exemplary trio: Johnson, Rousseau, Burns. That which, apart from their heroism, the three have in common, though Carlyle wisely never says so, is their finding or making room for some scepticism about heroes, hero-worship, and the heroic in history. Scepticism; not cynicism, which Carlyle deprecates and pities.

Many of the most acute remarks by Chapman, Man of Letters, turn upon heroism—turn upon it both as revolving it in mind and (on occasion) as rounding upon it. Generously, he is even able to admit the presence of the heroic in traditions that he felt bound to warn the world against. He does not pause when he speaks of 'the conservative and heroic spirit in which modern commentators have dealt with the recovery of Greek literature', and he is sufficiently in earnest about heroism to be able to make sharp jokes about it, as when he summarizes 'a masterpiece of the pathetic':

Alcestis begs Admetus not to marry again, for fear lest a stepmother should maltreat the children. Admetus consents, and proceeds to lift a long-drawn tragic wail, precisely as if he were a moral hero.

How fleetly this establishes the proper limits of our moral awe, and how floatingly the heroic line—'proceeds to lift a long-drawn tragic

42. 'The Hero as Man of Letters', *On Heroes, Hero-Worship, and the Heroic in History*, 154–5.

wail', with its *cadence* that *lifts*—lifts and draws not only a wail but a veil. Chapman can even do what not all of us find it easy to do: delight in the wit of others who banter socially in our neck of the sacred wood. It is to Chapman that we owe the Boston *bon mot* of Mrs Bell. 'She had been taken to Cambridge to attend a Greek play, and on being asked about it, replied, "Oh, it was one of those Greek tragedies where one of the characters on the stage says to another, 'If you don't kill mother, I will.'"'[43] The play's the thing. But then the great player is a great thing too. 'Your bright boy of six is taken to see the great actor in *Hamlet*. He ought, if you can manage it, to be taken to see every great man who passes through town.'[44]

Chapman found himself needing to account for Emerson's greatness. 'Emerson represents a protest against the tyranny of democracy. He is the most recent example of elemental hero-worship.'[45] When Chapman sought to make good his judgement that Emerson was a hero, it was to the memory of Tennyson's King Arthur, and of the life in the dying King's admonition, that he turned: 'But the hero may enslave his race by bringing in a system of tyranny; the battle-cry of freedom may become a dogma which crushes the soul; one good custom may corrupt the world.'

> And slowly answered Arthur from the barge:
> 'The old order changeth, yielding place to new,
> And God fulfills Himself in many ways,
> Lest one good custom should corrupt the world···'
>
> (*Morte d'Arthur*, 239–42)

Emerson was aware that 'every hero becomes a bore at last'. Carlyle appreciated that, in these matters, addition may mount to multiplication. 'Thou and I, my friend, can, in the most flunkey world, make, each of us, *one* non-flunkey, if we like; that will be two heroes to begin with.'[46] Chapman despised the ways of the flunkey world, as is clear from one of his apophthegms: 'I'll tell you my philosophy—that there's only one real joy in life—but fortunately there's likely to be lots of it—the joy of casting at the world the stone of an unknown world.'[47] Unknown, but known not to be flunkey.

---

43. 'Retrospections', in *Chapman and His Letters*, 195.
44. 'Our Universities', in Chapman's *New Horizons in American Life* (1932), 14–17.
45. *Selected Writings of Chapman*, 150–1.   46. *Past and Present*, ed. Traill, 36.
47. *Chapman and His Letters*, to Mrs Henry Whitman (9 October 1896), 120.

I am grateful to this man, George Thompson. He stood for courage in 1835 in Massachusetts. He typified courage also at a later time during the Civil War when he stood with John Bright and W. E. Forster as the expounders of the cause of the North before the people of Great Britain.[48]

He stood for courage ··· he stood with John Bright. No less, he stood by his principle.[49]

The Duke of Wellington had been for the people of Great Britain 'that tower of strength | Which stood four-square to all the winds that blew'.[50] He had courage. 'In Spain, and also in France, I used continually to go alone and reconnoitre almost up to their Piquets. Seeing a single horseman in his cloak, they disregarded me as some Subaltern. No French General, said Soult, would have gone without a guard of at least a thousand men.'

DeLancey was with me and speaking to me when he was struck. We were on a point of land that overlooked the plain, and I had just been warned off by some soldiers; (but as I saw well from it, and as two divisions were engaging below, I had said 'Never mind,') when a ball came leaping along *en ricochet* as it is called, and striking him on the back, sent him many yards over the head of his horse. He fell on his face, and bounded upward and fell again. All the Staff dismounted, and ran to him; and when I came up he said, 'Pray tell them to leave me, and let me die in peace.' I had him conveyed into the rear; and two days afterwards when, on my return from Brussels, I saw him in a barn, he spoke with such strength that I said, (for I had reported him among the killed) 'Why, DeLancey, you will have the advantage of Sir Condy in *Castle Rackrent*; you will know what your friends said of you after you were dead.' 'I hope I shall,' he replied. Poor fellow! We had known each other ever since we were boys. But I had no time to be sorry; I went on with the army and never saw him again.[51]

'Never mind.' 'But I had no time to be sorry.' These are nods of a kind, but neither is of the kind that John Jay Chapman was imagining when he wrote that 'the nod of the Duke of Wellington was insufferable'—that is, the nod to the vanquished from a condescending victor. Yet Wellington's badinage will have steadied the wounded DeLancey.

---

48. *Selected Writings of Chapman*, 50.
49. On 'standing by each other' as against 'standing around each other', see the poem by Carmen Bugan, p. 287 below.
50. Tennyson, *Ode on the Death of the Duke of Wellington* (1852), 38–9.
51. Colonel Sir William Howe DeLancey (1778–1815). Wellington's conversation, as recorded by Samuel Rogers, *Table-Talk & Recollections*, ed. Christopher Ricks (2011), 127–8, 130–3.

In Maria Edgeworth's novel, Sir Condy Rackrent played dead—'I've a notion I shall not be long for this world any how, and I've a great fancy to see my own funeral afore I die'—only to grumble it away ('I've had enough of this; I'm smothering, and can't hear a word of all they're saying of the deceased'): 'So the night passed off very merrily, but, to my mind, sir Condy was rather upon the sad order in the midst of it all, not finding there had been such a great talk about himself after his death as he had always expected to hear.'[52]

Wellington did right by DeLancey in all this. ~'I had reported him among the killed'~. DeLancey had not been killed, but he was to die of his wounds. The Battle of Waterloo was June 1815; in July 1916, the Great War saw a real life sequel. Robert Graves set it down.[53]

It was about ten o'clock on the 20th that I was hit. Late that night the colonel came to the dressing-station; he saw me lying in the corner and was told that I was done for··· That morning the colonel wrote the usual formal letters of condolence to the next-of-kin of the six or seven officers who had been killed. This was his letter to my mother:

22/7/16

DEAR MRS. GRAVES,

I very much regret to have to write and tell you your son has died of wounds. He was very gallant and was doing so well and is a great loss···

But Graves was alive, and was doing as well as could be expected at Queen Alexandra's Hospital, Highgate. 'I heard here for the first time that I was supposed to be dead; the joke contributed greatly to my recovery. The people with whom I had been on the worst terms during my life wrote the most enthusiastic condolences to my parents: my housemaster, for instance.' There seemed no end to the sardonic possibilities. 'Some letters written to me in France were returned to him [Graves's father] as my next-of-kin. They were surcharged: "Died of wounds—present location uncertain."'

Graves lived to tell the tale not only in the fine lean prose of *Good-Bye to All That*—'The only inconvenience that my death caused me was that Cox's Bank stopped my pay and I had difficulty in persuading it to honour my cheques'—but in his poem *The Second-Fated*:

---

52. *Castle Rackrent* (1800), ed. Ryan Twomey (New York, 2015), 53–4. Seven pages later, Sir Condy is dead. ('He had but a very poor funeral after all.')
53. *Good-Bye to All That* (1929), chapter XX, pp. 273–82.

> Fortune enrolled me among the second-fated
> Who have read their own obituaries in *The Times*,
> Have heard 'Where, death, thy sting, Where, grave, thy victory?'
> Intoned with unction over their still clay,
> Have seen two parallel red-ink lines drawn
> Under their manic-depressive bank accounts · · ·[54]

The Duke of Wellington figured within Chapman's thoughts on sacrifice and 'absolute heroism'. In the *North American Review* in October 1918, a month before the Armistice was signed, Chapman issued a warning: *The President's Dictatorship*. He knew better than to limit himself to fear of any personal exceptionalism in or from President Woodrow Wilson, for Chapman knew that there has never been a nation that has not laid claim to exceptionalism. The incipient tragedy is the combination of exceptionalist hubris with not just possessing but being the most effective fighting machine in the world. The fire this time—just as in the times of earlier World Powers—would not be that of failure but that of success, a nation's perilous power in the face of other nations. And over the face of the earth.

The United States is to be tried in the fire of success as other nations have been—and no one of them has come out scathe-less. The ambition and cruelty of the Spaniard in the sixteenth century were proverbial. The insolence of Frenchmen in the age of Louis XIV was wounding to the pride of all other nations. At a later date the nod of the Duke of Wellington was insufferable · · · And now we face this situation: that the United States will probably soon possess the most effective fighting machine in the world. I suppose it is impossible that the consciousness of this fact should not show upon the lip of every American in the near future; and I look with some dread for the symptom, because it is a symptom of decay. Nineveh and Babylon rise up before me when I see it. There is something in the exertion of power which is not good for human nature; and war is only wholesome when it means pure sacrifice, absolute heroism · · · At any rate, let us not rejoice in becoming a World Power. Let us be weary at the very thought of it. Let us adopt no tone of bettering humanity or pushing our sacred institutions over the face of the earth.

> ~Because it is a symptom of decay
> Nineveh and Babylon rise up before me
> Weary at the very thought of it~

---

54. *The Second-Fated*, in *5 Pens in Hand* (1958); *Complete Poems*, ed. Beryl Graves and Dunstan Ward, vol. 2 (Manchester, 1997).

When in 1992 General Norman Schwarzkopf, of the Gulf War, gave to his autobiography the title *It Doesn't Take a Hero*, he conceded too much when he spoke with modesty. 'It doesn't take a hero to order men into battle. It takes a hero to be one of those men who goes into battle.'[55] But this, though well meant, is not well judged. For it is a bleak truth—the penalty for disobeying a military order necessarily being what it is—that not every man who obeys the order is a hero, and, conversely, that to order men into battle may ask great resolve of a different kind. 'It doesn't take a hero ⋯'. Yet in some sense it does take one to know one. 'We will also take the liberty to deny altogether that of the witty Frenchman, that no man is a Hero to his valet-de-chambre.'[56] For Carlyle knew that cynicism has a way of inadvertently telling the truth. 'The Valet does not know a Hero when he sees him! Alas, no: it requires a kind of *Hero* to do that;—'.

T. S. Eliot when young chose to end a poem with a sigh:

> A hero! And how much it means;
> How much—
> The rest is merely shifting scenes.   (*Mandarins* I)

Later, he thought again about what it means.[57] 'It has often been said that no man is a hero to his own valet; what is much more important is that no honest man can be a hero to himself; for he must be aware how many causes in world history, outside of abilities and genius, have been responsible for greatness.'

55. Chris Walsh's *Cowardice: A Brief History* (2014) is very wise on courage, on deserters, and on honour (which the book breathes as its element).
56. 'The Hero as Man of Letters', in *On Heroes, Hero-Worship, and the Heroic in History*, 183–4. '*that of* [the witty Frenchman]': OED 8c, 'referring to a statement or saying cited immediately after; usually in *that of* (the author)'; 1662 'according to that of Macrobius'.
57. *The Varieties of Metaphysical Poetry*, ed. Ronald Schuchard (London, 1993), 289.

9

T. S. Eliot, Byron, and
Leading Actors

'Byron (1788–1824)', by T. S. Eliot (1888–1965), was written as an act of friendship. Not towards Byron; rather, Eliot towards *son ami bien-aimé*, Bonamy Dobrée, who had solicited a contribution to *From Anne to Victoria* (1937).[1] Eliot ruefully recalled 'the days of my schoolboy infatuation' and 'the first boyhood enthusiasm', with Byron's 'imposture' (even in *Don Juan*) finding itself duly disparaged. Nothing needed to be acknowledged by way of the help to 'a beginner in 1908' that Byron's insouciant *noblesse* had furnished, although Eliot's intriguing poems of 1908–14 had made evident whence the lordly manner.

> He said: this universe is very clever
>   The scientists have laid it out on paper
> Each atom goes on working out its law, and never
>   Can cut an unintentioned caper.[2]

The intentioned clever caper is thanks to Byron, with the nobility—gracing what Eliot called 'that monstrous house-party'—moving to 'what is called mobility'.

> This makes your actors, artists, and romancers,
>   Heroes sometimes, though seldom—sages never;
> But speakers, bards, diplomatists, and dancers,

---

1. 'Byron', in *On Poetry and Poets* (London, 1957), 193–206. A short essay, not in need of page-references here.
2. Written March 1911. *The Poems of T. S. Eliot,* ed. Christopher Ricks and Jim McCue, (London, 2015), i. 259, 1127–8.

> Little that's great, but much of what is clever;
> Most orators, but very few financiers · · ·[3]

(Don Juan, Canto XVI, 98)

> And wherefore this exordium?—Why, just now,
>   In taking up this paltry sheet of paper,
> My bosom underwent a glorious glow,
>   And my internal Spirit cut a caper · · ·   (Don Juan, Canto X, 3)

The second-stage Byronic glow faded for the young Eliot as soon as he realized that the wry spry art of Jules Laforgue offered even more than Byron by way of delight, opportunity, and rescue—Laforgue, 'to whom I owe more than to any one poet in any language'.[4] Nevertheless, Eliot had understood that he needed to read, mark, learn, and inwardly digest Byron. 'I also like to dine on becaficas': it was by courtesy of *Beppo* that this epigraph to *The Sacred Wood* (1920)—unidentified, unlike the companion epigraph from Petronius—was served.

> The waiter brings in oranges
> Bananas figs and hothouse grapes;

(Sweeney Among the Nightingales)

But it is Byron who brings in fig-peckers.

Much of Eliot's chivvied essay on Byron was at a loss. Two full empty pages were devoted to plot-summary in hope of clarifying any *Giaour*-power. One of the matters that looked fertile was Byron's nationality. 'I therefore suggest considering Byron as a Scottish poet— I say "Scottish", not "Scots", since he wrote in English.' 'Of a Scottish quality in Byron's poetry, I shall speak when I come to *Don Juan*.' But when Eliot came to speak of this, he had nothing to say. (A pity, given his having put so well in 1919 a penetrating question: 'Was There a Scottish Literature?'[5]) 'I cannot think of any other poet of his distinction who might so easily have been an accomplished foreigner writing English.' But then if Byron is to be considered 'a Scottish poet', he *was* a foreigner when writing English. Eliot himself—like, say, Henry James— was an accomplished foreigner, one who, *naturaliter* (again like James), had come to embody a nationality question. Eliot might have found or

---

3. As in the Eliot edition, raised ellipses · · · mean an omission here and now.
4. *To Criticize the Critic* (London, 1965), 22. *The Poems of T. S. Eliot*, i. 355-62, on 'A Beginner in 1908'.
5. *Athenaeum*, 1 August 1919.

made something here. But all that happens is that when the thought returns, nothing turns on it. 'He was right in making the hero of his house-party a Spaniard, for what Byron understands and dislikes about English society is very much what an intelligent foreigner in the same position would understand and dislike.'

Eliot did come to divine a possible *raison d'être* for his Byron essay, but only when he let his life of the mind be invaded by real-life (and *realpolitik*) foreigners: Hitler and Mussolini. A time-warp (1937 or 1927?) both led Eliot to, and half-concealed from him, one aspect of the rolery of leading actors. This entails identifying now the animus as to Byron—whose 'acute animosity sharpened his powers of observation'.

Sir Walter Scott had an air of nobility, magnanimity, and serenity (the chime setting itself against the ensuing 'triviality').

But Byron—that pudgy face suggesting a tendency to corpulence, that weakly sensual mouth, that restless triviality of expression, and worst of all that blind look of the self-conscious beauty; the bust of Byron is that of a man who was every inch the touring tragedian. Yet it was by being so thorough-going an actor that Byron arrived at a kind of knowledge: of the world outside, which he had to learn something about in order to play his role in it, and of that part of himself which was his role. Superficial knowledge, of course, but accurate so far as it went.

Of course. Eliot's hostility is all too plain, but fortunately he found that he could not but fret valuably about the relations between a *role* and the *real*. Eliot was pressed towards the salutary intractabilities that constitute not only our personal but our political lives. 'Every inch the touring tragedian.' 'Ay, every inch a king.' Mad, King Lear, but a king, withal. And when a king was later described—as Andrew Marvell described King Charles the First—as a 'royal actor', any distinction between pretending to be brave on the scaffold and actually being brave would sour into a mean-minded jeer. Off with his head. 'Come off it, you're only pretending to be brave': vulgar spite.

> That thence the *Royal Actor* born
> The *Tragick Scaffold* might adorn:
>   While round the armèd Bands
>   Did clap their bloody hands.
> *He* nothing common did or mean
> Upon that memorable Scene:
>   But with his keener Eye

> The Axes edge did try:
> Nor call'd the *Gods* with vulgar spight
> To vindicate his helpless Right,
> But bow'd his comely Head,
> Down as upon a Bed.

(An Horatian Ode upon Cromwell's Return from Ireland, 1650)

There, the paradox had been a tragic one. In Goldsmith's *Retaliation* (1774), it would prove to be a comic realization of how teasingly laminated a great actor might prove to be, incarnating the contrary truths that lurk in the verb *to act*.

> Here lies David Garrick, describe me who can,
> An abridgment of all that was pleasant in man;
> As an actor, confessed without rival to shine:
> As a wit, if not first, in the very first line;
> Yet, with talents like these and an excellent heart,
> The man had his failings, a dupe to his art.
> Like an ill-judging beauty, his colours he spread,
> And beplastered with rouge his own natural red.
> On the stage he was natural, simple, affecting:
> 'Twas only that, when he was off, he was acting.

As for Byron, he was never on stage—or off it, come to that. Eliot's sense of him had to turn, again and again, to the word *pose*. But (Eliot's restlessness) this is a word that poses a question, many difficulties.

It would be difficult to say whether Byron was a proud man, or a man who liked to pose as a proud man—the possibility of the two attitudes being combined in the same person does not make them any less dissimilar in the abstract.

With Byron, if you like, everything was pose, but the existence of a pose implies the possibility of a reality to which the pose pretends.[6]

Among the give-aways that paradoxically are also holding-operations, there is the quasi-concession *if you like*, itself a touch actorly. 'With his pose, he is also a *poète contumace* in a solemn country.'[7]

Byron was the 'thorough-going actor'. And how thoroughly far did he go? To the Greek War of Independence (for Eliot, drily, 'the Greek

---

6. *The Varieties of Metaphysical Poetry*, ed. Ronald Schuchard (London, 1993), 209, the Clark Lectures, 1926.
7. Tristan Corbière's 'Le Poète contumace' contributed to Eliot's poems in French, 'Petit Epître' and 'Tristan Corbière'.

adventure'), and to death. The stakes had been real and had been high. Personal, national, international.

Such was still the case in 1937, a year that saw two solicited publications that engage 'leading actors' and that would have been the stronger as a single persevering argument: 'Byron (1788–1824)', published in February, and then a piece—published November/December—on Wyndham Lewis's *The Lion and the Fox*.

In December 1936, Lewis had inscribed a copy for Eliot, who soon declared, 'Lewis's book is tremendously interesting.'[8] Eliot commissioned a review, of which he promptly acknowledged receipt ('I like your Lewis very much: and he is a very difficult man to review'),[9] and the five-page (signed) review was published in *The Monthly Criterion* in June 1927.

Ten years later, when Eliot had to come up with something for Dobrée, the *Monthly Criterion* review of *The Lion and the Fox* will have come to mind, not least because it was by Dobrée. The coinciding prompted a Byron/Wyndham Lewis coinciding, with then a further convergence: Byron as a thorough-going actor, and the great dictators (in whom Wyndham Lewis took an interest scarcely healthy) as leading actors. *Entre deux guerres* in 1927, Dobrée had invoked the Great War; had reported that, for Lewis, Shakespeare was 'a despiser of his heroes, notably so in the case of Coriolanus'; and had found Lewis at 'his most stimulating' on Machiavelli. Dobrée closed with a corrugated compliment to the book: 'it is doubtful if it will find its way into the schools: there is too much reality about it'. Eliot was to pay *Don Juan* a similar compliment. For Lord Henry and Lady Adeline 'have a reality for which their author has perhaps not received due credit', and Aurora Raby is 'a character too serious, in a way too real for the world he knew'.

For Byron in *Don Juan*, and for Eliot on *Don Juan*, the *real* keeps coming up against a *role*. Dobrée had quoted the sub-title of *The Lion and the Fox*: *The Rôle of the Hero in the Plays of Shakespeare*. Eliot says of Don Juan that 'he exhibits a kind of physical courage and capacity for heroism which we are quite willing to attribute to Byron himself'. Neither Eliot nor Byron could cut the part to be played by 'role' (or by 'rôle'). Both recognized the intransigence of the relations between the

8. To Ottoline Morrell, 7 February 1927. *The Letters of T. S. Eliot, vol. 3: 1926–1927*, ed. Valerie Eliot and John Haffenden (London, 2012), 412.
9. 28 February 1927. Ibid. 432.

real and a *role*. Eliot proffered 'an attempt to start that ball rolling', though just what ball was never clear unless it was *role* that was the name of the game. An intelligent foreigner will register the ascending degrees of foreign-ness: role, and rôle, and *rôle*.[10] In the essay, Eliot has the least foreign form—'He was an actor who devoted immense trouble to *becoming* a role that he adopted'—which dances along with the conviction of 'a touch of unreality: to a man so occupied with himself and with the figure he was cutting nothing outside could be altogether real'. This accords with Byron's having *role* and *real* be immediate of vicinity and teasingly akin. As in *Don Juan* Canto XVI, where the rhymes turn elegantly, and where the theatrical figures of speech play their part within the company (and where 'pose' relaxes surreptitiously within 'supposed').

96
Though this was most expedient on the whole,
    And usual—Juan, when he cast a glance
On Adeline while playing her grand role,
    Which she went through as though it were a dance,
    (Betraying only now and then her soul
    By a look scarce perceptibly askance
Of weariness or scorn) began to feel
Some doubt how much of Adeline was *real*;

97
So well she acted, all and every part
    By turns—with that vivacious versatility,
Which many people take for want of heart.
    They err—'tis merely what is called mobility,
A thing of temperament and not of art,
    Though seeming so, from its supposed facility;
And false—though true; for surely they're sincerest,
Who are strongly acted on by what is nearest.

98
This makes your actors, artists, and romancers,
    Heroes sometimes, though seldom—sages never;
But speakers, bards, diplomatists, and dancers,
    Little that's great, but much of what is clever;
Most orators, but very few financiers···

10. *OED* originally had || Rôle. Later: delete || [not naturalized] and add: Now usu. spelt **role**.

Actors, heroes, bards, diplomatists, orators: and, admittedly, dema-
gogues. Dictators, too. All of these *mobilistas* make play with what is
real and what is role, within the Byronic worlds of tragicomedy and
comi-tragedy. As embodied by the young Eliot in *Suite Clownesque*
(written 1910).

> Here's the comedian again
> With broad dogmatic vest, and nose
> Nose that interrogates the stars,
> Impressive, sceptic, scarlet nose;
> The most expressive, real of men · · ·
>
> Here's one who has the world at rights
> Here's one who gets away with it
> By simple spreading of the toes,
> A self-embodied rôle, his soul
> Concentred in his vest and nose.

Gets away with it ... Eliot remarked of *The Giaour* that Byron 'not only
gets away with it, but gets away with it *as narrative*'. The art of Eliot
had always been to get away with it *without* narrative. Or with very
precious little narrative. As he said of Jonson and *Volpone*, 'it is not so
much skill in plot as skill in doing without a plot'.[11]

Eliot in 1927 had been moved to dissent from Mario Praz (who in
1937 was to figure in Eliot's Byron essay), regretting 'that you have
given so much space to *The Lion and the Fox* which, apart from many
brilliant incidental observations is, I think, not only an inferior book
but a by-product on which he ought not to have wasted so much
time'.[12] There was by 1937 something compensatory in Eliot's explor-
ing *The Lion and the Fox* ten years after it was published.[13] But a
remarkable creativity had intervened: *Coriolan* I. *Triumphal March* and
II. *Difficulties of a Statesman*, first published as one in 1936.

Coriolanus, in fact, has a peculiar pertinence. For Mr. Lewis has seen (what the
French public, a few years ago, seems to have missed) that *Coriolanus* is not a
defence of aristocracy, or a mere attack on the mob. Shakespeare is, in fact,
completely critical and detached from any partisanship; in this play his own
emotion is very strong indeed, but cannot be associated with that of any

---

11. 'Ben Jonson' (1919); *Selected Essays*, 3rd edn (London, 1951), 155.
12. 11 November 1927. *The Letters of T. S. Eliot*, vol. 3, 815.
13. *The Complete Prose of T. S. Eliot* heads it 'A retrospective review of *The Lion and the
    Fox*'. (Belated, rather? But best left as originally published, simply headed THE LION
    AND THE FOX.)

character or group in the play—and it is this detachment which makes the ordinary reader find this most violent play rather frigid. *The Lion and the Fox* is also a book about politics; but instead of calling it a 'political book' we should do better to call it an 'anti-political' book. And for this reason it is very pertinently concerned with Machiavelli.

—and (as Machiavelli had been) with Dictators, ancient and modern. (*Coriolanus* II. ii makes mention of 'our then Dictator, | Whom with all praise I point at'.) Eliot was furthering Lewis's venture, under cover of *perhaps worthwhile.*[14]

It is perhaps worthwhile at this point to mention the difference between the *aristocratic* ruler (seldom quite so aristocratic as he is imagined to be) who is an extinct type, and the demagogue. Frederick the Great, to whom Mr. Lewis devotes a chapter of this book, was an aristocratic ruler; with the advantage of being an exceptionally intelligent tyrant over an exceptionally docile people. Frederick the Great was therefore able to be a kind of artist, playing a part for his own amusement and in conformity with his own private and very unpleasant ideal. The modern 'dictator,' a Hitler or Mussolini, must be thought of rather (I am not professing to interpret Mr. Lewis's opinion, but venturing my own) as a highly paid *leading actor*, whose business is to divert his people (individually, from the spectacle of their own littleness as well as from more useful business). (I wonder whether the more retired life of other dictators, Josef the Terrible or the gentle Salazar, is not perhaps a token that they have more power).[15]

Eliot makes dark play with those powerful useful business-like lunulae (   ), turning in a dance of death, cheek to cheek—or is it back to back, a duel of death?

(I · · · venturing my own) >
(individually · · · more useful business). (I wonder whether · · · more power)[16]

'One object of Mr. Lewis's attention', we learn from Eliot, is 'the ruler as dramatic star'. By 1937 the great dictators were starring, disastrously. Stalin, since 1924. Mussolini, since 1925. Salazar, since 1932. Hitler, since 1933. Franco, since 1936. 'The gentle Salazar'? Why gentle with

---

14. 'And his conversation, so nicely | Restricted to What Precisely | And If and Perhaps and But' (*Five-Finger Exercises* V).
15. *Twentieth Century Verse*, November/December 1937. A contribution by Eliot to this Wyndham Lewis number had been solicited by the editor, Julian Symons.
16. Eliot shares Byron's feeling for them: 'His genius for digression, for wandering away from his subject (usually to talk about himself) and suddenly returning to it.' *But I Digress*, by John Lennard (1991), shows how much these little moons (lunulae is Erasmus's term) can illuminate.

Salazar? Well, at least he did not go in for histrionics. Anyway there will prove to be an *at most* tacitly but conclusively at hand.

The Christian News-Letter, 14 August 1940

PORTUGAL

In recent weeks there have been frequent references in the Press to Portugal, first in connection with the Colonial Exhibition held in Lisbon to celebrate the anniversary of the nation's independence,[17] and second in connection with our own Mediterranean problems.[18] Much of this matter has been repetitive, but at least, the name and eminence of Dr. Salazar, the Prime Minister for the last twelve years, is now well known to the British public. Dr. Salazar—whose chief, as President, is General Carmona—has never encouraged the adoption of the 'Leader Principle,' and no leader has ever won his position with less personal ambition, or less appeal to mass emotion. Nor did he rise to power through a 'party.' He simply happens to be the ablest statesman in Portugal, all the more distinguished by never appearing in a uniform or wearing a decoration. He looks what he is by profession, a university professor: but a very brief meeting with him gave me the impression of a university professor who is also an extremely acute judge of men. His interest and importance for us is that without being in any dubious political sense pro-clerical he is a Christian at the head of a Christian country.

Some appeal to Mass emotion, then. The rhetoric of 'He simply happens to be ⋯' is dubious, and Eliot's uncharacteristic failures of agreement ('the name and eminence ⋯ is', 'His interest and importance for us is ⋯') may betray an honourable unease. But the nub is the credit to be given to a ruler who is not an actor, does not pose. Not that it really was the case (*pace* Eliot) that Salazar recognized the President of Portugal as his 'chief'.[19] A pose. But this or such was Salazar's way. There was, Eliot assures us, no encouraging of 'The

17. Portuguese Independence of Spain had been gained in 1640. (Byron had not lived to see Greek Independence of the Ottoman Empire, 1832.)
18. A diplomatic nod to, for instance, the Battle of the Mediterranean (the Italian Navy vs. the Royal Navy), which began on 10 June 1940.
19. *Wikipedia*: 'Carmona nominated Salazar as Prime Minister in 1932, and largely turned over control of the government to him. In 1933, a new constitution officially established the "Estado Novo". On paper, the new document codified the dictatorial powers Carmona had exercised since 1928. However, in practice he was now little more than a figurehead; Salazar held the real power. On paper, the president's power to dismiss Salazar was the only check on his power. However, Carmona mostly allowed Salazar a free hand.' (There is no such thing as a free hand, even on paper. 'The hand that signed the paper felled a city ⋯ A hand rules pity as a hand rules heaven; | Hands have no tears to flow'. Dylan Thomas, written 1933, published 1935.)

Leader Principle' from Dr Salazar; it was elsewhere, with Hitler and
Mussolini, that the Leader Principle was acted out by highly paid (and
paid-for) leading actors.[20]

The year 1927, the year of *The Lion and the Fox* and of Dobrée's
review of it, had seen Eliot paying his utmost attention to the power
and servitude of the histrionic.[21] 'Shakespeare and the Stoicism of
Seneca', with its grasp upon self-dramatization and self-deception,
starring Othello, was delivered in March. In May, Eliot remarked of
Baudelaire: 'Experience, as a sequence of outward events, is nothing in
itself; it is possible to pass through the most terrible experiences protected by histrionic vanity.' In June: 'It is easy to admire Machiavelli in
a sentimental way. It is only one of the sentimental and histrionic poses
of human nature—and human nature is incorrigibly histrionic—to
pose as a "realist".'[22] Praising *The Lion and the Fox* as 'extremely interesting', and accusing sentimentalists of 'a form of self-satisfaction and
self-deception', Eliot exempted Machiavelli ('He had none of the
instinct to pose'), where the immediately preceding contrast—of a
writer given to 'indulgences'—was Byron. 'The ethic of Seneca is a
matter of postures' (September 1927). Pose is held to expand into posture, itself always in danger of imposture.

Come 1937, Byron is to be seen as the posturing touring tragedian.
(*Europe he saw, and Europe saw him too.*) Adverted by Charles Du Bos
to 'a long passage of self-portraiture from *Lara*', Eliot concedes and
recedes:

This passage strikes me also as a masterpiece of self-analysis, but of a self that
is largely a deliberate fabrication—a fabrication that is only completed in the
actual writing of the lines. The reason why Byron understood this self so well,

20. Eliot's inflections might in another country have been the death of him. In 'The
Literature of Fascism', of a Napoleonic Concordat in Italy: 'the position of the Roman
Church, facing a Roman Dictator a few yards away, is much more difficult than when
it faced a European Dictator in Paris' (*The Criterion*, December 1928). 'Civilization has
almost too many friends · · · I am sure that all our great leaders—not only Stalin and
Hitler and Mussolini and Kemal Ataturk, but · · · even General Franco, would be willing to stake everything in the cause of civilization' (*The Criterion*, October 1936).
21. Eliot's 1927 writings on self-dramatization and self-deception are compacted in
'T. S. Eliot and "Wrong'd Othello"', pp. 98–101 above.
22. Byron: 'It will readily be imagined that the prejudices which have passed the name of
Machiavelli into an epithet proverbial of iniquity, exist no longer at Florence. His
memory was persecuted as his life had been for an attachment to liberty, incompatible
with the new system of despotism, which succeeded the fall of the free governments
of Italy' (Note to *Childe Harold's Pilgrimage*, Canto IV).

is that it is largely his own invention; and it is only the self that he invented that he understood perfectly. If I am correct, one cannot help feeling pity and horror at the spectacle of a man devoting such gigantic energy and persistence to such a useless and petty purpose: though at the same time we must feel sympathy and humility in reflecting that is a vice to which most of us are addicted in a fitful and less persevering way; that is to say, Byron made a vocation out of what for most of us is an irregular weakness, and deserves a certain sad admiration for his degree of success.

Eliot had spent a dozen stray lines comparing busts. 'Were one a person who liked to have busts about, a bust of Scott would be something one could live with'. But Byron... Byron himself remembered in 1813 what the bust of a certain hero had meant to him in his first boyhood enthusiasm.

Buonaparte! Ever since I defended my bust of him at Harrow against the rascally time-servers, when the war broke out in 1803, he has been a 'Héros de Roman' of mine—on the continent; I don't want him here. But I don't like those same flights—leaving of armies, &c. &c. I am sure when I fought for his bust at school, I did not think he would run away from himself. But I should not wonder if he banged them yet.[23]

Where Eliot chose Byron as the recipient of his pity and horror, Byron chose a man of gigantic energy and persistence: Napoleon. Byron could not get his mind or his heart all round Napoleon, any more than could Robert Lowell in *History*, resisting but never quite bringing himself to repudiate the collusion of the self-dramatizing and the self-deceiving in Napoleon,

> a man... not bloodthirsty, not sparing of blood,
> with an eye and *sang-froid* to manage everything;
> his iron hand no mere appendage of his mind
> for improbable contingencies · · ·
> for uprooting races, lineages, Jacobins—
> the price was paltry... three million soldiers dead,
> grand opera fixed like morphine in their veins.
> Dare we say, he had no moral center?
> All gone like the smoke of his own artillery?[24]

One moral centre in any engagement with heroism and heroics is suicide, as in the case of Othello, whom Byron summons in his *Ode to*

---

23. Journal, 17 November 1813. *Byron's Letters and Journals*, vol. 3: '*Alas! The Love of Women*', ed. Leslie A. Marchand (London, 1974), 210.
24. The revised text from *Collected Poems*, ed. Frank Bidart and David Gewanter (2003).

Napoleon Buonaparte. In 1814 Napoleon, defeated, chose to commit abdication.[25] Byron's journal seethes.[26]

Saturday, April 9th, 1814

I mark this day!

Napoleon Buonaparte has abdicated the throne of the world. 'Excellent well.' Methinks Sylla did better; for he revenged and resigned in the height of his sway, red with the slaughter of his foes—the finest instance of glorious contempt of the rascals upon record · · · but Napoleon, worst of all · · · The 'Isle of Elba' to retire to! · · · Oh that Juvenal or Johnson could rise from the dead! 'Expende—quot libras in duce summo invenies?'[27]

The entry ends: 'But I won't give him up even now; though all his admirers have, "like the Thanes, fallen from him." '

The Dictator Sylla had succeeded, in defeat, in besting and worsting Napoleon. 'I have always looked upon Sylla as the greatest Character in History—for laying down his power at the moment when it was "too great to keep or to resign" and thus despising them all.'[28] But Byron had higher hopes (*loftier*, it may be feared) than could any longer be vested in Napoleon. 'To be the first man—not the Dictator—not the Sylla, but the Washington or the Aristides—the leader in talent and truth—is next to the Divinity!'[29]

> I don't want to see no Shakespeare or Napoleon,
> I don't want to see no Lincoln or George Washington.

Eliot in 1952, choosing instead that the spiritualist trance summon Jack Johnson, the first black heavyweight world champion.[30] But it was the

---

25. Susan J. Wolfson and Peter J. Manning in *Selected Poems* (2005) add a dimension: 'The decision of the heroic figure, in whom he saw himself and with whom he was paired in the popular imagination, to capitulate rather than nobly to commit suicide left Byron "utterly bewildered and confounded"; he could not know that on 12 April, two days after he composed his first draft, Napoleon did attempt to poison himself.'
26. '*Alas! The Love of Women*': *Byron's Letters and Journals*, 256. Marchand helps with the Shakespearean (for instance, 'the Thanes', from *Macbeth*). 'Excellent well' would have profited. 'Do you know me, my Lord?', with Hamlet's: 'Excellent, excellent well: y'are a Fishmonger' (I. ii).
27. 'Weigh [Hannibal]; how many pounds' weight will you find in that greatest of commanders?' (Marchand).
28. Journal, 1 May 1821. *Byron's Letters and Journals*, vol. 8: '*Born for Opposition*', ed. Marchand (London, 1978), 106. Byron's quotation, unidentified: Johnson, *The Vanity of Human Wishes*, 133–4: 'What but their Wish indulg'd in Courts to shine, | And Pow'r too great to keep or to resign?'
29. Journal, November 1813. '*Alas! The Love of Women*': *Byron's Letters and Journals*, 218.
30. *The Poems of T. S. Eliot*, ii. 200–1.

dictator Sylla whom Eliot found haunting. Of *Catiline*, he wrote: 'Jonson makes Sylla's ghost, while the words are spoken, a living and terrible force. The words fall with as determined a beat as if they were the will of the morose Dictator himself.'[31] A twist was given to scholar/ dictator-ship by Felix Schelling's dubbing Jonson 'the first literary dictator', with a further twist by Eliot: 'We have been taught to think of him as the man, the dictator (confusedly in our minds with his later namesake).' Samuel Johnson was the Great Cham; Eliot became, for those who accused him of pontification, 'the Pope of Russell Square'. Dictators preyed on him; there is something both acute and askew in his determining the Mississippi to be one. 'A river, a very big and powerful river, is the only natural force that can wholly determine the course of human peregrination.' At sea, or in the prairie, or among mountains, one may have a choice. 'But the river with its strong, swift current is the dictator to the raft or to the steamboat. It is a treacherous and capricious dictator.'[32]

'But I won't give him up even now.' But the *Ode to Napoleon Buonaparte* did give Napoleon up to contempt. Juvenal and Johnson were made to rise from the dead (and from the journal-entry), with the *Ode*'s first epigraph being the line from Juvenal's Tenth Satire. Johnson had envisaged a modern Hannibal in Charles XII of Sweden:

> His Fall was destin'd to a barren Strand,
> A petty Fortress, and a dubious Hand;
> He left the Name, at which the World grew pale,
> To point a Moral, or adorn a Tale.
>
> (*The Vanity of Human Wishes*, 219–22)

Eliot: 'These lines, especially the first two, with their just inevitable sequence of *barren*, *petty*, and *dubious*, still seem to me among the finest that have ever been written in that particular idiom.'[33] Byron had quoted the last line in a letter of 1820, subsequently recording: 'Read Johnson's "Vanity of Human Wishes," – all the examples and mode of giving them sublime···'tis a grand poem—and *so true!*—true as the 10th of Juvenal himself.'[34]

---

31. 'Ben Jonson'; *Selected Essays*, 150, 154.
32. Introduction to *The Adventures of Huckleberry Finn* (1950).
33. Introductory Essay to *London: A Poem and The Vanity of Human Wishes* (1930). Eliot hailed the section on Charles XII as, 'in itself, quite perfect in form' ('Johnson as Critic and Poet', 1944; *On Poetry and Poets*, 180).
34. Journal, 9 January 1821. *'Born for Opposition': Byron's Letters and Journals*, 19.

Johnson, Juvenal... A third great writer had to be raised: Gibbon. Byron's other epigraph for the *Ode* is from *The History of the Decline and Fall of the Roman Empire.*[35] 'The Emperor Nepos was acknowledged by the *Senate*, by the *Italians*, and by the Provincials of *Gaul*', but within a year a seditious army was in full march from Rome to Ravenna. 'Nepos trembled at their approach; and, instead of placing a just confidence in the strength of Ravenna, he hastily escaped to his ships, and retired to his Dalmatian principality.'

By this shameful abdication, he protracted his life a few years, in a very ambiguous state, between an Emperor and an Exile, till—

At which point Byron cuts off the syntax and the life. Gibbon had proceeded, 'till he was assassinated by the ungrateful Glycerius, who was translated, perhaps as the reward of his crime, to the archbishopric of Milan'.

Napoleon's abdication had brought it about that 'Contempt could thus make mirth | Of these, the Conquerors of the earth' (107–8). Yet there was nothing in life that Byron could not make mirth of, so next year (1815) his readers were to join him in taking leisurely jaunty pleasure in Napoleon's having eluded Elba.

> Once fairly set out on his party of pleasure,
> Taking towns at his liking and crowns at his leisure,
> From Elba to Lyons and Paris he goes,
> Making *balls for* the ladies, and *bows to* his foes.[36]

Byron may himself have been 'every inch the touring tragedian', but now it was thumbs up for Napoleon, every *pouce* the touring comedian. 'With rings on her fingers and bells on her toes, | She shall have music wherever she goes.' The anapaests dance along on the tips of their toes, with 'toes' as the word unsung. The world is Byronic, and Napoleon may take not only towns but ladies at his and their liking, perhaps.

That Napoleon should put in a cameo appearance in Eliot's correspondence was to Eliot's liking. He could thus make mirth of a final

35. Ed. David Womersley (London, 1994), chapter XXXVI, ii. 400–1. (Gibbon has 'about five years'; Byron, 'a few years'.)
36. All the more respected as a great city when (like Paris) it is pronounced *à l'anglaise*, Lyons—when spelt with an *s*—is to be heard as *Lions*. Napoleon was being lyonized (he, a lion and a fox). The *OED* cites Scott (1809): 'They cannot lionize me without my returning the compliment and learning something from them.'

problem, while granting that the case of Napoleon was 'not quite parallel to mine'.

I have your letter of 13 June [1938], asking me whether I am an American or an English writer··· It might be argued that this question is one which cannot be decided by itself, but is only a special case in a general category. Is Napoleon, for instance, to be considered as an Italian or a Frenchman? We know that his native language was Italian, and that his Corsican family were probably of Genoese extraction. His case however is not quite parallel to mine, because he changed the spelling of his name, which I have not done.[37]

George Gordon Byron had been for a while George Byron Gordon, until 'Lord Byron' happily settled the matter. Eliot went by many names but did not change the spelling of Eliot.[38] As for the name of Napoleon, it rings out in the work of Old Possum (unlike Bonaparte/Buonaparte).[39] For Macavity is 'the Cat who all the time | Just controls their operations: the Napoleon of Crime!' 'He is the Napoleon of crime, Watson.'[40] But there needs no Sherlock Holmes to tell us where the sobriquet—with its rhyme—had been purloined from.[41] 'Even I', Byron half-boasted,

> Was reckoned, a considerable time,
> The grand Napoleon of the realms of rhyme.
>
> (*Don Juan*, Canto XI, 55)

Adducing 'the Napoleonic idea', Eliot wrote:

The feeling towards a dictator is quite other than that towards a king; it is merely the consummation of the feeling which the newspapers teach us to have towards Mr. Henry Ford, or any other big business man. In the *success* of a man like Mussolini (a man of 'the people') a whole nation may feel a kind of self-flattery; and the Russian people deified itself in Lenin. Both Italy and Russia seem to me to be suffering from Napoleonism.[42]

37. To Nelson Lansdale, 22 June 1938; *The Poems of T. S. Eliot*, i. 886.
38. After the attribution of *Ash-Wednesday* III to "T. S. Eliott", Eliot wrote, on 21 January 1930: 'I was Angry about the spelling of my name, but it is a Venial rather than a Deadly Sin: Elyot, Eliott or Aliot have been used at various periods; the only real insult is to spell it Elliot or Elliott, which is Scotch.' *The Poems of T. S. Eliot*, i. 1207.
39. But 'I might mention Griddlebone', called on to play a boney part (*Macavity: the Mystery Cat*, 40).
40. Of Moriarty. 'The Final Problem', in *The Memoirs of Sherlock Holmes*.
41. *The Poems of T. S. Eliot*, ii. 66.
42. 'Mr. Barnes and Mr. Rowse', *The Criterion*, July 1929.

Byron felt a kind of self-flattery. General Suwarrow did not, and although he suffered from Napoleon, he did not suffer from Napoleonism. Byron is at his greatest as a poet when he contemplates, in such another, this rising above posing and posturing and the figure he was cutting. For me, the greatest tragic moment in *Don Juan* is this, consummately realized:

> Suwarrow, who had small regard for tears,
>   And not much sympathy for blood, surveyed
> The women with their hair about their ears
>   And natural agonies, with a slight shade
> Of feeling; for however habit sears
>   Men's hearts against whole millions, when their trade
> Is butchery, sometimes a single sorrow
> Will touch even Heroes, and such was Suwarrow.

(Don Juan, Canto VII, 69)

The lines mean exactly what they say exactly. Not 'no regard for tears'; not 'no sympathy for blood'; not 'no shade of feeling'. Slight, no slighting. No sentimentality, and no cynicism either. With 'regard' coming to be seen somewhat differently when 'surveyed' arrives, and with 'their hair' and their 'agonies' bringing the sensation of a dispassionate yet compassionate zeugma. Suwarrow, a hero in this. Not coldness precisely, but coolth, yes. With all this being brought about by what Swinburne praised so duly in *Don Juan*: 'There is in that great poem an especial and exquisite balance and sustenance of alternate tones.'[43]

Reviving in 1937 *The Lion and the Fox*, Eliot said of Machiavelli and *The Prince*: 'What gives his book its terrifying greatness is the fact that he *does not seem to care.*' Napoleon, with his terrifying greatness, did not seem to care. Though his trade was butchery, he was not one to offer common commiseration; he played out his own kind of down-playing, courting the charge of callousness, head haught. Byron could not but note this.

The great error of Napoleon, 'if we have writ our annals true' [*Coriolanus*, V. vi], was a continued obtrusion on mankind of his want of all community of feeling for or with them; perhaps more offensive to human vanity than the active cruelty of more trembling and suspicious tyranny. Such were his speeches to public assemblies as well as individuals; and the single expression which he is said to have used on returning to Paris after the Russian winter had destroyed his army, rubbing his hands over a fire, 'This is pleasanter than

---

43. *Swinburne as Critic*, ed. C. K. Hyder (London, 1972), 39.

Moscow', would probably alienate more favour from his cause than the destruction and reverses which led to the remark.[44]

The bitter comedy of Napoleon's stylized aside is set against the bitter cold that formed part of Russia's defence against the King of Sweden (and, in due course, against Napoleon and against Hitler):

> Stern Famine guards the solitary Coast,
> And Winter barricades the Realms of Frost.
>
> (*The Vanity of Human Wishes*, 207–8)

'A grand poem—and *so true!*' On this, Byron and Eliot were at one.

44. *Childe Harold's Pilgrimage,* Canto III, xli.

10

Geoffrey Hill's Grievous Heroes

I

Geoffrey Hill paid tribute to Coleridge and Ruskin as 'my mind's heroes'. Posthumous on purpose, *The Book of Baruch by the Gnostic Justin* (2019) was to consist of as many poems—prose-poems—as Hill would live to complete. In the event (the event to which the whole creation moves), there were to be two hundred and seventy-one. Hill's death on 30 June 2016, at the age of 84, summoned the awe with which Boswell contemplated Samuel Johnson contemplating the end:

His mind resembled the vast amphitheatre, the Colisæum at Rome. In the centre stood his judgement, which, like a mighty gladiator, combated those apprehensions that, like the wild beasts of the *Arena*, were all around in cells, ready to be let out upon him. After a conflict, he drove them back into their dens; but not killing them, they were still assailing him. To my question, whether we might not fortify our minds for the approach of death, he answered, in a passion. 'No, Sir, let it alone. It matters not how a man dies, but how he lives'.[1]

The Book of Baruch attends upon heroes, hero-worship, and the heroic in history. 'You were heroic in your day and had great style'; 'fame and metaphor and things in that way heroic'; 'eight or nine hundred other heroes, bruisers, losers, and skivers'; 'I count them among my grievous heroes'.[2] My mind's heroes would not have to be my grievous heroes, but they might well be, and Coleridge and Ruskin were. What our minds should register is that the line that precedes 'my mind's heroes' has at its centre the word 'incomprehensible'.[3]

---

1. *Boswell's Life of Johnson*, ed. George Birkbeck Hill, rev. L. F. Powell (Oxford, 1934–1950), ii. 106–7.
2. *The Book of Baruch*, ed. Kenneth Haynes (Oxford, 2019), 29, 55, 84, 186.
3. Ibid. 261. Seamus Perry's prompt illumination of *The Book of Baruch* was outstanding, especially as to Hill's politics in relation to his theology (*London Review of Books*, 12 September 2019).

It often seemed that Hill could not write a single poem that did not accommodate this particular word-formation (*indescribable, impossible, unalterable, intolerable, unconscionable*...). More, he often associates such formations with the hero and the heroic. He insists on the vicinity of two things that look distant from one another: a compact suffix, *-ble*, and a capacious noun, *heroes*. Very different, the features of a hero and the functions of a suffix (in Hill's case, an indispensable suffix), yet the paired attentions, I now notice from *The Book of Baruch*, are made to seek one another's company. If a Royal Air Force poem (141) imagines 'some unheroic crew', you will find, a few lines later, that a claim is 'indelibly in your name'.

This suffix confronts not just 'the art of the possible' (the Politician's Tale) but the art of the impossible, both within art itself and within all else. For the hero may be thought of as someone who acknowledges, and who lives by, contrarieties that are both underfoot and aloft. To one side, a greater-than-usual refusal to grant the world's insistence that such-and-such is impossible (or indisputable or inescapable or inevitable...). To the other, a greater-than-usual refusal to be broken—or broken in—by the insistence of things, the fact that such-and-such is, yes, impossible (or indisputable...). Heroism may be characterized by an exceptionally imaginative courage in the face of these pincer-jaws. The unremarkable suffix *-ble* is the outward and visible sign of an inward and spiritual grind.

In 2012, I published an essay on Hill's life of the mind, the 'unrelenting, unreconciling mind'.[4] The present pages are a revision, relating Hill's unrelenting use of *-ble* to a sense of what this suffix was especially needed for. 'Rhyme is the grand enforcer': this was one of the *Expostulations on the Volcano*.[5] A mere two words later, the word that Hill enforced was 'hero', a forced off-rhyme with 'here I', two lines earlier. Here I had the answer: 'hero'.

Enter Thomas Carlyle.

The author of *On Heroes, Hero-Worship, and the Heroic in History* enters poem 259 of *The Book of Baruch*. The contrast is with Coleridge and Ruskin, both of whom Hill again honours, this time as 'honest', in

4. In *Geoffrey Hill: Essays on his Later Work*, ed. John Lyon and Peter McDonald (Oxford, 2012); my essay included some commentary and some lists that I now leave there. Hill: 'balk the strength | of Gillray's unrelenting, unreconciling mind', *To the High Court of Parliament: November 1994*.
5. *Expostulations on the Volcano*, 36; *The Daybooks* I, in *Broken Hierarchies: Poems 1952–2012*, ed. Kenneth Haynes (Oxford, 2013).

the immediately preceding sentence. The first of his lines on Carlyle enjoys its twisting; the next line wonders whether to go straight, as to what Hill owes and really ought to own.

> Carlyle was ever a malign twister, clad awhile like Nestor.
> These no doubt merely the smoke and mirrors of my debt.

Twisters, these, 'twister' into 'Nestor', and 'no doubt' into 'my debt'. This poem that summons Carlyle had opened with debts at once flaunted and flouted, flanked by the indispensable suffix: 'With debts insoluble ⋯'.

Carlyle's writings are as -ble-based as are Hill's, most notably in the three incarnations of the hero that are the closest to Carlyle and to Hill. 'The Hero as Prophet' is a babble of -ble, all too vulnerable to its own epithets, intolerable, unspeakable, insupportable, and unreadable. 'The Hero as Poet' pinions 'indestructible' between 'unheroic' and 'heroism': 'Such, in spite of every perverting influence, in the most unheroic times, is still our indestructible reverence for heroism.' The Poet is 'Heroic', even though 'reading rhyme' might be 'insupportable'.[6] As for 'The Hero as Man of Letters', this lecture topped the -ble stakes, reaching superlatively for two formations or deformations unadmitted by the *OED*, 'indispensablest' and 'indisputablest'. These, from the creator of 'impossiblest', or rather of this: 'how near it bordered on the absolutely insuperable! certainly the impossiblest-looking literary problem I ever had'. It is understandable that Carlyle was exclamatory. Heroically, he was writing for the second time the first volume of *The French Revolution*, inadvertently burnt by one of John Stuart Mill's servants.[7]

But then Hill's art engaged all six of Carlyle's embodiments of heroism, the others being 'The Hero as Divinity', 'The Hero as Priest', and 'The Hero as King'. Hill would probably have welcomed The Hero as Soldier, The Hero as Martyr, and The Hero as Scientist, all of whom he honoured in poems. In his *Collected Critical Writings*, the Index (no place for smoke and mirrors) makes clear that Carlyle vexed him and mattered to him.[8] But it is in *The Book of Baruch* that this particular convergence of the heroic and the -ble suffix is most telling.

6. *On Heroes, Hero-Worship, and the Heroic in History* (1841); *Works*, ed. H. D. Traill (London, 1896–1907), 85, 90–1.
7. Carlyle, in *Letters and Memorials of Jane Welsh Carlyle*, ed. J. A. Froude (London, 1883), i. 13.
8. On the achievement of this Index (by Hill and Kenneth Haynes), see Matthew Sperling, 'The Trouble of an Index', in *Essays in Criticism* (October 2011).

Carlyle's is the only *OED* citation for *irrecognizably*, *irrecognizability*, and *irrecognizant*, and is the first for *irrecognizable*. Hill, too, enjoyed such sustainability: 'sustain the intractable··· that unrecognizable man'.[9] *Oraclau / Oracles* (2010) had spoken of 'a word' when its game was really the formation of many a word:

> murderers
> In a word if it's a word we're after
> And not near-unrecognizable laughter.[10]

Oraclau had listened for 'the heroic song', had watched how 'ambition guides heroes', and had admitted Carlyle's best-known turn of phrase, the French Revolution's Robespierre as 'sea-green incorruptible'.

> I admit, I have not the least
>   Idea what *sea-green*
> *Incorruptible* means, knowing the man;
> What ironies a-dribble from what pen—
> Yes, *yes,* Carlyle, wife Welsh!—[11]

Hill knows perfectly well what Carlyle's phrase means. He pretends not, and begins the next poem (no. 94) with 'Well, to come clean, it makes me think of snot'.[12]

The *OED* is clear: 'In phr. *sea-green incorruptible,* applied to Robespierre by Carlyle (see quot. 1837) and now commonly used allusively··· to designate a person of rigid honesty or uncompromising idealism. Also in extended use and *absol.*, impervious to moral corruption.' What I had forgotten till I obeyed the instruction *see quot. 1837* was Carlyle's husky sportful laugh (rather in the manner of *The Book of Baruch*). For Carlyle's chapter, *Attitude,* concludes with the preparing of men's minds for a Republic. ' "A Republic?" said the Seagreen, with one of his dry husky *un*sportful laughs, "What is that?" O seagreen Incorruptible, thou shalt see!'[13]

> *O seagreen Incorruptible, thou shalt see!*

From *sea* to *see*, with *dry* as a stepping stone. Hill's *-ible* acknowledges that it may be degenerating into a-dribble, but 'Yes, *yes,* Carlyle'.

Hill was aware of his own reputation (personal, professional, and poetical) as sea-green incorruptible, even while creating poems that

---

9. *The Book of Baruch*, 123.   10. *Oraclau,* 84.   11. *Oraclau,* 49, 79, 93.
12. James Joyce, *Ulysses,* 'the snotgreen sea', smirching the wine-dark one.
13. *The French Revolution: The Constitution,* Book IV, ch. iv; ed. Traill, ii. 168.

acknowledge both the difficulty and the impossibility of living up to it. As for his sporting some laughs in *The Book of Baruch*, the instances tease. The internal rhyme within the prose line, *minor key / Charles Péguy*, hooks the heroic and the mock-heroic: 'Something famous and heroic in a minor key, by Charles Péguy'. The line with the internal rhyme *pierrot / no hero* is to reel in Eliot: 'To say "Eliot should have quit, still the out-of-line pierrot, in nineteen twenty-eight" is less than adequate even if we are agreed he was no hero.'[14] Is this the editorial *we*, the warm-shoulder *we*, the royal *we*, or the schizophrenic *we*? Rather, a reminder that, in this judgement on Eliot, F. R. Leavis had been a precise precursor of Hill.

But then Leavis's judgements on Eliot are likewise 'less than adequate', not least because they change and chop without any account of the changed grounds. In 1966, Leavis insisted on the 'heroic integrity of his poetic career':

I see Eliot's creative career as a sustained, heroic and indefatigably resourceful quest ··· The heroism is that of genius ··· What I am intent on is justifying my attribution to Eliot of a heroic quality in the exercise of his genius.[15]

Half a dozen years later, the case is altered: 'Eliot himself was in no danger of being a tragic hero of that kind, or a hero at all.'[16] *In no danger* is good, in its way. When Hill made laconic mention of 'our scant heroes',[17] he had the adjective *scant* ('Existing or available in adequate or barely sufficient amount, quantity, or degree') be flecked with the verb, 'To treat slightingly or inadequately; to neglect, do less than justice to'.

A posthumous publication, *The Book of Baruch* brings to mind the very last publication of Hill's lifetime: his version of *Peer Gynt*, of which copies became available on the day of his death.[18] Heroism revisited and revalued.

The Triumph of Love CXXXVIII had been fired by Hill's anger at critics who deplored his deploying of the Great War:

> Confound you, Croker—you and your righteous
> censure! I have admitted, many times,

14. *The Book of Baruch*, 95, 258. Prose-poems throughout the book, so no lineation to mark.
15. 'Eliot's Classical Standing', in *Lectures in America* (London, 1969), 30, 40.
16. *The Living Principle* (London, 1975), 184.
17. *Liber Illustrium Virorum* XLIX, in *The Daybooks* II.
18. *Peer Gynt and Brand* (London, 2016). With 'Afterword: Translating and Recreating Ibsen: An Interview with Geoffrey Hill', by Kenneth Haynes.

> my absence from the Salient · · ·
>   At Arras I sacrificed
> Edward Thomas (the chief cause of your
> hostility—why can't you say so?). I find
> your certitudes offensive. My cowardice
> is not contested. I am saying (simply)
> what is to become of memory? Yes—I know—
> I've asked that before.

That was 1998. 2016 was to hear Hill saying it again but anew, in the voice of Peer Gynt, who cannot live without the thought of heroism, and who cannot live heroism.

> I will swim like a feather on the stream of history,
> knowing that the story of greatness is my story;
> heroic battling for what is great and good,
> though at a safe distance, as an observer merely · · · [19]

(Act Four, Scene 9)

Such a concession as 'safe distance' has a touch of distaste and has its farcical side. (When Kenneth Haynes asked Hill in the interview, 'Did Yeats' subtitle "An Heroic Farce" for *The Green Helmet* help you to situate what you were doing?', the answer was comically staid: 'I think it may well have done.') There is comedy in Hill's speaking of his 'remit' for his *Brand* as 'making the unactable actable'. His *Peer Gynt* shows no sign of disillusionment with the indispensable suffix, for it puts in a good many appearances, including this exchange:

PEER   Could you but see into my heart and soul
                   you would discover
                   Peer, Peer, the one and only Peer,
                   the irreducible entity
                   indissoluble to mere quantity.
BUTTON MOULDER   Such is not possible.   (Act Five, Scene 7)

---

19. 'Heroism without Risk' is the motto of the brigands in *The Mountebanks* (Gilbert and Collier); Shaw, *Music in London* (London, 1931), ii. 1, 6 February 1892. Shaw wrote of Peer Gynt's ending: 'In the imagination of this old woman he finds the ideal Peer Gynt; whilst in himself, the loafer, the braggart, the confederate of sham magicians, the Charleston speculator, the false prophet, the dancing-girl's dupe, the bedlam emperor, the thruster of the drowning man into the waves, there is nothing heroic' (*The Quintessence of Ibsenism*, 1891, in *Major Critical Essays* (London, 1932), 47).

In the interview, Hill welcomed Haynes's suggestion as to the particular passage with which the conversation should reach conclusion, 'one of the most moving and lyrical passages in the whole play':[20]

> So unutterably poor a soul can return
> to pristine nothingness in the dense grey.
>
> ⋆ ⋆ ⋆
>
> Inviolable sun and you, dear, violated earth
> was it wise to bear and shed light on her who gave me birth?
>
> ⋆ ⋆ ⋆
>
> Inconsolably the soul gathers where it is from.   (Act Five, Scene 10)

Of the three pivots—unutterably, inviolable, inconsolably—in these lovely lines of Hill's, at once heroic and elegiac, only the first is to be found in what he calls the 'faithful' version, by Janet Garton, that the interview juxtaposes with Hill's own rendering. Of which he says 'The internal rhyme ("inconsolably", "soul") is deliberate', turning then immediately to his old retainer: 'I wanted the melancholy to be aurally unmissable.'

Equally unmissable in translating Ibsen had been the opportunity afforded by the word 'impassable'. It was to this that Hill had turned for pity and for understanding of young Einar's cowardice in *Brand*, with the face of the storm at sea becoming the surge of Agnes's rebuke to him:

EINAR   Life is so very sweet,
        Agnes; I daren't do it.
AGNES   [*shrinking away from him*]
        Einar, what do you mean?
EINAR   I mean ... I'm afraid.
AGNES   Then you have made
        an impassable ocean
        rage between us for ever.   (Act Two, Scene 1)

Carlyle, who knew very well what it was for an impassable ocean to rage between him and his belovèd for ever ('Yes, *yes*, Carlyle, wife Welsh!'), had mustered his own kind of pity for Johnson, Burns, and Rousseau. Heroes must travel on from the tolerable to the impassable.

---

20. The words of Janet Garton (quoted in the interview), the scholar of Scandinavian literature who supplied the introduction to Hill's *Peer Gynt and Brand*.

The worst element in the life of these three Literary Heroes was, that they found their business and position such a chaos. On the beaten road there is tolerable travelling; but it is sore work, and many have to perish, fashioning a path through the impassable![21]

II

Hill's inaugural lecture at the University of Leeds in 1977 initiated not only his first volume of criticism (*The Lords of Limit*, 1984), but some permanent persuasions, and it at once adumbrated and illuminated, with dark and light, his sense of the limits within which the art of poetry can and can not realize its hopes: 'Poetry as "Menace" and "Atonement"'. By his third paragraph, Hill was moved, first, to speak of 'a reconciling', and then to quote T. S. Eliot, 'The Three Voices of Poetry' (1953):

when the words are finally arranged in the right way—or in what he comes to accept as the best arrangement he can find—[the poet] may experience a moment of exhaustion, of appeasement, of absolution, and of something very near annihilation, which is in itself indescribable.

The highly descriptive word 'indescribable' is where this thought, Eliot's and now Hill's, was destined to arrive. It is a thought to which Hill would return.

> Indescribable,
> a word accustomed through its halting
> promptness, comes to be inscribed.   (*The Orchards of Syon* XX)

> But when I
> say poetry I mean something impossible
> to be described, except by adding lines
> to lines that are sufficient as themselves.

> (*In Memoriam: Gillian Rose*)

The suffix -*ble* urges the contemplation in all honesty of what is and what is not possible. The formation *possible* itself has the matter doubly compacted, there in both elements of the compound, since the Latin

21. 'The Hero as Man of Letters', in *On Heroes, Hero-Worship, and the Heroic in History*; *Works*, ed. Traill, 159. As against Carlyle's gravity, there is the level levity with which the words of Marianne Moore move. *I May, I Might, I Must*: 'If you will tell why the fen | appears impassable, I then | will tell you why I think that I | can get across it if I try.'

posse means 'to be able to', with the suffix *-ble* then seconding it. Awareness of this would press Hill to such exactitudes as 'the finest-possible light', not exactly the same as 'the finest possible light' (*The Bibliographers*). Or, again with the twofold support of *-ble*, the soul as 'possibly | Indestructible' (with the split-second pause for contemplation, at the line-ending). Or the reiterated scruple of *And if not*:

> Add the irrefutable
> grammar of Abdiel's defiance.
> And if not wisdom, then something
> that approaches it nearly. And if not faith,
> then something through which it is made possible
> to give credence—   (*The Triumph of Love* XXIII)

Beginnings to ends: one of the epigraphs to *The Lords of Limit* (1984) had called up the words of Chinua Achebe, 'saying yes now when his first unalterable word had been no', and the final page of Hill's *Collected Critical Writings* (2008) arrives at an 'intolerable condition'. What Eliot called 'the intolerable wrestle | With words and meanings' (*East Coker* II) was itself to be wrestled with by Hill, both in poetry and in prose.[22]

The progress of Hill's poetry was an intense understanding that all will lapse into the progress of error unless error itself be unrelentingly admitted and then probed, tented. (Yet 'a manageable hypothesis' may enter upon 'irredeemable error'.) His earliest grasp of this gist was never rescinded by him, rightly, but there was something erroneous in his calling upon the word 'atonement'.[23] For the word 'atonement' obdurately will not return to its radical roots, to 'at-one-ment'. At-one-ment is simply and finally, and unanswerably, not a word in the English language; and it will not do to intimate that the technical perfecting of a poem is 'an act of atonement, in the radical etymological sense—an act of at-one-ment, a setting at one, a bringing into concord, a reconciling,

---

22. 'It will be objected that Hobbes, like Bacon, regarded equivocation, all forms of ambiguity in language, as "intolerable" and worked for their eradication; and, from that, it may be concluded that he and Bacon were at liberty to stand aloof from the "intolerable wrestle | With words and meanings"'. Empirical observation confirms that this is not so'. The preceding sentence in Hill began: 'It is not absolutely invulnerable to Hobbes's charge···' (*Collected Critical Writings*, ed. Kenneth Haynes, 193).

23. 'Geoffrey Hill: At-one-ment', in *The Force of Poetry*, 320–1. Matthew Sperling records the caveats both of Richard Chenevix Trench (of the *OED*), and of Hill; *Visionary Philology: Geoffrey Hill and the Study of Words* (2014), 42–3. As so often, Coleridge is crucially to Hill's point; on Reconciliation, Atonement, and translations of such terms, see, for instance, *Collected Works: Aids to Reflection*, ed. John Beer, ix (Princeton, 1993), 320.

a uniting in harmony': it will not do to intimate this unless, in the very moment, it is conceded that there can be no reconciling, no bringing into harmony, of words like 'a reconciling, a uniting in harmony' and the non-word 'at-one-ment'; more radically (despite the etymology), that there can be no atonement of atonement and at-one-ment. For one thing, even if the latter were alive in our language, it would now be pronounced differently from atonement. The Index to Hill's *Collected Critical Writings* precludes any easy exit from one particular entry, even as the sound-effect finds itself pivoting:

> atonement
> attainability of

'Seeing how they stand': so begins the fourth of the *Psalms of Assize*, in *Canaan*. Hill let stand his earlier hope in this matter. In this poem he abides by it with a difference, assisted by the indispensable suffix, and by a touch of fetching comedy, there in how the words stand there on the page:

> loving kindness
>   and mercy
> righteousness
> patient abiding
> and whatever good
> is held
>   untenable
> the entire complex dance
> of simple atonement

The complex dance that is Hill's achievement makes manifest that the possibilities and impossibilities of reconciliation continued to be the heart of his art but that at this heart there was a deepening darkness. Abiding by the contrariety of scale with which Hill worked wonders, the distinctly small suffix -*ble* became unavoidable because of what it intimates as to the possibility of reconciliations.

Recalling Pope's dextrous pleasure in 'How Index-learning turns no student pale, | Yet holds the Eel of science by the Tail',[24] we might start where Hill's *Collected Critical Writings* comes to an end. Browsing in the Index, we see that -*ble* is indispensable, one entry dubbing *centre* 'indispensable' (James, Henry); another, for *circumstances*, identifying 'inextricable

---

24. *The Dunciad*, i. 279–80.

part of' and 'intractabilities of'; and the entry for 'imagination' characterizing it as 'constrained and inviolable at once'.

'Double-takes': the appreciation of Hill's poems that must always be borne in mind is by Hill himself, the three pages that he was long tempted to disown but that are as powerfully germane today as they were more than fifty years ago: the vivid, exasperated, surging commentary that brought to its climactic end *The Penguin Book of Contemporary Verse* in 1962.[25] The chosen poems, chosen by Hill (not by Allott), were the paired sonnets *Annunciations* I and II. Hill at once gritted our teeth: 'I suppose the impulse behind the work is an attempt to realize the jarring double-takes in words of common usage: as "sacrifice" (I) or "Love" (II).' (Why didn't we all see at once that the author of *The Sacrifice* and of *Love*, George Herbert, was one of the presiders?) The continuity with the later Hill is audible within the 'Touchable' of the first sonnet, 'the changeable | Soldiery' of the second, and the sardonic overarching of the standard complacencies:

but this can be put behind us (as it is in the imagery) because Art is 'decent': it 'reconciles the irreconcilable'.

The suffix -*ble* is itself remarkable for its jarring double-takes.

Hill's 'version' of Ibsen's tragedy *Brand* (1978) was a crucial stage and station for him. Reflecting on the play many years later, he mustered a battery of the -*ble*, adducing Ibsen's 'flexibility' and the play's 'inevitability', its being 'ineluctably "Promethean"', and its having 'brought unchallengeably to an end a long period of failure and neglect which must, to Ibsen, have seemed interminable'.[26] The 'culpable', the 'incapable', the 'fallible', and (more than once) the 'inescapable': such is the explicit invocation that sounds and resounds in Hill's *Brand*. 'Ibsen, to my mind, here enjoys a self-made latitude verging on licence, demonstrating one of many ways in which an aggressively iron will to resist may be quietly reconciled with options and conditions.' The character Brand, as against the play *Brand*, neither sought nor found reconciliation

25. *The Penguin Book of Contemporary Verse 1918–60*, ed. Kenneth Allott, new rev. edn (Harmondsworth, 1962).
26. Preface to the Penguin edition (1996), pp. vii–x. Later, *Peer Gynt and Brand* (Penguin, 2016), where Hill reported on the several texts of his *Brand*: 'It was performed with cuts, and the first publication of the translation, by Heinemann [1978], had those cuts also. A restored translation appeared in 1981 (Minnesota), and a revised and further restored translation came out in 1996 (Penguin). In the current edition [2016] there are further revisions, aimed at bringing it even closer to the literal.'

or quiet, leave alone the possibility of being quietly reconciled. Sacrifice, upon which *Brand* turns at every moment, may function as one obdurate reminder that, although there are Lords of Limit, limits are lord. Whereas Carlyle was long to remain an unacknowledged avatar, Ibsen was an acknowledged one, joining Charles Péguy. 'Péguy, stubborn rancours and mishaps and all, is one of the great souls, one of the great prophetic intelligences, of our century.' There is some glancing at himself by Hill—including some glancing blows (repeatedly laying about with -*ble*)—in his Péguy, 'this much-snubbed irascible man': 'A man of the most exact and exacting probity, accurate practicality, in personal and business relations, a meticulous reader of proof, he was at the same time moved by violent emotions and violently afflicted by mischance. Like others similarly wounded, he was perhaps smitten by the desirability of suffering.'[27] *The Mystery of the Charity of Charles Péguy* concluded the *Collected Poems* of 1985. It celebrates 'Inevitable high summer' and (on its very last page) 'the Virgin of innumerable charities'.

In *Canaan* (1996), *A Song of Degrees* committed itself to 'inescapable witness', while in *A Treatise of Civil Power* XXI, 'Testimony without | witness is conceivable'[28]. But what is not conceivable, what is inescapable, when it comes to bearing witness, is -*ble*. As witnesses to its truths, *King Log* (1968) had called upon 'A workable fancy', 'an equable contempt for this world', 'impalpable bitterness', and the variously 'vulnerable'— an epithet applied to such very different things as a mole, a poem's form, and the pieties.[29] Hill put questions not just about but to the unanswerable.

> so we bear witness,
> Despite ourselves, to what is beyond us,
> Each distant sphere of harmony forever
> Poised, unanswerable.   (*Funeral Music* 8)

He wrote and spoke of the unspeakable, and he heard the chit-chat charity with which the unspeakable may find itself spoken of:

27. From the prose tribute that originally accompanied *The Mystery of the Charity of Charles Péguy* (1983).
28. Clutag edition (2005), dropped from the Penguin *A Treatise of Civil Power* (2007).
29. *Annunciations*; *The Songbook of Sebastian Arrurruz* 4; *Funeral Music* 1; *Three Baroque Meditations* 2; *The Assisi Fragments*; *Funeral Music* 3; *Three Baroque Meditations* 2; *Cowan Bridge*.

Yes: and he will weaken, scribbling, at the end,
Of unspeakable desolation. Really? Good Lord!

(Fantasia on 'Horbury')

Mercian Hymns (1971) furnished 'the desirable new estates', it recalled 'unattainable toys' and the 'irreplaceable', and it gave currency to 'accountable tact'. It soldered variably-resistant hyphens, there in 'the variably-resistant soil'.[30] *Tenebrae* (1978) held to the 'untenable belonging', and 'marked | visible absences'; 'brilliance made bearable'; sleep and waking as 'Vulnerable to each other'.[31] A serene reconciliation was to vail its head in prayer, within the first of the three *Hymns to Our Lady of Chartres* (1984):[32]

> Through what straits might we come to worship this,
> and kneel before you, and be reconciled,

—but to come to this place of worship, the Hymn has had to file past the suffix-regiment, stationed there as risible, visible, invisible. A trinity, of a kind, but then so were Satan, Sin, and Death. Perdition manifested its own unearthly reconciliations: 'the stricken faces damnable and serene' (*Florentines*). No light but rather darkness risible.

III

When, as is the case with Carlyle, formations like *untenable, undeniable, unquestionable, insupportable*, and *intolerable* are enlisted to form part of an armoury or army, they have a way of self-destructing, for their repetition precipitates the resistance that they aim to crush. Everyone's favourite goddess, Nemesis, is happy to take responsibility and revenge.

Again and again F. R. Leavis showed himself to possess extraordinarily attentive percipience. The crux in the action of a novel, the precise turn of phrase or of line, in verse or in prose, the vivid demonstration of the unexpected relations between the very different things that he noticed: all of this was his and therefore became ours. But his rhetoric

30. *Mercian Hymns* I, VI, VII, XI, XII.
31. *The Pentecost Castle* 12; *Terribilis Est Locus Iste*; *The Masque of Blackness*; *Loss and Gain*.
32. *Broken Hierarchies* has 'might I come' (in what had become Hymn 6). The most recent poems in the *Collected Poems* of 1985, the *Hymns*, 'were composed in 1983–4 shortly after the completion of *The Mystery of the Charity of Charles Péguy*'. *Broken Hierarchies* expanded the three to twenty-one Hymns, with the dates 1982–2012.

of indisputability precluded there being value in his remarking for us what can only be self-evident. If the critical case is always *undeniable, incontestable, unanswerable,* and *indisputable*—more, is 'most unquestionable', is 'more indubitably' and 'more inescapably' and 'most unmistakably' so—what imaginative powers of mind had been needed by someone who noticed, yes, that such-and-such is the case? Whereupon *anyone* can be seen to be for Leavis a weapon of mass self-destruction.

It would be of no use to try and argue with anyone who contended that · · ·
To anyone not wearing these blinkers it is plain that · · ·
Anyone capable of profiting by · · ·
It should be obvious at once to any one capable of being convinced at all · · ·
As anyone who cares to open his Wordsworth may see · · ·
Any reader not protected by a very obstinate preconception would · · ·

Joined by a further recruit, *No one*:

No one who has responded perceptively would · · ·
But no one worth arguing with · · ·

For when Leavis posits that there could be such a thing as the 'critically impregnable',[33] there comes to mind an entry about General Moltke in Madan's *Notebooks.*[34]

Moltke, only laughing twice in his life.
[Once, when his mother-in-law died, and once when a certain fortress was declared to be impregnable.]

There was much that was heroic about Leavis's dedication and his faith, but the heroic includes his tragically wronging himself. For he was driven—by the needs of his rhetoric—to scant his own extraordinary powers as a noticer, someone who felicitously draws to our attention things that are by no means plain and unequivocal, but that, on the contrary, needed his trained and profoundly observant imagination for their apprehension.

The polemical *-ble* misguides. But then the wider ways of the suffix *-ble* (*-able, -ible*) turn out to be far from straightforward. Fortunately they also turn out to be fertile, a rich vein for a writer who delights in cross-currency and may honourably exploit it. For instance, *washable*

---

33. *New Bearings in English Poetry* (London, 1932), 64.
34. *Geoffrey Madan's Notebooks*, ed. J. A. Gere and John Sparrow (Oxford, 1981), 90.

sometimes won't wash—and moreover we had better agree just what we mean by *agreeable.*

'This shirt is *washable*' [= 'can (safely) be washed']; 'This ink is *washable*' [may = 'can be washed out/away' though in fact it may indicate a guarantee that water can be applied without the writing being washed out.]

With *agreeable,* there are three uses: 'companionable', 'willing to agree', 'can be agreed *to*'; in this last sense it is predicative only:

I have *agreeable* friends.
Eventually, my friends were *agreeable.*
We must find a formulation that is *agreeable* to everyone.[35]

And what, for business'-sake, does *payable* mean? Is it, too, on the double-take?

> The Poles are heroes living as they have to
> (put PAYABLE TO BEARER) ···   (*Speech! Speech!* 40)

For PAYABLE is pliable, which may make it all the more business-like.

1. That is to be paid; due, owing; falling due.
2. That can be paid; capable of being paid. *Rare.*
3. Hence *transf.* in general sense: Capable of yielding profit, commercially profitable; paying.[36]

Although the modality of most passive *-able* adjectives is usually potential ('can be'), with some it is intentional or obligational ('will be', 'must be'). Compare:

The deposit is *refundable.*   ['will']
The money is *payable* on delivery.   ['must']
The money is *payable* by cheque.   ['can']

We think of the English language as wielding the sibling-suffix *-ive* when it intends the active: *of the kind that can do such-and-such.* And we think of this as arched against *-ble* when it intends the passive (though the suffix *-ive* then feels odd in 'passive'): *of the kind that can be such-and-such-ed.* Have something done to it, as against doing something. Yet this sturdy scheme has for centuries accommodated a great many

---

35. *A Comprehensive Grammar of the English Language,* ed. Randolph Quirk, Sidney Greenbaum, Geoffrey Leech, and Jan Svartvik (1985), in particular Appendix I [Word-formation], sub-section 40. 'This has the effect of making *washable* capable of two interpretations', where '*washable* capable' has a lifelike undulatory effect à la Liffey.

36. T. S. Eliot says of the poet who invokes 'inspiration' that 'he has shirked the labour of smelting what may have been payable ore'; Valéry, *The Art of Poetry* (London, 1958), Introduction, p. xii.

exceptions. So the grammarian makes immediate room for manoeuvre, happy to posit 'a polar contrast' but then hiring 'fundamentally':

> Two common suffixes are used to form adjectives ··· from verbs and they are in polar contrast in respect of verbal voice: *-ive* is fundamentally related to the active, 'of the kind that can V'; *-able* is fundamentally related to the passive, 'of the kind that can be V-ed' ··· *supportive* 'can support', *supportable* 'can be supported'.

At once there is an opportunity to remonstrate. For does *supportive* really mean *can support*? Not according to the *OED*, which moves from 'Having the quality of supporting' (which is not the same as *can support*) to that which is crucially different from *can support*: 'affording support; sustaining'. Which is what we mean by 'supportive' these days.

Open for ever to misconstruction is a particular turn in the language which the *OED* suggests may be behind the proliferation of *-able* words: the feeling ('due to form-association') that *-able* words derive from the adjective *able*, so that *eatable*, for example, 'is taken as *eat* + *able*, able to be eaten'. But we learn that the suffix has a different etymology: it derives from the adjective which comes from the Latin *habe-re*, 'to hold, lit. "easy to be held or handled, handy," hence "pliant, suitable, fit for a purpose"'. No relation therefore to the suffix, but handily sounding as though it were very closely related, and therefore able to have an ineradicable effect upon our language.

The suffix *-ble* does look as though it goes with the adjective *able*, so that *tolerable* would mean 'able to be tolerated'; this puts pressure on all *-ble* formations even though this concurrence rests on a mistake. Then there is another warping, an intriguing time-warp: 'Many adjectives in -ABLE *suffix* have negative counterparts in UN- *prefix*, and some of these are attested much earlier than their positive counterparts, the chronological difference being especially great in the case of UNTHINKABLE.' The *OED* at this point withholds the dates, but here they are: *unthinkable*, *c.*1430; *thinkable*, 1805. For not only the grammarian but the lexicographer must make clear that all is not as schematized as one might suppose.

> *-able*: Forming adjectives denoting the capacity for or capability of being subjected to or (in some compounds) performing the action denoted or implied by the first element of the compound. (*OED*)

Which must mean that *-ble* sometimes, when it is doing the *performing*, functions as *-ive*. Which is co-operative, but does complicate everything.

Yet at the same time it may resist the lockstep rally of the binary. Hill's practice permits of a writer's resorting to -ble creatively, as against his or her possessing the force only of habit, the comfort only of routine ('invariable routine'[37]) or of addiction.

Hill's achievement derives from his welcoming such of the -ble words as enjoy an irregularity of some sort or other, being resistant to the binary totality of *can X / can be X-ed*.[38] Cases where, for instance, the variation may derive from the fact that the base for this -ble is not the usual one, of a verb, but that of a noun, and where the meaning is not the usual passive sense of *can be X-ed*. The grammarian can list for us such instances as '*peaceable, fashionable, seasonable*, etc.'[39]

> I did not anticipate the marriage
>
> that I destroyed. It was not then the fashion.
> The Ludlow Masque was far from fashionable
> though fashioned well. To up the bid, superbly.

> (*Scenes from Comus*, 1.16)[40]

Fashionable no longer means 'Capable of being fashioned' (*OED* 1, *obs*.) though Hill fashions his lines from these very changes of usage, as Milton had fashioned (with the help of anachronisms) his risky masque. For *fashionable*, as Hill brings out, observes the sense 'observant of or following *the fashion*'. What then comes next in the *OED* is no longer at one with prevailing usage, because persons of the upper class are no longer the vogue-setters, celebrities are. But all the same we need the *OED*'s line of thought: 'Conformable to fashion; in accordance with prevailing usage; of the kind in vogue among persons of the upper class.' The same is true when Hill resorts to another of the grammarian's instances, at the opening of *On Reading 'The Essayes or Counsels, Civill and Morall'*:

37. *The Triumph of Love* XLVII.
38. The *OED*'s examples of the active -ble include *capable, comfortable, suitable, agreeable, conformable, companionable, durable,* and *equable.* Hill has 'the durable covenant' (*Vocations*), 'Mystic | durables' (*The Orchards of Syon* II), and 'an equable contempt' (*Funeral Music* I), 'equably' (*In Ipsley Church Lane* I).
39. The poet Jon Silkin (Hill's colleague, friend, and advocate) brought to his own book of poetry, *The Peaceable Kingdom* (1954), the painting by Edward Hicks (1780–1849) of which Hicks made 62 versions.
40. *OED*: *anticipate*: To observe or practise in advance of the due date. ('What is euphemistically called "anticipating Marriage"', *The Expository Times*, 1 May 1965.)

> So many had nothing; *we* have orchards
> sometimes *ill-neighboured*, and are driven
> to untimely harvest, simply to thwart thieves.
> Our galleries may or may not be places
> of seasonable resort.

Timber and food are to hand, but *seasonable* does not mean capable of being seasoned, whether as timber or as food. For *seasonable* is altogether active: 'occurring at the right season, opportune', 'suitable to the time of year' (where *suitable* is itself one that the grammarian lists as not passive).

A grammarian fulfils a duty to the instances that diverge, when (say) '-*able* yields no passive meaning but rather has a sense paraphrasable as "apt to V": *changeable, perishable, suitable,* etc.' The poet fulfils this afresh, one resource being the ways in which 'changeable' is itself changeable. Apt to change? Liable to, tending to, susceptible to? Or (lining up with 'Soldiery') the Changing of the Guard?

>   the changeable
> Soldiery have their goings-out and comings-in
> Dying in abundance.   (*Annunciations* 2)

A grammarian will need to be alert to the difference between 'must' and 'may':

Given that -*able* adjectives may be active as well as passive, some items can be either:
> The weather is *variable*. [must be *active*]
> The date is *variable*. [may be *passive*]

A lexicographer will welcome the extended family: 'Liable or apt to vary or change; (readily) susceptible or capable of variation.' Meanwhile the poet will create more than one music of theme and variation. 'Fear is your absolute, yet in each feature | infinitely variable···' (*The Triumph of Love* LXIX)

> Mortal beauty is alienation; or not,
> as I see it. The rest passagework,
> settled beforehand, variable, to be lived through
> as far as one can, with uncertain
> tenure.   (*The Orchards of Syon* XX)

Clearly, *variable* declines to be settled beforehand and clarified (reliably) as *can be varied*.

But then *reliable* was judged at first to be far from reliable. These days, a grammar is careful to be imperturbable, politic and correct: 'Prepositional and phrasal verbs usually form *-able* adjectives with omission of the particle: "We can rely *on* John" ~ "John is *reliable*".' But in the old days, they reserved the right to be perturbed. Since *reliable* means 'that may be relied upon', why is it not a sin of omission to omit 'upon'? The answer is slackly specious, like pleading that there were other drivers who were also exceeding the speed limit:

> In current use only from about 1850, and at first perhaps more frequent in American works, but from 1855 freely employed by British writers, though often protested against as an innovation or an Americanism. The formation has been objected to (as by Worcester in 1860) on the ground of irregularity, but has analogies in *available, dependable, disposable, laughable* (Webster 1864). The question has been fully discussed by F. Hall in his work *On English Adjectives in -able with special reference to Reliable* (1877).

All the better to word you with.

Inflammable / flammable? Sir Thomas Browne's word *flammability* was 'revived in modern use to avoid the possible ambiguity of *inflammability*, in which the prefix *in-* might be taken for a negative' (*OED*). The committee in 1963 was 'particularly anxious that we should standardize on *flammability* in order to prevent such misunderstanding'. (Others of us would be particularly anxious about *standardize on*.) The previous year, Hill had set his face—as a poet often will need to—against standardization but was so good as to be mild about the peril:

> Lion and lioness, the mild
> Inflammable beasts,
> At their precise peril kept
> Distance and repose   (*The Assisi Fragments*)

Distance, but *-ble* stands by to be of service with personal relations, the affections and their amiable relaxedness. This, though, can work only if we recognize that *-ble* doesn't have to give salience to *can*, and very often doesn't. The *OED* rightly moves on promptly from *likeable / likable* as 'that can be liked' to the more generous sense that is its usual intimation: 'pleasing; agreeable'. More forcefully, for *lovable / loveable* the *OED* does without *can* altogether, moving at once to 'deserving of being loved; amiable; attractive, pleasing'. For *lovable* does not function as a grudging *able to be* (merely that? at a pinch?). In a programme about Charles Laughton, the interviewer asked Christopher Isherwood whether Laughton was lovable. Isherwood's lilted flat-tongued reply was along the right lines: Well, *I* managed to love him.

The same goes for a clutch of commendations, among them *com-mendable* which does not mean able to be commended but 'proper to be commended, deserving of commendation or approval, praiseworthy, laudable'. Then *laudable* is 'praiseworthy, commendable'. Which means that although it is true that Hill's poem *History as Poetry* ends by compounding *-ble*, this is not wasteful or a tic since its two instances are crucially different, are performing very different services in history as well as in poetry.

> Thus laudable the trodden bone thus
> Unanswerable the knack of tongues.

For though *unanswerable* shoulders the responsibility of 'Can this or can this not be answered?', *laudable* does not operate so. It speaks directly of—and on behalf of—that which is due, that which is worthy. In this, it is at one with the most honourable of such formations: *honourable*. 'Worthy of being honoured; entitled to honour, respect, esteem, or reverence.'

By now we are all comfortable—which does not mean 'able to be comforted'—with *reliable*, and there is equanimity all round. In one of Hill's most tender cadences, perfectly rounding a prose-poem, 'The lamps grew plump with oily reliable light'. One reason for welcoming these irregulars is to guard against a rabble, what Ralph Cudworth in 1678 called 'a bundle of incomprehensibles, unconceivables, and impossibles'. The indispensable suffix has a way of taking things into its own hands. It is certainly indispensable, but then *indispensable* is smutched with irregularity, verging on the illegitimate (dispense *with*, no?), so the word is lucky not to find itself simply thrown away, 'that indispensable throwaway phrase which is a revelation and no surprise'.[41]

IV

Yet ought not Hill himself to have thrown away many a *-ble*?

He acknowledged that there is such a thing as *overuse* (though he did simply leave it at that, with the help of parentheses that tuck things away). Of Robert Herrick's *Hesperides*:

41. *The Book of Baruch*, 32.

Its politics *de trop*
even when you allow for our own cant.
(Cant: how I love the word and overuse it.)[42]

The *un*loved overused word, in Hill's eyes and ears, was *accessible*.
Overused by criticizers of Hill's poems; overused, I should submit, by
Hill in the flagrancy of retort. 'Take accessible to mean | acceptable,
accommodating, openly servile'. 'ACCESSIBLE | traded as
DEMOCRATIC.'[43] The Index to the *Collected Critical Writings* identifies ten of its pages as bearing upon 'accessible/accessibility', and adds
'commodity, accessibility as'; also 'context, and accessibility'; plus
'reader, and accessibility'. *A Treatise of Civil Power* XXI has it in for the
accessible ('the accessible | is past redemption'), but the particular
poem, though then dropped, was not itself past redemption in that Hill
reconceived it as *A Précis or Memorandum of Civil Power*.

Adducing his countless instances of *-ble* draws attention to a linguistic phenomenon central to his art, but then raises the critical question
of overuse. A poet's liberties are his or hers to take, but a critic has
other responsibilities, for instance to differentiate the real thing from
what (from overuse) sometimes became no more—or no other—than
a habit, a recourse, a tick, a tic, or even a pathology, addiction to a diction.[44] That the suffix *-ble* might suffocate, this was left to the very end
of the Note at the end of my 2012 essay as a matter for banter:

Confessio Amantis (in the series *Old Members at Work*) was Geoffrey Hill's contribution to *Keble College: The Record 2009*. At one point, a run of fifteen lines
for the Record has *ineluctable, insoluble, intractable, tractable, unpredictable yet
unassailable, 'accessibility', insolubility, probably unsustainable*, and *predictable*. The
final prose-paragraph addresses 'the intractable ideal and the manageable but
inadequate praxis'.[45]

We can grant that all of us stand every day in need of such words without acquiescing in there being no such thing as too much of this
often-good thing. For the *-ble* effect sometimes mounts to apoplexy.
Clavics 17, explicitly on 'Logorrhea', ends:

42. *The Triumph of Love* XLI: 'For hardness of heart read costly dislike of cant'. The Index
to Hill's *Collected Critical Writings* offers twelve entries under cant | canting.
43. *The Triumph of Love* XL, and *Speech! Speech!* 118.
44. Jon Glover, reviewing *The Book of Baruch*: 'The changes of direction might seem
worrying at first, but soon they become addictive' (*PN Review* 249, September–
October 2019). But addiction should be worrying at last.
45. An Old Member, nourished by his alma mater (Ke*ble* College), at work on his *Confessio
Amantis,* nodding to good old Gower.

> Ingrate, veritable
> Core, thy pulsings irritable
> Gifts grantable yet out of hand mere prize.

Since we may perfectly well deplore coagulators no less than blood-thinners in poetry, we do not have to be grateful for those lines, or prize them. It may not be that we are lacking in gratitude if we find impossible such lines as these:

> Impossibles that beguile paradigm;
> Triumph turned contest of ingratitude;[46]

—or if we find intolerable the style of such a concluding line as 'Intolerable burdens reared on style.'[47]

Admittedly there is courage in Hill's throwing down all these iron gloves: *intolerable, unconscionable, unbearable, unspeakable, unreasonably*. The *Orchards of Syon* VII has within its first eleven lines not only *incorrigible* and *unreadable* but *ineradicable* and *arguably*. Then there is the other iron glove, the one that hurls back some further charges specifically levelled at Hill's poems: to *inaccessible* and *unreadable*, add *unintelligible, unfathomable, impenetrable*, and *incomprehensible*, 'the *politique* | of incomprehensible verse-sequences'.[48]

The poet is daring, and he dares us. But might not the floor be becoming pestered with gloves and gauntlets? *Scenes From Comus* (2.68) has 'implausible, credible muse', with 'Unbelievable' in the next line. *Without Title*—which prompted Eric Ormsby to call Hill 'incomparable'—has 'incontrovertibly', 'unarguably', and 'not answerable' (in *Pindarics* 2), while *In Ipsley Church Lane* 3 has 'immeasurably', 'immoveable', and (yes) 'insufferably'. Such prompt compounding of -*ble* was ever at hand, but at some point this turns into the emptiness that is visited upon the over-and-over.

The Book of Baruch maintained, to the last, Hill's investment in -*ble*. 'Poem as cradle of the unbiddable name', and as cradle of -*ble* (bearing a virus from the author of *Liber Illustrium Virorum*). 'Unbelievable the credible reality of wealth'; 'bearable because irreparable', alongside 'The unimaginable power of the neutron'; 'mutely audible, darkly lucent, impenetrable'; and 'motive is inaccessible', seconded and then thirded by 'The radical incompatibility of those spiritually able'.

---

46. *Liber Illustrium Virorum* LI. 47. *Liber Illustrium Virorum* XIX.
48. *The Triumph of Love* LVI.

Crucially, excruciatingly, there is in Purcell, we are told, 'nothing unsingsingsingable'.[49]

A due attention to the *-ble* phenomenon would juxtapose a few embodiments. In 1959 there was the greatness of the poem *Of Commerce and Society*. It ends with the line 'At times it seems not common to explain'.

> Many have died. Auschwitz,
> Its furnace chambers and lime pits
> Half-erased, is half-dead; a fable
> Unbelievable in fatted marble.

There, *there*, is the grossly burgeoning unimaginability of Auschwitz, with the very sounds moving from delicacy ('a fable') into the fattened slabs of monumental evil:

> a fable
> Unbelievable in fatted marble.

For '*fable*' into 'Unbelie*vable*', like '*fat*ted mar*ble*', is a gross distending, and 'fatted' is the ancient sacrifice.[50]

But the realized terror of such wording impugns Hill's subsequently resorting to the word 'fable' (again in the company again of 'pits', now 'those entombing pits'); no longer a taut knot but slackened to a cluster:

> Fable or not it is unbearable.
> Nye died of cancer; surprised-by, terrible.   (*Oraclau*, 144)

It is itself something of a fable that an abrupt six-word sentence, with 'Intolerable' centred so as to constitute a line to itself, can command anything more than an off-key jingle.

> Intolerable
> much that passes for fable.   (*Ludo*, 18)

---

49. *The Book of Baruch*, 126, 33, 51, 71, 75, 189. Further compoundings: 'unpredictable times ··· undeniably there' (67); 'reprehensible ··· sustain the intractable ··· that unrecognizable man' (123); 'invariably ··· undemonstrable' (148); 'unreasonably ··· impenetrably' (149); 'feasible like invisible rope-tricks' (166); and 'the soul indelibly stamped: immoveable that snarl' (197).

50. 'Geoffrey Hill: "The tongue's atrocities"', in *The Force of Poetry*, 289. *September Song* (1968) opens with the profoundly tragic apprehension of the unremitting formation: 'Undesirable you may have been, untouchable | you were not' (*The Force of Poetry*, 296–300).

Or, with 'fable' yet again on call (as *in* but not *of* these words), there is too usual a combining of the known components: 'one vulnerable chance, becoming fable', to be enforced in the next line by 'incapable'.[51]

How does the suffix come to constitute a field of force, a mind-field? By its engagement with reconciliation.

> That weight of the world, weight of the word, is.
> Not wholly irreconcilable. Almost.   (*Scenes From Comus*, 1.20)

'Not wholly irreconcilable': the double negative, with its caution and then with the further caution (not *wholly*), at once a caveat and a precision, must bring out the doubleness that lives in *irreconcilable*, of all words.

V

One preoccupation of Hill's, as of every writer, is the claim of the eye as against that of the ear, not (on this occasion) as the claim of literature meeting that of music, but the claims within literature itself, when what is seen on the page is set against what is heard either in the auditorium of the head or at a reading-aloud. Possibility wrestles with impossibility, each needing to listen to *-ble* in its countless incarnations. Eye and ear. 'Not wholly irreconcilable. Almost.'

Take Hill's ways with two conventions, both of which have eye and ear at odds, even while trusting in the power of imagination that 'reveals itself in the balance or reconciliation of opposite or discordant qualities'.[52] The conventions are those that entail beginning or not beginning a line of verse with a capital letter, and that entail choosing between arabic and roman numerals. Both conventions proffer something that is at once clear to the eye and unutterable to the ear. Seen, but not heard. They test the possibilities, and are obliged to bear what they find.

Throughout Hill's first book, *For the Unfallen*, lines of verse begin with capital letters. Not altogether so with *King Log*.[53] Then with

51. *The Book of Baruch*, 209.
52. Coleridge, *Biographia Literaria*, ch. XIV.
53. *September Song*, and two of the *Four Poems Regarding the Endurance of Poets*, formally different from the book's other poems, have their lines begin in lower-case.

Tenebrae there becomes established what will be Hill's practice (lower-case line-openings) for several volumes.[54] With the early prose-poem *A Letter from Armenia*, the question in one sense cannot arise and in another sense cannot but. The same is true of *Mercian Hymns* and *The Book of Baruch*, two sequences of prose-poems.

But does the practice, whichever it is, have to mean that the reader is to be blind to the convention, and that whether there is or is not a capital letter has become invisible or without significance? It is an aspect of Eliot's engagement with *his* convention that we as readers sometimes find valuably withheld from us a clear assurance that there would, or there would not, be a capital letter on this word if it were elsewhere than at the head of the line. It ministers to Hill's respect for conventions that there is a manifest contrariety between his *Lachrimae* sequence (with its lower-case line-openings) and the Renaissance poems that it honours, echoes, and yet would not wish to be mistaken for, despite all its sonorities of archaism.

> Loves I allow and passions I approve:
> Ash-Wednesday feasts, ascetic opulence,
> the wincing lute, so real in its pretence,
> itself a passion amorous of love.   (*Pavana Dolorosa*)

The necessary capital letter of the poem's opening line, followed at once by the differently necessary capital letter of the second line ('Ash-Wednesday'), gives to the ensuing lower-case, 'the wincing lute', a sense of something being doffed.

Along these same lines, an effect is achieved on the last page of *Scenes From Comus* that is a matter not solely of syntax but of a convention so resisted, albeit passingly, as to make us for a moment glimpse (with the help of the eternal unremitting suffix) the Elizabethan and Jacobean world and *its* conventions:

> Nothing is unforgettable but guilt.
> Guilt of the moment to be made eternal.
> Reading immortal literature's a curse.

54. *Without Title*, *Pindarics*, and *A Treatise of Civil Power*, plus the section *Ludo* (Epigraphs and Colophons to *The Daybooks*), but not the six *Daybooks* themselves, where lines of verse return to Hill's initial practice and begin with capital letters.

> Beatrice in *The Changeling* makes me sweat
> even more than Faustus' Helen, let alone
> Marlowe's off-stage blasphemous fun with words[55]

It is those opening capitals, five out of the six lines, that succeed in bestowing upon the line

> even more than Faustus' Helen, let alone

its trans-historical stationing. Against the old convention, the new convention strikes up again taut wintry vibrations. Similarly, the third stanza of *On Reading 'Milton and the English Revolution'* will never read quite the same as the stanzas before and after it, for it finds a way to satisfy both the old and the new conventions:[56]

> Wiped the old slur between liberty and licence.
> Wisdom is back. How did it go, Wisdom?
> *The soul knows there no difference of sex.*
> Sympathy flows, utterance is end-stopped.
> As if that stopped collusion. Perhaps it does.
> Memory too returns, her key still in the lock.

In *Speech! Speech!* the fifty-fifth poem ends: 'This is more end-stopped than usual. WHY?' Because the end-stopping permits of a run of openings, by which, of the twelve lines of this poem, nine begin with capitals, as though an earlier convention still put in something of a claim.

The nub is this: that the eye can see but the voice cannot utter the difference between the one and the other. The same is true of the other instance: numerals arabic or roman? From the beginning, Hill would often counterpoint or alternate the numerals. His first volume, *For the Unfallen*, opened with roman for *Genesis*, then went largely to arabic. His posthumous volume, *The Book of Baruch*, has arabic. *The Triumph of Love* was a triumph in that the roman numerals of the poems exactly matched the arabic page-numbers.

But it is not true that one can't *say* the difference between arabic and roman numerals. I need to add to something I wrote long ago (1960) when contrasting the date MCMXIV that is the title of a Larkin poem with the dates at the head of a Hill poem (*September Song*):

> born *19.6.32–deported 24.9.42*

---

55. *Broken Hierarchies* recomposes this as 'even more than Faustus' Helen. Recompose |
Marlowe's off-stage blasphemous fun with words'.
56. Of the eight lines that comprise stanza XIII of *A Treatise of Civil Power*, seven begin with capital letters; the lower-case exception begins, aptly, 'despite ⋯'.

The imaginative probity of both poets' artistic decisions found anti-
thetical incarnations. Hill inscribed a terrible dehumanized bureau-
cratic numeracy. The effect is of professionalized dishonour, whereas
Larkin's *MCMXIV* evokes a departed honour. I cannot say MCMXIV,
yet I cannot think it right of the BBC, in a programme of Larkin's
poems, to say 'nineteen fourteen'. You sympathize, since some wording or other has to usher in the poem, yet how much of the sense of
loss is lost. How enduring had been the continuity with ancient wars
and with immemorial commemoration; how sharp, the passing of an
era. 'Never such innocence again.'[57]

But what I should have acknowledged is that the BBC reader—or,
come to that, Larkin himself—could (ill-advisedly) have said *anno mil-
lesimo nongentesimo quarto decimo*. The education of, say, Alfred Tennyson
would have meant only a few moments' pondering had he wished to
say 'In Memoriam AHH OBIIT MDCCCXXXIII', even if *anno mil-
lesimo octingentesimo tricesimo tertio* would not have come as trippingly
to his tongue as 'eighteen thirty-three'. Larkin would not have immediately known how to say MCMXIV in Latin words, as distinct from
how to apprehend the numerals in England. Would Geoffrey Hill,
when giving a reading from *The Triumph of Love*, be fluent at voicing,
for instance, CXXXIX in Latin words? But of course he should do no
such thing. He should leave it as unspeakable yet comprehensible.

Similarly with another nexus of conventions that has its own com-
plexities, that of the diacritical marks in late Hill. Such, from one point
of view, is the evident mark of the some of the last few volumes. Not
just the usual things, italics, caps. small and large, accent-marks, abbre-
viations ('yr death wish' is something other than 'your death wish'),
and editorial square-brackets [ED]. For to these must be added a few
still-unusual new things, such as the vertical | that hovers. As a word
for all such writerly devices, here in the work of a poet who dwells
much upon his troubled senescence, we should reconcile ourselves to
prosthetic. 'Check my prosthetic tears'. 'Edna | with her prosthetic jaw
and nose | prevails over these exchanges'.[58]

It is from Hill's imaginative erudition that some of us are now aware
that T. H. Green 'criticized Butler for being "content to leave the

57. The closing line of Larkin's poem. The point made in '*Geoffrey Hill: At-one-ment*'
(1960) is slightly modified in 'Philip Larkin: "Like something almost being said"'
(1982); *The Force of Poetry*, 302, 280.
58. '*Speech! Speech!* 67, and *In Memoriam: Gillian Rose*.

moral nature a cross of unreconciled principles" '.[59] A few lines later in Hill, Coleridge appears, though not in order to quote his great tribute to imagination: that it 'reveals itself in the balance or reconciliation of opposite or discordant qualities' (*Biographia Literaria*, ch. XIV). In his comments for the *Penguin Book of Contemporary Verse*, the young Hill had been sceptical not of this in itself but of any smooth accommodation of it:

but this can be put behind us (as it is in the imagery) because Art is 'decent': it 'reconciles the irreconcilable'.

Yet Coleridge valued 'Rafael's admirable Galatea' for 'the balance, the perfect reconciliation, effected between these conflicting principles of the FREE LIFE and of the confining FORM'.[60] True, he also warned his hearers as to 'how far they might be seduced by the best feelings to transfer that facility of forgiveness and reconciliation which is so natural to generous minds, from the events of private life, where it is most amiable, to public men and public events, where it would be error and apostacy'. This is the iron hand of Coleridge that raises itself against 'quacks, administering the "poppy and mandragora" of oblivion and unnatural reconciliation, at the moment, when the knife and the cautery alone can prevent the foam of a mad faction from being taken up into the blood, and carried into the very heart of the Constitution'.[61] 'To watch the Tiber foaming out much blood' (*Mercian Hymns* XVIII).

No more than Coleridge can Hill reconcile himself to unnatural reconciliation. Naturally unreconciling, such minds. But not blankly so, and reconciliation may need no more than the caveat or prophylaxis of *perhaps*.

> You could say
> that to yourself in the darkness before sleep
> and perhaps be reconciled. Nothing true
> is easy—is that true? Or, how true is it?
> It must be worth something, some sacrifice.
>
> (*The Triumph of Love* CIV)

59. ' "Perplexed Persistence": The Exemplary Failure of T. H. Green' (1975); *Collected Critical Writings*, 110; a few lines later, 'the ineluctable fact···'.
60. 'The Principles of Genial Criticism' (1814); *Collected Works: Shorter Works and Fragments*, ed. H. J. Jackson and J. R. de J. Jackson, vol. xi (1995), 374.
61. *The Morning Post*, 3 and 11 December 1801; *Collected Works: Essays on His Times*, ed. David V. Erdman, vol. iii (1978), 285, 296.

Before Senility entertains what is clearly neither more nor less than a hope:

> In plainer style, or sweeter, some figment
> of gratitude and reconciliation
> with the near things, with remnancy and love:[62]

—some figment? The wishful and the wistful remain the things of which Hill is very wary.

> He could not reconcile,
> he said, either Pity or Terror with the justice
> of their dereliction: (*The Triumph of Love* XII)

Nothing is to balk the strength of Hill's unrelenting, unreconciling mind. He is sensitive not only to there being some overlap of reconciliation and reconcilement (both include 'the fact of being reconciled') but to their differentiations.[63]

> The reconcilement of these explosions
> With a mysterious Providence, with God,
>   Perplexes all good talk abroad
>   Among the difficult persuasions.[64]

Many of Hill's difficult persuasions are brought about by courtesy of the suffix *-ble* and the power that it can possess and yield. *The Triumph of Love* XII darkly plays *-ble* against *-bble*, where 'the wind | bore an unmistakable sour tang | of paper-rubble', and where 'He could not reconcile···' is the cold key. The very next poem reinforces this with its 'reinforceable | base cinderblocks'. There is for Hill no escaping *-ble* : 'So what is faith if it is not | inescapable endurance?', and there is no forgetting it: 'Nothing is unforgettable but guilt', 'the flawless hubris of heroic guilt'.[65]

Above all, there is the poem that is inconceivable without *irreconcilable* and *inconceivable*, the heroic poem that had in 2005 brought to a close the first section of *Scenes From Comus*:

62. These lines in *Before Senility* were salvaged from the final stanza of the poem called *A Treatise of Civil Power*, dropped by Hill.

63. OED, *reconcilement*: The fact of reconciling or being reconciled to another or to each other. *reconciliation*: The action of reconciling persons, or the result of this; the fact of being reconciled.

64. The opening of *Oraclau / Oracles* 48.

65. *The Triumph of Love* CXXI; *Scenes From Comus* 3.19; *A Short History of British India* I.

> That weight of the world, weight of the word, is.
> Not wholly irreconcilable. Almost.
> Almost we cannot pull free; almost we escape
>
> the leadenness of things. Almost I have walked
> the first step upon water. Nothing beyond.
> The inconceivable is a basic service.
>
> Hyphens are not-necessary for things I say.
> Nor do I put to strain their erudition—
> I mean, the learned readers of J. Milton.
>
> But weight of the world, weight of the word, is.

Having maintained in 1984 that hyphens had proved necessary for things that Hill had had to say, I met this of his in 2005 with mixed feelings and thoughts. Hill was to think again, and his saying this about hyphens duly became itself something not-necessary for things he said. *Broken Hierarchies* (2013) conceived, yet once more, the basic service that is revision:

> The inconceivable is a basic service;
>
> Not to be too Parnassian about it;
> And not to put to strain their erudition
> (I mean the learned readers of J. Milton);
>
> And weight of the word, weight of the world, is.

For 'Hyphens are not-necessary for things I say', read now 'Not to be too Parnassian about it'.[66] For 'But weight of the world, weight of the word is', read now 'And weight of the word, weight of the world, is'. Till the very end, Hill was weighing anew his words (and his suffixes, his hyphens) in the light of his myriad-mind.

A Coda

On what often closes a prose-poem by Hill.

Hill esteemed the conviction that Walt Whitman expressed: 'the English language · · · is the medium that shall well nigh express the inexpressible'. The author of *Mercian Hymns* learnt much from the poet-prose-man who hymned everything. For even while *Leaves of Grass* was 'an attempt to give the spirit, the body, the man, new words, new potentialities of speech' (since 'the new world, the new times, the

---

66. For Hopkins's principle of the 'Parnassian', see p. 137.

new peoples, the new vista, need a tongue according'[67]), Whitman could sound what Hill speaks of: a tenderness towards 'the witness and achievement of the past'.

Whitman knew (as the end of a singular sentence) a cadence's credentials, its music at the close:

> When I heard the learn'd astronomer,
> When the proofs, the figures, were ranged in columns before me,
> When I was shown the charts and diagrams, to add, divide,
>   and measure them,
> When I sitting heard the astronomer where he lectured with
>   much applause in the lecture-room,
> How soon unaccountable I became tired and sick,
> Till rising and gliding out I wander'd off by myself,
> In the mystical moist night-air, and from time to time,
> Look'd up in perfect silence at the stars.

The more-than-a-thousand pages of Hill's poems make clear that the English heroic line did wonders for him. But then what measure did not? So the place for isolating one particular pleasure of Hill's heroic lines is his prose-poems. Admittedly this amounts to little more than a footnote to the present essay.

Of the thirty prose hymns or canticles that constitute *Mercian Hymns* (1971), eighteen arrive in the end—some of them vaulting there—at the rhythm valued not only by poetry but by prose.

I

> King of the perennial holly-groves, the riven sandstone:
>   overlord of the M5: architect of the historic rampart
>   and ditch, the citadel at Tamworth, the summer hermitage
>   in Holy Cross: guardian of the Welsh Bridge and the Iron
>   Bridge: contractor to the desirable new estates: saltmaster:
>   moneychanger: commissioner for oaths: martyrologist:
>   the friend of Charlemagne.

'I liked that,' said Offa, 'sing it again.'

★

> I   'I liked that,' said Offa, 'sing it again.'
> III   ⋯sealing his brisk largesse with 'any mustard?'
> IV   ⋯the long-unlooked-for mansions of our tribe.

---

67. Hill quoting Whitman, 'Alienated Majesty: Walt Whitman', in *Collected Critical Writings*, 508, 513, 515.

     V   ···a king of some kind, a prodigy, a maimed one.
    VI   ···wrists and knees garnished with impetigo.
  VIII   I dedicate my awakening to this matter.
    IX   ···lived long enough to see things 'nicely settled'.
    XI   ···his snout intimate with worms and leaves.
   XII   I have accrued a golden and stinking blaze.
  XIII   ···his possession, cushioned on a legend.
   XIV   ···whenever it suited him, which was not often.
  XVII   He lavished on the high valleys its haleine.
 XVIII   To watch the Tiber foaming out much blood.
   XXI   ···the harp-shaped brooches, the nuggets of fool's gold.
 XXIII   The lamps grew plump with oily reliable light.
  XXIV   ···dust in the eyes, on clawing wings, and lips).
 XXVII   ···dripped red in the arena of its uprooting.
   XXX   ···coins, for his lodging, and traces of red mud.

★ ★ ★

The line that concluded the last poem of *Mercian Hymns* (1971) was in
due course to colour the line that concludes the first poem of Hill's
other book of prose-poems, *The Book of Baruch* (2019), with 'red flags'
hailing 'red mud'. We are to listen for and to the cadence.

     1   ···tread to strange tunes under the red flags.
     2   ···Entertain me to your antiphon.
    23   ···deep poets are like divers with the bends.
   147   ···magnified by sun through spindrift-rime.
   197   ···sustaining of its near subliminal song.
   208   ···similitudes by no means watertight.
   216   ···claimed to have undergone or understood.
   222   ···illumination that's both bound and blind.
   232   ···the 'simply divine' understood by none.
   235   ···as a disincentive it will do.
   253   ···not a sigh but an exultant snarl.
   257   ···Dryden, Purcell, and their 'Fairest Isle'.
   271   ···the afterglow of each brief thunder-shower.

This last, the last words of *The Book of Baruch*.

II

Norman Mailer, Just Off
the Rhythm

I

As sweet as anything he had ever known,
Their happy delirium may perhaps remain,
Inhabiting an empty midnight plain
While glints of light came to each alone.
No, never had she been more luminous—
Scenes that extolled the beauty of her soul.
I removed the stone and felt into the hole;
He looked off into the jungle, righteous, envious.
Sweat was breaking out along his back,
Blood on his face, but he felt no pain.
The sun clouded over, and it began to rain,
Stacks of such clauses fed the sky with smoke.
    And then a cloud shattered overhead.
    Not so easy for the timid when all is said.

The construct of his own security
Murmured words more real than her lips.
His feelings were now caustic as a whip—
All of them blend and lose identity.
'I'm going. You can frig this goddam war.'
Couple of benches along the two long walls,
Fireflies over the great shrub of the Mall,
And the big team couldn't get to score.
He knew that was the best and simplest way.
Henry looked up. 'I'm sorry,' Henry said.
Didn't want to be in the papers dead,
There was no money in them anyway.
    Mailer was not unhappy he was there—
    Not often could Mailer count on such sweet air.

258

ALONG HEROIC LINES

These sonnets are and are not by Norman Mailer, with every line—
every heroic line—coming verbatim from Mailer's works in prose.[1] As
sonnets, they are brought about in the spirit of David Ferry's poem *Of
Rhyme*: 'The discovering is an ordering in time.'

Mailer was not unhappy he was there, particularly if *there* meant
Provincetown, Massachusetts. The cadence of both of those lines of
Mailer's about Mailer endeared Provincetown to him, and him to
Provincetown. From three different books of his, the old town and the
old dance:

~Besides it was the Wild West of the East
No, it was the Wild West of the East
Provincetown the Wild West of the East~[2]

Tough Guys Don't Dance, the detective story set in Provincetown, does
not require that we *detect* the heroic line. For the book opens:

~At dawn, if it was low tide on the flats~

Mailer has rhythm: better, he has a feeling for the mnemonic power of
certain rhythms, along with an intuition as to how they are not only
memorable but memory-charged. With spurts of feeling, he can stain
the English heroic line so that it is alive to primeval fears:

I removed the stone and felt into the hole in front of the footlocker, my fingers scraping and searching into this soft loam like field mice at the edge of
food, and I felt something—it could be flesh or hair or some moist sponge—
I didn't know what, but my hands, fiercer than myself, cleared the debris to
pull forward a plastic garbage bag through which I poked and saw enough at
once to give one frightful moan, pure as the vertigo of a long fall itself. I was
looking at the back of a head. The color of its hair, despite all the stains of
earth, was blond.[3]

1. The first sonnet = *The Naked and the Dead* (1948), 513; *Portrait of Picasso as a Young Man:
An Interpretive Biography* (1995), 176, 61; *The Armies of the Night: History as a Novel, the
Novel as History* (1968), 280; *Marilyn: A Biography* (1973), 193, twice; *Tough Guys Don't
Dance* (1984), 47; *The Naked and the Dead*, 259, 26, 31, 504; *The Prisoner of Sex* (1971), 62;
The Naked and the Dead, 95; *The Armies of the Night*, 281. The second sonnet = *The
Naked and the Dead*, 77; *The Deer Park* (1955), 130; *The Armies of the Night*, 145;
The Naked and the Dead, 480; *Advertisements for Myself*, 58; *The Naked and the Dead*, 159,
162; *Advertisements for Myself*, 51; *The Armies of the Night*, 200; *Advertisements for Myself*,
48, 53, 40; *The Armies of the Night*, 198, 212.
2. *The Presidential Papers* (1963), 99. *Of a Fire on the Moon* (1971), 398 (in UK, *A Fire on the
Moon*). *Tough Guys Don't Dance*, 33. Michael Lennon evoked, retaining the cadence,
Norman Mailer's Provincetown: The Wild West of the East (2005).
3. *Tough Guys Don't Dance*, 47.

~I removed the stone and felt into the hole
Scraping and searching into this soft loam
It could be flesh or hair or some moist sponge
But my hands, fiercer than myself
A plastic garbage bag through which I poked
Enough at once to give one frightful moan
Pure as the vertigo of a long fall
I was looking at the back of a head~

There is a fierce sponge-like power, soaked with the Jacobean flow that had brought blood to *Gerontion* for Eliot. Mailer knows that there is need of a *cordon sanitaire*, and he creates it in the dashes and the rhythmical demarcation:

~it could be flesh or hair or some moist sponge~

'I removed the stone and felt into the hole'—how narrowly this escapes 'and fell into the hole'.

But do the cadences themselves fall into pastiche, or become an embalming of what once had moved? More than fifty years ago, Gabriel Pearson raised the level of discussion. 'Dickens's use of blank verse has always been automatically censured, as though its occurrence in a prose work must be wrong. Yet there is no reason, on principle, why it should be. The query as to its quality, which is really a query about function, does not get raised.' In bringing to life *The Old Curiosity Shop*, the tragic matter for Dickens had been the death of Mary Hogarth.

Nell was an unsuccessful attempt to grope and feel a way through this crisis, to locate death as a human event. Dickens probes and rummages around the grave. He attempts to feel what it is like being dead · · · Blank verse and pathetic fallacy meanwhile secretly give the game away. Dickens could not after all feel what death is like. He could only feel what it was like to try to feel it. This is surely how his blank verse should be understood.[4]

~To grope and feel a way through this crisis
To locate death as a human event
Probes and rummages around the grave
To feel what it is like being dead
Feel what it was like to try to feel it~

Pearson, in his staminal inaugurative essay, feels his way to probe this event, literary and human:

4. On *The Old Curiosity Shop*, in *Dickens and the Twentieth Century*, ed. John Gross and Gabriel Pearson (London, 1962), 79–80.

Often, a blank verse line will act as a kind of charged formula which Dickens hopes will gather resonance and elevate wish-fulfilment and elegiac self-pity into significant statement. 'Death does not change us more than life, my dear' (Ch. 19) is a good example. Well, it is a thought; but a pretty blank one which conducts little meaning from what goes on in the novel, while having an air of asking to be taken seriously as valid consolation, which it isn't.

For 'blank verse line', better to read 'the heroic line', given that such lines within the prose from which they are excerpted do sometimes rhyme. Moreover, there would then be a thread towards Pearson's words 'heroic' and 'hero'. For Nell's flight from London, as he shows, was 'an effort to recover a pre-urban innocence, to redeem the waste land of the city where men live "solitary...as in the bucket of a human well". There is something mythic, if not heroic, as well as regressive in this search; and in one aspect Nell comes close to being a sort of folk hero.'

> ~The waste land of the city where men live
> As in the bucket of a human well~

The temptation to write 'where men *dwell*' was resisted by Pearson, for this would have been to tease. It was for Mailer to play a serious hand in his tribute (jealous, intrigued) to Robert Lowell and his 'remarkable sense of rhythm'. What in *Tough Guys Don't Dance* is ugly below ground is felt here in *The Armies of the Night* as positively redeemed:

> Lowell's poetry
> ~gave one the sense of living in a well,~
> the echoes were deep,
> ~and sound was finally lost in moss on stone;
> down there the light had the light of velvet,
> and the ripples were imperceptible.~[5]

The Old Curiosity Shop toys with the idea that Nell could be the child as heroine. The Dickensian child as hero, though, would be Oliver Twist, the hero of his story. A brave boy, and all the more a-hero-in-the-making because of the polite prudence with which he twice says *Please, sir*.

Child as he was, he was desperate with hunger, and reckless with misery. He rose from the table; and advancing to the master, basin and spoon in hand, said: somewhat alarmed at his own temerity:

---

5. Preserving Mailer's continuous sequence of words (though the lineation is imposed here), from *The Armies of the Night*, 141–2. Mailer's 'Lowell · · · a well' echoes Lowell's own saying: 'All's well that ends'. (Lowell's name ends well.)

'Please, sir, I want some more.'

The master was a fat healthy man; but he turned very pale. He gazed in stupefied astonishment on the small rebel for some seconds, and then clung for support to the copper. The assistants were paralysed with wonder; the boys with fear.

'What!' said the master at length, in a faint voice.

'Please, sir,' replied Oliver, 'I want some more.'

(Oliver Twist, Chapter II)

There is courage in his tenaciously saying exactly the same again, though this time (for us readers, not for Oliver or the master) his words are interrupted by the narrative that suspends his speaking: ' "Please, sir," replied Oliver, "I want some more." '[6] Respectful, but the rhythm is quietly obdurate, the equal stresses saying levelly, once more, 'I want some more.'

When Mailer told of a child's being sent to an orphanage, the child—Norma Jean Baker—was not an orphan. (And she was not yet Marilyn Monroe.) 'There is a moment when Norma Jean goes through the portals for the first time which tolls a bell as loudly as any sentimental event since Charles Dickens wrote, "Please, sir, can I have some more?" '[7] Given that Mailer once deplored an early work of his own with the judgement, 'Such sentimentality was Dickensian',[8] it is a pity that he plies the rhythm, suborning Oliver's steadfast words into a touch of the ingratiating, 'Please, sir, can I have some more?'

Mailer has the last words of his *Marilyn* be a return to Dickens, this time Mr. Dickens. The portals are no longer those of an orphanage. General William Booth Enters into Heaven? No, Marilyn Monroe. Salvation, perhaps, at last.

Goodbye Norma Jean. Au revoir Marilyn. When you happen on Bobby and Jack, give the wink. And if there's a wish, pay your visit to Mr. Dickens. For he, like many another literary man, is bound to adore you, fatherless child.[9]

~Like many another literary man~

Numbered among those literary men is not only Mr Arthur Miller but Mr Norman Mailer. The line is an intimation that Marilyn Monroe

---

6. See Mark Lambert's critical masterpiece, *Dickens and the Suspended Quotation* (New Haven, 1981). Further, for Dickens and the heroic line, see Ch. 6, 'The Novelist as Critic', above, pp. 120–50.

7. *Marilyn: A Biography*, 35.   8. *The Prisoner of Sex*, 90.

9. *Marilyn: A Biography*, 248. This biography has much on the Kennedy brothers and Miss Monroe; also in *The Presidential Papers*.

can stand as the heroine of her tragedy. A friend of hers 'tells her to put on underwear, for Marilyn wears nothing beneath her dress, as if her skin is the true undergarment'.[10] (The caveat 'as if' is to preserve decorum.) On just one page (p. 173) of *Marilyn*, the line goes winding its way, flexible and indeflectible, catching different lights and darks, risking plangency:

~But he will write a movie script for her
Either the highest offering of his love
The wind of death is in the winding sheet
Instead, he seeks 'immediate medical help'
He will have to save it more than once again~

More than once again, yes. Both for her and for Mailer, who had long maintained for Marilyn Monroe a duly level tone, there (for instance) in two consecutive heroic lines of *The Presidential Papers*:[11]

~Probably she was like that by the end. Sleeping pills are the great leveler.~

Mailer's openness to the dangerous amenability of the heroic line (the heroic line is a great leveller) made his phrasing again and again at once a tribute, a warning, and a threat. For the line, like any other measure, is corruptible, versatile in luring and alluring, and so in degrading and humiliating. When responsibly enlisted within creative resistance to romance, the cadences will realize ~all the symphonic flatulence of hindsight~; ~the final lines of marital misery~; and nightmares ~like unfed scorpions in the unsettled flesh~.[12]

Her illness is made up of all that oncoming accumulation of ills she has post-poned from the past, all that sexual congress with men she has not loved, and all those unfinished hours with men she has loved, all the lies she has told, all the lies told about her, all unavenged humiliations sleeping like unfed scor-pions in the unsettled flesh.

Yet such cadences can be in touch with dreams that are quite other than nightmares. 'If your taste combined with her taste, how nice, how sweet would be that tender dream of flesh there to share.'[13]

~How sweet would be that tender dream of flesh~

—where 'tender' is as variously ample (moved to sympathy, and touch-ingly bruisable) as Tennyson and his hero dreamt of it, in *Maud*: 'And

10. *Marilyn: A Biography*, 79.   11. November 1962; in *The Presidential Papers*, 103.
12. *Marilyn: A Biography*, 65, 184, 167.   13. *Marilyn: A Biography*, 5.

dream of her beauty with tender dread' (I. xvi). Elsewhere in Mailer, the sleep of scorpions might, with luck and pluck, yield to the sleep that knits up, not ravels.

Long after he had failed to be lulled by the quiet rhythms of her breathing, Eitel got up and visited Victor's room, and looked at his child sleeping, but there was only a small emotion he could feel, and so putting on an overcoat, he stepped out on the balcony of their house and looked down to the checkerwork of houses and streets which filled the valley of the capital, and beyond, far in the distance was the ocean and the lights of automobiles on the highway which bordered it.[14]

> ~Lulled by the quiet rhythms of her breathing
> Only a small emotion he could feel
> Which filled the valley of the capital~

The quiet; even more, the silence. 'The silence was intense again, laving itself in layers of somnolence.' From (of all unexpectedly apt settings) *The Naked and the Dead*, the phrasing is intense in its feeling for what lay there, the layers that can further fold 'silence' into 'intense' and extendedly into 'somnolence'.[15] T. S. Eliot wrote that 'Milton's poetry is poetry at the farthest possible remove from prose; his prose seems to me too near to half-formed poetry to be a good prose.'[16] Of Mailer's best writing it might be said that it is so near to fully-formed poetry as to be a good prose.[17]

A good prose will need to recognize and resist the seduction that a cadence like 'laving itself in layers of somnolence' may practise. Take the cadence with which tears fall. It is often of danger, including— back then in the world of the young Marilyn Monroe—to the future bridegroom, Jim Dougherty.

We need only remember it is *Marilyn* we are talking about. So we know he has to be—more than he will ever admit—has to be secretly and hopelessly entangled in the insane sexual musk which comes off a fifteen-year-old who

---

14. *The Deer Park*, 373.
15. *The Naked and the Dead*, 509. The sleep of peace is yearned for again in *The Naked and the Dead*, 518: the sun '~laving his body with a pleasant heat.~' But the danger of relapsing into surrender is sounded. '~We would die with deadened minds and twilight sleep~' (*The Presidential Papers*, 174).
16. 'Milton II' (1947), in *On Poetry and Poets* (1957), 154.
17. Yet Mailer swims along with the old canard: 'And that, indeed, may be why good poetry is more magical than good prose—the message is more elusive, more compressed, and more responsive to sensuous study' (*Picasso*, 167). On public-relations for the poetry people (indeed magical), see 'The Best Words in the Best Order', Chapter 1 above.

talks to him with eyes as soft and luminous as a deer's and then become eyes that have just gone dead in a pouted painted mouth, a presence that comes down upon his own mouth like velvet, then withdraws into a veil of mist and tears tender as a warm and rainy fog.[18]

> ~Secretly and hopelessly entangled
> With eyes as soft and luminous as a deer's
> Withdraws into a veil of mist and tears
> Tender as a warm and rainy fog~

For the heroic line can lend itself to the unworthy service of self-dramatization at one with self-deception. Just like tears. 'This gave him a vindictive pleasure, and he imagined himself in prison, a killer, while tears of pity came into his eyes.'[19]

> ~While tears of pity came into his eyes~

A vindictive pleasure, laced with a self-deceiving vindication. Tennyson had recognized the phenomenon and its rhythmical insinuation, heard and seen in a corrupt lachrymosity:

> '···O pardon me! the madness of that hour,
> When first I parted from thee, moves me yet.'
> At this the tender sound of his own voice
> And sweet self-pity, or the fancy of it,
> Made his eye moist; but Enid feared his eyes,
> Moist as they were, wine-heated from the feast···[20]

The heroic line may be chosen to promulgate a true or a false sense of an escape from fear and danger. When Wilfred Owen opens *Strange Meeting* with 'It seemed that out of battle I escaped', the possibility—though not the likelihood—of an escape can be heard in what the

18. *Marilyn: A Biography*, 45–6. The word 'fog' precipitates this placing and this cadence: '~the harbor sounds that float in on the fog~', *The Naked and the Dead*, 352.
19. *The Naked and the Dead*, 362.
20. *Geraint and Enid*, 345–50, in *Idylls of the King*. Self-pity, and then self-congratulation of a sort. Pity often takes pleasure in this cadence: '~He listened to the downpour on the tent'~, followed by 'and thought ~with pleasurable pity of the men~ in the platoon who would be awakened in their damp blankets to sit shivering in the muddy machine-gun hole while the rain penetrated their clothing. "Not for me," he said.' *The Naked and the Dead*, 354, where the salutary next words, opening a paragraph, are these: '~But then he remembered what the doctor had said'. The verbs *to listen* and *to hear* co-operate with this cadence: '~Listen, America, listen to your shame....~' (*Advertisements for Myself*, 36); '~When my voice came on, I had a shock ···~ to listen to myself with a cool ear~' (*Advertisements for Myself*, 405); '~he hears the liquid slapping sounds of love~' (*The Naked and the Dead*, 273).

cadence may seem to promise. Which is why Mailer's great war-novel, *The Naked and the Dead*, so often records in a rhythm the hankering for some such escape. Perhaps at leisure in the past, perhaps tantalizingly in the future, on leave: '~the dance band at the summer bathing club~', '~the world of long green lawns, and quiet beaches~', even how unexpectedly exquisite it was when the bullets '~whirred past with an ineffable delicate sound~'. Or there is the rueful admission that this time things may not altogether work out, audible in the edgy equanimity of '~The jungle looked almost pretty from the water~'.[21]

Sometimes the temptation to be gullible about the pretty can be staved off by the manifest discrepancy between the appeal of the cadence and the repellence of the materials:

~Covered with nothing less than an old slime~

But hygiene—there is always need to resist putrefaction as well as petrification—had already prescribed something for the stomach, -*er* being heard to mutter five times (yes, 'foam rubber' is the queasy feeling): 'I despised the shelter. I let it molder. The foam rubber of the bunk mattresses has gone to powder. The stone floor is covered with nothing less than an old slime.'[22]

When Mailer calls up the positive pace of which those lines are the negative stumbling, he will nevertheless, yet again, bring about the consummation by courtesy of the heroic line, in the vicinity of 'rhythms'. Sometimes this is too courteous by half, acquiescent. Of harmony: 'It means that separate parts function in a lively set of rhythms with one another. No organ is too fast or too slow vis-à-vis another organ. The pleasant relation inspires proportions in the outer forms which are healthy, harmonious, and beautiful.'[23] ~Healthy, harmonious, and beautiful~. This is the cadence complaisant, an Advertisement for Itself.

II

The very short early story *The Notebook* (1951) pitches in with 'rhythm'—the word points to a weapon wielded by 'the young lady' and by 'the writer' as well as by the narrator. The rhythm of walking is

21. *The Naked and the Dead*, 334, 332, 511, 244.   22. *Harlot's Ghost* (1991), 8.
23. *The Presidential Papers*, 302–3.

set against that of talking (*arguing*, QUARRELLING), and of writing, there in The Notebook. The story starts:

The writer was having a fight with his young lady. They were walking toward her home, and as the argument continued, they walked with their bodies farther and farther apart. The young lady was obviously providing the energy for the quarrel. Her voice would rise a little bit, her head and shoulders would move toward him as though to add weight to her words, and then she would turn away in disgust, her heels tapping the pavement in an even precise rhythm which was quite furious.
The writer was suffering with some dignity. He placed one leg in front of the other, he looked straight ahead, his face was sad, he would smile sadly from time to time and nod his head to every word she uttered.[24]

~The writer was having a fight with his young lady
Their bodies farther and farther apart
As though to add weight to her words
The writer was suffering with some dignity
And nod his head to every word she uttered~

Rather as it is crucial not to suppose that poetry is a matter of rhythm but prose is not, so it is with dancing against walking. Every day there is something to be learnt from the everyday. From *The Deer Park*:

She seemed to bounce when she walked, her shoulders swayed in a little rhythm with her hips, her neck curved, her hair tumbled in gold ringlets over her head, and her husky voice laughed at everyone's jokes.[25]

~Swayed in a little rhythm with her hips~

This laughs along with her, her laughing not at others but at their jokes. Eric Griffiths helped us understand what it is to share (when real, not just the current wheedling).

We laugh at a book but we more importantly laugh *with* it; we see that we were meant to find this bit funny, and we are pleased that we can and do laugh. As we recognize the appropriateness of our response, we take pleasure in that appropriateness itself; we are sharing a joke with a book, and with its author who may have been dead for years ··· And laughing over Flaubert runs continuously into laughing with a friend (it would be strange if someone saw all the jokes in literature but never understood a joke that somebody made in day-to-day relations).[26]

24. *Advertisements for Myself*, 150.   25. *The Deer Park*, 90.
26. Eric Griffiths, *The Printed Voice of Victorian Poetry* (1989), 86–7.

What is true of jokes is no less true of griefs and grievances, not comedy but tragedy. Mailer's masterpiece, *The Executioner's Song*, is a trilogy or tetralogy of tragedies from beginning to end. The rhythms are the telling thing.

Coming down the courthouse corridor, Gilmore looked like a man coming in with hope. To Schiller's eye, Gary didn't seem nearly so frail as during the hunger strike. He might be just two days off his fast, but he was carrying himself well. Had a little cadence to his walk, as if even with the shackles, he could take small, prancing steps that were a little faster, a little more stylish, than the plodding pace of the guards next to him. Something nice about the way he moved, as if hearing an inner beat.[27]

~Coming down the courthouse corridor
Like a man coming in with hope
Nearly so frail as during the hunger strike
He might be just two days off his fast
Had a little cadence to his walk
Small, prancing steps that were a little faster
The plodding pace of the guards next to him
Something nice about the way he moved
He moved, as if hearing an inner beat~

Gary Gilmore retained something, something at odds with his murderous brutality, throughout his campaign of hope, the hope to be put to death, whereas Richard Gibbs, the police informer, sounds as though he never had anything to retain.

~A guy who would stick a shiv under your armpit.~
                                        Farrell liked him even less.
~He looked like a poor old weasel sitting there.
The total stamp of jail was on the man.~[28]

There is a poem by Robert Lowell in *History* (1973) that is headed 'Norman Mailer', the title exhausting the poem's engagement with Norman Mailer. Lowell had written to Alfred Kazin in 1962: 'I like what you say about Mailer. I find an elephantiasis in him that is contemptible, then a real mind and real energy that leaves me envious and empty.'[29] Mailer got under Lowell's skin. This was reciprocated. It was

---

27. *The Executioner's Song* (1979), 743.
28. Preserving Mailer's continuous sequence of words (though the lineation is imposed here), from *The Executioner's Song*, 755.
29. *The Letters of Robert Lowell*, ed. Saskia Hamilton (London, 2005), 403; 18 March 1962.

a good bodyscape for each of them, this subcutaneous other. Mailer on
Lowell in 1967:

He was not a splendid reader, merely decent to his own lines, and he read from
that slouch, that personification of ivy climbing a column, he was even diffi-
dent, he looked a trifle helpless under the lights. Still, he made no effort to win
the audience, seduce them, dominate them, bully them, amuse them, no, they
were there for him, to please *him*, a sounding board for the plucked string of
his poetic line, and so he endeared himself to them. They adored him—for his
talent, his modesty, his superiority, his melancholy, his petulance, his weakness,
his painful, almost stammering shyness, his noble strength—*there* was the
string behind other strings.[30]

> ~He was not a splendid reader, merely decent
> He looked a trifle helpless under the lights
> For the plucked string of his poetic line
> There was the string behind other strings~

Mailer's summary judgements on his contemporaries were repeatedly
couched in terms of rhythm: 'yes, even if Lowell's remarkable sense of
rhythm drew one deep into the poems, nonetheless hypnotic they
resolutely were not, for the language was particular, with a wicked
sense of names, details, and places.'[31] ~A wicked sense of names, details,
and places~.

Wicked, Mailer on Truman Capote: 'He is tart as a grand aunt, but
in his way he is a ballsy little guy, and he is the most perfect writer of
my generation, he writes the best sentences word for word, rhythm
upon rhythm.' 'Saul Bellow knows words, but writes in a style I find
self-willed and unnatural. His rhythms have a twitch.' Of Jack Kerouac:
'His rhythms are erratic, his sense of character is nil, and he is as pre-
tentious as a rich whore, as sentimental as a lollypop.'[32] ~As sentimental
as a lollypop~. Or as Dickens in his off-again moments.

Mailer's writing, like his apprehension, is wide and it is open. 'All the
pleasure of boxing was in my fingers. Like nearly everything else, good
boxing is what is done with the rhythm and even more what is done
just off the rhythm.'[33] Within his own writing, and particularly his revisions, it is *movement* of which he most needed to be confident, hoping

30. *The Armies of the Night*, 55.
31. *The Armies of the Night*, 141. Conjuring up a name and a place from *The Waste Land*:
    Madame Sosostris, 'the wisest woman in Europe, | With a wicked pack of cards'.
32. *Advertisements for Myself*, 465–6.   33. *The Deer Park*, 236.

that he 'came close to the meanings of sound.'[34] Re-writing is re-hearing, rhythm-wise:

the style of the work lost its polish, became rough, and I can say real, for there was an abrupt and muscular body back of the voice now. It had been there all the time, trapped in the porcelain of a false style · · ·

~Trapped in the porcelain of a false style~

Or of a cadence. The real thing rings true. 'Consider that a good half of writing consists of being sufficiently sensitive to the moment to reach for the next promise which is usually hidden in some word or phrase just a shift to the side of one's conscious intent.' ~Usually hidden in some word or phrase~. For 'consciousness, that blunt tool, bucks in the general direction of the truth; instinct plucks the feather.'[35] ~The general direction of the truth~. No more has to be claimed, at first, than that.

What held Mailer to the general direction of the truth for so much of the time of his time was, first and foremost, a deep rhythmical sense of how variegated movement is, how differently—despite the similitude of cadence—movement is alive in, say, dancing ('~sharp little heels beating out the rhythm~'), as against floating ('~his mind drifted slowly like a torpid stream~'), or wading ('~through a thick resistant medium like oil~').[36] Possessing an idiosyncratic yet authentic understanding of rhythms, 'Mailer, minor poet',[37] was sensitive to how prose could accommodate poetry's measures and moves, could resist them or invite their presence. He had room within himself, and within the amplitude of his books, to incorporate the tension that set rhythm against sentiment—and thereby set itself against complacency. Such phrasing as '~to stand erect and be original~' stands by the fact that the heroic line is traditional before being original. '~The empty pit where there should be a man~' is filled by its respect for the longstanding line, even as '~dragged on through empty apathetic hours~' is neither empty nor apathetic since it is filled with what is felt along the line. And the retrospective is at one with the prospective, since the cadence keeps on keeping on: '~dragged on through empty apathetic hours while glints of light came to each alone~'.[38]

34. On his revising *The Deer Park*, in *Advertisements for Myself*, 236.
35. *The Armies of the Night*, 38.
36. *The Deer Park*, 182; *The Naked and the Dead*, 143, 85.
37. *The Armies of the Night*, 50; Mailer on himself in comparison with Lowell.
38. *Advertisements for Myself*, 23; *The Naked and the Dead*, 322; *The Armies of the Night*, 308.

'~They were merely envelopes of suffering~'. Not so—the envelope itself, as though black-edged in mourning, refuses to endorse *merely*. '~A man was really a very fragile thing~'. Yes, but the memorial construction that incarnates the thought is not a fragile thing, it is an enduring thing, it strengthens the things that remain.[39]

The Naked and the Dead attends to heroism in war. It does not attend *upon* heroism, for heroism needs to be differentiated from heroics, even while it is the case that without at least a touch of heroics there would often be no hope of heroism. *The Fight* (1975) weighs the pitting of Muhammad Ali against George Foreman, while conscious that Mailer, 'just off the rhythm', is for no more than seconds out of the ring. In boxing, the quickness of the hand must deceive the eye, but how to have the context be not only the ring but the page? Here is Mailer on revising *The Deer Park*, again:

···and all this was to the good, or would have been for a reader who went slowly, and stopped, and thought. But if anyone was in a hurry, the little sentence 'Older sister' was like a finger in the eye, it jabbed the unconscious, and gave an uncomfortable nip of rhythm to the mind.

I had five hundred changes of this kind. I started with the first paragraph of the book, on the third sentence which pokes the reader with its backed-up rhythm, 'Some time ago,' and I did that with intent, to slow my readers from the start, like a fighter who throws his right two seconds after the bell and so gives the other man no chance to decide on the pace.[40]

~Uncomfortable nip of rhythm to the mind
I had five hundred changes of this kind
Pokes the reader with its backed-up rhythm~

When Mailer calls upon the word 'rhythm', he often braces it against a nearby heroic line, even if the occasion is forthright narrative.[41] *The Naked and the Dead*: 'Their bodies were outraged; they had been eating and sleeping with no rhythm at all for the last few hours.'[42] ~No rhythm at all for the last few hours~. Yet not 'no rhythm'; the very instance resists acquiescence.

He felt only a vast grief which mellowed him, dissolved the cysts of his bitterness and resentment and fear and left him spent and weeping on the sand. The softer gentler memories of Mary were coming back to him; he recalled the

39. *The Naked and the Dead*, 658, 216.   40. *Advertisements for Myself*, 239.
41. *Picasso*, 241 (of Matisse): '"Goldfish and Sculpture", from 1911, stripped of its palette, gives up nearly all of its rhythm'. ~Gives up nearly all of its rhythm~.
42. *The Naked and the Dead*, 144.

sweltering liquid rhythms of their bodies against each other in heat and love · · ·[43]

> ~And left him spent and weeping on the sand
> The softer gentler memories of Mary
> The sweltering liquid rhythms of their bodies~

'Against each other', yet the opposite of adversarial. Memories and rhythm include the memory inherent in rhythm and the rhythm inherent in memory. 'The years pass into the years and we count our time in lonely private rhythms which have little to do with number or judgment or the uncertain shifting memory of friends.'[44]

> ~The uncertain shifting memory of friends~

Therefore we are obliged, most of us, to meet the tempo of the present and the future with reflexes and rhythms which come from the past. It is not only the 'dead weight of the institutions of the past' but indeed the inefficient and often antiquated nervous circuits of the past which strangle our potentiality for responding to new possibilities which might be exciting for our individual growth.[45]

> ~Weight of the institutions of the past
> Exciting for our individual growth~~

But here Mailer sentimentalizes (*exciting!*), and so—as happens in such slippage—he slights. For the institutions of the past have not only a dead but a living weight, found and pondered in rhythms and in constructions, 'if one believes, as I sometimes do, that the secrets of existence, or some of them anyway, are to be found in the constructions of language which have come down to us'.[46]

As with boxing, there may be the need for a quick feint, with the unit of sense turning out not to be 'my fear of homosexuality' but rather

I must have known that my fear of homosexuality as a subject was stifling my creative reflexes, and given the brutal rhythms of my nature, I could kill this inhibition only by jumping into the middle of the problem without any clothes.[47]

> ~Given the brutal rhythms of my nature~

43. *The Naked and the Dead*, 285.   44. *The Deer Park*, 348.
45. *Advertisements for Myself*, 345.   46. *The Presidential Papers*, 302–3.
47. *Advertisements for Myself*, 222. The brutal rhythms of Mailer's nature were acted out in his life, lethally. Jack Henry Abbott (1944–2002), killer early and late; Mailer assisting Abbott's release on parole, 1981. But Mailer, 'kill this inhibition', back in 1959.

In his writing, he was often able to 'place' the brutal rhythms, although to put it like that may suggest an implausible figure, a Jamesian Mailer. Yet when Mailer commented on *The Executioner's Song*, he did justice: true, 'you wouldn't want Henry James to describe the life of Gary Gilmore'. But.

For what Henry James wanted to do, however, his language was ideal. He recognized before anyone else that polite social life, despite its ridiculous or affected aspects, also presents a spectrum of small options present at every moment. In social life, a person often chooses among three or four equally agreeable alternatives, even to making the choice of being little warmer or a little cooler than he or she originally expected to be toward a given person. James had an extraordinary sense of that unforeseen vibration in the almost wholly expected, and he created a fictional world out of such insight, a world that depended altogether on his unique voice.[48]

In James, the vibration; in Mailer, there are jolts, for us as well as for him: 'jolted clear to the seat of my semen by the succession of rhythmic blows which my heart drummed back to my feet'.[49] Alongside easy rhythms that spoke of rhythms, there were dark verbal compacts ('fluxed' might flummox us, courting obscenity): 'and left the lovers fluxed with the rhythms and reflexes of one another'.[50] There were also persuasive languors: time as '~the tropical envelopments of love~'.[51] And even a waiving, a relief of a weird kind, felt in the rhythm, just before the big fight: 'It is like being at a vast party in Limbo—there is tremendous excitement, much movement and no sex at all. Just talk.'[52]

~Much movement and no sex at all. Just talk.~

The corpus of Mailer is exercised by the body.

I had given my working hours of the early morning to dissolving a few of the inhibitions, chilled reflexes~and dampened rhythms of the corpus before me~[53]

—and often the body is involved in a collision of some kind. 'So she was capable of using her encyclopedic knowledge of the colliding congesting rhythms in the bodies of the strangers she met.'[54]

~The colliding congesting rhythms in the bodies~

48. *The Spooky Art: Thoughts on Writing* (2003), 77.
49. 'The Time of Her Time', in *Advertisements for Myself*, 492.
50. *Advertisements for Myself*, 528.   51. *Advertisements for Myself*, 521.
52. *The Presidential Papers*, 217, on the Paret/Griffith fight.
53. 'The Time of Her Time', in *Advertisements for Myself*, 487.
54. *Advertisements for Myself*, 522.

What Mailer brings home from the various rhythm-contexts of which he has encyclopedic knowledge, and to which he is attuned, is the odd fact that though there are many cognate forms of the word 'rhythm' as different parts of speech,[55] there is no verb to go along with the noun—and this despite the fact that the sense of 'rhythm' is so at one with action, movement, the kinetic, pace, timing. When we imagine *dance*, the verb and the noun are most happily one, and other cognate parts of speech join in.[56] But *rhythm* withholds the verb-form that one would have thought that it would be eager for. True, the *OED* will grant us *to rhythm* as a verb, but only as 'rare' and as meaning 'to rhyme', with this verb underpinning *rhythmer* and *rhythming* yet with both of them similarly at the service of *rhyme*. The same is true of *rhythmed* (obsolete, and meaning rhymed), except insofar as it did in 1863 have a shot at meaning 'Marked by rhythm; rhythmical'. But none of these candidates were sustainably up to a verb's job, whether *to rhythmize* (1885, to put into rhythm), or *to rhythmicize*: '1907, rare. To make (a song) rhythmical; to endow with rhythm. Also to establish a steady rhythm.' As for *rhythmist*, the *OED*'s covert pun on 'versed' was not enough to gain it a foothold (1864, 'one who is versed in, or has a true sense of, rhythm').

The rhythmist Mailer enjoys tracing swing and the swing of things:

> For to swing is to communicate, is to convey the rhythms of one's own being to a lover, a friend, or an audience, and—equally necessary—be able to feel the rhythms of their response. To swing with the rhythms of another is to enrich oneself—the conception of the learning process as dug by Hip is that one cannot really learn until one contains within oneself the implicit rhythm of the subject or the person.[57]

~Convey the rhythms of one's own being
Rhythm of the subject or the person~

The person is to be physically unignorable, with Mailer—given his body-memory (which is more ample than the muscle-memory of a golfer)—having some claim to two of those extended nouns that the language had hoped to engraft, nouns that exude corporeality to the

---

55. Adjectives (rhythmal, rhythmetric, rhythmetrical, rhythmic, rhythmical, rhythmo-poetic), adverb (rhythmically), and enlarged nouns (rhythmicality, rhythmicity, rhythmopœia, rhythmus).
56. Danceable, dancer, dancingly, dancitive, and (US, 1967, at first a proprietary term), dancercise.
57. *Advertisements for Myself*, 350.

point of being medical. One is *OED*, *rhythmicity*: 'Rhythmical quality
or character; the capacity for maintaining a rhythm', where the earliest
citations are these:

1901 Buck's *Handbook Med Sci* The pulse rate presents more or less regular
and extensive variations in the course of a day... They are hardly the expression of an inherent rhythmicity.

1910 *Heart* The ventricles are freed of the influence of their pace-maker, and
their rate of beat is consequently slow until the dormant rhythmicity becomes
fully awakened.

1944 *Mind* Variability in size, number, direction, space, distance and rhythmicity is probably the most important characteristic in the primitive visual field.

1969 *Nature* Cutting the nerves .. which connect the corpora cardiaca to the
sub-oesophageal ganglion .. caused a gradual loss of rhythmicity in otherwise
intact cockroaches.

The second is *rhythmicality*: 'rhythmical property'. 1885, Romanes, *Jelly-
fish*: 'The contractile tissues which have longest retained their primitive
endowment of rhythmicality'. The primitive visual field and the primitive endowment: Mailer would deepen this to the primeval. '~Primeval
fears inspire primeval thoughts~'.[58] The line and its thought are inspired
not only by fears and thoughts but by the endowment of rhythmicality.
Or rhythmicity in the case of otherwise intact cockroaches.

He was looking at a corpse which lay almost naked on its back. It was an
eloquent corpse, for there were no wounds on its body, and its hands were
clenching the earth as if to ask for a last time the always futile question. The
naked shoulders were hunched together in anguish, and he could easily conceive the expression of pain that should have been on the corpse's mouth. But
the corpse lay there without a head, and Red ached dully as he realized the
impossibility of ever seeing that man's face.[59]

Not the Naked and the Dead, the almost naked altogether dead.

In 'Advertisements for Myself on the Way Out', Mailer's narrator
declares that 'There is a master pimp in our presence who is a candidate
for the role of hero (his rivals for your vote, a television celebrity and
a psychoanalyst ···', and then he juxtaposed, in a list of the party-goers,
'a war hero' and 'a movie star'.[60] But war heroes, these Mailer respected
and inspected (and suspected).

---

58. *Of a Fire on the Moon*, 416.   59. *The Naked and the Dead*, 216.
60. *Advertisements for Myself*, 515, 528.

'Maybe I'd rather be anything else than a soldier, maybe, Lieutenant, I'd rather be a...a...' Dalleson searched for a sufficiently damning word, and then clenching his fist powerfully he shouted, 'Maybe it would be more natural for me to be a *poet*.'[61]

~More natural for me to be a poet~

This moment subsumes memories that are both within the great expanse of the novel and are continuous with even larger memories: 'A thinker, a poet; there were many Japanese like him. And yet they died like anything but poets, died in mass ecstatic outbursts, communal frenzies.'[62]

~And yet they died like anything but poets~

Tag ends of all the stories of Jap torture flicked his brain. Sonofabitch, they'll cut mah nuts off. He felt his breath escaping through his nose, slowly, with compression, stirring the hairs in the nostril. He could hear them puttering around, their words slicing abruptly against his ears.[63]

~The stories of Jap torture flicked his brain
He felt his breath escaping through his nose
Slowly, with compression, stirring the hairs
He could hear them puttering around
Their words slicing abruptly against his ears~

This is a held breath, there in the hushed long-grass battleground of *The Naked and the Dead*.

In the semi-gloom of the cellar, they were crouched against the wall or under the window, firing the machine gun irregularly, being answered irregularly. They did not seem to know he was with them. He slumped feeling his resolution ebb. Three days before, in preparing the house they had dug a slit trench against one of the side walls. It would be better if he were to remain in it, where a chance bullet could not reach him. After all, he could not do the men any good if he were dead. And then mockingly, he felt his fear disappearing, as he dropped into the greater safety of the trench. He shut his eyes.[64]

The ears are open to wisdom at one entrance.

~They did not seem to know he was with them
He slumped feeling his resolution ebb
He could not do the men any good if he were dead
Into the greater safety of the trench~

61. *The Naked and the Dead*, 394.   62. *The Naked and the Dead*, 247.
63. *The Naked and the Dead*, 516.
64. 'A Calculus at Heaven', in *Advertisements for Myself*, 35.

War is experienced as not only killing but deadening, 'the deadening rhythms of war, its boredom, its concussion, and—let no one count this for too little—its injustice.'[65]

III

The real heroism, he thought, was to understand, and because one understood, be even more full of fear at the enormity of what one understood, yet at that moment continue to be ready for the feat one had decided it was essential to perform · · · But the astronauts, brave men, proceeded on the paradoxical principle that fear once deposed by knowledge would make bravery redundant.[66]

'The heroes of the time were technologists, not poets.'[67] Poets would listen for the music of the spheres, and Mailer hails the rhythms of the heavens—not war's deadening rhythms but enlivening ones. The silence of the infinite spaces is open to the cadence of the heavenly bodies. It had been audible in Mailer's first book. 'He wanted to live. ~A little man, tumbling through space~.'[68] *The Naked and the Dead* had not needed other planets, for it found the needed vastness here on this planet of ours, where the ocean, alive to the oceanic rhythms of Melville, informs the immense orchestration:

After a little while, there was only

~the gray-black ocean, the darkened sky,~

and

~the evil churning of the gray-white wake~.[69]

At the take-off of Apollo 11, Mailer was to hear and see a memory of Melville, 'the mysterious ship' being '~white as the white of Melville's Moby Dick · · · slow as Melville's Leviathan might swim~'.[70]

The enormity (in both senses) of war had its parallels in the enormity of Peace, peace, when there is no peace. The pretend-peace of politics had long gravitated naturally for Mailer to the largest imaginable figure of speech, one that was also a fact of life, in politics and in

65. *Advertisements for Myself*, 155.   66. *Of a Fire on the Moon*, 109.
67. *Of a Fire on the Moon*, 151.   68. *The Naked and the Dead*, 666.
69. Preserving Mailer's continuous sequence of words (though the lineation and italicization are imposed here). *The Naked and the Dead*, 454.
70. *Of a Fire on the Moon*, 100.

the scientific competitiveness of the cold war. He speaks of 'country-men', as against the men of other countries, for the space-race was far from co-operative.

Because our tragedy is that we diverge as countrymen further and further away from one another,

~like a space ship broken apart in flight~

which now

~drifts mournfully in isolated orbits,~

satellites to each other,

~planets none, communication faint.~[71]

Donne needed to plead with his loved one: 'O more then Moone, | Draw not up seas to drowne me in thy spheare'.[72] For the Prisoner of Sex, the moon draws up everything that is contrarious, so that the word 'dam', though it is right up against 'curse', is not a curse (and, despite 'women', is not a mother): 'women had that unmentionable womb, that spongy pool, that time machine with a curse, dam for an ongoing river of blood whose rhythm seemed to obey some private compact with the moon.'[73]

~Unmentionable womb, that spongy pool
Obey some private compact with the moon~

The compact with the moon has to include, for Mailer, a compact with the rhythm of the heroic in history. Yet among the thoughts are the exquisite, the delicate: '~a fan of feathers gliding to the floor~'.[74] 'The beginning of the trip to the moon was', we hear, '~as slow as the fall of the fullest flake of snow~'.[75] There is grace: 'But now he was out in the open endless lunar gravity, his body and the reflexes of his life obliged to adopt a new rhythm and schedule of effort, a new disclosure of grace.'[76] ~The open endless lunar gravity~. But then perhaps the whole story could be felt along these lines.[77]

71. The closing lines of 'The Existential Heroine' (on Jacqueline Kennedy, 1962), in *The Presidential Papers*, 98. Again preserving Mailer's sequence of words.
72. *A Valediction: of weeping.*
73. *The Prisoner of Sex*, 60–1. Not to be confused, Mailer insists, with 'such barbarities as the rhythm system of the Church' (p. 199).
74. *Of a Fire on the Moon*, 400.   75. *Of a Fire on the Moon*, 194.
76. *Of a Fire on the Moon*, 401.   77. *Of a Fire on the Moon*, 156, 183, 296, 414, 422.

~The somber shelves of a library at night
Flat on his back as a baby in his crib
To cater to the rhythm of their duties
The astronauts were in no shape to sleep
The liberty of this moon-conquered night~

Following the flag is one thing that patriotism trades on. When it came to a flag on the moon, the windlessness was against them. But necessity is the mother of ventilation.

It was at this point that patriotism, the corporation, and the national taste all came to occupy the same head of a pin, for the astronauts next proceeded to set up the flag. But that operation, as always, presented its exquisite problems. There was, we remind ourselves, no atmosphere for the flag to wave in. Any flag made of cloth would droop, indeed it would dangle. Therefore a species of starched plastic flag had to be employed, a flag which would stand out, there, out to the nonexistent breeze, flat as a slab of plywood. No, that would not do either. The flag was better crinkled and curled. Waves and billows were bent into it, and a full corkscrew of a curl at the end. There it stands for posterity, photographed in the twists of a high gale on the windless moon, curled up tin flag, numb as a pickled pepper.[78]

~The corporation, and the national taste
To occupy the same head of a pin
No atmosphere for the flag to wave in
Made of cloth would droop, indeed it would dangle
Starched plastic flag had to be employed
Waves and billows were bent into it
Curled up tin flag, numb as a pickled pepper~

Peter Piper is not the only tongued twister. In this worlds-wide story that invites us to ponder heroes, hero-worship, and the heroic in history, there is not only a further place for heroics, there is a cameo appearance by the villain, or at least by the villainous, the villain-ose.

Cue Wernher von Braun, quondam Nazi. He is, for Mailer, the corporate non-humanity that is the counterpart to the human benignity that is the Robert Lowell of *The Armies of the Night*. Von Braun, who 'was the heat in rocketry', ignites *Of a Fire on the Moon*.

A press conference, no matter how many he had had, was a putative den of menace. So his eyes flew left and right as he answered a question, flicking back

78. *Of a Fire on the Moon*, 405. Not that the story is as relatively simple, or as uncontested, as it might seem from Mailer; for the high comedy, follow Google, The flag [or The flags] on the moon.

and forth in their attention with the speed of eyes watching a Ping-Pong game, and his mouth moved from a straight line to a smile, but the smile was no more than a significator, a tooth-filled rectangle. Words were being mouthed like signal flags.[79]

~Words were being mouthed like signal flags~

But something other than Nelson's signal flags at the Battle of Trafalgar:

England Expects That Every Man Will Do His D U T Y

America [Germany Under Erasure] Expects That Every Man Will Cater to the Rhythm of Their Duties.

International politics is the art of the compromised: such is life. The life will sometimes be that which underlies Mailer's heroic lines, amenable to breaking into sonnetry again.[80]

> Some women are born to have a lot of men.
> Poised on the edge of a delicious bliss,
> Well within the shadow of the cliffs,
> The nervous needles pricked his flesh again.
> Their boots were covered with great slabs of muck.
> Laving itself in layers of somnolence,
> Two separate senses of a private silence,
> Like a wave of surf about to break,
> Like a hound uncertain of the scent—
> The open endless lunar gravity,
> The final lines of marital misery—
> He licked his lips, mourning his wife again.
> The rugged care provided by his wife?
> What a dreary compromise is life!

79. *Of a Fire on the Moon*, 67, 71.
80. *Advertisements for Myself*, 37; *The Naked and the Dead*, 625, 586, 601, 130, 509; *The Armies of the Night*, 129; *The Naked and the Dead*, 186, 11; *Of a Fire on the Moon*, 366; *Marilyn: A Biography*, 184; *The Naked and the Dead*, 447; *The Presidential Papers*, 233; with the last line, from *Advertisements for Myself*, 185, where these are the closing words of the thirty-page story, 'The Man Who Studied Yoga'.

12

Ion Bugan on the Iron Curtain

Commissioned for *Dead Ground 2018–1918*, edited by Andrew McNeillie and James McNeillie. ' "Dead ground" in military terms is terrain into which you cannot see', notes the Introduction, adding 'We use the term here as a kind of metaphor, in a wide-ranging way.'

> Arm in arm, my father and I return
> to the ground of his failed escape:
> it is now forty-eight years on.
>
> *(A walk with my father on the Iron Curtain)*

CARMEN BUGAN, writer of Romania. Born, 1970. Came to the United States of America (with her parents and her siblings), 1989.

NICOLAE CEAUŞESCU, dictator of Romania. Born, 1918. Came to absolute power (with his wife), 1965. Killed, 1989. Disinterred, to be interred afresh, 2010.

Carmen Bugan's well-founded memoir in prose, *Burying the Typewriter* (2012), opened with a poem of which the title, *Visiting the country of my birth*, constituted a heroic line. The country was of others' deaths, for then at once:

> The tyrant and his wife were exhumed
> For proper burial; it is twenty years since
> They were shot against a wall in Christmas snow.

Proper burial not only for the party-leader, but—some years earlier— for the anti-party machine. It had been proper, albeit illegal, to bury the typewriter. (Rather, to bury *a* typewriter, for secretly there was another typewriter that rested not in dead ground but in the living room; unhidden at a plain site; in terms of the hunt, a stalking horse.) 'Proper burial' as prudent, then. The authorities, finding the typewriter to be incriminating evidence of dissidence, would decline to confess that the incriminated party was not the courageous citizen but Ceauşescu and his Communist Party. Carmen Bugan brings all this to book, with photos of the hole dug in the ground and of its contents, alongside the wording of the secret police files (to all of which she has now been given access and to which she accords deeply imaginative resolution in both her memoir and her poems). From a page in the files headed: PHOTOGRAPHIC EVIDENCE.

'After we lifted the plastic sack we saw in the hole a plastic white container, buried 40 cm deep'. *Stamp of the Socialist Republic of Romania and the signature of Colonel Coman, in charge of penal research.*[1]

Burying the . . . might well have moved sharply to *Hatchet.* To lay down one's arms, to cease from hostilities; the resumption of hostilities being to dig up the hatchet. But no.

Then Father would take the hatchet from behind the stove and patrol the house, 'This is my house, no one comes into my house, or I'll kill him!' He'd wait with our key placed in the door so it couldn't be pushed out. (*At hour 1:32*)

The modest comma after the words *the house,* opening into *my house* · · · *my house,* is the key placed there by the poet. How simple, in the heat of anger, is the chilling wording of the thought of 'thoughts' that 'were banished | by men with keys to our house' (*Releasing the porcelain birds*).[2]

    Then Father, her father, was imprisoned, tortured. He made an escape but was seized. Secret police: 'The aforementioned objects belong to escapees Bugan Ion and P.T. who crossed the frontier from the People's Republic of Romania to the People's Republic of Bulgaria on the day of 21.02.1965.' But Ceauşescu sought to hold for Romania (in commerce with the United States) the 'most-favored nation' accreditation, so there was to come something of an amnesty.

> The dictator released the news of amnesty on his birthday
> 'To remain in history for his clemency,' Mother said
> Not knowing it was her irony that remained preserved:
> In our country people starved and friend informed on friend.
>
> (*Found in secret police records*)

---

1. *Burying the Typewriter,* p. vi.
2. The poems are from the volume *Releasing the Porcelain Birds* (2016).

The news was good, yet it could not but jar: amnesty, history, clemency, country, taking in but moving on from irony. Irony that knows the Iron Curtain (and that knows how tellingly askew is the preposition *on* in *A walk with my father on the Iron Curtain*). 'Found in secret police records' is in Part I—it too, headed FOUND IN SECRET POLICE RECORDS—of *Releasing the Porcelain Birds*, which bore a subtitle: 'poems after surveillance'. There the preposition does double-duty, *after* as the poet's having survived surveillance temporally (not temporarily) as well as the poet's being darkly grateful for a resource of an unexpected kind, unwelcome were it not that art welcomes uglinesses that it can transform.

'Ground of being on his ground of escape' (*A walk with my father on the Iron Curtain*). In Bugan's subsequent volume, *Lilies from America* (2019), one of the new poems recalls 'the sacred welcoming ground of our country, which had later become the betraying ground of our country' (*Christmas 2017*). Yet the grounds had proved anything but betrayed or dead. Nothing could have been more alive than this ground of being, this profound faith in freedom, honesty, probity (Carmen Bugan, having been short-listed in 2013, was in 2017 made a Fellow of the Orwell Prize) for which Ion Bugan with his heroic family suffered. Her father's typewriter—the family typewriter whatever the sacrifices and fears within the imperilled family—was a wordsmithy that is now possessed by an incorruptible woman of letters. Her words are in open view and in plain hearing for the eyes and ears of people who value every single tongue but not the forked one. *Preparing for the journey of return* (a title that returns to the heroic line) has something to add:

> and we have embraced new languages,
> starting from nothing in the middle of our lives.

That typewriter you planted last year in your garden, has it begun to sprout? What was planted (not by the secret police, this time) in the garden in Romania was no corpse. Dead ground within the garden, possibly, but only as not visible (it was to be hoped) and as not vulnerable from certain vantage-points. The world was supposed not to know of its existence, this ground of being, with its seasonable miracle of an unseen inhumed life. George Herbert, from *The Flower*:

> Who would have thought my shrivel'd heart
> Could have recover'd greennesse? It was gone

> Quite under ground; as flowers depart
> To see their mother-root, when they have blown;
> Where they together
> All the hard weather,
> Dead to the world, keep house unknown.

The hearts of neighbour-informers, fair-weather as against hard-weather friends, did shrivel, whereas none of the family hearts kept in the Bugan house (we hear every one of them in these writings) ever shrivelled. Yet every heart found itself, at some point, pleading to be shriven.

Since Herbert's day, since those seasons of his, the underground recovery of 'Dead to the world' has itself had shrivelling visited upon it. Where it had once compacted its sense into 'seeming, to the unimaginative ground-eyed world, to be dead, but no such thing, most truly alive', this 'Colloq. phr.' *dead to the world* has come since 1899 to mean, rather vacantly, 'unconscious or fast asleep; unaware of the external world'.

Unaware is the nub. The death-dealing dangers—and opportunities— of 'dead ground', in military terminology, are among the things of which you cannot beware (and of which you cannot avail yourself) unless you are aware of them. Much as you cannot *ignore* something the presence of which you were ignorant of.

The term *dead ground* itself had been very quietly ushered in by the *OED*, with 'Cf.' directing us from *dead*—

Mil. Denoting an area which cannot be fired on from a particular point because of the nature of the ground, intervening obstacles, etc.—

where the citations, all of which put 'dead' within quotation marks, are 1899, 1900, and 1919, pointing on to *angle*: '(Cf. *dead angle* in D. 2.)'

Special combs. *dead angle* (*Fortif.*), 'any angle of a fortification, the ground before which is unseen, and therefore undefended from the parapet', Stocqueler *Milit. Encycl.*

(1853, a date to be unearthed from the *OED*'s Bibliography.)

Dead ground is markedly unobtrusive, to be spotted from within *dead angle*, but in the words 'therefore undefended' there is a valuable complication of the military scene, even as 'cannot be fired on' is crucially different from, say, 'cannot be surveyed (or surveilled), may not even be recognized as dead ground'. As for that oppositely valuable thing, a simplification, we can be grateful that, under *dead ground*, one dictionary reminds us of the altogether usual fact: 'an area of ground hidden from an observer due to undulations in the land.'

For *undulations* does the trick in bringing home that, when not on
the battlefield, most of us have to beware of dead ground only when
we are at the wheel. Is it safe, at this very moment, to overtake (or be
overtaken)? We can't see what may be hiding within dead ground; we
may not have known or seen that there *is* dead ground. And what with
licensed rage and all, haven't roads become battlefields, lethally alive
with open hostilities that can make the worst of dead ground? Here
the masterpiece was created not by words alone but by the antagon-
isms and co-operations of different media that constitute the art of
film: Steven Spielberg's road-raging *Duel* (1971).

Childhood under the Eye of the Secret Police: the original subtitle (the
paperback was to have simply, *A Memoir*) felt the oppressive weight of
under as well as that of another sensing, another medium: under the *Ear*
of the Secret Police, too. Eyes and ears had been feared, way back in
the totalitarian world of Rome:

SILIUS   your State
Is waited on by Envies, as by Eyes;
And every second Guest your tables take,
Is a fee'd Spy, t' observe who goes, who comes,
What conference you have, with whom, where, when,
What the discourse is, what the looks, the thoughts
Of ev'ry person there, they do extract,
And make into a substance.

AGRIPPINA   Hear me, Silius.
Were all Tiberius body stuck with Eyes,
And ev'ry Wall and Hanging in my House
Transparent, as this Lawn I wear, or air;
Yea, had Sejanus both his Ears as long
As to my in-most Closet, I would hate
To whisper any thought, or change an act · · ·

                                   (Ben Jonson, *Sejanus His Fall*, Act II)

The very spies know that they too are spied upon. Tiberius sets Macro
upon Sejanus, 'to be our eye, and ear' (Act III). In Jonson's eyes, the
Roman sycophant would be at home in that sickening recency of our
corps.-speak, *reaching out*.

                          Look, look! is not he blest
          That gets a seat in eye-reach of him? More

> That comes in ear- or tongue-reach? Oh, but most
> Can claw his subtle elbow, or with a buzz
> Fly-blow his ears.   (Act V)

Centuries after not only Sejanus but Jonson, Rome returns to be bruised anew as Romania, with eye-reach and ear-reach monstrously augmented by totalitarian technology.

> The Roman race most wretched, that should live
> Between so slow laws, and so long a bruising.   (Act III)

The most degrading moments in *Burying the Typewriter* and in the poems uncoil from what the secret police hear (and say), thanks to their microphones; what they record and transcribe; then succeeded by a further uncoiling of what Bugan herself now has come to hear and to say, to record and to transcribe—better, to translate from Romanian to English and to transpose it all from the grey inhumanity of the documents to the deep colours of her art. *Legends* has on facing pages—confronting pages—both the secret police document [Strictly Secret / Ex.[Exemplary] Unique / Transcribed P.A.] and her own helpless remonstration that its record simply has to be false ('He could not have known that code-name'):

> Your words, P.A., are in my father's mouth
>
> and today it seems I read a version of ourselves
> narrated in your own language that makes it
>
> plain to see how you recorded and transcribed
> our fears, how we lived without a choice.

Writing in English, Bugan is yet vigilant to honour her responsibilities to her native language. The epigraph to 'The house founded on elsewhere' is from *The Temptation to Exist*, by Emil Cioran (translated from Romanian by Bugan):

He who turns against his language, adopting that of others, changes his identity and even his deceptions. He tears himself—a heroic betrayal—from his own memories, and up to a point, from himself.

The Appendix to *Releasing the Porcelain Birds*, after the body of the book has presented the secret police transcripts that she has made into an art of truth, reproduces 'excerpts from the original copies of secret police surveillance files in Romanian', the aim being 'to give a visual sense of the historical material that led to the making of these poems, and a sense of the original secret police language for those who can read Romanian'. She honours, too, her other responsibilities:

I thank the Center for the Study of the Archives of the Securitate (CNSAS) in Bucharest for giving me access to the archives of surveillance documents on my family and for reassuring me that I can publish these documents. I also thank my family for allowing me to publish the excerpts from our archive that appear in the current book in my literal translation. The language of the translations reflects the secret police-speak in the original files: I made no effort to correct the grammar or improve the flow of the transcripts.

Reassuring me! Drily punctilious, so straight the face that leaves it at that.

~Correct the grammar or improve the flow~

Within the heroic line with its Augustan balance of an antithesis (there in the plain prose) is audible the fall of a tyrant—brought about by the heroism of Romanian dissidents, among them Carmen Bugan's father.

Ceauşescu of Romania. His fall was destined to a firing squad. Charles XII of Sweden:

His Fall was destin'd to a barren Strand,
A petty Fortress, and a dubious Hand;
He left the Name, at which the World grew pale,
To point a Moral, or adorn a Tale.

(Johnson, *The Vanity of Human Wishes*, 219–22)

The tale is to be told again and again, for Charles XII is the haunted heir to the Hannibal of Juvenal.

The containment in 'dead ground' would mean—would proffer— something to someone arriving at a new terrain, as Bugan did with English (and Beckett with French). There may be available to anglophones and francophones a benign counterpart—and counter-resistance— to those microphones of the secret police. (At the home of the Bugans, a conscience is suddenly visited upon inanimate objects: 'the microphones must have blushed | At our words after long silence'.[3]) We may speculate—while wishing that there were a verb that is based etymologically not on the eye of flesh but on the ear—about the ways of words that cross to other words, words that may be out of sight but are not necessarily out of mind; out of eyeshot but not always out of earshot; alive within what may prove to be dead ground. Words, though

---

3. *Found in secret police records.*

few, had succeeded in crossing from the rooms of the family home in
Romania to a location that is not exactly a *room* at all, being a cell.

> We hung onto those few words that could cross
> the clay-like murky territories between us.   (*A birthday letter*)

Could cross because of what it is, when you think about it, to double-
cross. It was as early as 1926 that T. S. Eliot deprecated the betrayal of
this feat of slang: 'This useful and expressive word is already in decay;
its original meaning of a betrayal of *both* sides is reduced to plain
betrayal, which renders it superfluous.'[4] And *territories*: not only because
of earth's clay, and disinterring, but because such a secure word can put
up some resistance to the prospect of terror?

The reader, this reader, may be imagining these intimations of a cel-
larage. True, and a warning may be in order. 'The jailer warned him
not to talk about what had happened there.' Understood. But then
exactly how much are we to understand, to gather, at a related moment
of *A birthday letter*?

> Each word was limitless,
>
> clothed our souls and warmed against despair,
> shielded us from *their* world of terror,

—*warmed* against? That, solely? The words of these poems are such
warnings and intimations.

> I see us in our small kitchen that first night standing around each other
> Not knowing what to say.   (*Found in secret police records*)

—but careful *not* to say 'standing *by* each other', for she knows that this
is not for her to say (even while she does well to intimate the thought,
and we know what she means).

> I said that life is hard,
> no wood for winter, no one to help,
> school year finished well, and I aim to go to University.[5]

No one to help me, but touched by No one for me to help. (Differently
poignant.) 'I aim to go', not *I am to*, for that would be counting
chickens.

4. *Times Literary Supplement* (2 September 1926), anonymously. In *The Double-Cross
   System* (1972), J. C. Masterman told of the turning of Germany's secret agents during
   the Second World War.
5. '*BUTNARU*' *at the visit with his daughter.* (= 'Grandpa'.)

> I sat in silence weighting apples, pears and plums
> against mesmerizing gallops across distant prairies.   (*'There'*)

—weighting, meanwhile *waiting* (without mentioning the matter), as well as weighing, to a scruple, the difference between what it is to weigh and what it is to weight. *Nomen est omen.* How should we weigh or weight the chances of Carmen Bugan's having turned—whether consciously or not, when she turned to English—to a reticent resource, something of a dead ground: her father's Christian name?

For my father, on his eightieth birthday

Ion.

Romanian has not only this form of the name John but science's atomic or molecular noun. The English language may be glimpsed— not overheard, for the pronunciation is other—as adding an extraordinary range of words, from *ion* (noun) itself to *-ion* as an indispensable ubiquitous suffix. I risk presumption, but.

The name *Ion* stands out more than once in the secret police transcripts that are reproduced, some in English, some in Romanian. 'The aforementioned objects belong to escapees Bugan Ion and P.T'—one such object being '(one) English–Romanian dictionary'. Here, obj. for object, as against obj. for 'objective', 'the objective', as Ion Bugan becomes when the police reports are translated. Subsequently 'the inmate Bugan Ion has to execute 3746 days of incarceration'. The poem in pain, *3746 days*, confronting the transcript, simply addresses her father as *you*. (But in the knowledge, and perhaps intimating, that Ion's pronunciation in Romanian is, roughly, *you-on*.)

Granted, she could very well have found herself translating into her English the Romanian word for 'incarceration' without ever catching sight of *Ion · · · incarceration*. Or of *aforementioned · · · Ion · · · dictionary*. But then she does write of herself (with prosecutors' curtness, no definite or indefinite articles for him and her) as '—daughter | of convict with a code-name'.[6] A convict with convictions, and with code-names in his world:'He could not have known that code-name.'[7] The honourable coding of a Christian name within a poem might incarnate discretion as well as valour. And other impulses: at news of the amnesty, 'In his prison cell my father's jubilation was recorded' (*Found in secret police*

6. '*BUTNARU*' *at the visit with his daughter.*   7. The poem, *Legends.*

records). Within these poetry-records there is the police record that sets down the name *Ion*. But whereas *Ion . . . incarceration* has a negative charge, *father's jubilation* is positively charged. And a simple candid sequence, 'the peeling blue | walls of the train station, my father, a puzzle', can silently station her father's name between 'my father' and 'a puzzle'. Or, *A walk with my father on the Iron Curtain*.

    ion: Electr. 'Any individual atom, molecule, or group having a net electric charge (either positive or negative).' Inmate Bugan Ion (*3746 days*):

> signing his own sentence by which atoms
> of his own blood, particles smaller still
>
> will be born from the combustion of his mind
> racing beyond the speed of light:

—a sentence that is signed (in its way), being born again from the combustion of Carmen's *mens sana*, in the moment when *Ion* is borne from *combustion*, a sequence itself born from the transcript's *Ion · · · incarceration*.

    The suffix is an axis not a direction. It permits of the highest of hopes, and the opening lines of the first of the new poems of 2019, *And now, the words*, knows as much:

> I struggle with the meaning of the word *resurrection*:
> Go do your work, word, I say,
> All the way back to your root.

And then the suffix -*ion* will come to compact both hope and fear in the opening lines of *Christmas 2017*:

I see the tumour wrappedsw around my father's aorta like a link in a chain. It cannot be touched by knife or radiation.

My father, Ion.

    Fear, again, with the sinister coincidences of the *ion trap*: 'a device designed to catch ions; *spec.* one in a cathode-ray tube or television camera that prevents ionized molecules from reaching the screen or the target'.

> Arm in arm in the old quarters searching for his hotel
> where he hid from police, the trap door that is
> no longer there.   (*A walk with my father on the Iron Curtain*)

    The hiding places of Carmen Bugan's power are truly hiding places. One of them is the fact that literature is itself an act of resistance, being a benign counterpart to the malign arts of surveillance. In a poem that opens as a prose-poem, *At hour 1:32*, we are ushered (by a heroic line) into 'the room equipped with listening devices'. Yet if the secret police callously exploit 'listening devices', then poets compassionately do so. A poem is a listening device, a recording device, and it too has a 'target' and even—in the case of a poet who, like Bugan, translates, including translating herself—a 'target language'. 'The dog was poisoned by informers.'[8] Unexpectedly early (from 1503–4), the corrupting sense:

One who informs against another; one who lays an information; *spec.* one who makes it his business to detect offenders against penal laws and to lay informations against them.

But a poet was and is an informer, in the several good senses of the word.

An instructor, teacher. *Obs.* From 1387–8.
    One who communicates information or intelligence; an informant. From 1422.
    One who or that which informs with life, etc.; an inspirer, animator, vitalizer.

> Nature! informer of the poet's art,
> Whose force alone can raise or melt the heart.
>
> *(Prologue to Sophonisba)*[9]

> Thou O Sun! · · ·
> Informer of the planetary train
> Without whose quickening glance their cumbrous orbs
> Were brute unlovely mass, inert and dead,
> And not as now the green abodes of life.
>
> (James Thomson, *Summer*, 94, 104–7)

Leave it to the secret police to avail themselves of the brute unlovely mass, inert and dead, of informers. And leave it to such poets as Carmen Bugan to inform the green abodes of life.

> Lush green clumps of trees, vineyards,
> A village church next to the river, and us,
> Children singing in the car (they always sing).   *(Cap d'Agde)*

Her opening poem closes like this:

---

8. *We are museums*, the opening poem of the book.
9. These lines are attributed by the *OED* to Pope; the Twickenham Pope informs us that they were 'presumably added' by David Mallet.

> even the illusion that
> There might have been *something* we could have kept for ourselves.

How touchingly this keeps to itself the force of a different preposition: could have kept to ourselves. Art's power is that it both does and does not keep things for itself and to itself. In this it conducts itself like a responsible family. Or a responsible society.

It is not solely for the secret police that people are, and should be, 'objects of observation'.

> Because we have become
> 'Objects of observation,' 'targets,' since nothing more has remained
> Of the people we were, we are now museums.

It is a duly humane thing that, in the course of the poems, the quotation-marks fall away from the phrase *objects of observation*.[10] The name of the crucial and excruciated *object of observation* was Ion. But let a poet's observation survey, not (an ugly back-formation) surveil.

> Let Observation with extensive View
> Survey Mankind, from *China* to *Peru*;
> Remark each anxious Toil, each eager Strife,
> And watch the busy Scenes of crouded Life;
> Then say how Hope and Fear, Desire and Hate,
> O'erspread with Snares the clouded Maze of Fate···
>
> (*The Vanity of Human Wishes*, The Tenth Satire of Juvenal Imitated, 1–6)

Snares, like the ion trap. Hope and Fear, Desire and Hate.

Edwin Morgan, a great translator-imitator from Russian (and from Hungarian, though not apparently from Romanian), has a twofold observation in *A View of Things*: 'what I hate about hate is its eyes', 'what I love about poetry is its ion engine'.[11] Geoffrey Hill, too, could contribute a coincidence here. For of great pertinence to Carmen Bugan's imaginative custody of Ion Bugan, of all her family, is the ending of the poem by Hill on tyrants and captivity that turns a rhyme of pure chance and of great moment:[12]

> Our fetters are struck off, the charged ions
> That held us | now as nothing to the aeons.
> Even so transfigured our captivity.

10. *We are museums* has them, on the first page of the poems; *A dream of return* does not, p. 48.
11. *The Second Life* (1968), in *Collected Poems* (1990).
12. 'Damning the tyrants', 'custody', 'captivity' (and 'Gramsci'), inhabit this poem, 21, of *Al Tempo De' Tremuoti* (*The Daybooks* VI).

13

Heroic Work by Samuel Johnson
and Samuel Beckett

~I know not how the days pass over me~

Samuel Johnson, Easter Day, 7 April 1765

~Nothing but the days passing over~

Samuel Beckett, 21 February 1938: 'It is the kind
of life that filled Dr Johnson with horror. Nothing
but the days passing over'

B eckett in his early thirties in the Thirties tried to set about his imagined play on Dr Johnson, *Human Wishes*.

I have not written a word of the Johnson blasphemy. I trust that acts of intellection are going on about it somewhere. Which will enable me eventually to see how it coincides with the Pricks, Bones and Murphy, fundamentally, and fundamentally with all I shall ever write or want to write. (1938)[1]

Its one scene was published, with Beckett's leave, in 1980.[2]

The interplay and interwork of Beckett's art with that of the artist Avigdor Arikha led to the single-page masterpiece that is Beckett's

---

1. To Mary Manning Howe, after 10 December 1937; *The Letters of Samuel Beckett*, vol. 1: *1929–1940*, ed. Martha Dow Fehsenfeld, Lois More Overbeck, George Craig, and Dan Gunn (Cambridge, 2009), 569. This high hope of Beckett's was first given imaginative attention by James Knowlson, *Damned to Fame: The Life of Samuel Beckett* (London, 1996), 250–1.
2. Ruby Cohn, *Just Play* (1980); then in Beckett's *Disjecta*, ed. Cohn (1983): 'Although Beckett filled three notebooks with material for a play on the relationship of Dr Samuel Johnson and Mrs Thrale, only this scenic fragment of 1937 was actually composed. Pauses, repetitions, and formal patterns are strikingly prophetic of his drama to come.' The manuscript of *Human Wishes* is at the Beckett International Foundation, the University of Reading. Rosemary Pountney wrote with appreciation of *Human Wishes* in her 1988 book *Theatre of Shadows: Samuel Beckett's Drama 1956–1976*.

Ceiling. Ceiling's affiliation with Arikha, for whom it was written in 1981, is manifest and secure. But is there any good reason to accommodate *Ceiling* (of all Beckett's works) within his fervent prophecy in 1937 that *Human Wishes*—'the Johnson thing', 'my Johnson fantasy', 'the Johnson blasphemy'[3]—would come to coincide fundamentally not only with *More Pricks than Kicks* (1934), *Echo's Bones* (1935), and *Murphy* (1937), but 'fundamentally with all I shall ever write or want to write'?

In 1984, the BBC invited me to assemble and conduct a quire of voices in tribute to Dr Johnson, for the bicentenary of his death. The spirit was to be that of Johnson on Shakespeare, 'without envious malignity or superstitious veneration'. Many of the remarks within the radio programme on Johnson had their filaments to Beckett, who was for ever grateful to and for Johnson and who shared the conviction that 'Human life is everywhere a state in which much is to be endured, and little to be enjoyed'[4]—a ruling that has all the authority of those who have as great a capacity for enjoyment as for endurance. 'They can put me wherever they want, but it's Johnson, always Johnson, who is with me. And if I follow any tradition, it is his.'[5]

I had invited Beckett to say or to supply a few words. He furnished a few, generously and courteously, but privately not publicly, on a crisp card.

SAMUEL BECKETT

Paris 21.1.84

Dear Christopher Ricks
   Thanks for yrs. of Jan. 16.
   I'm bereft of words these days and so must decline with regret your kind invitation.
   If you speak of his waifs & strays you might find some use for the fragment p.153 of enclosed.
You'd be very welcome.
   With all good wishes,
      yours ever
      Sam Beckett

3. *The Letters of Samuel Beckett*: to George Reavey, 26 April 1937 and 27 July 1937, i. 489, i. 522; to Mary Manning Howe, after 10 December 1937, i. 369.
4. *Rasselas*, ch.11.
5. Deirdre Bair, reporting Beckett in conversation; *Samuel Beckett: A Biography* (1978), 272.

The enclosed (*Disjecta*) had been published the previous year. 'Waifs & strays', not only as the people of Johnson's household, disjecta as they would have been for those who had nothing of Johnson's compassion, but as *Disjecta*, Beckett's waifs & strays.

Beckett knew what he hoped to show in *Human Wishes*, knew this perhaps too well for it ever to be consummated.

I also am very interested in the Johnson-Thrale-Piozzi arrangement, and often thought what a good subject was there, perhaps only one long act. What interested me especially was the breakdown of Johnson as soon as Thrale disappeared···Think of a film opening with Johnson dancing home to his den in Fleet Street after the last visit to Mrs Thrale, forgetting a lamppost & hurrying back. Can't think why there hasn't been a film of Johnson, with Laughton. But I think one act···would be worth doing. There are 50 plays in his life.[6]

The one scene—not even one act—would present three women of Johnson's household (and the cat Hodge) awaiting his return from the funeral of Mr Thrale on the evening of 14 April 1781.

Johnson's further lodger Dr Robert Levet (or Levett) makes an appearance ('slightly, respectably, even reluctantly drunk') but is mum. Not silent, exactly—'he remains a little standing as though lost in thought, then suddenly emits a single hiccup of such force that he is almost thrown off his feet.' (The force of a hiccup was to echo in Beckett's *Play*, 1964.) Dr Levet is to die in a year's time, in 1782, two years before his elegist. Johnson's poem *On the Death of Dr Robert Levet* evokes Levet's sheer goodness, concluding its sense of a life honourably concluded:

> Then with no throbbing fiery pain,
> No cold gradations of decay,
> Death broke at once the vital chain,
> And free'd his soul the nearest way.[7]

6. To Mary Manning Howe, 13 December 1936. *The Letters of Samuel Beckett*, i. 396–7. *Life of Johnson*, from S. Whyte: 'Upon every post as he passed along, I could observe he deliberately laid his hand; but missing one of them, when he had got at some distance, he seemed suddenly to recollect himself, and immediately returning back carefully performed the accustomed ceremony, and resumed his former course, not omitting one till he gained the crossing' (*Life of Johnson*, ed. George Birkbeck Hill, rev. L. F. Powell, 1934–50, i. 485). James Knowlson is characteristically informative and perceptive as to Beckett's being possessed by Johnson, and on *Human Wishes* and its anticipations of Beckett's completed plays (*Damned to Fame*, 249–51).

7. Johnson's respect for Levet has been further illuminated by Arthur Freeman (*TLS*, 25 May 2007). He brought to light Johnson's notice of Levet's death in *The Gentleman's Magazine* (January 1782): 'In Bolt-Court, Fleet-str. at the house of his friendly patron Dr. Johnson, Mr. Rob. Levet, a very useful, skilful, and charitable practicioner in physic, in

'The peevishness of decay is not provoking', announces Mrs Desmoulins in *Human Wishes*, a scene that opens in decay and with delay.

MRS DESMOULINS   He is late.
Silence.
MRS DESMOULINS   God grant all is well.

The prayer will return. Johnson will not, not in the one scene we have. Waiting for Pomposo? (But Beckett was to tell Ruby Cohn that 'Johnson was planned to appear towards end of Act 1'.[8])

MISS CARMICHAEL   And the doctor, is the doctor....
Silence.
MRS DESMOULINS   He is late.
Silence.
MRS DESMOULINS   God grant all is well.

Johnson is awaited from the funeral of Mr Thrale, for whom now all is well—though Johnson is the last person who would ever be able to see death so. *Human Wishes* is one of Beckett's lifelong contemplations of the thought, so classically firm in the ancient world, so impossible to Johnson (whom Beckett revered, all his life), that it is better to be dead than alive, best of all never to have been born. Beckett said of Cowper's wish that he 'had never been': 'Into such a wish J. [Johnson] could never have entered.'[9]

> 19 October 1769
> BOSWELL. 'But is not the fear of death natural to man?'
> JOHNSON. 'So much so, Sir, that the whole of life is but keeping away the thoughts of it.'

---

full possession of every power both of body and mind, though supposed to have been 80 years old. He was born near Hull in Yorkshire.' As Freeman points out, this confirms its humanity with a benign use of the word *patron*, which elsewhere was often, for Johnson, pejorative: 'commonly a wretch who supports with insolence, and is paid with flattery'.

8. 21 November 1972. *The Letters of Samuel Beckett*, vol. iv: *1966–1989*, ed. George Craig, Martha Dow Fehsenfeld, Dan Gunn, and Lois More Overbeck (Cambridge, 2016), 315.

9. *Letters*, i. 529, 531, from notes by Beckett (now at Reading). To Thomas McGreevy, 4 August 1937: 'there can hardly have been many so completely at sea in their solitude as he was or so horrifiedly aware of it—not even Cowper. Read the Prayers & Meditations if you don't believe me.' (And, we must add, re-read Cowper's *The Cast-Away*, to feel the full horror of *at sea*.)

15 April 1778
MISS SEWARD. 'There is one mode of the fear of death which is certainly absurd; and that is the dread of annihilation, which is only a pleasing sleep without a dream.' JOHNSON. 'It is neither pleasing, nor sleep; it is nothing. Now mere existence is so much better than nothing, that one would rather exist even in pain, than not exist.'

JOHNSON. 'The lady confounds annihilation, which is nothing, with the apprehension of it, which is dreadful. It is in the apprehension of it that the horrour of annihilation consists.'[10]

Beckett to Mary Manning Howe, 11 July 1937:

There won't be anything snappy or wisecracky about the Johnson play if it is ever written. It isn't Boswell's wit and wisdom machine that means anything to me, but the miseries that he never talked of, being unwilling or unable to do so. The horror of annihilation, the horror of madness, the horrified love of Mrs Thrale,[11] the whole mental monster ridden swamp that after hours of silence could only give some ghastly bubble like 'Lord have mercy upon us.' The background of the *Prayers and Meditations*. The opium eating, dreading-to-go to bed, praying-for-the-dead, past living, terrified of dying, terrified of deadness, panting on to 75[,] bag of water, with a hydracele on his right testis.[12]

The compassion in 'panting on to 75[,] bag of water' is a tribute to Johnson's straightness of face: 'My diseases are an asthma and a dropsy, and, what is less curable, seventy-five.' 'The water' (Johnson's ensuing cadence feeling for the boundary that is the English heroic line)~breaks its boundaries in some degree~. Boswell was rightly in awe of the courage of Johnson, who 'united his own efforts with those of the gentlemen who attended him; and imagining that the dropsical collection of water which oppressed him might be drawn off by making incisions in his body, he, with his usual resolute defiance of pain, cut deep, when he thought that his surgeon had done it too tenderly'.[13]

Heartfelt, from both Boswell and Beckett. But 'the miseries that he never talked of'? Bringing to bear the wisdom of William Empson

10. *Life of Johnson*, ii. 93, iii. 295–6.
11. 'His horror at loving her I take it was a mode or paradigm of his horror at ultimate annihilation, to which he declared in the fear of his death that he would prefer an eternity of torment.' (To Thomas McGreevy, 4 August 1937; *Letters*, i. 529.)
12. Knowlson (*Damned to Fame*, 250) gave us this, all the more valuably in that it is not included in the *Letters* (despite its falling within the brief for the edition: 'those passages only having bearing on my work', Beckett, 18 March 1985).
13. October, December 1784; *Life of Johnson*, iv. 362–3, 399.

('Usual for a man | Of Bunyan's courage to respect fear'[14]), we can see
that Johnson, being a man of heroic courage, did bring himself to talk
of the miseries, though he was deeply unwishing to do so. It was
Boswell's adhesive importunity at which Johnson erupted, Boswell's so
nagging Johnson to *go on* talking of them.

When we were alone, I introduced the subject of death, and endeavoured to
maintain that the fear of it might be got over ··· [here, ten lines of exchanges]
'But may we not fortify our minds for the approach of death?'—Here I am
sensible I was in the wrong, to bring before his view what he ever looked
upon with horrour ··· he answered, in a passion, 'No, Sir, let it alone' ··· [but
four sentences of reply by Johnson] I attempted to continue the conversation.
He was so provoked, that he said, 'Give us no more of this;' and was thrown
into such a state of agitation, that he expressed himself in a way that alarmed
and distressed me; shewed an impatience that I should leave him, and when
I was going away, called to me sternly, 'Don't let us meet to-morrow'.[15]

Don't let us meet Johnson at all in the one scene of *Human Wishes*.

MRS DESMOULINS   He is late.
Silence.
MRS DESMOULINS   God grant all is well.

Halfway through the scene, something is spelt out. Oliver Goldsmith
has just been the last-mentioned of three playwrights: 'The dear doctor's debt to nature' has been 'discharged'.

MISS CARMICHAEL   His debt to nature?
MRS WILLIAMS   She means the wretched man is dead.
MISS CARMICHAEL   Dead!
MRS WILLIAMS   Dead. D-E-A-D. Expired. Like the late Queen
                   Anne and the Rev. Edward—
MISS CARMICHAEL   Well I am heartily sorry indeed to hear that.[16]

He is late. The late Queen Anne. To the succession from 'late' as tardy to
'late' as deceased, there is added the lively proverb that had long taken
Queen Anne's death in 1714 to be the type of being in ignorance of

---

14. *Courage means Running*, in *The Gathering Storm* (1940).
15. 26 October 1769; *Life of Johnson*, ii. 106–7.
16. Perhaps such a spelling-out returned to Beckett when he wrote *Mort de A.D.* (pub-
    lished 1955), a poem in French about Arthur Darley of the Irish Hospital. (Lawlor and
    Pilling (eds), *The Collected Poems of Samuel Beckett* (2012), 398, remark 'the use of
    Darley's initials in the title to give us the English word "dead" and the redundancy of
    "mort" / "dead" '.)

something—particularly a death. As the *Oxford Dictionary of English Proverbs* has it:

1722 He's as dead as Queen Anne the day after she dy'd.
1840 Lord Brougham, it appears isn't dead, though Queen Anne is.
1859 Thackeray: On which my lady cried petulantly, 'Oh, Lord, Queen Anne's dead, I suppose.'
1885 May happen thee hasn't heard th' other piece o' news. Queen Anne's dead.

As for the interruptus,

Like the late Queen Anne and the Rev. Edward—

it is a great stroke that has the mature women leaving *Edward* forever unconsummated by its *Young*.[17]

But it is time to contemplate Beckett's *Ceiling*, where a preternatural consciousness is bent down upon what it is to return to consciousness.[18]

Great gratitude is owed to Avigdor Arikha, for the depth and passion of his art, and for what his friendship with Samuel Beckett meant to each of them, and to Anne Atik Arikha, whose memoir, *How It Was*, is informed with respectful love. She tells of her first sight of *Ceiling* on 7 September 1981:

17. In *Murphy*, Beckett relished the thought of 'night's young thoughts' (chapter 5), as against Young's *Night Thoughts*. Edward Young (1683–1765) was known, too, for his *Conjectures on Original Composition*; Beckett's turn of phrase in *Murphy* is both a conjectural emendation and an original composition. Given that the aposiopesis 'Edward—' happens in *Human Wishes*, it may be apt that in *London* the author of *The Vanity of Human Wishes* has this exclamation: 'Illustrious EDWARD! from the Realms of Day, | The Land of Heroes and of Saints survey' (99–100). But then a King—Edward III, victor at Crécy—spurns a surname.

18. *Ceiling* was published in the monograph *Arikha* (Richard Channin and others, Thames & Hudson, 1985), and in the book-catalogue *Avigdor Arikha: From Life: Drawings and Prints 1965–2005*, ed. Duncan Thomson and Stephen Coppel (British Museum Press, 2006). Beckett's French text, *Plafond*, appeared in the Arikha monograph as published by Hermann, (Paris, 1985); made known to me by the kindness of Avigdor Arikha. *Ceiling* was left out of *Samuel Beckett: The Complete Short Prose 1929–1989*, ed. S. E. Gontarski (New York, 1995), but fortunately appears in *Company / Ill Seen Ill Said / Worstward Ho / Stirrings Still*, ed. Dirk Van Hulle (London, 2009), from which I learnt of Beckett's poem, *ceiling* (9 April 1981). Six consecutive versions of *Ceiling* (eight pages), and three typed manuscripts (three pages), are documented in *No Symbols Where None Intended* (Humanities Research Center, the University of Texas at Austin), selected and described by Carlton Lake (1984), 169–72. Within *Disjecta*, *Ceiling* both would and would not have been at home: would, as in the company of Beckett's other tributes to Arikha; would not, since there is a difference between such tributes and the ephemeral or incomplete works that *Disjecta* valuably gleaned—among them, *Human Wishes*.

While A. went upstairs to the loggia to get more paintings, Sam slipped into my hands the text he'd written for A. together with Eugene Istomin's letter. [There was a secret project, organized by Eugene, for the publisher, Jovanovitch, to bring out a special edition, and originally Sam had planned to write about A.'s work for him, but decided to write a text about seeing, instead, which became *Ceiling*, as having much more to do with A.'s approach. It ended up being published by Pierre Berès.] Talk. Sat down to dinner. I'd looked quickly through *Ceiling*. He said: 'Will it do? Has nothing to do with anything. Hope it's all right.'[19]

There, 'the text he'd written for A.' is the tribute to Arikha's 'double awareness' that Beckett was to publish next year, with his own awareness manifesting itself in double texts, French and English. *Ceiling* is then the further creation, deepening Beckett's insight into seeing. Anne Atik reproduces a typescript that has Beckett's second thoughts about the title: the typed *Ceiling* was struck through, and he wrote *Somehow again*. His third thought was the wise reversion to *Ceiling*.

Ceiling is a painful paean to what it is to *come to*. One draft has the deleted title *On coming to*, which felt the possibilities of *On* [as *Upon*] there too.[20] A remarkable locution, *coming to*, when you come to think of it.

★ ★ ★

Ceiling

For Avigdor
September 1981

On coming to the first sight is of white. Some time after coming to the first sight is of dull white. For some time after coming to the eyes continue to. When in the end they open they are met by this dull white. Consciousness eyes to of having come to. When in the end they open they are met by this dull white. Dim consciousness eyes bidden to of having come partly to. When in the end bidden they open they are met by this dull white. Dim consciousness eyes unbidden to of having come partly to. When in the end unbidden they open they are met by this dull white. Further one cannot.

On.

No knowledge of where gone from. Nor of how. Nor of whom. None of whence come to. Partly to. Nor of how. Nor of whom. None of anything. Save dimly of having come to. Partly to. With dread of being again. Partly

19. *How It Was* (London, 2001; 2005), 108–9.
20. *No Symbols Where None Intended*, 170.

again. Somewhere again. Somehow again. Someone again.
Dim dread born first of consciousness alone. Dim
consciousness alone. Confirmed when in the end the eyes
unbidden open. To this dull white. By this dull white.
Further one cannot.

On.

Dim consciousness first alone. Of mind alone. Alone
come to. Partly to. Then worse come of body too. At the
sight of this dull white of body too. Too come to. Partly
to. When in the end the eyes unbidden open. To this dull
white. Further one—

On.

Something of one come to. Somewhere to. Somehow to.
First mind alone. Something of mind alone. Then worse
come body too. Something of body too. When in the end
the eyes unbidden open. To this dull white. Further—

On.

Dull with breath. Endless breath. Endless ending
breath. Dread darling sight.

* * *

~On coming to the first sight is of white~. Every way of putting the
matter is immediately found to stand in need of reservation, of quali-
fication, of a further degree of specification, or—with a full sense of
what a warning is—of a caveat.

These are the movements, the 'stops and steps of the mind' (in
Eliot's phrase, *Ash-Wednesday* III), the shifts to which consciousness
is both reduced and expanded. Notable are four particular stages of
phrasing and re-phrasing: words that are subsequently modified;
words that are not; words that modify and will themselves in turn be
modified; words that modify their immediately previous appearance.
Inexorably *on*, revolving and yet advancing meticulously (with 'dread'
as that word's etymological root), advancing our feeling for the con-
cept, what it is to *come to*. Determined to follow where the expression goes: if *comes to*, then where has it *gone from*, where, whither,
whence?

No knowledge of where gone from. Nor of how. Nor of
whom. None of whence come to. Partly to. Nor of how.
Nor of whom. None of anything.

Whereupon something is saved—in a way—by the word *Save*:[21]

> None of anything. Save dimly of having
> come to. Partly to. With dread of being again. Partly
> again. Somewhere again. Somehow again. Someone again.

Beckett had long nursed these scrupulosities. In *Murphy*: 'He lit the radiator, undressed, got into the chair but did not tie himself up. Gently does these things, sit down before you lie down. When he came to, or rather from, how he had no idea, the first thing he saw was the fug···'.[22]

For upon reflection, *come to* is intriguing. *OED*: 'To recover (from a swoon, etc.); to revive, come round'. (*round* = *to*?) But coming to *what*, exactly? In the vicinity, but fended off, there are many other claimants: come to mind, come to life, come to light, come to ruin, come to nothing... (Quentin Skinner pointed out to me that *to come to*—given Beckett's sense of it all—is to come to grief.[23]) These, though, all need to be capped with their noun, whereas *come to*, if left at that, *tout court*, enjoys a final vacancy. Johnson's *Dictionary* has a specific entry for a turn that has a different end in mind:

> To COME *to himself*. To recover his senses.
> 'He falls into sweet ecstacy of joy, wherein I shall leave him 'till he *comes to himself.*' *Temple*

We know very well that *come to* does have *consciousness* standing by, there in our minds and three times on Beckett's page, but one of the striking things about *come to* is its not quite bringing itself to arrive at *consciousness*. Beckett, alive to what English and French can differently do, was aware that his *Plafond* was different from his *Ceiling*, since the French idiom is not equivalent to *come to* but is something else.

> ~On coming to the first sight is of white.
> Revenu à lui il voit d'abord du blanc.~

---

21. 'Sinon' in *Plafond*; see the French edition of Richard Channin's Arikha monograph, published by Hermann (Paris, 1985).
22. *Murphy* (1938), ch. 9, p. 191. In *Watt*, 'the coming to' declines to be solely a physical location as though consciousness were not at all in mind: 'Watt will not | abate one jot | but of what | | of the coming to | of the being at | of the going from | Knott's habitat' (1953, Addenda, 250). There is at Dartmouth College a recording of Beckett's uttering this poem, his delivery doing everything to not-settle the matter as to *the coming to*.
23. 'Time and grief and self so-called. Oh all to end.' (The closing words of *Stirrings Still*.)

The same cadence (surprisingly, given that in French, such would not be the heroic line), but a different story, not least in being gendered: 'lui il'. It is not just at first sight, then, but at second and third sight, that *coming to* is what the body of the work comes to. Not as skeleton but as tissue, throughout. Or all but throughout; for something happens at the very end.

On coming to the first sight is of white. Some time after coming to the first sight is of dull white. For some time after coming to · · · having come to · · · having come partly to · · · having come partly to · · · whence come to. Partly to · · · having come to. Partly to · · · Alone come to. Partly to · · · come to. Partly to · · · Something of one come to. Somewhere to. Somehow to.

And then, finally, what a discomposing relief it is to come to the end, an end that speaks both of the endless and of the ending, without— any longer—any mention of *coming to*. Or of *to* (as meaning 'closed', as when you check that the door is to, *Plafond*'s 'clos'), or of *too* (as meaning 'also', *Plafond*'s 'aussi'). For what is so delectably maddening about the perseverance of *Ceiling* is its refusing to evade the taxing tension that juggles the threesome. Everywhere there is the *to* of *come to*, abetted by the simple preposition ('To this dull white'). There is the *too* which (as *also*) opens, and the *to* which closes: 'Expressing contact: so as to come close to something; *esp.* with verbs forming phrases denoting shutting or closing' (*OED*), where the citations include Chaucer: 'Teehee, quod she, and clapt the window to'. (*Tee* to *to*.) *The Miller's Tale*, Alisoun's tail.

All this unremitting need for differentiation was actively sought by Beckett, for he had at first been happy (*happy!*) to make things easier for us. The final wording was to be 'For some time after coming to the eyes continue to.' The earlier draft had been more obliging: 'For some time after coming to the eyes continued closed.' Again, the end-process brought this: 'Consciousness eyes to of having come to', whereas the early wordy draft had misguidedly given us clear guidance, asking less of us: 'Conscious with closed eyes of having come to he left them so.'

Beckett, by the time he was in his seventies, well knew that to write obdurately, making no concessions, would be judged not just vexatious but mad. One of the citations in Johnson's *Dictionary*, under 'Heroically: after the way of a hero', is Dryden on Elkanah Settle ('Doeg'), who wrote—as some were to accuse Beckett of doing—'without knowing how or why':

Free from all meaning whether good or bad,
And, in one word, heroically mad.

(Absalom and Achitophel, Part II)

In two words, actually, but with the two often being at one, since there may be a madness in the hero, whether that of Ajax in his world, or that of James Joyce or Samuel Beckett in theirs. 'Free from all meaning'? This, but also something no less objectionable: making free with all meaning, in the pursuit of 'mystification and outrage'. Such is Philip Larkin's charge against modernism, and he called as a witness for the prosecution Dr Johnson. 'This is my essential criticism of modernism, whether perpetrated by Parker, Pound or Picasso: it helps us neither to enjoy or endure.'[24] Johnson: 'The only end of writing is to enable the readers better to enjoy life, or better to endure it.'[25] As Beckett's writing does.

The enduring exactitudes of two sixteenth–seventeenth century divines illuminate how *Ceiling* is written, and why. Commentators on Beckett have remarked, for instance, those 'stops and steps of the mind' in Lancelot Andrewes (1555–1626), audible in both the poetry and the prose of T. S. Eliot.[26] Beckett is sure to have been aware of Eliot's title, *For Lancelot Andrewes* (1928), and of the essay that Eliot then included in his *Selected Essays* (1932). Andrewes's movements of thought had received from the editor of his *Preces Privatae* a tribute to which Eliot gave salient quotation. Canon Brightman:

Andrewes develops an idea he has in his mind: every line tells and adds something. He does not expatiate, but moves forward: if he repeats, it is because the repetition has a real force of expression; if he accumulates, each new word or phrase represents a new development, a substantive addition to what he is saying.[27]

Eliot paid his own tribute to Andrewes and to 'this extraordinary prose, which appears to repeat, to stand still, but is nevertheless proceeding in the most deliberate and orderly manner':

Andrewes takes a word and derives the world from it; squeezing and squeezing the word until it yields a full juice of meaning which we should never have

24. Introduction to *All What Jazz* (1970); *Required Writing* (1983), 293, 297.
25. On Soame Jenyns's *A Free Enquiry into the Nature and Origin of Evil*, in the *Literary Magazine* (1757).
26. Comparison of Beckett with Andrewes as to style was engaged by Brian Vickers in *Repetition* (ed. Andreas Fischer, 1994), 98; and by Richard Harries in *A New Companion to English Renaissance Literature and Culture* (ed. Michael Hallaway, 2010), 436.
27. Eliot's essay 'Lancelot Andrewes' (1926) quotes this from F. E. Brightman; in *Selected Essays*, 335–6.

supposed any word to possess. In this process the qualities which we have mentioned, of ordonnance and precision, are exercised.[28]

In due course, such creative individuality would need to be distinguished from a critical school that Eliot deprecated: criticism determined to analyse 'stanza by stanza and line by line, and extract, squeeze, tease, press every drop of meaning out of it that one can. It might be called the lemon-squeezer school of criticism.'[29] And the Beckett of such thinking as *Ceiling* is moved to? The lemon-squeezer school of creation, lemon-squeezer but also birth-contractor, as the Unnamable knows.[30]

I was given a pensum, at birth perhaps, as a punishment for having been born perhaps, or for no particular reason, because they dislike me, and I've forgotten what it is. But was I ever told? Squeeze, squeeze, not too hard, but squeeze a little longer, this is perhaps about you, and your goal at hand. After ten thousand words?

The other such divine, this one known to have been read by Beckett, is Jeremy Taylor (1613–67).[31] Of *The Rule and Exercises of Holy Living* (1650) and *The Rule and Exercises of Holy Dying* (1651), the young Beckett had asked 'Why two books, Holy Living & Holy Dying, when one would have done the trick. Surely the classical example of literary tautology.'[32]

BOSWELL: 'I mentioned Jeremy Taylor's using, in his forms of prayer, "I am the chief of sinners," and other such self-condemning expressions' · · ·
JOHNSON: 'Taylor gives a very good advice: "Never lie in your prayers; never confess more than you really believe; never promise more than you mean to perform." '[33]

In *Human Wishes*, Jeremy Taylor—*ghostly father*, so *ghostly adviser, director*—haunts not only the world of Johnson (and of Mrs Williams,

---

28. *Selected Essays*, 339, 337.
29. 'The Frontiers of Criticism' (1956), in *On Poetry and Poets* (1957), 113.
30. *The Unnamable* (1958), 30.
31. There is, as always, a very helpful entry in *The Grove Companion to Samuel Beckett* (New York, 2004), ed. C. J. Ackerley and S. E. Gontarski.
32. To Thomas McGreevy, 6 [for 5] December 1933; *The Letters of Samuel Beckett*, i. 172. Fifty years later, to the month, Beckett wondered 'Why two' New-Year-resolutions/ hopes: To the Editor, The Times, London: RESOLUTIONS COLON ZERO STOP PERIOD HOPES COLON ZERO STOP BECKETT Such a thought gave Beckett lifelong pleasure. 'She wore by way of ear-rings two long ivory crucifixes · · · he thrust Moll's face away from his on the pretext of examining her ear-rings. But as she made to return to the charge he checked her again with the first words that came into his head, namely, Why two Christs?, implying that in his opinion one was more than sufficient. To which she made the absurd reply, Why two ears?' (*Malone Dies*, 86, 93).
33. *Life of Johnson*, iv. 294–5.

Mrs Desmoulins, and Miss Carmichael) but of Beckett. The final two pages of the one scene that constitutes all we have of *Human Wishes* consist of a reading-aloud, with loud interruptions. After the stage direction *Silence*, Miss Carmichael suddenly, without notice, utters death.

MISS CARMICHAEL	'Death meets us everywhere, and is procured by every instrument and in all chances, and enters in at many doors; by violence—'
MRS WILLIAMS	What twaddle is this Miss Carmichael?
MISS CARMICHAEL	I am reading from my book, Madam.
MRS WILLIAMS	I did not suppose you were inventing it.
MISS CARMICHAEL	'By violence and secret influence; by the aspect of a star and the stink of a mist—'
MRS WILLIAMS	The stink of a mist?
MISS CARMICHAEL	Yes, Madam, the stink of a mist.
MRS WILLIAMS	Continue, continue.

On they duel, Miss Carmichael and Mrs Williams (with Mrs Desmoulins presumably resigned to not getting a word in edgeways). Mrs Williams places a wager as to the author: 'Brown for a guinea.'[34] And there duly arrives the conclusion, in which nothing is concluded. (Apart from the wager.)

MRS WILLIAMS	Is it possible she reads and does not know what she reads.
MISS CARMICHAEL	I read so little, madam, it is all one to me.
MRS WILLIAMS	Turn to the title page, my child, and tell me is it Brown.
MISS CARMICHAEL	*(turning to the title page)*. Taylor.

34. Dr Johnson read Sir Thomas Browne attentively, death-wise. 'As easily may we be mistaken in estimating our own courage, as our own humility; and, therefore, when Browne shews himself persuaded, that "he could lose an arm without a tear, or with a few groans be quartered to pieces," I am not sure that he felt in himself any uncommon powers of endurance; or, indeed, any thing more than a sudden effervescence of imagination which, uncertain and involuntary as it is, he mistook for settled resolution. "That there were not many extant, that in a noble way feared the face of death less than himself," he might likewise believe at a very easy expence, while death was yet at a distance; but the time will come to every human being, when it must be known how well he can bear to die; and it has appeared, that our author's fortitude did not desert him in the great hour of trial.' Sir Thomas Browne's *Christian Morals*; *Biographical Writings*, The Yale Edition of the Works of Samuel Johnson, vol. xix, ed. O. M. Brack, Jr, and Robert DeMaria, Jr (2016), 336. The English heroic line: ~ the time will come to every human being ··· our author's fortitude did not desert him ~.

Like Samuel Johnson, Samuel Beckett was in a position to report that he had 'Read Jeremy Taylor'. But that those particular death-dealings of Taylor's would stake a claim to *Human Wishes*? This will have owed something (I would wager) to the fact that *The History of the English Language* in Johnson's *Dictionary* had come to include the reader's being met there by those dozen lines beginning 'Death meets us everywhere, and is procured by every instrument and in all chances, and enters in at many doors; by violence—'.[35]

Coincidences abound, and Beckett could avail himself and his art of them. Names, for instance. Do nine tailors make a man? The Index to the Hill/Powell edition of Boswell's *Life of Johnson* enumerates eighteen Taylors, with John Taylor abutting and abetting Jeremy Taylor. Beckett: 'All this would come in quite naturally in the last act, i.e. the fear of his death, when he was being reproached by his clerical friend Taylor for holding the opinion that an eternity of torment was preferable to annihilation.'[36]

Memorably, Beckett in 1937 had hoped that something would enable him eventually to see how *Human Wishes* would coincide with all that he had published and with all that he would ever write or want to write. The wording of *Ceiling* on the page, like the dramatic wording of *Human Wishes* on the stage, 'appears to repeat, to stand still, but is nevertheless proceeding in the most deliberate and orderly manner'. *Ceiling* turns repeatedly upon 'coming to', and *Human Wishes* upon 'coming to one's notice'.

MRS DESMOULINS It is impossible that the creator of *False Delicacy* should have been laid to rest and the fact not come to my notice.

★ ★ ★

MRS DESMOULINS Should however Mr Kelly, by some extraordinary haphazard, be no longer alive—
MRS WILLIAMS Nor drawing his pension without encumberland.

35. Within the ample additions made to Johnson's pages by the Revd H. J. Todd, who ushers in the dozen lines of Jeremy Taylor's litany of death: 'His painting of the various ways, in which the last enemy that shall be destroyed, accosts us, is perhaps unrivalled.'
36. To Joseph Hone, 3 July 1937; *The Letters of Samuel Beckett*, i. 509. Dr John Taylor, author of *A Letter to Samuel Johnson on the Subject of a Future State* (1787). 'In the advertisement he wrote that "having heard that his friend Dr. Johnson had said, that he would prefer a state of torment to that of annihilation, [he] told him that such a declaration, coming from a person of his weight and character, might be productive of evil consequences.' *Life of Johnson*, iii. 296 note (under 1778).

MRS DESMOULINS	And the fact not have come to my notice, I...I...
(*Weeps*).	
MRS DESMOULINS	I shall regret it bitterly...bitterly... (*Exit, closing door softly*).

★ ★ ★

MRS WILLIAMS (*in a strong decided tone*)	What will the woman bitterly regret, if she does not do so already, the death of Kelly or the fact not having come to her notice.
Silence.	
MRS WILLIAMS	There is a notice of the mind and there is a notice of the heart. The first is nothing. And the heart is cold.

★ ★ ★

MRS WILLIAMS	I know they are dead, their deaths are come to the notice of my mind.

★ ★ ★

MRS WILLIAMS	But it did not come to the notice of my heart until the Christmas following.

One's having *come to* may be thought of as a necessary but not a sufficient condition of having something come to one's notice, whether of mind or of heart. There may then be something of a second coinciding in the matter of consciousness, which is conspicuous in *Ceiling*—where it is then seen to dim as no longer standing in need of announcement. The first paragraph proffers the word three times, the next twice, the next once, and the two subsequent paragraphs not at all. Meanwhile the need for differentiation is felt to be pressing:

> Dim consciousness first alone. Of mind alone. Alone come to. Partly to. Then worse come of body too. At the sight of this dull white of body too. Too come to. Partly to.

This need is in touch with an earlier differentiation within consciousness and self-consciousness, one that had been set to shape *Human Wishes* for Johnson and for Mrs Thrale:

And if the play is about him and not about her, it does not mean that he was in the right, or any nonsense like that, but simply that he being spiritually self conscious was a tragic figure, i.e. worth putting down as part of the whole of which oneself is a part, & that she, being merely physically self conscious is less interesting to me personally.[37]

The escapes and trammels of consciousness formed Beckett's sense of life in particular ways during those days of 1937. It was very telling of James Knowlson to give salience to a Beckett letter of that same month:

The real consciousness is the chaos, a grey commotion of mind, with no premises or conclusions or problems or solutions or cases or judgments. I lie for days on the floor, or in the woods, accompanied & unaccompanied, in a coenaesthesia of mind, a fullness of mental self-aesthesia that is entirely useless · · · I used to pretend to work, I do so no longer.[38]

Cœnaesthesis: 'The general sense or feeling of existence arising from the sum of bodily impressions, as distinct from the definite sensations of the special senses; the vital sense' (*OED*), including Ribot, 1882: 'The undefined consciousness, the product of all the vital processes, constituting bodily perception'. In short, where one finds oneself *on coming to*. Knowlson moves from this letter immediately to Beckett at work on Johnson in the National Library of Ireland, 'as he watched "the seagulls stalking high overhead" and bringing a bone or a stone onto the glass roof of the reading room'.

That glass roof constituted a ceiling. Beckett, though, was to prove determined not to yield to a particular temptation. 'Help, help, if I could only describe this place, I who am so good at describing places, walls, ceilings, floors, they are my speciality.'[39] Beckett changed his mind about the title *Ceiling*, which heads a typescript but was struck through, with *Somehow again* substituted by pen. The third thought, not to use this phrase from the piece but to revert to *Ceiling*, was blessedly right. *Ceiling* as a title has the particular authority that derives, not from within the piece, but from above it. The word does not appear as we read on, though Beckett had briefly admitted the word, one draft speaking of 'A patch of ceiling'.[40] It is a title perfectly judged, and perfectly placed, there where a ceiling is to be found. The pure triumph of *Ceiling* is in its feeling no wish whatsoever to *describe* the ceiling; all

37. *Partly to* · · · *Partly to*. From *part* · · · *part*. To Thomas McGreevy, 4 August 1937; *Letters*, i. 529.
38. To Mary Manning Howe, 30 August 1937; *Letters*, i. 546. Knowlson, *Damned to Fame*, 249 (there reading *coenaesthesic*).
39. *The Unnamable*, 157.   40. *No Symbols Where None Intended*, 170.

it wants to do is to describe what it is like to come to, seeing the ceiling.

It is the white or whitewashed ceiling that supervises the coming to. 'With dread of being again.' Rudyard Kipling knew of this:

> Every secret, self-revealing on the aching whitewashed ceiling,
> Do you wonder that we drug ourselves from pain?
>
> (*Gentlemen-Rankers*)

T. S. Eliot knew his Kipling and his ceiling:

> You dozed, and watched the night revealing
> The thousand sordid images
> Of which your soul was constituted;
> They flickered against the ceiling.
> And when all the world came back · · ·   (*Preludes* III)

For Beckett, a ceiling's revealing does not have to be of anything sordid or divine, unless *to come to* is itself either divine or a sort of sordor. When all the world comes back, there has to have been a coming to. To what, again? To consciousness. The second of Eliot's *Preludes* had started there:

> The morning comes to consciousness
> Of faint stale smells of beer · · ·⁴¹

A glass roof, a ceiling, a *bourne*. It is this last that haunted Beckett from first to last.

The bourne or limit for him is the word *bourne* itself, the thought of it and of what Beckett could make of what Shakespeare had made of it. There is scarcely any limit to what Shakespeare variously made of the word, but there is one instance that has haunted the world at large and Beckett's world: that of *Hamlet* (III. i), with 'Borne' there at the bourne of the line, keeping in touch with 'beare' (as in 'borne') at the end of *its* line as well as within a later line:

> Who would these Fardles beare
> To grunt and sweat under a weary life,
> But that the dread of something after death,

---

41. (Not 'comes to consciousness / With' but 'comes to consciousness / Of'.) Eliot chose *comes to* for the tragic return to consciousness in Seneca's *Hercules Furens* after he has killed his family (Eliot's epigraph to *Marina* is from this scene, the poem opening with a dawning consciousness): 'Hercules comes to, · · · and spies his dead wife and children'. 'Seneca in Elizabethan Translation' (1927), in *Selected Essays*, 69–70.

> The undiscovered Countrey, from whose Borne
> No Traveller returnes, Puzels the will,
> And makes us rather beare those illes we have · · ·

This has itself often puzzled the will, since after all the Ghost of Hamlet's father does return from beyond that bourne. It is *Hamlet*, not surprisingly, that supplies one of the citations for *bourn* ('a bound; a limit') given by Johnson in his *Dictionary*. It is this allusion that precipitates another of the great cuttings-short in *Human Wishes*. Should Mrs Williams's anger pursue someone who is dead? No, 'For English vengeance *wars not with the dead*', as Johnson himself wrote of Hugh Kelly (who is one of the four dramatists summoned in *Human Wishes*).[42]

MRS DESMOULINS   There are many, Madam, more sorely disappointed, willing to forget the frailties of a life long since transported to that undiscovered country from whose—

MRS WILLIAMS (*striking the floor with her stick*)   None of your Shakespeare to me, Madam. The fellow may be in Abraham's bosom for aught I know or care.

The wit of this is plural. First, that of all words, it should be the limitary *bourne* that is never reached, is for ever unsounded. Second, that the impassioned cry 'None of your Shakespeare to me, Madam' can no more escape Shakespeare than any of us can. For what follows the cry, namely the allusion to Abraham's bosom, cannot rest simply on the Bible's bosom, being Shakespeare's again, too. 'The Sonnes of *Edward* sleepe in *Abrahams* bosome' (*Richard III*, IV. iii), with Shakespeare's Edward royal, not reverend (the occasion of the immediately preceding interruption: 'Like the late Queen Anne and the Rev. Edward—'). Nor is there an end to the Shakespearean inescapabilities, since Abraham's bosom has been for ever changed by the inspired malapropism of the Hostess in *Henry V* (II. iii).

PISTOLL   For *Falstaffe* hee is dead · · ·

---

42. *Prologue to 'A Word to the Wise'* (1777). 'Hugh Kelly had died in February 1777 at the age of thirty-eight, and on 29 May the management of Covent Garden gave a performance of his *Word to the Wise* for the benefit of his widow and children. To add importance to the occasion Johnson was asked to write a Prologue. He complied out of kindness, for his opinion of Kelly was not high, and they were not well acquainted' (*The Poems of Samuel Johnson*, 210). Johnson italicized the allusion to Pope's *Iliad*, vii. 485 ('I war not with the dead').

HOSTESS   · · · hee's in *Arthurs* Bosome, if ever man went to *Arthurs* Bosome.

The *Oxford Dictionary of English Proverbs* is right to tuck this, Arthur's bosom, within Abraham's.

The bourne, then, is a pregnant silence in *Human Wishes*. In the late works of Beckett, *bourne* knows no limits. In *Company* (1980):

So as he crawls the mute count. · · · Be that as it may and crawl as he will no bourne as yet. As yet imaginable. Hand knee hand knee as he will. Bourneless dark.[43]

'What should such Fellowes as I do, crawling betweene Heaven and Earth', mused Hamlet (III. i). Beckett's paragraph crawls towards the limit that it craves: 'no bourne as yet', 'Bourneless dark'.[44]

In *Stirrings Still* (1988):

For he could recall no field of grass from even the very heart of which no limit of any kind was to be discovered but always in some quarter or another some end in sight such as a fence or other manner of bourne from which to return.[45] Nor on his looking more closely to make matters worse was this the short green grass he seemed to remember eaten down by flocks and herds but long and light grey in colour verging here and there on white.[46]

Among the things recalled or remembered here are Shakespeare's words and Beckett's recalling of them. Together they constitute a bourne from which to return.

some end in sight · · · verging here and there on white.
On coming to the first sight is of white.

That *Ceiling* is alive to the bourne is not solely a matter of a ceiling's being a bourne, but of the interplay of *bourne* with *born* that the English language (unlike French) not only permits but encourages. Life, with its birth/death pangs, has two bournes. 'I am being given, if I may

43. *Company* / *Ill Seen Ill Said* / *Worstward Ho* / *Stirrings Still*, 32–3.
44. Beckett's French, *Compagnie*, 'aucune borne' and 'Du noir sans borne'. But there are limits to what French can do with 'borne', since the Shakespearean allusion does not inform it.
45. *Compagnie*: 'borne à ne pas dépasser'. Quentin Skinner pointed out that 'manner of bourne' opens towards Hamlet's words (I. iv) just before the Ghost appears: 'to the manner borne'.
46. *Company* / *Ill Seen Ill Said* / *Worstward Ho* / *Stirrings Still*, 112.

venture the expression, birth to into death, such is my impression.'[47]
John Keats gave consummate expression to such lacings:

> Then in a wailful choir the small gnats mourn
> Among the river sallows, borne aloft
> Or sinking as the light wind lives or dies;
> And full-grown lambs loud bleat from hilly bourn···
>
> (*To Autumn*)

This says 'lives or dies', and *borne* finds itself joined in a wailful
choir with *bourn* (seconded by *mourn*), these then intimating the
mortality of *born* (those full-grown lambs). Here in Keats it is not—
as in *Human Wishes*—*bourn* that is actively tacit, but *born*. *Company*
and *Stirrings Still* say *bourne*. *Ceiling* limits itself to saying *born*, right next
to *dread*: 'Dim dread born first of consciousness alone.' (The music of
the English heroic line, to adopt Johnson's words and cadence.)

> But that the dread of something after death,
> The undiscovered Countrey, from whose Borne···

And there is always (well, blessedly not *always*, not for ever) the dread
of something before death. And of nothing, before or after death. And
of there being no such nothing, no such release into annihilation. When Beckett gave *Ceiling* to Anne Atik Arikha in 1981, he
asked 'Will it do? Has nothing to do with anything.'

Yet great art may be an invaluable realization of nothing's having to
do with anything, even perhaps with everything. Carlyle praised the
Hero as Man of Letters in the conviction that Johnson's wording 'has
always something within it. So many beautiful styles and books, with
nothing in them.'[48] But there can be a positive turn to this last, this
wrestling with nothing or with Nothing. The poem by John Wilmot,
Earl of Rochester, that Samuel Johnson praised as 'the strongest effort
of his Muse' is *Upon Nothing*.[49]

> Nothing, thou elder brother even to Shade,
> Thou hadst a being ere the world was made,
> And (well fixed) art alone of ending not afraid.

47. *Malone Dies* (1956), 114. See Christopher Ricks, *Beckett's Dying Words* (1993), 39–40, on
   Beckett's way of putting it.
48. *On Heroes, Hero-Worship, and the Heroic in History* (1841); *Works*, ed. H. D. Traill (1896–
   1907), i. 400–6.
49. Its opening lines; Rochester, *The Complete Works*, ed. Frank H. Ellis (Harmondsworth,
   1994).

Ere time and place were, Time and Place were not,
When primitive Nothing, Something straight begot;
Then all proceeded from the great united what.

Something, the general attribute of all,
Severed from thee, its sole original,
Into thy boundless self must undistinguished fall.

When Johnson found something to say about *Upon Nothing*, it was by
teasing out Rochester's teasing ways with the positive and the negative:

In examining this performance, *Nothing* must be considered as having not
only a negative but a kind of positive signification; as [i.e. as in] I need not fear
thieves, I have *nothing*; and *nothing* is a very powerful protector. In the first part
of the sentence it is taken negatively; in the second it is taken positively, as an
agent···The positive sense is generally preserved, with great skill, through the
whole poem; though sometimes, in a subordinate sense, the negative *nothing* is
injudiciously mingled.[50]

The terms 'positive' and 'negative' refuse to stay narrow, as is intimated
in those words of Beckett about Johnson and *Human Wishes*, in 1937:

All this would come in quite naturally in the last act, i.e. the fear of his death,
when he was being reproached by his clerical friend Taylor for holding the
opinion that an eternity of torment was preferable to annihilation. He must
have had the vision of *positive* annihilation. Of how many can as much be said.[51]

Human Wishes (1937) was in the distant past by the time that *Ceiling*
dawned in 1981. What might then have brought *Human Wishes* back to
mind? For one thing, Beckett's having been in correspondence with
Ruby Cohn about it, issuing in his allowing her to publish its sole scene
in *Just Play* in 1980 (furthermore, before long, allowing her to include it
in her edition of his *Disjecta*, 1983). For another thing, a bicentenary. 1981
is two hundred years from the signal day celebrated (if only that were the
word) in *Human Wishes*. 'He is late', the opening words, are said of
Johnson and of his not yet having returned from Mr Thrale's funeral.

The editors of the *Letters* often recognize what the rest of us would
have failed to recognize: say, a specific source in Johnson. 'My memory
grows confused, and I know not how the days pass over me.'[52] Beckett:

50. *The Lives of the Poets*, ed. Lonsdale, ii. 13–14.
51. To Joseph Hone, 3 July 1937; *The Letters of Samuel Beckett*, i. 509. *Beckett's Dying Words*,
    15–16, remarks some filaments to 'positive'.
52. Johnson's *Diaries, Prayers and Annals*, ed. E. L. McAdam, Jr, with Donald and Mary
    Hyde (1958), Easter Day, 7 April 1765, p. 92.

'It is the kind of life that filled Dr Johnson with horror. Nothing but the days passing over. It suits me all right.'[53] Trust Beckett. Trust him, too, to realize the power of a cadence.

~I know not how the days pass over me.
Nothing but the days passing over~

With flexible good grace, the English heroic line adapts itself to an elegiac impulse for both writers. As it does again for Johnson, nearing death in December 1784, when he arrived at such a final cadence: 'As he opened a note which his servant brought to him, he said, "An odd thought strikes me: we shall receive no letters in the grave".'[54]

~We shall receive no letters in the grave~

The word that *Ceiling* finally concludes with is *sight*.[55] What had opened was this: 'On coming to the first sight is of white.' The arc of *Ceiling* constitutes a heroic couplet:

On coming to the first sight is of white.
Endless ending breath. Dread darling sight.

A triplet effect, too, in that *white* / *sight* accommodates *sight* / *white* / *sight*. Cheek by jowl with *Dread,* as the very end, is *darling*, the most *outré* word in the piece. It arrives to mitigate—not that it can ever annul—*Dread*. The return to consciousness may be dreaded ('With dread of being again') but, when all is said and done (or rather when all is not yet quite said or quite done), consciousness—which costs us dear—cannot but be dear to us. Johnson's *Dictionary*, *darling*: 'regarded with great kindness and tenderness'. Beckett, for all the pertinacity with which he respects the longing for oblivion, does not pretend *and there's an end on 't.* 'Yes, there is no good pretending, it is hard to leave everything.'[56]

One word that Beckett found it hard, or even impossible, to leave was 'fundamental'. His fervent hope in 1937 as to *Human Wishes* (I quote it this last time) had been that something would enable him 'eventually to see how it coincides with the Pricks, Bones and Murphy, fundamentally, and fundamentally with all I shall ever write or want to write.' But that run of words, 'fundamentally, and fundamentally', is markedly odd. So there comes to mind what has become a famous moment in a letter of 1957 to Alan Schneider: 'My work is a matter of

53. To McGreevy, 21 February 1938; *Letters*, i. 606, 608.
54. Boswell's *Life of Johnson*, iv. 413.   55. *Plafond*: 'vision'.
56. *Malone Dies* (1956), 107.

fundamental sounds (no joke intended), made as fully as possible.'[57] All the more fully in that Beckett was writing to congratulate Schneider on having directed for CBS-TV *The Life of Samuel Johnson* (by James Lee). 'Congratulations on TV Great Cham. Yes, I always had a passion for that crazy old ruffian.'

Whereupon there surfaced the fundamental reason for Beckett's calling upon the word 'fundamentally' in 1937 and in 1957: Boswell's rich evocation of Johnson in his element.

(Then looking very serious, and very earnest.) 'And she did not disgrace him;— the woman had a bottom of good sense.' The word *bottom* thus introduced, was so ludicrous when contrasted with his gravity, that most of us could not forbear tittering and laughing; though I recollect that the Bishop of Killaloe kept his countenance with perfect steadiness, while Miss Hannah More slyly hid her face behind a lady's back who sat on the same settee with her. His pride could not bear that any expression of his should excite ridicule, when he did not intend it; he therefore resolved to assume and exercise despotick power, glanced sternly around, and called out in a strong tone, 'Where's the merriment?' Then collecting himself, and looking aweful, to make us feel how he could impose restraint, and as it were searching his mind for a still more ludicrous word, he slowly pronounced, 'I say the *woman* was *fundamentally* sensible;' as if he had said, hear this now, and laugh if you dare. We all sat composed as at a funeral.[58]

~All sat composed as at a funeral~

This, on 20 April 1781. Mr Thrale's funeral, the occasion of *Human Wishes*, had been 14 April 1781, less than a week earlier.

Coincides? Beckett in 1937 had called up Johnson, 'past living, terrified of dying, terrified of deadness, panting on to 75'. Beckett's own panting-on reached 75 in April 1981. Come July 1981, there were versions of *Ceiling* (panting the word 'On'), and come September 1981—'in the end—its presentation to Anne Atik and to Avigdor Aikha.

Human Wishes had its particular understanding of what *to* can succeed in doing.

MRS WILLIAMS	Words fail us.
MRS DESMOULINS	Now this is where a writer for the stage would have us speak no doubt.
MRS WILLIAMS	He would have us explain Levett.
MRS DESMOULINS	To the public.

57. 29 December 1957; *No Author Better Served: The Correspondence of Samuel Beckett & Alan Schneider*, ed. Maurice Harmon (Cambridge, MA 1998), 24–5.
58. *Life of Johnson*, 20 April 1781, iv. 99.

MRS WILLIAMS   To the ignorant public.
MRS DESMOULINS   To the gallery.
MRS WILLIAMS   To the pit.
MISS CARMICHAEL   To the boxes.

Ceiling came to its own understanding of what *to* can succeed in doing.

> Dim consciousness first alone. Of mind alone. Alone
> come to. Partly to. Then worse come of body too. At the
> sight of this dull white of body too. Too come to. Partly
> to. When in the end the eyes unbidden open. To this dull
> white. Further one—

> On.

> Something of one come to. Somewhere to. Somehow to.
> First mind alone. Something of mind alone. Then worse
> come body too. Something of body too. When in the end
> the eyes unbidden open. To this dull white. Further—

Further? The further destination (*Too come to*) might be Boswell's humane dramatization—in pages which had come to Beckett's notice and on which he took capacious notes for *Human Wishes*—of Johnson's singularities[59]:

In the intervals of articulating he made various sounds with his mouth, sometimes as if ruminating, or what is called chewing the cud, sometimes giving a half whistle, sometimes making his tongue play backwards from the roof of his mouth, as if clucking like a hen, and sometimes protruding it against his upper gums in front, as if pronouncing quickly under his breath, *too, too, too;* all this accompanied sometimes with a thoughtful look, but more frequently with a smile.

'At the sight of this dull white of body too. Too come to. Partly to.'

Such intervals of articulating would have 'wrung from Dante one of his rare wan smiles',[60] Dante another of the heroic figures who coincide with all that Beckett ever wrote or would want to write. As did always James Joyce, for the centenary of whose birth Beckett sent a sentence:

I welcome this occasion to bow once again, before I go, deep down, before his heroic work, heroic being.

---

59. *Life of Johnson*, Spring 1764, i. 485–6.
60. *The Lost Ones* (1972); *Texts for Nothing and Other Shorter Prose*, ed. Mark Nixon (London, 2010), 103.

Acknowledgements

There has been substantial revision or augmentation of previous publications, as follows:

The Best Words in the Best Order, deriving from 'Prose and the Best Words in the Best Order', Inaugural Lecture as the Oxford Professor of Poetry (*Times Literary Supplement*, 25 February 2005). Reproduced with permission.

The Anagram, deriving from 'Shakespeare and the Anagram', *Proceedings of the British Academy* (Volume 121, 2002 Lectures. Copyright © 2003, The British Academy).

Dryden's Heroic Triplets, deriving from 'Dryden's Triplets', *The Cambridge Companion to John Dryden*, ed. Steven N. Zwicker (© Cambridge University Press, 2004).

T. S. Eliot and 'Wrong'd Othello', deriving from *Decisions and Revisions in T. S. Eliot* (Faber & Faber and the British Library, © British Library Board 2002).

Congratulations, deriving from *Re-Constructing the Book: Literary Texts in Transmission*, ed. Maureen Bell et al. (Copyright © 2003 Ashgate). Reproduced by permission of Taylor & Francis Group.

The Novelist as Critic, deriving from *The Oxford Handbook of the Victorian Novel*, ed. Lisa Rodensky (Oxford: Oxford University Press, © 2013, Oxford University Press. https://doi.org/10.1093/oxfordhb/9780199533145.013.0031). Reproduced with permission of the Licensor through PLSclear.

Henry James and the Hero of the Story, Part II, deriving from 'Derogation from "The Next Time"', *Cambridge Quarterly*, 37 (1): 64–78 (Copyright © 2008, Oxford University Press. https://doi.org/10.1093/camqtly/bfm031).

John Jay Chapman and a Vocation for Heroism, deriving from 'On Heroes and Anti-Hero-Worship' © 1992 Christopher Ricks, which first appeared in *Arion: A Journal of Humanities and the Classics*, 2.2&3, 19–26.

Geoffrey Hill's Grievous Heroes, deriving from 'Geoffrey Hill's Unrelenting, Unreconciling Mind', *Geoffrey Hill: Essays on his Later Work*, ed. John Lyon and Peter McDonald (Oxford: Oxford University Press. Copyright © 2012, Oxford University Press). Reproduced with permission of the Licensor through PLSclear.

Ion Bugan on the Iron Curtain, deriving from 'Ground of being on his ground of escape', *Dead Ground: 2018–1918*, ed. Andrew McNeillie and James McNeillie (Clutag Press, 2018).

Heroic Work by Samuel Johnson and Samuel Beckett, deriving from 'Samuel Beckett's *Human Wishes* and *Ceiling*', *Fulcrum*, Number 6 (2008).

Now first published: *Henry James and the Hero of the Story* [*The Modern Warning*]; *T. S. Eliot, Byron, and Leading Actors*; and *Norman Mailer, Just Off the Rhythm*.

For extracts by T.S. Eliot: All permissions/quotations are from *The Poems of T. S. Eliot*, ed. Christopher Ricks and Jim McCue (London: Faber & Faber; Baltimore: Johns Hopkins University Press, 2015).

Rannoch by Glencoe from *The Poems of T. S. Eliot*, ed. Christopher Ricks and Jim McCue (London: Faber & Faber; Baltimore: Johns Hopkins University Press, 2015).

Excerpt from *Rannoch by Glencoe* from *The Poems of T. S. Eliot*, ed. Christopher Ricks and Jim McCue (London: Faber & Faber; Baltimore: Johns Hopkins University Press, 2015). All rights reserved.

Little Gidding from *The Poems of T. S. Eliot*, ed. Christopher Ricks and Jim McCue (London: Faber & Faber; Baltimore: Johns Hopkins University Press, 2015).

Excerpt from *Little Gidding* from *Four Quartets* by T. S. Eliot from *The Poems of T. S. Eliot*, ed. Christopher Ricks and Jim McCue (London: Faber & Faber; Baltimore: Johns Hopkins University Press, 2015). All rights reserved.

Preludes III, from *Preludes* from *The Poems of T. S. Eliot*, ed. Christopher Ricks and Jim McCue (London: Faber & Faber; Baltimore: Johns Hopkins University Press, 2015).

Excerpt from *Preludes* III, from *Preludes* from *The Poems of T. S. Eliot*, ed. Christopher Ricks and Jim McCue (London: Faber & Faber; Baltimore: Johns Hopkins University Press, 2015). All rights reserved.

The following extracts are reproduced by permission:

Extracts of *Welsh apocalypse (VI)*, *The Triumph of Love*, Psalms of Assize, Funeral Music, *Scenes from Comus*, The Assisi Fragments, Pavana Dolorosa, On Reading Milton and the English Revolution, *Wilkins scripsit, 1888*, and *Mercian Hymns*, reproduced from Geoffrey Hill, *Broken Hierarchies, Poems 1952–2012*, ed. Kenneth Haynes (Oxford: Oxford University Press. Copyright © 2013, Oxford University Press). Reproduced with permission of the Licensor through PLSclear.

Extracts from *A walk with my father on the iron curtain, Visiting the country of my birth, At hour 1:32, Found in secret police records, Preparing for the journey of return, Legends, A birthday letter, BUTNARU at the visit with his daughter, There, 3746 days, And now, the words, Christmas 2017, Cap d'Agde*. Reproduced by kind permission of Carmen Bugan.

Every effort has been made to trace and contact copyright holders prior to publication. If notified, the publisher will be pleased to rectify any errors or omissions at the earliest opportunity.

For advice, promptings, and more, I am grateful to John Barnard, Al Basile, Owen Boynton, Nuzhat Bukhari, Carmen Bugan, Archie Burnett, Greg Delanty, Martin Dodsworth, David Ferry, William Flesch, Jennifer Formichelli, Bryan Garner, Charles Griswold, Jeff Gutierrez, Mark Halliday, Saskia Hamilton, Kenneth Haynes, Geoffrey Hill, Philip Horne, Steven Isenberg, James Johnson, George Kalogeris, Daniel Karlin, Marcia Karp, Paul Keegan, Vicky Kimm, Emily Kramer, Hermione Lee, William Logan, Jim McCue, Andrew McNeillie, Julie Nemrow, Lisa Nemrow, Tim Parks, Anita Patterson, Tim Peltason, Adrian Poole, Michael Prince, William H. Pritchard, Laura Quinney, Anna Razumnaya, Lisa Rodensky, Quentin Skinner, Peter Swaab, Harry Thomas, John Tobin, Meg Tyler, Alissa Valles, Chris Walsh, Rosanna Warren, Frederick Wiseman, Susan Wolfson, David Womersley, and Ellen Wrigley.

Index

Friedländer, Paul 33
Fuller, Margaret 66
Fuller, Roy 7

Gard, Roger 177 n
Garrett, John 7
Garrison, William Lloyd 197–8, 199
Garton, Janet 231
Gaskell, E. C. 135
Gaultier, Jules de 92
Gibbon, Edward 221
Glover, Jon 245 n
Goffman, Erving 96 n
Goldsmith, Oliver 297
 Retaliation 54–5, 211
Graham, Kenneth 128
Graves, Robert 6–7, 205–6
Green, T. H. 251
Grierson, Herbert 94
Griffin, Sir Lepel 154
Griffiths, Eric 266

Haigh-Wood, Maurice 99
Harari, Josué V. 33 n
Harcourt, Simon 72
Hardy, Thomas 138
 Far From the Madding Crowd 148
Hartman, Geoffrey 43–4
Hawthorne, Nathaniel 149–50
Haynes, Kenneth 230, 231
Herbert, George 19, 45, 235
 Anagram 37–41
 The Flower 282–3
Herrick, Robert: Hesperides 244–5
Hicks, Edward 241 n
Hill, Geoffrey
 Annunciations 235, 236 n, 242
 The Assisi Fragments 236 n, 243
 Before Senility 253
 The Bibliographers 233
 The Book of Baruch 225–9, 241 n,
  245 n, 246, 247 n, 248 n, 250,
  256, 259
 Broken Hierarchies 237 n, 250 n, 254
 Canaan, A Song of Degrees 236
 Clavics 245–6

 Collected Critical Writings 233, 234,
  245, 252 n, 255 n
 The Daybooks 249, 291 n
 T. S. Eliot, critique of 229
 Expostulations on the Volcano 226
 Fantasia on 'Horbury' 237
 Florentines 237
 For the Unfallen 248, 250
 Four Poems Regarding the Endurance
  of Poets 248 n
 Funeral Music 236, 241 n
 Genesis 250
 History as Poetry 244
 Hymns to Our Lady of
  Chartres 237
 Ibsen, versions of:
  Brand 30, 230, 231, 235–6
  Peer Gynt 229, 230
 The Imaginative Life 179
 In Ipsley Church Lane 241 n,
  246
 In Memoriam: Gillian Rose 232,
  251 n
 King Log 236, 248
 Lachrimae 249
 Letter from America 249
 Liber Illustrium Virorum 246
 The Lords of Limit 232, 233
 Ludo 247, 249
 Mercian Hymns 237, 249, 252,
  254, 255
 The Mystery of the Charity of
  Charles Péguy 236
 Of Commerce and Society 247
 On Reading 'Milton and the English
  Revolution' 250
 On Reading 'The Essays or
  Counsels, Civill and
  Morall' 241–2
 Oraclau 228, 247, 253 n
 The Orchards of Syon 30, 232, 241 n,
  242, 246
 Pavana Dolorosa 249
 The Penguin Book of Contemporary
  Verse (ed. Kenneth Allott
  1962) 235, 252